Fodor's 2009

NEW ORLEANS

Where to Stay and Eat
for All Budgets

Must-See Sights
and Local Secrets

Ratings You Can Trust

Fodor's Travel Publications   New York, Toronto, London, Sydney, Auckland
www.fodors.com

FODOR'S NEW ORLEANS 2009

Editor: Michael Nalepa, Paul Eisenberg

Editorial Contributors: Michelle Delio, Jeanne Faucheux, Kandace Power Graves, Paul A. Greenberg, Molly Jahncke, Russell McCulley, Sue Strachan

Editorial Production: Tom Holton

Maps & Illustrations: David Lindroth and Mark Stroud, *cartographers*; Bob Blake, Rebecca Baer, and William Wu, *map editors*

Design: Fabrizio LaRocca, *creative director*; Guido Caroti, Siobhan O'Hare, *art directors*; Tina Malaney, Chie Ushio, Ann McBride, *designers*; Melanie Marin, *senior picture editor*; Moon Sun Kim, *cover designer*

Cover Photo: (French Quarter): Bill Heinsohn/Alamy

Production/Manufacturing: Angela L. McLean

ISBN 978–1–4000–1951–9

ISSN 0743–9385

SPECIAL SALES

This book is available at special discounts for bulk purchases for sales promotions or premiums. Special editions, including personalized covers, excerpts of existing books, and corporate imprints, can be created in large quantities for special needs. For more information, write to Special Markets/Premium Sales, 1745 Broadway, MD 6-2, New York, New York 10019, or e-mail specialmarkets@randomhouse.com.

AN IMPORTANT TIP & AN INVITATION

Although all prices, opening times, and other details in this book are based on information supplied to us at press time, changes occur all the time in the travel world, and Fodor's cannot accept responsibility for facts that become outdated or for inadvertent errors or omissions. So **always confirm information when it matters,** especially if you're making a detour to visit a specific place. Your experiences—positive and negative—matter to us. If we have missed or misstated something, **please write to us.** We follow up on all suggestions. Contact the New Orleans editor at editors@fodors.com or c/o Fodor's at 1745 Broadway, New York, NY 10019.

PRINTED IN THE UNITED STATES OF AMERICA

10 9 8 7 6 5 4 3 2 1

Be a Fodor's Correspondent

Your opinion matters. It matters to us. It matters to your fellow Fodor's travelers, too. And we'd like to hear it. In fact, we need to hear it.

When you share your experiences and opinions, you become an active member of the Fodor's community. That means we'll not only use your feedback to make our books better, but we'll publish your names and comments whenever possible. Throughout our guides, look for "Word of Mouth," excerpts of your unvarnished feedback.

Here's how you can help improve Fodor's for all of us.

Tell us when we're right. We rely on local writers to give you an insider's perspective. But our writers and staff editors—who are the best in the business—depend on you. Your positive feedback is a vote to renew our recommendations for the next edition.

Tell us when we're wrong. We're proud that we update most of our guides every year. But we're not perfect. Things change. Hotels cut services. Museums change hours. Charming cafés lose charm. If our writer didn't quite capture the essence of a place, tell us how you'd do it differently. If any of our descriptions are inaccurate or inadequate, we'll incorporate your changes in the next edition and will correct factual errors at fodors.com immediately.

Tell us what to include. You probably have had fantastic travel experiences that aren't yet in Fodor's. Why not share them with a community of like-minded travelers? Maybe you chanced upon a beach or bistro or B&B that you don't want to keep to yourself. Tell us why we should include it. And share your discoveries and experiences with everyone directly at fodors.com. Your input may lead us to add a new listing or highlight a place we cover with a "Highly Recommended" star or with our highest rating, "Fodor's Choice."

Give us your opinion instantly at our feedback center at www.fodors.com/feedback. You may also e-mail editors@fodors.com with the subject line "New Orleans Editor." Or send your nominations, comments, and complaints by mail to New Orleans Editor, Fodor's, 1745 Broadway, New York, NY 10019.

You and travelers like you are the heart of the Fodor's community. Make our community richer by sharing your experiences. Be a Fodor's correspondent.

Happy traveling!

Tim Jarrell, Publisher

CONTENTS

PLANNING YOUR TRIP

About This Book. 6
1 EXPERIENCE NEW ORLEANS . .7
New Orleans Today 8
New Orleans Planner 10
What's Where. 12
Top New Orleans Attractions. . . . 14
Local for a Day. 21
New Orleans with Kids 22
Best Fests & Parades. 23
Free & Almost Free 25
Offbeat New Orleans. 26
Get Outta Town 27
Great Itineraries. 28
2 EXPLORING
NEW ORLEANS. 31
The French Quarter 34
Faubourg Marigny & Bywater 52
Tremé 55
CBD & Warehouse District. 59
Garden District. 66
Uptown. 76
Bayou St. John & Mid-City. 83
Metairie & the Lakefront 90
Algiers Point. 91
3 MARDI GRAS & JAZZ FEST. . . 93
Mardi Gras 94
Jazz & Heritage Festival. 103
4 WHERE TO EAT 113
5 WHERE TO STAY 145
6 NIGHTLIFE & THE ARTS. 173
Nightlife 176
The Arts 192
7 SHOPPING. 195

NEW ORLEANS IN FOCUS

Remembering Katrina 15

8 SIDE TRIPS FROM
NEW ORLEANS. 223
Plantation Country. 225
Cajun Country 240
NEW ORLEANS
ESSENTIALS 263
Getting Started. 264
Booking Your Trip. 267
Transportation 269
On The Ground 273
INDEX 278
ABOUT OUR WRITERS 288

MAPS

The French Quarter & Faubourg
Marigny 36–37

CBD & Warehouse District. 60

Garden District. 67

St Charles Avenue Uptown 78

Lakefront & City Park. 84

Algiers Point. 91

Where to Eat in the French Quarter
& Faubourg Marigny 119

Where to Eat in CBD & the
Warehouse District 130

Where to Eat Outside the
Downtown Area 134

Where to Stay in Downtown
New Orleans. 148-149

Where to Stay Outside the
Downtown Area 168

Downtown Nightlife. 180-181

French Quarter Shopping . . 198-199

CBD & Warehouse District
Shopping. 211

Magazine Street
Shopping. 216-217

Maple Street/Riverbend
Shopping. 221

Southern Louisiana 226

Plantation Country. 228

Cajun Country 241

Lafayette. 242

ABOUT THIS BOOK

Our Ratings

As travelers we've all discovered a place so wonderful that its worthiness is obvious. And sometimes that place is so unique that superlatives don't do it justice: you just have to be there to know. These sights, properties, and experiences get our highest rating, **Fodor's Choice**, indicated by orange stars throughout this book.

Black stars highlight sights and properties we deem **Highly Recommended,** places that our writers, editors, and readers praise again and again for consistency and excellence.

By default, there's another category: any place we include in this book is by definition worth your time, unless we say otherwise. And we will.

Disagree with any of our choices? Care to nominate a place or suggest that we rate one more highly? Visit our feedback center at www.fodors.com/feedback.

Budget Well

Hotel and restaurant price categories from ¢ to $$$$ are defined in the opening pages of each chapter. For attractions, we always give standard adult admission fees; reductions are usually available for children, students, and senior citizens. Want to pay with plastic? **AE, D, DC, MC, V** following restaurant and hotel listings indicate whether American Express, Discover, Diners Club, MasterCard, and Visa are accepted.

Restaurants

Unless we state otherwise, restaurants are open for lunch and dinner daily. We mention dress only when there's a specific requirement and reservations only when they're essential or not accepted—it's always best to book ahead.

Hotels

Hotels have private bath, phone, TV, and air-conditioning and operate on the European Plan (aka EP, meaning without meals), unless we specify that they use the Continental Plan (CP, with a continental breakfast), Breakfast Plan (BP, with a full breakfast), or Modified American Plan (MAP, with breakfast and dinner) or are all-inclusive (including all meals and most activities). We always list facilities but not whether you'll be charged an extra fee to use them, so when pricing accommodations, find out what's included.

Many Listings

★	Fodor's Choice
★	Highly recommended
✉	Physical address
✛	Directions
🏠	Mailing address
☎	Telephone
🖷	Fax
⊕	On the Web
✉	E-mail
🎟	Admission fee
☉	Open/closed times
Ⓜ	Metro stations
🖃	Credit cards

Hotels & Restaurants

🏨	Hotel
⇲	Number of rooms
⚲	Facilities
⦿|	Meal plans
✕	Restaurant
⌂	Reservations
↘	Smoking
৪⦿	BYOB
✕🏨	Hotel with restaurant that warrants a visit

Outdoors

⅄	Golf
⚠	Camping

Other

⊙	Family-friendly
⇨	See also
✉	Branch address
☞	Take note

Experience
New Orleans

WORD OF MOUTH

"All in all, still one of my top places to visit. I love NOLA and I'm glad to see downtown & the Quarter looking so good. Plus, the people could not have been friendlier and more welcoming."

—laurelt

"It's sure a great choice if you really want to get away to a U.S. city that's TOTALLY different and doable without a car. It's on my list of weekend escapes now, for sure!"

—jayne1973

NEW ORLEANS TODAY

As much as people here would like to move on, there's no getting around Hurricane Katrina—which not only devastated New Orleans, but also reshaped the rest of the world's perception of the city. Three years after the disaster, many people still think that New Orleans is A) still underwater, or B) completely fine. Neither impression is accurate. The water is gone, but heavily flooded neighborhoods are still rebuilding. The levees that guard the city from storms have been repaired and improved, and big conventions and sporting events have returned—but New Orleans still has a long way to go. The good news for visitors is that virtually all of the attractions that make it such a fun place to be, including the famous French Quarter, are intact. Downtown is buzzing during the day, music pours from clubs every night, and the indomitable spirit and easy manner of the city's residents still make even the most jaded visitor feel welcome.

Today's New Orleans

. . . is still in recovery mode. Three years after Katrina, much work remains to be done. Hospitals and schools have reopened (though not as many as before the storm); and federal money to help New Orleans rebuild its ravaged infra-structure has been freed up, allowing the city to embark on a major program to repair streets, rebuild police and fire stations, and revitalize ravaged neighborhoods. It seems unlikely, however, that New Orleans will ever regain its former population, which was in decline long before Katrina. At the beginning of 2008, there were roughly 300,000 people living in the city itself—about two-thirds as many as before the storm. But the city worked hard to get its tourism infrastructure back together, and has successfully hosted big events (Mardi Gras and Jazz Fest among them), as well as smaller meetings and conventions. Some building projects announced before the storm, including a glitzy Donald Trump hotel and condominium tower, have resumed, and flood-ravaged neighborhoods like the Lower Ninth Ward and Lakeview are rebuilding. But it will be years before New Orleans puts Katrina behind it.

. . . is proud of its traditions. Red beans and rice on Monday, St. Joseph's altars, jazz funerals—this is a place steeped in tradition, one that guards its peculiar customs fiercely. Take Mardi Gras, fir example: some of the parading organizations, known as krewes, have been

WHAT WE'RE TALKING ABOUT

Where's Ray? The city's enigmatic, colorful, at times infuriating mayor has been the subject of a lot of speculation, from how many hours he actually puts in at work each week to his plans for his own political future. Will he run for the congressional seat that may become vacant following the corruption trial of incumbent Bill Jefferson? Or will he move to Dallas, where he owns a second home, after his term ends?

The New Orleans Saints gave long-suffering fans something to cheer about when they made it to the NFC Championship—one win away from the NFL's Super Bowl—in 2006. They faltered the following season, but the L.S.U. Tigers picked up the slack by winning the 2008 BCS National Championship in the Superdome. This football-crazed city also around for 150 years or more, dutifully building elaborate floats each year and parading through the streets in masks. The Mardi Gras Indian tradition, likewise, is shrouded in secrecy and ritual: "tribes" of mostly African-American revelers spend months constructing fanciful, Native American–influenced costumes, in tribute to actual tribes that once helped escaped slaves find freedom.

. . . is one giant movie set. Or that's how it seems at times, with multiple film projects going on at any given moment. The scenic backdrop is one reason for all the activity; generous tax credits and a growing local film industry are the other drivers behind what civic boosters have dubbed "Hollywood South." In 2008 there was a lot of buzz surrounding The Curious Case of Benjamin Button and its star (and part-time resident) Brad Pitt, and Cirque du Freak with Selma Hayek and John C. Reilly. And on the small screen This Old House, the Food Network, and BET, among others, have been filming here lately.

. . . is like no other place in America. It sounds like a tourist brochure cliché, but it's true: New Orleans does feel like a place out of step with the rest of the country. Some of

that is due to geography: this port city has seen an influx of many cultures over the course of its long history. It welcomes diversity and tolerates lifestyles that deviate from the norm—a big reason artists and other creative types have long put down roots here. The fact that the city lies mostly below sea level lends it a certain degree of fatalism and probably, if unconsciously, informs the New Orleans's live-for-today attitude. At times, all that quirkiness can make it a frustrating place to live—but fascinating nonetheless.

. . . is on the verge of ____. Fill in the blank; your guess is as good as anybody's. Will the coming months be "more than a tipping point" in the city's recovery, as Mayor Ray Nagin recently promised? Or will a national economic slowdown ensure that rebuilding continues in fits and starts, as it has for the first three post-Katrina years? There are some encouraging signs, including a revitalized medical district, rising enrollment at local universities, and a sense that life is slowly returning to normal. Our advice: come see for yourself, and be part of the revival of one of the world's great cities.

has a new love: the NBA's Hornets, permanently back in town after a post-Katrina stint in Oklahoma City.

Sightings are rare, but Brad Pitt and Angelina Jolie bought a place in the French Quarter after Katrina, lending a bit of Hollywood glamour to the town. Pitt has been active in affordable housing initiatives in the Lower Ninth Ward, where his Make it Right organization is raising money for the hurricane-ravaged community's reconstruction efforts.

What's that strange smell in the French Quarter? Lately, it's been a floral-scented spray a local sanitation company uses to clean the streets. The streets of the Quarter are indeed cleaner, and the spray's television commercials have made its owner, Sidney Torres IV, a local celebrity (his pal Lenny Kravitz stars in one). All of this has led to speculation that the handsome garbage man may make a run for mayor.

NEW ORLEANS PLANNER

Getting There

By air: Most major and a few regional airlines serve Louis Armstrong International Airport in Kenner, 15 mi east of downtown New Orleans. A taxi from the airport costs $29 for two people (fixed rate to the Central Business District (CBD); each additional person is an extra $12), and shared-ride shuttles are available to hotels. If you're traveling light and have a lot of extra time, you can also take Jefferson Transit's airport bus, which runs between the main terminal entrance and the CBD. Fare is $1.60.

By train: Three Amtrak lines serve New Orleans: the City of New Orleans, from Chicago; the Sunset Limited service between New Orleans and Los Angeles; and the Crescent, which connects New Orleans and New York by way of Atlanta. For tickets and schedules, call 800/872–7245 or visit www. amtrak.com.

Getting Around

On public transportation: Streetcars are a great way to see the city. The St. Charles line runs from Canal Street to the intersection of Claiborne and Carrollton avenues; along the way, it passes the Garden District, Audubon Park, Tulane and Loyola universities, and other worthy destinations. The Riverfront line skirts the French Quarter along the Mississippi, from Esplanade Avenue to the Ernest N. Morial Convention Center. Some Canal line streetcars make a straight shot from the Quarter to the cemeteries at City Park Avenue others take a spur at Carrollton Avenue that goes to City Park and the New Orleans Museum of Art. Ask the driver which one you're boarding if it is not clear.

At present, bus travel in New Orleans is a pretty depressing experience (although the Regional Transit Authority has pledged to update its aging fleet in the coming months), but a few lines are of use to visitors. The Magazine bus runs the length of shopping mecca Magazine Street, from Canal and Camp streets to the Audubon Zoo entrance at the far edge of Audubon Park. The Esplanade bus serves City Park, and drops Jazz Fest passengers off a few blocks from the Fair Grounds.

Fares for streetcars and buses are $1.25, and visitors' passes are available. For route maps, timetables, and more information, visit www.norta.com.

By car: Several agencies rent cars at the airport and at downtown locations; reserve in advance to get the best deal. If you don't plan to drive outside the city limits, you probably won't need one—you'll probably save money traveling by streetcar, cab, and on foot. If you do decide to drive, keep in mind that streets are in ragged condition, traffic lights routinely malfunction, and parking in the Quarter is tight (and parking regulations vigorously enforced).

Safety

Much of the post–Hurricane Katrina media coverage has focused on New Orleans's escalating crime rate. Sadly, this isn't just sensationalism—gangs operate in the city's underpopulated neighborhoods, there's a growing homelessness problem, the murder rate is among the highest in the nation, and armed robberies occur all too frequently. These grim statistics should not dissuade you from visiting, but you need to exercise caution if you venture outside the well-touristed areas—especially at night.

The French Quarter is generally safe, but use caution in the areas near Rampart Street and below St. Philip Street at night.

The CBD and Warehouse District are safe, but take a cab at night if there aren't many other pedestrians around.

Do not walk around in the Bywater or the lower part of Faubourg Marigny at night, and avoid Garden District side streets after dark.

Algiers Point is reasonably safe to walk around in by day—but the neighborhoods surrounding it can get sketchy very quickly.

All that said, the New Orleans Police Department does take pains to keep violent crime out of the tourist zones, with many uniformed and plainclothes police stationed throughout the Quarter and at special events.

Helpful Web Sites

www.fodors.com: Log on to the Travel Talk Forums to get advice from New Orleanians and travelers who have recently visited the Crescent City.

www.nola.com: Find out what's happening in the city from the city's daily newspaper, the New Orleans Times-Picayune.

www.neworleanscvb.com: Head here for up-to-date information from the New Orleans Convention & Visitors Bureau.

www.offbeat.com: The Web site for the monthly magazine Offbeat has extensive club and live music listings, along with features covering the local music scene.

www.nolafugees.com: This Web site offers an irreverent (and frequently off-color) slice of post-Katrina life in New Orleans. Warning: not for the sensitive or easily offended.

When to Go

In New Orleans, May through September is hot and humid. Just mustering the energy to raise a mint julep to your lips may cause exhaustion. These long hot summers may explain why things are less hurried down here. If you visit during these sticky months, you'll find that all hotels and restaurants are air-conditioned and, in July and August, hotel prices are lower.

June through November are the months to watch for heavy rains and occasional hurricanes. These conditions occur mainly with quick changes in temperature that accompany cold fronts. Although winters are mild compared with those in northern climes, the high humidity can really put a chill in the air December through February. Don't be surprised to see women wearing fur coats in many of the city's finer establishments.

Perhaps the best time to visit the city is early spring. Days are pleasant, except for seasonal cloudbursts, and nights are cool. The azaleas are in full bloom and the city bustles from one outdoor festival to the next. Below are average daily maximum and minimum temperatures for New Orleans.

WHAT'S WHERE

1 The French Quarter.
The geographic and cultural heart of the city since the early 1700s, the Quarter is a commercial and residential hodgepodge of wrought-iron balconies, beckoning court-yards, shops—and, of course, tawdry Bourbon Street.←

2 Faubourg Marigny & Bywater. The Marigny, New Orleans's first suburb, has nightclubs, cafés and some lovingly restored Creole cot-tages; grittier Bywater, despite gentrification, retains its work-ing-class credentials.

3 Tremé. The cradle of jazz, second-line parades, and other hallmarks of New Orleans culture was eroded by a freeway and Armstrong Park, but a trip to the tiny Backstreet Cultural Museum conjures memories of the historically African-American neighborhood's heyday.

4 CBD & Warehouse District. Most of the city's newer hotels are clustered here, near Canal Street or the sprawling Morial Convention Center. Other draws are classy museums, fine restaurants, a bustling casino, and adventur-ous art galleries.

5 The Garden District. Go ahead and gawk: stunning, early-19th-century mansions, gardens, and the shops of Mag-azine Street make this a great neighborhood for walking.

6 Uptown. Audubon Park and the campuses of Tulane and Loyola universities anchor oak-shaded Uptown; hop on the St. Charles streetcar to survey it in period style.

7 Bayou St. John & Mid-City. Rambling City Park and the New Orleans Museum of Art, reachable by streetcar, are the main draws here, as are some lively bars.

8 Metairie & the Lake-front. The south shore of Lake Pontchartrain is a good place for a bike ride or picnic; suburban Metairie is mostly Anywhere, USA.

9 Algiers Point. Drink in the views from the ferry to this neighborhood across the Mis-sissippi River from the French Quarter, then take a stroll amid handsome 19th-century cottages.

10 Plantation Country. Hit the tour bus trail up the Mis-sissippi to see how Louisiana's wealthy planters (and their not-so-fortunate slaves) once lived, and take time to explore towns like St. Francisville along the way.

11 Cajun Country. Awesome food and festivals, rockin' dance halls,—and in Lafayette, a surprisingly sophisticated cultural scene—await in nearby Cajun Country.

TOP NEW ORLEANS ATTRACTIONS

Jackson Square

Flanked by St. Louis Cathedral, the antebellum Pontalba apartment buildings, and the Mississippi River, postcard-pretty Jackson Square has been the hub of New Orleans life since the city's colonial start. Artists, musicians, and fortune-tellers congregate on the plaza surrounding the square, but the manicured park itself—with its famous bronze equestrian statue of Andrew Jackson—is a peaceful oasis in the midst of the French Quarter bustle.

Bourbon Street

Crude and crass, New Orleans's most famous entertainment strip isn't to everyone's taste, but you have to see it at least once—preferably at night, when the neon-lighted street swells with music and alcohol-fueled conventioneers. Tawdry strip clubs and souvenir shops scream for attention, but look closer and you'll find local jazz musicians showing off their chops, elegant restaurants, and faded bars where luminaries like Mark Twain and Tennessee Williams imbibed.

St. Charles Avenue Streetcar

Three streetcar lines converge on Canal Street, but this one packs the most bang for the buck-and-a-quarter. Following a route in use since a steam train first plied the avenue in 1835, streetcars clatter through the CBD, then roll along the oak-shaded median through some of the city's most-exclusive addresses. The views from the vintage cars alone are worth the trip, but the route includes several great destinations, including Audubon Park, the Garden District, and the Riverbend shopping district.

Garden District

A field day for architecture buffs and gardeners, the leafy Garden District is a remarkably intact collection of 19th-century Greek Revival mansions and raised cottages, many built by wealthy merchants during New Orleans's cotton heyday. Cap a visit here with lunch at Commander's Palace and a visit to adjacent Lafayette Cemetery, and check out the shops and cafés on busy Magazine Street.

The Parks

New Orleans is home to two impressive urban parks, each with its own character and attractions. Audubon Park, across from the campuses of Tulane and Loyola universities, sports waterfowl-filled lagoons, a world-class zoo, and great views of the Mississippi River from atop the levee. Across town, City Park is home to the New Orleans Museum of Art and an adjacent sculpture garden, along with the New Orleans Botanical Gardens and a mini-amusement park for kids.

French Market

French trappers, seafood vendors, and more than a few rowdy sailors traipsed through these open-air stalls once upon a time. Today the place more resembles a bazaar, and instead of vegetable stalls and charcuteries you'll find stands packed with jewelry, bags, cheap sunglasses, and antiques. The quality of the merchandise varies, but the scene is a lot of fun—especially on weekends.

Plantation Country

Tucked among the chemical plants and oil refineries that generate Louisiana's new money, remnants of the Old South aristocracy line the banks of the Mississippi River from New Orleans to north of Baton Rouge. Many stately old plantation homes have been carefully restored, filled with period furnishings and opened to the public. However brutal the history, there's no denying the beauty of the mansions and their accompanying gardens.

REMEMBERING KATRINA

It took New Orleans 300 years to etch its image on the public consciousness—a city known around the world for food and music, pageantry and debauchery, and an irreverent, *laissez-faire* culture more attuned to the Caribbean than the Heartland. But it took one great storm a matter of hours to sear a new picture.

Katrina,
August 29th
8:20am

The site of the nation's worst natural disaster and, for a few terrifying days, a pit of human suffering, New Orleans is the first major American city to be nearly drained of its population. Three years after Hurricane Katrina struck, the city has regained about ⅔ of its former population. Yet large swaths of New Orleans remain in a kind of limbo. Small businesses and some residents have trickled back into the heavily damaged neighborhoods, but many more are waiting for a number of factors to kick in— insurance settlements, federal and state assistance, and direction from city officials—before they return.

Visitors have come back, and they find that the city retains its sense of joy and hospitality. French Quarter and Mo-rial Convention Center areas are vital. For many, however, it's important to see first-hand the places millions of people came to know through news reports and images: neighborhoods like the Lower Ninth Ward, where a torrent of water tossed houses and cars, and the 17th Street Canal, where brackish Lake Pontchartrain poured through a collapsed floodwall and inundated much of the city.

The following pages include a recap of the disaster and a self-guided driving tour that provides a glimpse of the physical scars Hurricane Katrina left behind. They will be with the city for years.

Evacuee arrives at New Orleans airport

AUGUST 29, 2005

Just before sunrise, Hurricane Katrina, a Category 4 hurricane, makes landfall at Buras, LA., 65 miles southeast of New Orleans. Four hours later, the city's levee system is riddled with holes, and severe flooding engulfs nearly 80% of the city.

Lake Pontchartrain

London Ave Canal

Orleans Ave Canal

17th St Canal

17TH STREET CANAL BREACH

Canal No 2

W Esplanade Ave

LONDON AVENUE CANAL BREACHES

6. Minutes later, floodwaters punch holes in the floodwalls on the east side of the London Street Canal, flooding homes in Gentilly.

LAKESHORE

Peoples Ave

Robert E

7. Almost four hours after landfall, the 17th Street Canal floodwall fails, sending a wall of water into Lakeview, Mid-City, and parts of Metairie.

LAKEVIEW

GENTILLY

City Park

Wisner Blvd

Orleans Ave

Pontchartrain Blvd

17th Street Canal Levee

Orleans Ave Canal Levee

London Ave Canal Levee

St Bernard Ave

Elysian Fields Ave

Gentilly Blvd

610

610

5. The storm surge from Lake Pontchartrain pushes down the Orleans Avenue Canal, overtopping levees and pouring water into City Park and Mid-City.

City Park Ave

Peoples Ave

SEVENTH WARD

New Orleans International Airport

Airline Dr

61

Earhart Expy

Palmetto St

N Carrollton Ave

10

61

N Broad St

NEW MARIGNY

St Claude Ave

90

39

46

Brooklyn Ave

Dakin St

Saint Charles Ave

S Claiborne Ave

Fontainebleau Dr

Earhart Blvd

TRÉMÉ

10

S Rampart

Tulane Ave

FRENCH QUARTER

FAUBOURG MARIGNY

Decatur St

♦ Jackson Square

S Carrollton Ave

MID-CITY

S Broad St

M.L. King Jr Blvd

♦ Superdome

CENTRAL BUSINESS DISTRICT

Pontchartrain Expy

Tchoupitoulas St

ALGIERS POINT

General Meyer Ave

Saint Charles Ave

Calhoun St

S Claiborne Ave

Washington Ave

Louisiana Ave

Felicity St

WAREHOUSE DISTRICT

90

Audubon Park

Exposition Blvd

UPTOWN

Upperline St

Napoleon Ave

Saint Charles Ave

LOWER GARDEN DISTRICT

Franklin Ave

UPPER GARDEN DISTRICT

Mississippi River Levee

GRETNA

Tchoupitoulas St

River Rd

Barataria Blvd

4th St

Destrehan Ave

Peters Rd

Belle Chasse Hwy

Westbank Exp

90

Mississippi

River

WESTWEGO

River Rd

HARVEY

4. More than two hours after landfall, the storm surge swells Lake Pontchartrain, overtopping the floodwall on the south side of Lakefront Airport, adding to the rising floodwaters in New Orleans East.

2. Twenty minutes later, the surge overtops the floodwalls and levees in the Industrial Canal.

1. Nearly 30 minutes after landfall, Katrina's storm surge pushes up the Intracoastal Waterway. Water flows over tops and through breaches of the levees protecting New Orleans East; the area begins to flood.

3. The levees hold for roughly an hour until the west side wall breaches, flooding the Upper Ninth Ward, Bywater, and Tremé. Some 15 minutes later, two sections on the east side collapse; a torrent rushes in, flooding the Lower Ninth Ward, Arabi, and Chalmette. Some residents seek refuge on rooftops.

The days that followed

August 30
The breach at the 17th Street Canal gets larger; Lakeview floodwaters rise to nine feet. Many people climb onto roofs to escape. Crowds build at the Superdome, seeking refuge. Rescuers in helicopters and boats pick up hundreds of stranded people, and reports of looting begin to emerge.

August 31
The first buses arrive at the Superdome to take refugees to the Astrodome in Houston.

September 1
Looting, carjacking, and other violence spreads. Crowds at the Superdome swell to 30,000, with another 25,000 at the New Orleans Convention Center.

September 2
Congress approves $10.5 billion for immediate rescue and relief efforts.

September 4
Superdome is fully evacuated. Nearly 45,000 refugees.

September 8
An additional $52 billion in aid approved by Congress.

September 17
Business owners are allowed back into Algiers, French Quarter, the CBD, and Uptown.

September 23
A storm surge from Hurricane Rita overtops an Industrial Canal levee, reflooding the Lower Ninth Ward; surge also tops the London Avenue Canal, reflooding Gentilly.

September 26
After suspending re-entry due to Hurricane Rita, the city allows residents to return.

February 18, 2006
The first official Mardi Gras parade (in Orleans Parish), Pontchartrain, rolls.

February 28
Amid controversey, thousands turn out to celebrate Mardi Gras.

April 28
First day of New Orleans Jazz and Heritage Festival.

May 20
C. Ray Nagin is re-elected Mayor of New Orleans.

June 24
Approximately 20,000 attend American Library Association meeting, the largest conference in the city post Katrina.

Hurricane Katrina was the third-strongest landfalling U.S. hurricane ever recorded.

Nearly 80% of the city was flooded.

Almost 200,000 homes, 71%, were damaged by flooding.

A POST-KATRINA DRIVE

To truly understand the devastation of Hurricane Katrina, you need to see it at the neighborhood level. This tour will give you a sobering glimpse of the formidable challenges the city faces as it rebuilds its levees and neighborhoods and restores its population. As you tour the flood-destroyed areas, you may encounter debris, potholes, malfunctioning traffic signals, and construction. Bring a map, and be prepared to alter your route. Use appropriate caution; as some neighborhoods have repopulated, crime, unfortunately, has also returned. This tour is not for everyone: Heed warnings in the city and don't drive at night.

Car and levee in the Lower Ninth Ward.

TO MID-CITY & 17TH ST. CANAL

Start at the intersection of Canal and North Rampart streets. Driving on Canal, away from the Mississippi River, alongside the streetcar tracks, you'll pass under the Interstate 10 elevated freeway at North Claiborne Avenue and into Mid-City. You will pass many buildings that are still boarded up, some bearing the ominous stain of the flood line. At just over 2 miles, you'll reach the intersection of Canal and South Carrollton Avenue, where a cluster of restaurants has reopened. Another 0.8 miles, at the end of the streetcar tracks, you'll reach City Park Avenue and a pair of historic cemeteries. Take a right, then a quick left onto Canal Boulevard. Past Interstate 610, you'll enter the Lakeview neighborhood, inundated with up to 9 feet of water when floodwalls on the 17th Street Canal collapsed.

At 4.5 miles, you'll come to Harrison Avenue and, to the right, a revived business corridor. Proceed 1 mile farther on Canal Boulevard, then turn left on Robert E. Lee Boulevard. Follow Robert E. Lee as it crosses West End Boulevard, first curving left and then veering right. Six blocks past West End, you'll come to Bellair Drive, the last street before a bridge over the 17th Street Canal. Turn left. After one block, the spot where the floodwall break occurred is visible to the right.

FREQUENTLY ASKED QUESTIONS

Is New Orleans really ready for tourists? Hotels, restaurants, and shops who depend on visitors are certainly ready and want tourists to return. Faced with a severe worker shortage, however, many businesses are struggling to provide the level of service visitors enjoyed before Katrina. But those tourists willing to endure a few inconveniences will find that much of what they like about the city—food, music, and history—are still here.

Is it safe to go? People were understandably shaken by reports of widespread looting and (sometimes exaggerated) mayhem that followed in Katrina's immediate wake. The tourist areas and populated neighborhoods are generally considered safe, but the city has seen rising crime rates, and looting continues in some of its underpopulated neighborhoods.

New Orleans population: 462,269 (August 2005), 295,450 (December 2007).

16 hospitals in the New Orleans metropolitan area are now open.

Louis Armstrong International Airport is up to 82% of pre-Katrina daily departures, serving 88% of pre-Katrina destinations.

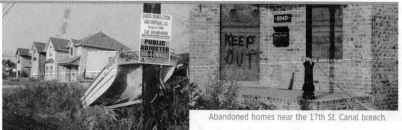

Abandoned homes near the 17th St. Canal breach.

ACROSS THE LAKEFRONT THROUGH GENTILLY

Drive five more blocks, through a stand of oak trees, and turn left. Take another left on Fleur de Lis Drive, a wide boulevard, then right back on to Robert E. Lee. Drive for four blocks, then turn left at the second traffic signal, between a bank and shopping center, and enter the West End. Past a row of apartments and restaurants, Lake Pontchartrain comes into view (mile 8).

Drive along Lakeshore Drive until the road crosses back over the levee and Bayou St. John. (Note that Lakeshore Drive can be closed to traffic for no apparent reason; Robert E. Lee can be used as an alternate route.) At the traffic circle, take a right on Paris Avenue; here, you'll pass through a neighborhood that escaped relatively unscathed. After Paris Avenue crosses Robert E. Lee, the damage quickly becomes apparent. Eight blocks past Robert E. Lee, pass Fillmore Avenue, make a U turn, turn right on Fillmore, and cross the London Avenue Canal. Storm surge from the canal was responsible for destroying much of the surrounding neighborhood. At 12.6 miles, turn right on Elysian Fields Avenue. Drive 1 mile, and continue through the large intersection at Gentilly Boulevard. Then, make a U-turn, and turn right on Gentilly Boulevard (a shady ridge that stayed mostly above water).

At mile 14, turn right on Franklin Avenue. The street passes under a freeway and through a hard-hit section of the 7th Ward before arriving at North Claiborne Avenue.

What shape is the French Quarter in? The neighborhood did not flood, and damage to its collection of historic buildings was relatively mild. Shops, restaurants, clubs, and museums have reopened, but hours may have changed—always call ahead.

What other parts of the city are open? The parts of the city that did not take on floodwaters after Katrina—the French Quarter, Faubourg Marigny, Bywater, the CBD/Warehouse District, and Uptown—have quickly repopulated. All other neighborhoods except some parts of the Lower Ninth Ward are now deemed safe for rebuilding.

Is it safe and appropriate for children? Parents ought to bear in mind the safety concerns we note here and limit their touring with children to the parts of the city mentioned above that did not take on flooding. Bourbon Street at night is hardly appropriate for kids. But then, was it ever?

90% of businesses have reopened in downtown New Orleans.

There are now 888 restaurants open in the New Orleans metropolitan area.

Almost all of New Orleans major hotels have reopened; 32,000 of 38,000 rooms are now available.

Scenes from Tennessee street, in the Lower Ninth Ward.

TO THE LOWER NINTH WARD

Cross North Claiborne, then North Robertson. Go one-half block, make a U-turn, then take a right on North Robertson. This street takes you into the Upper Ninth Ward and, in about 1.5 miles, over the Industrial Canal. To the left is the Lower Ninth Ward. One block past the foot of the bridge make a U turn, then turn right on Tennessee Street. To the left is the site of the levee breach that destroyed the neighborhood; it has since been repaired. Go seven blocks to North Tonti, turn right, then drive one block and take a right again on Reynes. Most of the houses and debris have long been cleared, so there are few reminders that this was once a densely populated neighborhood. Cross North Claiborne and, five blocks later, take a right on St. Claude Avenue, where you will cross another drawbridge.

St. Claude Avenue proceeds through the Upper Ninth Ward; Bywater, which did not flood, is on the left as you make your way back Downtown. A little over a mile past the Industrial Canal, you'll cross a series of railroad tracks. Just past Elysian fields Avenue, St. Claude curves to the left and merges with North Rampart Street before arriving at Esplanade Avenue and the French Quarter's edge. From here, it's less than a mile on North Rampart to your Canal Street starting point.

FREQUENTLY ASKED QUESTIONS

How do I get around the city? Taxis are available, if not as plentiful as they once were, and the city's transit system is up and running again in many neighborhoods. The historic streetcars are rolling along the Mississippi River, Canal Street, and elegant St. Charles Avenue. All roads are open to vehicles, although many are in disrepair.

What health concerns should I be aware of? Tap water is safe to drink and bathe in, and trash has been cleared in the French Quarter, CBD, and Garden District, as well as parts of Uptown and Faubourg Marigny. Emergency medical services are available.

LOCAL FOR A DAY

Tired of time-share hawkers and tap dancers? Want to spend some time enjoying New Orleans the way locals do? Step one: get out of the Quarter.

Get Some Exercise

Go for a jog along the St. Charles Avenue streetcar tracks. You'll have plenty of company anywhere between Jackson Avenue and the university area—just follow the well-worn trails along the wide median (to really pass for a local, refer to it the "neutral ground"). Keep an eye out for streetcars (duh) as well as vehicles crossing the tracks. If that sounds too risky, hit the track at Audubon Park or the paths in City Park. Or rent a bicycle and head for the Lakefront or Audubon Park, where you can get on a paved jogging and bike trail that runs along the Mississippi River levee well into Jefferson Parish.

Find a Market

The Crescent City Farmers Market sets up at the corner of Girod and Magazine streets in the CBD on Saturday mornings; on Tuesday from 9 AM to 1 PM, it's held Uptown at Tulane Square, on Leake Avenue at Broadway. While you may not want to lug a bag of broccoli back to your hotel, there's always some good prepared food for sale, local chefs foraging for ingredients, and an entertaining bunch of vendors. If you happen to be around the third Saturday of the month, check out the Bywater Art Market at Palmer Park (at Royal and Piety streets in the Bywater), where the merchandise is high quality and the crowd never less than colorful.

Queue Up for Breakfast

Contrary to the impression you may have gleaned from Hollywood's version of New Orleans, locals as a rule do not start the morning with café au lait and a plate of beignets—but they do have their favorite spots, where on weekends you'll find lines of hungry customers stretching onto the sidewalk. Both Bluebird Café (*3625 Prytania St., Uptown, 504/895–7166*) and Slim Goodies Diner (*3322 Magazine St., Uptown, 504/891–3447*) are open weekdays, when there's less chance of a wait. Thanks to word-of-mouth advertising, Elizabeth's (*601 Gallier St., Bywater, 504/944–9272*) gets its share of tourists, but the Saturday and Sunday brunch crowd still mostly consists of neighborhood denizens.

Hang Out by the River

Locals love Riverview Drive—better known as the Fly—the riverside stretch of Audubon Park behind the zoo, even if they have no idea how it got its nickname (probably from a butterfly-shape building that used to stand here). There are a couple of baseball diamonds and a football/soccer field, but most people are content to spread out on a blanket, have a picnic, and watch the ships go by on the Mississippi. The nearby dog park, on the levee just upriver from the park, is another popular gathering spot, especially in late afternoon.

NEW ORLEANS WITH KIDS

Get Out & Play

City Park. There's plenty to do here for the younger set, including two free playgrounds: one with swings near the Peristyle, and a new playground for older kids, just off Marconi Drive, that has more challenging things to clamber on. Storyland, a fairy tale–theme park, is open on weekends year-round, and features a number of sculptures created by Blaine Kern Studios, the maker of Mardi Gras floats. Adjacent Carousel Gardens Amusement Park has low-impact rides, a miniature train that tours the park, and a beautiful 100-year-old carousel as a centerpiece. It's open weekends from March through December.

Barataria Preserve. Let the kids burn off some excess energy on the trails in this swamp outpost of the Jean Lafitte National Historic Park, about 15 mi from the French Quarter. Come when it's warm and you'll see lots of creepy-crawlies, including alligators.

Animals Everywhere!

Audubon Zoo. A well-designed showcase for animals from all over the world, the zoo also has a hands-on area for kids—where young volunteers show off real live zoo residents—and a petting zoo with docile goats, among other beasts.

Aquarium of the Americas. Loads of exotic sea creatures, a penguin exhibit, and an interactive area where kids can get their hands wet make the aquarium a favorite family destination. There's a fun museum shop and an IMAX theater next door.

Kiddie Culture

Louisiana Children's Museum. The Warehouse District museum tries to sneak in a little education while giving kids a place to romp, role-play, and dabble in the arts.

Rivertown. It's a bit of a haul out to Kenner, near the airport, but worth the effort to catch a Saturday-afternoon performance in the Children's Castle or to visit the Louisiana Toy Train Museum.

Summer Stages Children's Theater. This drama school for young actors stages kid-friendly fare in summer and a holiday program.

For Kids of All Ages

Blain Kern's Mardi Gras World. The city's most famous float-building family offers tours of the their company's vast studio, where kids can try on costumes and watch the artists at work. Call ahead, though; at press time, the company had just announced plans to relocate its Algiers studio to a site near the convention center by late 2008.

Streetcars. You can't leave New Orleans without taking the kids for a ride in a streetcar, which you can also use to get to several of the sites listed above, including City Park (on the Canal Street line) and Audubon Park (St. Charles Avenue).

BEST FESTS & PARADES

New Year's Eve
You'd expect a party town to throw a big New Year's bash, right? Join the crowd on the Mississippi River near Jax Brewery for fireworks, live music, and the annual countdown to midnight.

Mardi Gras, February or March
There's simply nothing quite like Mardi Gras. The biggest event in the city's busy festival calendar has been around for well over a century, and for a celebration of frivolity, people here take Carnival very seriously. There are almost daily parades—even one for dogs, the Krewe of Barkus—in the two weeks leading up to Fat Tuesday, when pretty much the entire city takes the day off, gets in costume, and hits the streets.

St. Patrick's Day, March
A couple of big parades roll on the weekend closest to March 17: one that starts at Molly's in the Market and winds through the French Quarter, and an Uptown parade that rolls on Magazine Street. On St. Paddy's Day, the streets around Parasol's Restaurant & Bar, in the Irish Channel neighborhood, turn into one big, green block party.

Easter
Three fun parades hit the streets of the French Quarter on Easter Sunday: one led by local entertainer Chris Owens, another dedicated to the late socialite Germaine Wells, and a gay parade that takes the bonnet tradition to a whole new level.

Tennessee Williams/New Orleans Literary Festival, March
This annual tribute to the *Streetcar Named Desire* playwright, who spent much of his career in New Orleans, draws well-known and aspiring writers, lecturers, and a handful of Williams's acquaintances. It closes with contestants reenacting Stanley Kowalski's big "Stella-a-a!" moment. *504/581–1144, www. tennesseewilliams.net.*

French Quarter Festival, April
A lot of locals consider this festival one the best. With stages set up throughout the Quarter and on the river at Woldenberg Park, the focus is on local entertainment—and, of course, food. *504/522–5730, www.fqfi.org.*

Louisiana Strawberry Festival, April (Ponchatoula, LA)
They grow 'em big and sweet north of Lake Pontchartrain, and this annual berry-theme bash draws big crowds. Expect rides, a parade, beauty contests, music, and lots of dessert. *985/370–1889 or 800/917–7045, www.lastrawberryfestival.com.*

Festival International de Louisiane, late April (Lafayette, LA)
Lafayette's pretty downtown becomes one big stage for musicians from Louisiana and throughout the French-speaking world. There's art, theater and dance, great food—and, best of all, the entertainment is free. *337/232–8086, www. festivalinternational.com.*

New Orleans Jazz & Heritage Festival, April-May
Top-notch local and international talent take to several stages the last weekend of April and first weekend of May. The repertoire covers much more than jazz, with big-name pop stars in the mix, and there are dozens of lectures, quality arts and crafts, and awesome food to boot. Next to Mardi Gras, Jazz Fest is the city's biggest draw. *504/410–4100, www.nojazzfest.com.*

BEST FESTS & PARADES

Breaux Bridge Crawfish Festival, early May (Breaux Bridge, LA)

The hard-partying Cajun may be a stereotype, but this festival in Breaux Bridge, 12 mi east of Lafayette, only reinforces it. There's lots of great Cajun and zydeco music to go with the mudbugs. *337/332–6655, www.bbcrawfest.com.*

New Orleans Wine & Food Experience, May

Winemakers and oenophiles from all over the world converge for five days of seminars, tastings, and fine food. The Royal Street Stroll, when shops and galleries host pourings and chefs set up tables on the street, is especially lively. *504/529–9463, www.nowfe.com.*

Essence Music Festival, July

Held around Independence Day, this three-day festival draws top names in R&B, pop, and hip-hop to the Louisiana Superdome. The event also includes talks by prominent African-American figures and empowerment seminars. *www.essence.com/essence/emf.*

Southern Decadence, early September

Labor Day means picnics, a long weekend, and—in New Orleans, at least—hundreds of drag queens–for-a-day parading through the Quarter. What began as a small party among friends has evolved into one of the South's biggest gay celebrations. The parade rolls (and as the day wears on, staggers) on Sunday, but Decadence parties and events start Thursday evening.

Art for Art's Sake, early October

Art lovers and people-watchers pack the Warehouse District and Magazine Street galleries for this annual Saturday evening kickoff to the arts season. What's on the walls usually plays second fiddle to the party scene, which spills out into the streets.

Celebration in the Oaks, late November–early January

City Park's majestic oaks, Botanical Gardens, Carousel Garden, and Storyland amusement park are awash in holiday lights and decorations during this popular weeks-long event. There's food and rides, a miniature train decked out for Christmas, and entertainment by local school groups. *504/482–4888, neworleanscitypark.com.*

A New Orleans Christmas, December

The lighting of Canal Street kicks off this monthlong celebration. Royal Street shops and historic homes don holiday decorations, restaurants feature special *reveillon* menus, and thousands of carolers gather in Jackson Square for a candlelit sing-along. Around Christmas, bonfires are lighted on the levee at various points along the Mississippi, from below New Orleans up into Cajun Country. Legend says the bonfires were lighted by the early settlers to help Papa Noël (the Cajun Santa Claus) find his way up the river. Steamboat tour companies offer special cruises for the occasion.

FREE & ALMOST FREE

Free Museums & Galleries

Unless you're a dues-paying member or a Louisiana resident, you won't get a break at most New Orleans museums. It costs nothing, however, to browse the Warehouse District galleries on and around Julia Street, where you'll find works by established and up-and-coming artists. Make a detour through the lobby and mezzanine of the Renaissance Arts Hotel (*700 Thcoupitoulas St.*), which has an impressive collection on display.

The Sydney and Walda Besthoff Sculpture Garden in City Park, next to the New Orleans Museum of Art, has major work by important 20th-century artists, including Henry Moore, Jacques Lipchitz, Barbara Hepworth, and Seymour Lipton, dramatically set among lagoons and moss-laden oak trees.

Uptown, on the Tulane University campus, the Newcomb Art Gallery hosts shows featuring work by internationally known artists—like the photographer Diane Arbus and master silversmith William Spratling, two recent examples—as well as themed exhibitions and work by Newcomb's art school alumni.

Free Music

Outdoor festivals like the Satchmo Summer Fest and French Quarter Festival are great places to hear live music for free. Street bands also serenade visitors daily in the French Quarter—although if you linger, you'll be asked to toss a few bucks into the hat.

Drop by the Jean Lafitte National Historic Park's French Quarter visitor center to get a schedule of upcoming shows; the park hosts concerts by Louisiana musicians in the courtyard. *419 Decatur St., 504/589-3882.*

The New Orleans Jazz National Historical Park sponsors live performances and lectures Tuesday–Saturday at its French Market office (*916 N. Peters St., 504/589-4806*). The performers—who are invariably good—cover the jazz spectrum, from traditional brass band music to modern jazz.

If you happen to be in town on a Wednesday from early April to late June, check out the free Wednesday at the Square concert series at Lafayette Square in the CBD, across from Gallier Hall. Around 5 PM, a horde of downtown workers converges on the square to hear good local bands, dance, and socialize. There's plenty of food and drink available (not free, alas).

Free Ride

The Canal–Algiers ferry offers some of the best views of the city, and there's no charge if you're not in a car. It's a fun thing to do with kids, and a great way to get a sense of the Mississippi River's magnitude. The pedestrian entrance is on the plaza at the foot of Canal Street, across from Harrah's Casino; it docks on the West Bank at Algiers Point, a quaint historic neighborhood that makes for a good daytime stroll. At night, though, stay on board for the return trip.

OFFBEAT NEW ORLEANS

Cemeteries

It may sound odd, but the old cemeteries in and around New Orleans, where tombs have to be built above the boggy ground to keep the remains of loved ones from drifting away, are fascinating places to visit. Those near the French Quarter (St. Louis No. 2 and St. Roch, for example) aren't safe to visit alone, however; it's best to go on a tour or with a large group. Lake Lawn Metairie Cemetery (*5100 Pontchartrain Blvd., 504/486–6331*), on the other hand, is safe to tour; the office even offers audio guides to help motorists find their way around the stately cemetery, the final resting place of luminaries like Al Hirt, Louis Prima, and Civil War general P. G. T. Beauregard. Guided tours are available by appointment. One note: because it's a very busy cemetery, officials prefer that people visit between 8:30 and 10:30 AM or after 3:30 PM, when there's less chance of disrupting a funeral in progress.

Sno-balls

Generations of New Orleanians who grew up in the days before air-conditioning developed a method for coping with stifling summers: the sno-ball, shaved ice served in a cup or Chinese take-out container and topped with everything from simple syrup to fat-laden condensed milk. Hansen's Sno-Blitz Sweet Shop (*4801 Tchoupitoulas St., 504/891–9788*) has been dishing them out since 1934; another stalwart is Plum Street Snowball at 1300 Burdette Street (*504/866–7996*). For visitors, the fun lies less in the actual product (although a sno-ball can be pretty darn refreshing on a hot summer day) than in being part of a local ritual.

Weird Museums

At the New Orleans Historic Voodoo Museum (*724 Dumaine St., 504/680–0128*), the owner might greet you at the door with a pet albino boa constrictor draped around his neck, the first sign that this is no stuffy cultural institution. The collection of masks, paintings, and voodoo artifacts is small, but offers some insight into a curious religious practice that found a foothold in South Louisiana in colonial days—and, in some quarters, persists.

Louis Dufilho, America's first licensed pharmacist, operated an apothecary, La Pharmacie Francaise, in this 1823 town home. Today it holds the New Orleans Pharmacy Museum (*514 Chartres St., 504/565–8027*), an interesting collection of ancient medicine bottles, a huge leech jar, eyeglasses, and some truly unsettling surgical instruments. The house and spacious courtyard alone are worth the price of admission.

Tiny Abita Springs, north of Lake Pontchartrain, is notable for three things: artesian spring water, Abita Beer, and an oddball institution, the U. C. M. Museum (*22275 Hwy. 36, at Grover St., Abita Springs, 985/892–2624*). Artist John Preble's strange vision—sort of a Louisiana version of Watts Towers—is an obsessive collection of found objects (combs, old musical instruments, paint-by-number art, taxidermy experiments gone horribly awry . . .) set in a series of ramshackle buildings, including one covered in broken tiles. Truly odd and entertaining, but not for the clutter-phobic.

GET OUTTA TOWN

Cajun Country

The land that gave the world one of its great cuisines—and a refuge for French-Canadian exiles in the 18th century—is worth at least one overnighter. Lafayette, with its attractive downtown and plentiful accommodations, makes a good hub for exploring the region. The Cajun kitsch can be a bit much at times, but there are some outstanding restaurants and museums, including the Paul and Lulu University Art Museum and Acadian Village, a recreation of an early-19th-century Acadian settlement. Venture south to picturesque Abbeville, where restaurants serve up some mean oysters on the half shell, or to New Iberia and nearby Avery Island, home of the famous Tabasco hot sauce and a gorgeous 250-acre garden. Breaux Bridge, site of the annual Crawfish Festival, has antiques shops and some excellent Cajun restaurants, including Café des Amis and Mulate's. St. Martinville, south of Breaux Bridge, is an attractive small town and home of the Evangeline Oak, immortalized in Longfellow's classic poem "Evangeline."

To the north lie Grand Coteau, a quaint, historic village set on a natural bluff, and Opelousas, a hotbed of zydeco music; nearby Plaisance hosts the annual Southwest Louisiana Zydeco Music festival each Labor Day weekend. A bit farther afield, the normally quiet town of Mamou goes bonkers on Fat Tuesday, when the traditional Courir de Mardi Gras takes to the streets; Saturday mornings, little Fred's Lounge gets packed to the gills with locals and more than a few tourists two-stepping and waltzing to live Cajun music.

Plantation Country

For *Gone with the Wind* fans, the stretch of the Mississippi north of New Orleans is the ultimate Southern experience. Tour buses ply the highway on both sides of the river, but with a car and a map, it's easy to explore on your own. Fortunes were made here in the 18th and 19th centuries—on the backs of the slaves that worked these plantations—and vestiges of the Old South's wealthy heyday remain in the region's lavish homes, many lovingly restored and open to the public. Highlights include Oak Alley, with its procession of ancient oak trees that flank the entrance, and Nottoway, the largest extant plantation house. Several homes offer accommodations and dining for those who want to linger.

Many of the small towns that dot Plantation Country are fun to explore, but St. Francisville, about 25 mi north of Baton Rouge, deserves special mention. The historic town center is a well-preserved collection of antebellum homes and buildings, and the river landing there is one of the few places in South Louisiana where the Mississippi isn't hemmed in by levees. A cluster of fine plantation homes are nearby, including Rosedown Plantation and Gardens and the attractive Oakley House at Audubon State Historic Site, where John James Audubon taught drawing to the plantation owner's daughter while executing some of the works in his Birds of America series. Baton Rouge itself is worth a visit to see the Old State Capitol (and the new one, where Governor Huey P. Long met his untimely end) and its lively downtown.

GREAT ITINERARIES

HIGHLIGHTS OF NEW ORLEANS

Including a Trip to Plantation Country

Day 1: The French Quarter

Start by getting to know the city's most famous neighborhood. Sure, it's a cliché, but the café au lait and beignets at Café du Monde are a good place to begin, followed by a stroll around Jackson Square and St. Louis Cathedral. Cross the seawall and take in the views of the Mississippi River from Woldenberg Riverfront Park. Wander along North Peters Street to the shops and market stalls in the French Market, followed by a stroll around the mostly residential Lower Quarter and Faubourg Marigny. After lunch, explore the antiques stores and art galleries on Royal and Chartres streets, winding it all up with a cocktail in a shady courtyard; try Napoleon House, an atmospheric bar and café that makes a mean Pimm's Cup, or the French Quarter mainstay Pat O'Brien's. Save Bourbon Street for later in the evening; like anything that's lived hard and been around as long, it's much more attractive in low light.

Day 2: Uptown & the Garden District

The St. Charles Avenue streetcar rumbles past some of the South's most-prized real estate; take a seat in one of the antique wooden seats, raise a window, and admire the scenery on the way to leafy Audubon Park. Follow the paved footpath to the Audubon Zoo, keeping an eye out for the zoo's white tigers, a pair of albino brothers named Rex and Zulu. Board an inbound Magazine Street bus near the zoo entrance and take it a couple of blocks past Louisiana Avenue, where a number of restaurants, some with sidewalk tables, are clustered. Continue on Magazine to Washington Avenue and head left through the Garden District. Prytania Street, just past Lafayette Cemetery No. 1 (Anne Rice fans, take note), is a good axis from which you can explore the neighborhood's elegant side streets. Catch a Downtown-bound streetcar on St. Charles, or wrap up the afternoon shopping and dining on Magazine Street.

Day 3: Remembering Katrina

It may strike some as macabre, but touring neighborhoods that were devastated by Hurricane Katrina and its subsequent floods has become a ritual for many visitors, not unlike the hordes that have made Lower Manhattan's Ground Zero a pilgrimage site. You can opt for a guided bus tour, which takes you to Lakeview and the infamous 17th Street Canal levee breach; some companies also travel to the Ninth Ward and Chalmette. If you have your own transportation, follow a drive through Katrina's aftermath on page 25 in our Remembering Katrina feature. After a somber tour of Katrina's devastation, a good antidote is to look for signs of renewal and rebirth. City Park, which sustained extensive wind and flood damage, has reopened its stately botanical gardens; nearby stands the venerable New Orleans Museum of Art and the adjacent Sydney and Walda Besthoff Sculpture Garden. Wrap the day up with dinner and live music downtown at one of the clubs on Frenchmen Street, in the Faubourg Marigny neighborhood, where the city's diehard party spirit soldiers on.

Day 4: Art, History & Culture

Dedicate one day to a deeper exploration of the city's cultural attractions. Art lovers shouldn't miss the Warehouse District, where a pair of fine museums—the Ogden Museum of Southern Art and the Contemporary Arts Center—anchors a vibrant strip of contemporary art galleries, most of which feature local artists. History buffs will want to check out the National World War II Museum, also in the Warehouse District, and the Historical Collection of New Orleans in the French Quarter, which hosts changing exhibits in a beautifully restored town home. New Orleans music aficionados can browse the bins at the Louisiana Music Factory, which has a wide selection of CDs—and occasional in-store performances—by Louisiana musicians.

Day 5: Heading Out of Town

Consider a day trip out of town to visit one of the region's elegant plantation homes, explore Cajun Country, or take a guided swamp tour. Some tour companies offer a combination of these destinations, with lunch included. Many of the antebellum mansions between New Orleans and Baton Rouge have been painstakingly restored and filled with period furniture; nature lovers will want to set aside time to explore the grounds and lush flower gardens. Swamp tours may sound hokey, but they're actually a good way to see south Louisiana's cypress-studded wetlands (and get up close and personal with the alligators and other critters who live there). Continue the nautical theme in the evening with a ride to Algiers Point aboard the Canal Street ferry for lovely sunset views of the New Orleans skyline.

TIPS

Call ahead for hours and days of operation. In the wake of Katrina, many businesses still have not returned to their full pre-storm schedules. The city has a lot to offer, but some patience and understanding is called for while it rebuilds.

If you're venturing out in your own vehicle, be aware that street conditions, which weren't great to begin with, are still in disrepair in some places. Many bridges and neighborhood streets may be closed for repairs. Traffic signals can be erratic, and debris and roofing nails left behind by contractors can be hazardous to tires.

Summers in New Orleans arrive early and stick around longer than most people would like. If visiting in the hot months, stay hydrated, limit your midday outdoor activities, and be prepared for sudden, sometimes violent downpours.

Exploring
New Orleans

WORD OF MOUTH

"Walk all around the French Quarter. And walk around the Garden District. Take a cemetery tour. Drink a Pat O'Brien's hurricane. Have a muffuletta sandwich in Central Grocery. Buy cheap (but fun) things to bring home (beads, hot sauce, etc.) at the French Market!"

—BuffaloGirl

By Molly
Jahncke &
Michelle Delio

SOMETIME DURING YOUR VISIT TO New Orleans, find a wrought-iron balcony, an oak-shaded courtyard, or a columned front porch and sit quietly, favorite beverage in hand, at 6 AM. At this hour, when the moist air sits most heavily on the streets, New Orleans is a city of mesmerizing tranquillity. By noon, early-morning calm confronts big-city chaos: with all there is to see and hear and eat and drink and do.

The spiritual and cultural heart of New Orleans is the French Quarter, where the city was settled by the French in 1718. You can easily spend several days visiting museums, shops, and eateries in this area. Yet the rest of the city's neighborhoods, radiating out from this focal point, also make for rewarding rambling. The mansion-lined streets of the Garden District and Uptown, the aboveground cemeteries that dot the city, and the open air along Lake Pontchartrain provide a nice balance to the frenzy of the Quarter. Despite its sprawling size, residents treat New Orleans like a small town, or perhaps like a collection of small towns. Families have lived in the same neighborhoods for generations; red beans and rice is served throughout the city on Monday; people visit the tombs of their departed on All Saints' Day; and from the smartest office to the most down-home local bar, New Orleanians are ready to celebrate anything at the drop of a hat.

To experience this fun-filled city, you can begin with the usual tourist attractions, but you must go beyond them to linger in a corner grocery store, sip a cold drink in a local joint, or chat with a stoop-sitter. New Orleanians, for all their gripes and grumbling, love their city. They treasure custom and tradition, take in stride the heat and humidity of a semitropical climate, and face life with a laid-back attitude, despite the ravages from Hurricane Katrina, which caused heavy damage to the city in late August 2005.

GETTING YOUR BEARINGS

The city occupies an 8-mi stretch between the Mississippi River and Lake Pontchartrain, covering roughly 365 square mi of flat, swamp-drained land. The heart of the city, downtown, includes the famous old area called the Vieux Carré (Old Square), or the French Quarter; the historic African-American district of Tremé; the Central Business District (CBD); and the Warehouse District. Across the river from downtown is an extension of New Orleans known as the Westbank, which includes the neighborhood of Algiers Point.

Downriver from the sights-packed French Quarter are the Faubourg Marigny and the Bywater districts, neighborhoods developed in the early 1800s. This mainly residential area is also home to eateries, cafés, music clubs, and collectibles shops. Across Rampart Street from the French Quarter lies Tremé. A couple of small museums add to the allure of this historic residential area. Although parts of this neighborhood saw significant flooding from Hurricane Katrina, most of the damage was caused by wind, rather than water. The museums have now returned, along with many residents.

Canal Street divides the French Quarter from the "American Sector," as it was designated in the early days following the Louisiana Purchase. Americans built their homes in increasing extravagance as they began to make money in the city and moved farther upriver. Eventually, a business district overtook what had been the residential blocks just uptown from Canal, and now the lawyers and artists of the CBD and Warehouse District share the area, taking advantage of the bars, clubs, and loft apartment buildings in this burgeoning neighborhood. Since Katrina, the CBD has seen a faster recovery and more growth—including new music venues and bars—than practically any part of the city.

Canal Street, which was undergoing a revival before the storm, has seen a slower recovery than other parts of the CBD. Although a few new stores have opened along the street, quite a few remain shuttered. Some new clothing stores have moved in, replacing businesses unable to recover from Katrina. The historic streetcar continues to run down the center of the street. The foot of Canal Street, where the French Quarter, the CBD, the Warehouse District, and the Mississippi River converge, is the site of major attractions such as the Aquarium of the Americas, Woldenberg Riverfront Park, Harrah's New Orleans Casino, and the Riverwalk shopping-and-entertainment complex.

WHICH WAY?

Directions in a city that bases its compass on the curve of the river can be hopelessly confusing. Canal Street, a long avenue that runs from the river to the lake, divides the city roughly into uptown and downtown sections. Streets to the north of Canal are named North and run downtown; those to the south of Canal are named South and run uptown. Only the French Quarter is laid out in a grid pattern. Ask a New Orleanian for directions and you are likely to hear about so many blocks downtown or uptown and on the lake or river side. The best advice is to keep a map handy at all times.

The St. Charles Avenue streetcar parallels the Mississippi River on a route several blocks inland along St. Charles Avenue, home to antebellum mansions, the Garden District, and the university sector Uptown. It is usually the best way to get to these areas.

Metairie, hurricane-damaged Mid-City, and the lakefront are accessible primarily by automobile. City Park, within Mid-City, covers a vast area that includes the New Orleans Museum of Art, the Botanical Garden, and an outdoor sculpture garden, plus miles of lagoons, golf courses, and recreation areas. The park was significantly damaged by Katrina, but groups of volunteers have joined with park employees to make it once again a worthwhile place to while away the afternoon.

The Mississippi River dominates New Orleans, even passing through one corner of it. The point across the river from downtown, Algiers, was settled in the late 1800s and remained fairly isolated until a modern bridge and regularly scheduled ferries connected it with the east bank in the 1960s. Algiers continues to maintain a small-town flavor, with pocket parks surrounded by Victorian cottages and oak-canopied streets.

GETTING AROUND

Downtown, the Garden District, and Algiers are best explored on foot, because sites are near one another and should be experienced at a slow pace. For other areas, biking, driving, or riding the streetcar is recommended because of the long distances covered.

If you should want to visit the areas damaged by Hurricane Katrina, you will have to do it by car. Many of these areas are still deserted and should not be toured on foot or at night.

TAKE CARE

Be alert to conditions around you, taking precautions not to wander alone on deserted streets or in questionable areas. New Orleans has a high crime rate. If in doubt about the safety of sights to visit, ask hotel personnel for advice, tour areas in groups when possible, and take a cab at night. (Areas requiring special precautions are noted throughout this chapter.)

THE FRENCH QUARTER

The French Quarter was largely spared Katrina's destruction. Although flooding and disorder touched its Canal Street edge, you'll have to look closely to find signs of damage elsewhere within its well-defined borders, as its many ornate cast- and wrought-iron balconies that look out onto town houses and storefronts remained intact. In the weeks and months following Katrina, the French Quarter became a focal point of media coverage and recovery operations. In this center of New Orleans cuisine and culture, a great commissary for emergency personnel was erected beside the old Jackson Brewery.

Although the crowds have been lighter since the storm, the nightlife returned here almost immediately. Contractors and relief workers quickly found their way to the Bourbon Street clubs, reviving the raucous, bawdy spirit of that strip. Since Katrina, the French Quarter has resumed its role as a major center of tourism and entertainment, where music pours from the doorways of bars as freely as the drinks flow within them. On an ordinary evening, a stroll through the French Quarter is also a moving concert, where the strains of traditional jazz, blues, classic rock and roll, and electronic dance beats all commingle.

During the day, the Quarter offers several different faces to its visitors. The streets running parallel to the river all carry distinct personas: Decatur Street is a strip of tourist shops and hotels uptown from Jackson Square; downtown from the square, it becomes an alternative hangout for leather-clad regulars drawn to shadowy bars, vintage clothing resellers, and novelty shops. Chartres Street is a relatively calm stretch of inviting shops and eateries. Royal Street is the address of sophisticated antiques shops and many of the Quarter's finest homes. Bourbon Street claims the sex shops, extravagant cocktails, and music clubs filmmakers love to feature. Dauphine and Burgundy streets are more residential, with just a few restaurants and bars serving as retreats for locals.

The French Quarter is the only section of New Orleans in which you will find an easily navigable grid pattern to the streets, so take advantage of it. The city curves with the river, so locals generally describe locations based on relative proximity to the river or the lake and to uptown or downtown. Thus, "it's on the downtown, lakeside corner" of a given intersection indicates that a destination is more or less on the northeast corner. As local directions also often refer to the number block that a site is on (as in the 500 block of Royal Street), block numbers are included in the French Quarter blocks of the French Quarter and Faubourg Marigny map. The numbers across the top of the map are applicable to all the streets parallel to North Rampart Street. Those streets in the French Quarter that are perpendicular to North Rampart Street all start at 500 at Decatur Street and progress at increments of 100 at each block in the direction of North Rampart.

Numbers in the margin correspond to numbers on the French Quarter and Faubourg Marigny map.

JACKSON SQUARE & THE RIVERFRONT

WHAT TO SEE

Aquarium of the Americas. Power failures during Katrina resulted in the major loss of the Aquarium's collection of more than 7,000 aquatic creatures. In a dramatic gesture of solidarity, aquariums around the country joined together with the Aquarium of the Americas in an effort to repopulate its stock, and this wonderful family attraction has fully reopened. The museum has four major exhibit areas—the Amazon Rain Forest, the Caribbean Reef, the Mississippi River, and the Gulf Coast—all of which have fish and animals native to that environment. A special treat is the Seahorse Gallery, which showcases seemingly endless varieties of these beautiful creatures. The aquarium's spectacular design allows you to feel part of the watery worlds by providing close-up encounters with the inhabitants. A gift shop and café are on the premises.

Woldenberg Riverfront Park, which surrounds the aquarium, is a tranquil spot with a view of the Mississippi. Package tickets for the aquarium and a river cruise are available outside the aquarium. You can also combine tickets for the aquarium and the **Entergy IMAX Theater,** a river cruise, and the **Audubon Zoo** in a package, or take the river cruise by itself. Note that the zoo cruise halts operation for several weeks around December each year for maintenance. ⊠ *1 Canal St., French Quarter* ☎*504/581–4629 or 800/774–7394* ⊕*www.audubon institute.org* ⊠*Aquarium $17.50; combination ticket with IMAX $22.50; combination ticket for aquarium, zoo, and round-trip cruise $41* ⊙*Aquarium Tues.–Sun. 10–5*

The Cabildo. Dating from 1799, this Spanish colonial–style building is named for the Spanish council—or *cabildo*—that met there. The transfer of Louisiana to the United States was made in 1803 in the front room on the second floor overlooking the square. This historic transaction was reenacted in the same room for the 200th anniversary of the

St. Louis
Cemetery
No. 1

52 Louis
    Armstrong
    Park

Basin St.

← TO STORYVILLE
  SITE

53

♦ Congo Square

N. Rampart   St.

100   200   300   400   500   600   700   800   900   1000

51

FRENCH QUARTER

Burgundy   St.

Conti   St.

1

St. Louis   St.

Orleans   St.

St. Ann   St.

Dumaine   St.

St. Philip   St.

← TO CBD/
  WAREHOUSE
  DISTRICT

Bienville   St.

2

Dauphine   St.

Streetcar
Stop

3

31

Bourbon   St.

Iberville   St.

Toulouse   St.

St. Peter   St.

4

Streetcar
Stop

Royal   St.

Exchange Pl.

5

21

30

19

20

29

18

27

28

8

17

Napoleon
House

Père
Antoine
Alley

Pirate's Alley

22

Chartres   St.

6   7

16

Jackson

23

25

Dorsiere St.

9

Wilk Row

15

Square

24

Decatur   St.

Clinton St.

N. Peters St.

10

Canal   St.

Clay St.

14

26

♦ Café
  du Monde

N. Front St.

Streetcar
Stop

Moon Walk

Streetcar
Stop

13

Woldenberg
Riverfront
Park

Streetcar
Stop

11

Entergy
IMAX Theater

Mississippi River

Algiers
Point

12

Canal Street
Ferry Terminal

American Aquatic
Gardens 41

Aquarium of the
Americas 12

Backstreet Cultural
Museum 48

Beauregard-Keyes
House 34

The Cabildo 16

Canal Place 11

Christopher
Porché-West Galerie 47

Customs House 10

Dr. Bob 42

1850 House 24

Faulkner House 18

French Market 32

Gallier House 36

Gauche House 38

Germaine Wells
Mardi Gras Museum 2

Haunted House 35

Hermann-Grima
House 3

Historic New Orleans
Collection 4

J & M Music Shop 51

Jackson Brewery 14

Jackson Square 23

Jean Lafitte National Park
Visitor Center 9

LaBranche Houses 19

Lafitte's
Blacksmith Shop 31

Latrobe House 37

Le Petit Théâtre 17

Louis Armstrong Park 52

Louisiana Office
of Tourism 25

The French Quarter & Faubourg Marigny

St. Claude Ave.

N. Rampart St.

1100   1200   1300

Burgundy St.

Dauphine St.

Bourbon St.

Royal St.

Chartres St.

Decatur St.

French Market Pl.

N. Peters St.

Streetcar Stop

Streetcar Stop

Ursulines St.

Gov. Nicholls St.

Barracks St.

Esplanade Ave.

900

800

700

600

500

Kerlerec St.

St. Anthony St.

Pauger St.

Touro St.

Frenchmen St.

N. Rampart St.

Burgundy St.

Dauphine St.

Royal St.

Elysian Fields Ave.

Marigny St.

St. Claude Ave.

Chartres St.

Decatur St.

N. Peters St.

Mandeville St.

Spain St.

Franklin St.

FAUBOURG MARIGNY

TO BYWATER NEIGHBORHOOD

KEY

🚊 Streetcar

Latrobe Park

0   1/4 mi

0   1/2 km

50 · 48 · 37 · 38 · 36 · 35 · 34 · 33 · 32 · 39 · 40 · 41 · 47 · 45 · 46 · 42 · 44 · 43 · 49

Louisiana Supreme Court Building 5
Madame John's Legacy ... 28
Maspero's Exchange 6
Mercury Injection Studio Arts 45
Michalopoulos Galleries ... 8
Miltenberger Houses 29
Musée Conti Wax Museum 1

New Orleans African-American Museum 50
New Orleans Historic Voodoo Museum 30
New Orleans Center for Creative Arts (NOCCA) ... 43
New Orleans Pharmacy Museum 7
Old Mint 39
Old Ursuline Convent 33

Our Lady of Guadalupe ... 53
Pontalba Buildings 15
The Presbytère 27
Quadroon Ballroom 21
Rodrigue Studio 20
St. Augustine Catholic Church 49
St. Louis Cathedral 22

Studio Inferno Glassworks 46
Venusian Gardens and Art Gallery 44
Washington Artillery Park 26
Washington Square Park 40
Woldenberg Riverfront Park 13

purchase in 2003. The Cabildo later served as the city hall and then the Supreme Court. Three floors of multicultural exhibits recount Louisiana history—from the colonial period through Reconstruction—with countless artifacts, including the death mask of Napoléon Bonaparte. In 1988 the building suffered terrible damage from a four-alarm fire. Most of the historic pieces inside were saved, but the top floor, roof, and cupola had to be replaced. The Cabildo is almost a twin to the **Presbytère** on the other side of the cathedral. Having suffered only minor window and shutter damage, the Cabildo was the first of the Louisiana State Museum properties to reopen after Katrina. ⊠ *Jackson Sq., French Quarter* ☎ *504/568–6968* ⊕ *http://lsm.crt.state.la.us* ⊠ *$6* ⊗ *Tues.–Sun. 9–5.*

NEED A BREAK?

Café du Monde (⊠ *800 Decatur St., French Quarter* ☎ *504/525–4544* ⊕ *www.cafedumonde.com*) serves up café au lait and beignets (and not much else) in a style that hasn't varied for more than a century. It's open around the clock, for late-night treats or a sweet breakfast. This is an absolute must-visit spot.

⑪ **Canal Place.** The tony stores of this upscale shopping and office complex were significantly damaged by looting following the storm, but repairs and restocking soon began in earnest. With the reopening of Saks Fifth Avenue in late 2006, the return of the city's signature downtown shopping complex was complete. **Canal Place Cinema,** the only location in this area that screens first-run movies, has already reopened, much to the relief of art-house film fans in New Orleans. Artwork based on local novelist Walker Percy's *The Moviegoer* hangs in the theater's hallways. The **Southern Repertory Theater,** on the third floor, specializes in plays of local interest or written by local artists. Nearby, **Rhino Gallery** sells arts and crafts by top local artists. The **Wyndham New Orleans at Canal Place** tops the complex; its dining rooms and lobby have fantastic river views. ⊠ *333 Canal St., French Quarter* ☎ *504/522–9200* ⊗ *Mon.–Sat. 10–7, Sun. noon–6.*

Canal Street. Canal Street, 170 feet wide, is the widest main street in the United States and one of the liveliest—particularly during Carnival parades. It was once scheduled to be made into a canal linking the Mississippi River to Lake Pontchartrain; the plans changed, but the name remains. In the early 1800s, after the Louisiana Purchase, the French Creoles residing in the French Quarter were segregated from the Americans who settled upriver from Canal Street. The communities had separate governments and police systems, and what is now Canal Street—and, most

BORDERLAND

In New Orleans, street medians are known as "neutral grounds." Why? The term evolved in the days following the Louisiana Purchase, when the Europeans and Creoles who inhabited the French Quarter did little to welcome American immigrants into their neighborhood. Americans instead settled outside of the city center and established what is now the CBD/Warehouse and Garden Districts. Canal Street became the first "neutral ground" in the clash of cultures.

specifically, the central median running down Canal Street—was neutral ground between them. Today, animosities between these two groups are history, but the term "neutral ground" has survived as the name for all medians throughout the city.

Some of the grand buildings that once lined Canal Street remain, many of them former department stores and businesses now serving as hotels, restaurants, or souvenir shops. The Werlein Building (605 Canal Street), once a multilevel music store, is now the Palace Café restaurant. The former home of Maison Blanche (921 Canal Street), once the most elegant of the downtown department stores, is now a Ritz-Carlton hotel, with a ground floor devoted to an upscale mini-mall. One building still serving its original purpose is Adler's (722 Canal Street), the city's most elite jewelry and gift store. For the most part, these buildings are faithfully restored, so you can still appreciate the grandeur that once reigned on this fabled strip.

⑩ Customs House. From the time of its construction in 1849 until 2004, this massive building served as the customs house for the Port of New Orleans. It occupies an entire city block and replaces what had been Ft. St. Louis, which guarded the old French city. The building has identical entrances on all four sides, because at the time it was completed no decision had been made as to which side would be the main entrance. At this writing, the Customs House was slated to become the home of the new **Audubon Insectarium** in summer of 2007; the museum is to be the largest of its kind in the United States. Scheduled exhibits include displays of Louisiana swamp insects, prehistoric insect wonders, and even a cooking demonstration showcasing insect recipes from around the world. ✉ *423 Canal St., French Quarter.*

㉔ 1850 House. A docent leads you through this well-preserved town house and courtyard, part of the **Pontalba Buildings** and furnished in the style of the mid-19th century, when the buildings were built as upscale residences and retail space. Notice the ornate ironwork on the balconies of the apartments: the original owner, Baroness Micaela Pontalba, introduced cast (or molded) iron with these buildings, and it eventually replaced much of the old hand-wrought ironwork in the French Quarter. The initials for her families, *A* and *P*—Almonester and Pontalba—are worked into the design. A gift shop and bookstore run by Friends of the Cabildo is downstairs. Call ahead to find out when the house is open for tours; operating hours vary. The Friends of the Cabildo offer an informative two-hour walking tour of the French Quarter that starts at this location. ✉ *523 St. Ann St., on Jackson Sq., French Quarter* ☎ *504/568–6968* ✉ *$3, walking tour $12* ☉ *Tues.–Sun. 9–5; tours Mon. at 1:30, Tues.–Sun. at 10 and 1:30.*

⑱ Faulkner House. The young novelist William Faulkner lived and wrote his first book, *Soldier's Pay,* here in the 1920s. He later returned to his native Oxford, Mississippi, and became a Pulitzer prize–winning writer. The house is not open for tours, but accommodates **Faulkner House Books** (⇨ *Shopping, French Quarter)* and the literary group **Pirate's Alley Faulkner Society,** which specializes in local and South-

ern writers. ✉624 *Pirate's Alley,*
French Quarter ☎504/524–2940
🕐*Daily 10–6.*

㉜ French Market. The sounds, colors,
and smells here are alluring: street
performers, ships' horns on the
river, pralines, muffulettas, sugarcane, and creole tomatoes. Originally a Native American trading
post, later a bustling open-air
market under the French and
Spanish, the French Market historically began at Café du Monde
and stretched along Decatur and
North Peters streets all the way to
the downtown edge of the Quarter. Today the market's graceful
arcades have been mostly enclosed
and filled with shops and eateries, and the fresh market has been
pushed several blocks downriver,
under sheds built in 1936 as part of
a Works Progress Administration project. This area of the French Market, which begins at Ursulines Street and contains a large **flea market** as
well as a farmers' market area and its own praline and food stands, was
slated for major renovation even before Katrina tore away its awnings
and the 2005 hurricane season devastated the farming communities
that provided its produce. The newly renovated French Market is a
great place to shop for cheap souvenirs, sunglasses, or beads; it's also
home to an expanded farmers' market.

> ## CHESS CHAMPIONS
>
> Frances Parkinson Keyes's his-
> torical novel The Chess Players is
> based on the life of Paul Morphy,
> a New Orleanian considered one
> of the greatest modern chess
> masters. The Beauregard-Keyes
> House was originally built for Mor-
> phy's grandfather, and the present
> location of Brennan's restaurant
> was once Morphy's residence. If
> you're interested in challenging a
> living chess master, stop by Jude
> Acer's sidewalk table outside the
> Gazebo Café on Decatur Street.
> The two-time world-record holder
> for simultaneous games, Acer is at
> his table most days and takes on
> all challengers for a small fee.

Latrobe Park, a small recreational area at the uptown end of the French
Market, honors Benjamin Latrobe, designer of the city's first waterworks. A modern fountain evoking a waterworks marks the spot where
Latrobe's steam-powered pumps once stood. Sunken seating, fountains,
and greenery make this a lovely place to relax with a drink from one
of the nearby kiosks. ✉*Decatur St., French Quarter* 🕐*Daily 6–6; hrs
may vary depending on season and weather.*

⑭ Jackson Brewery. Also called Jax Brewery, this former brewery was
remodeled in the 1980s to house a three-section shopping-and-entertainment complex. Outside are multilevel terraces facing the river, and
inside are more than 20 shops, a small museum preserving the history
of the brewery, a food court, and restaurants. The **Hard Rock Cafe** is
in a separate building. ✉*600 Decatur St., French Quarter* ☎*504/566–
7245* ⊕*www.jacksonbrewery.com* 🕐*Mon.–Sat. 10–6.*

★ ♻ ㉓ Jackson Square. Surrounded by historic buildings and plenty of the city's
atmospheric street life, the heart of the French Quarter is this beautifully landscaped park. Originally called the Place d'Armes, the square
was founded in 1718 as a military parade ground. It was also the site

of public executions carried out in various styles, including burning at the stake, beheading, breaking on the wheel, and hanging. A **statue of Andrew Jackson,** victorious leader of the Battle of New Orleans in the War of 1812, commands the center of the square; the park was renamed for him in the 1850s. The words carved in the base on the cathedral side of the statue—THE UNION MUST AND SHALL BE PRESERVED— are a lasting reminder of the federal troops who occupied New Orleans during the Civil War and who inscribed them.

Among the notable buildings around the square are **St. Louis Cathedral** and **Faulkner House.** Two Spanish colonial–style buildings, the **Cabildo** and the **Presbytère,** flank the cathedral. The handsome rows of brick apartments on each side of the square are the **Pontalba Buildings.** The park is landscaped in a sun pattern, with walkways set like rays streaming out from the center, a popular garden design in the royal court of King Louis XIV, the Sun King. In the daytime, dozens of artists hang their paintings on the park fence and set up outdoor studios where they work on canvases or offer to draw portraits of passersby. These artists are easy to engage in conversation and are knowledgeable about many aspects of the Quarter and New Orleans. You can also be entertained by musicians, mimes, tarot-card readers, and magicians who perform on the flagstone pedestrian mall surrounding the square, many of them day and night. ✉ *French Quarter* ۞ *Park daily 8* AM*–dusk; flagstone paths on park's periphery open 24 hrs.*

㉕ Louisiana Office of Tourism. In addition to maps and hundreds of brochures about sights in the city and its environs, this information center has guides who can answer questions. ✉ *529 St. Ann St., French Quarter* ☎ *504/568–5661* ۞ *Tues.–Sat. 9–5.*

Mississippi River. When facing the river, you see to the right the **Crescent City Connection,** a twin-span bridge between downtown New Orleans and the Westbank, and a ferry that crosses the river every 30 minutes. The river flows to the left downstream for another 100 mi until it merges with the Gulf of Mexico. Directly across the river are the ferry landing and a ship-repair dry dock in a neighborhood called **Algiers Point.** Downriver, a row of burned wharves and warehouses is visible stretching along the Faubourg Marigny and Bywater neighborhoods to the Industrial Canal. These riverside structures were consumed in a massive fire occurring in the days following Hurricane Katrina. (The city has grand plans for redeveloping the area into parks and public areas, but no date has been set for the project, and the burned warehouses remain.) Much of the rescue-and-recovery operation was based around the river; for months after the storm, responders and other government employees were housed on cruise liners anchored here. Today, the river has returned to its normal activity of steamboats carrying tour groups, tugboats pushing enormous barges, and oceangoing ships. Sometimes a dredge is visible, dredging the river's bottom of silt to keep the channel open for large ships.

⑮ Pontalba Buildings. Baroness Micaela Pontalba built these twin sets of town houses, one on each side of Jackson Square, in the late 1840s;

they are known for their ornate cast-iron balcony railings. Baroness Pontalba's father was Don Almonester, who sponsored the rebuilding of St. Louis Cathedral in 1788. The strong-willed Miss Almonester also helped fund the landscaping of the square and the erection of the Andrew Jackson statue in its center. She later moved to Paris, where she is buried. The Pontalba Buildings are publicly owned; the side to the right of the cathedral, on St. Ann Street, is owned by the state, and the other side, on St. Peter Street, by the city. In the state-owned side is the **1850 House,** and at 540-B St. Peter Street on the city-owned side is a plaque marking this apartment as that of Sherwood Anderson, writer and mentor to William Faulkner. ⊠*French Quarter.*

㉗ **The Presbytère.** One of twin Spanish colonial–style buildings flanking St.
Fodor'sChoice   Louis Cathedral, this one, on the right, was designed to house the priests
★   of the cathedral; instead, it served as a courthouse under the Spanish and later under the Americans. The building's cupola, destroyed by a hurricane in 1915, was restored in 2005 to match the one atop its twin. Fortunately, the new cupola withstood Katrina's winds, and the buildings once again mirror each other as they did throughout the 19th century. ⊠*Jackson Sq., French Quarter* ☎*504/568–6968* ⊕*http://lsm. crt.state.la.us* ☜*$5* ☾*Tues.–Sun. 9–5.*

㉒ **St. Louis Cathedral.** The oldest active cathedral in the United States, this church at the heart of the Old City is named for the 13th-century French king who led two crusades. The current building, which replaced two structures destroyed by fire, dates from 1794 (although it was remodeled and enlarged in 1851). The austere interior is brightened by murals covering the ceiling and stained-glass windows along the first floor. Pope John Paul II held a prayer service for clergy here during his New Orleans visit in 1987; to honor the occasion, the pedestrian mall in front of the cathedral was renamed Place Jean Paul Deux. Nearly every evening in December brings a free concert held inside the cathedral. The statue of the Sacred Heart of Jesus dominates **St. Anthony's Garden,** which extends behind the rectory to Royal Street. This statue was only mildly damaged during Katrina, losing the thumb and forefinger of one hand. The pieces have been recovered, but the statue's injuries have yet to be repaired. The garden is also the site of a monument to 30 members of a French ship who died in a yellowfever epidemic in 1857. ⊠*615 Père Antoine Alley, French Quarter* ☎*504/525–9585* ☜*Free.*

NEED A BREAK?   A great favorite among pensive French Quarter intellectuals, the tiny Pirates Alley Café (⊠*622 Pirates Alley, French Quarter* ☎*504/524–9332*) is an ideal setting for espresso, wine, or a light salad or sandwich alongside St. Louis Cathedral.

㉖ **Washington Artillery Park.** This raised concrete area on the river side of Decatur Street, directly across from Jackson Square, is a great spot to photograph the square and the barges and paddle wheelers on the Mississippi. The cannon mounted in the center and pointing toward the river is a model 1861 Parrot Rifle used in the Civil War. This monument honors the local 141st Field Artillery of the Louisiana National Guard

Micaela Pontalba

Every life has its little dramas, but how many of us can claim lives dramatic enough to inspire an opera? The Baroness Micaela Almonester de Pontalba is in that rarefied number, albeit posthumously. In 2003, on the 200th anniversary of the Louisiana Purchase, the New Orleans Opera Association commissioned an opera based on Pontalba and the mark she left on New Orleans—although you can encounter her legacy most readily in the Pontalba Buildings, the elegant brick apartment buildings lining Jackson Square.

Micaela Almonester was of Spanish stock, the daughter of the wealthy entrepreneur and developer Don Andres Almonester, who was instrumental in the creation of the Cabildo and Presbytère on Jackson Square. Don Almonester died while Micaela was still young, but not before passing on to his daughter a passion for building and urban design. The rest of her life became a tale of the impact a single will can have upon an urban environment, as well as a tragedy-torn drama of international scope.

At the time of the Louisiana Purchase, in 1803, New Orleans was in cultural upheaval. Following a period under Spanish rule during the late 18th century, the French had reacquired the colony—but only in time to sell it to the Americans. The blending of French and Spanish society was further complicated by the anticipated imposition of American laws and mores, so foreign to the population of New Orleans. Micaela Almonester was right in the middle of the confusion: daughter of Spanish gentry, she fell in love and married a Frenchman, who took her to Paris with his family to avoid coming under American rule in New Orleans.

The Pontalbas' marriage was particularly unhappy, and Micaela's relationship to her in-laws was poisoned by mistrust over family property. Control of her New Orleans inheritance became part of an increasingly bitter feud that included separation from her husband and, in its dramatic pinnacle, her attempted murder by her father-in-law. After the old baron inflicted four gunshot wounds on his daughter-in-law, he committed suicide, believing he had protected his son and his property. But Micaela, now Baroness de Pontalba following the old baron's death, survived her wounds. Within two years, she had recovered enough to conceive the plan for the buildings that bear her name, but a long series of delays, including a bitter divorce, halted the project. Micaela finally returned to New Orleans in the 1840s, in order to direct construction of the elegant apartment buildings that would complete the square her father had been so instrumental in developing during the previous century. The Pontalba Buildings, designed by James Gallier in the French style favored by Micaela, were dedicated in 1851 to great fanfare. Each building (one along each side of Jackson Square) contained 16 grand and lavishly detailed apartments.

Following the dedication of the buildings, Pontalba returned to France. She had been living in Paris for nearly 50 years by now, her children had grown up there, and it had become her home. Yet the pilgrimage she had made to New Orleans, in order to complete a dream in the name of her father's memory, hints that her heart had never really left her childhood home.

that saw action from the Civil War through World War II. Marble tablets at the base give the history of the group, represented today by the Washington Artillery Association. ⊠*Decatur St. between St. Peter and St. Ann Sts., French Quarter.*

⑬ Woldenberg Riverfront Park. This stretch of green from Canal Street to Esplanade Avenue overlooks the Mississippi River as it curves around New Orleans, giving the city the name the Crescent City. The wooden promenade section in front of Jackson Square is called **Moon Walk,** named for Mayor Moon Landrieu, under whose administration in the 1970s the riverfront beyond the flood wall was first opened to public view. Erected in 2003, the modest **Holocaust Memorial** has a spiral walkway clad in Jerusalem stone. At the center of the spiral are nine

sculptural panels by Jewish artist Yaacov Agam. The faces of the panels converge into different shapes when viewed from different angles, and a plaque at the top of the spiral describes the symbolic significance of each view. Woldenberg Park is named for its benefactor, local businessman Malcolm Woldenberg, whose statue is in the park. *Ocean Song,* a large kinetic sculpture near the statue of Woldenberg, was created by local artist John T. Scott. ⊠*French Quarter.*

INSIDE THE VIEUX CARRÉ

WHAT TO SEE

㉞ Beauregard-Keyes House. This stately 19th-century mansion with period furnishings was the temporary home of Confederate general P.G.T. Beauregard. The house and grounds had severely deteriorated by the 1940s, when the well-known novelist Frances Parkinson Keyes moved in and helped restore it. Her studio at the back of the large courtyard remains intact, complete with family photos, original manuscripts, and her doll, fan, and teapot collections. Keyes wrote 40 novels in this studio, all in longhand, among them the local favorite, *Dinner at Antoine's.* The house suffered some roof damage during Katrina, resulting in water stains along the dining room ceiling. Undaunted, the staff has reopened the site and continues its normal tour schedule. If you do not have time to tour the house, take a peek through the gates at the beautiful walled garden at the corner of Chartres and Ursulines streets. Landscaped in the same sun pattern as Jackson Square, the garden is in bloom throughout the year. ⊠*1113 Chartres St., French Quarter* ☎*504/523–7257* ⊡*$5* ⊙*Mon.–Sat. 10–3, tours on the hr.*

Bourbon Street. Ignore your better judgment and take a stroll down Bourbon Street, past the bars, restaurants, music clubs, and novelty shops that have given this strip its reputation as the playground of the South. The bars of Bourbon Street were among the first businesses of the city to reopen after the storm; catering to the off-duty relief workers, they provided a different form of relief. On most nights, the crowds remain lighter here than in recent years, but the spirit of unbridled revelry is back in full swing. The noise, raucous crowds, and bawdy sights are not family fare; if you go with children, do so before sundown. Although the street is usually well patrolled, it is wise to stay alert to your surroundings. The street is blocked to make a pedestrian mall at night; often the area is shoulder to shoulder, especially during major sports events and Mardi Gras.

> ### GET A "GO CUP"
>
> If you're on foot, you can get your beverage to go from any bar in the city. Open containers of alcohol are allowed on the streets, as long as they're not in glass containers. So when you're ready to leave, ask your bartender for a "go cup," pour your drink into the plastic cup, and head out the door to the next venue, drink in hand.

At Toulouse Street is the former site of the **French Opera House,** once one of New Orleans's most opulent public buildings, which burned down in 1919. There is probably a Lucky Dog vendor nearby, with a vending cart shaped like a hot dog. These carts were immortalized by John Kennedy Toole in his Pulitzer prize–winning novel about New Orleans, *A Confederacy of Dunces,* and their return after the storm was a welcome sight for visitors and locals alike. St. Ann Street marks the beginning of a short strip of gay bars, some of which retain links to the long history of gay culture in New Orleans.

36 **Gallier House.** Famous New Orleans architect James Gallier designed this as his family home in 1857. Today it contains an excellent collection of early Victorian furnishings. The tour includes the house, servants' quarters, and a gift shop. ⊠*1132 Royal St., French Quarter* ☎*504/525–5661* ✉*$6, combination ticket with Hermann-Grima House $10* ☉*Tours weekdays 10, 11, noon, 2, 3.*

38 **Gauche House.** One of the most distinctive houses in the French Quarter, this mansion and its service buildings date from 1856. The cherub design of the effusive ironwork is the only one of its kind. It was once the estate of businessman John Gauche and is still privately owned. This house is not open to the public. ⊠*704 Esplanade Ave., French Quarter.*

2 **Germaine Wells Mardi Gras Museum.** During a 31-year period (1937–68), Germaine Cazenave Wells, daughter of Arnaud's restaurant founder Arnaud Cazenave, was queen of Carnival balls a record 22 times for 17 different krewes, or organizations. Many of her ball gowns, in addition to costumes worn by other family members, are on display in this dim, quirky, one-room museum above Arnaud's restaurant. ⊠*Arnaud's restaurant, 813 Bienville St., 2nd fl. (enter through restaurant), French Quarter* ☎*504/523–5433* ✉*Free* ☉*Daily during restaurant hrs.*

③ Haunted House. Locals agree that this is the most haunted house in a generally haunted neighborhood. Most blame the spooks on Madame Lalaurie, a wealthy but ill-fated socialite who lost both parents as a child, then two husbands before finding a third and moving with him into this mansion on Royal Street. Madame Lalaurie fell out with society when a fire in her attic exposed atrocious treatment of her slaves: according to newspaper reports, well-wishing neighbors who rushed into the house found seven mutilated slaves in one of the apartments. Madame Lalaurie fled town that night, but occupants of the house have told of hauntings ever since. One tour guide claims that when clients faint from the heat it is always by this house, and that cameras often mysteriously refuse to function when pointed at the house, which is not open to the public. ⊠*1140 Royal St., French Quarter.*

☾ ❸ **Hermann-Grima House.** One of the largest and best-preserved examples of American architecture in the Quarter, this Georgian-style house has the only restored private stable and the only working 1830s creole kitchen in the Quarter. American architect William Brand built the house in 1831. The house fortunately sustained only minor damage during Katrina and is open for visits and tours. Cooking demonstrations on the open hearth are held here all day Thursday from October through May. You'll want to check the gift shop, which has many local crafts and books. ⊠*820 St. Louis St., French Quarter* ☎*504/525–5661* ☜*$6, combination ticket with the Gallier House $10* ☉*Tours weekdays 10, 11, noon, 2, 3.*

Fodor'sChoice
★

★ ❹ **Historic New Orleans Collection.** This private archive and exhibit complex, with thousands of historic photos, documents, and books, is one of the finest research centers in the South. It occupies the 19th-century town house of General Kemper Williams and the 1792 Merrieult House. Changing exhibits focus on aspects of local history. History tours and home tours of the houses, grounds, and archives are offered several times daily. A museum shop sells books, prints, and gifts. Children under 12 are not admitted. ⊠*533 Royal St., French Quarter* ☎*504/523–4662* ⊕*www.hnoc.org* ☜*Exhibit and research library (410 Chartres St.) free, tour of houses or archive galleries $4* ☉*Tues.–Sat. 9:30–3.*

★ ❾ **Jean Lafitte National Park Visitor Center.** This center has free visual and sound exhibits on the customs of various communities throughout the state, as well as information-rich daily history tours of the French Quarter. The one-hour daily tour leaves at 9:30 AM; tickets are handed out one per person (you must be present to get a ticket), beginning at 9 AM, for that day's tours only. Arrive at least 15 minutes before tour time to be sure of a spot. The office also supervises

ARRRRGH!

Pirate's Alley takes its name, in part, from the popular myth that Jean Lafitte met here with General Andrew Jackson before the Battle of New Orleans. During this meeting, Lafitte supposedly made his offer to double-cross the British. The legend apparently has no historical foundation, but its romance was so appealing that the name of the alley (originally Orleans Alley) was officially changed.

and provides information on Jean Lafitte National Park Barataria Unit, a nature preserve (complete with alligators) across the river from New Orleans, and the Chalmette Battlefield, where the Battle of New Orleans was fought in the War of 1812. Each year in January, near the anniversary of the battle, a reenactment is staged at the Chalmette site. ⊠ *419 Decatur St., French Quarter* ☎ *504/589–2636* ⊙ *Daily 9–5.*

⓳ LaBranche Houses. This complex of lovely town houses, built in the 1830s by Widow LaBranche, fills the half block between Pirate's Alley and Royal and St. Peter streets behind the Cabildo. The house on the corner of Royal and St. Peter streets, with its elaborate, rounded cast-iron balconies, is the most-photographed residence in the French Quarter. ⊠ *700 Royal St., French Quarter.*

㉛ Lafitte's Blacksmith Shop. The striking anvil no longer sounds in this ancient weathered building. You'll hear only the clinking of glasses at this favorite local bar for patrons from all walks of life. Legend has it that the pirate Jean Lafitte and his cronies operated a blacksmith shop here as a front for their vast illicit trade in contraband. The building, dating from 1772 and thus a rare survivor of the 18th-century French Quarter fires, is interesting as one of the few surviving examples of soft bricks reinforced with timber, a construction form used by early settlers. ⊠ *941 Bourbon St., French Quarter* ☎ *504/522–9377.*

�37 Latrobe House. Architect Henry Latrobe designed this modest house with Arsene Latour in 1814. Its smooth lines and porticoes started a passion for Greek Revival architecture in Louisiana, evidenced later in many plantation houses upriver as well as in a significant number of buildings in New Orleans. This house, believed to be the earliest example of Greek Revival in the city, is not open to the public. ⊠ *721 Governor Nicholls St., French Quarter.*

⓱ Le Petit Théâtre. Since 1916 this community-based theater group has entertained the Quarter with plays, musicals, and variety shows. The organization was originally housed in one of the Pontalba apartments on Jackson Square, but it quickly outgrew that space and moved to this building in 1922. Hosting the Tennessee Williams Festival every spring, Le Petit Théâtre attracts national attention. The flagstone patio with its fountain is postcard-perfect. The building next door is **Le Petit Salon** (⊠ *620 St. Peter St., French Quarter*), headquarters of a ladies' literary club since 1925. The house was originally built for a pair of French newlyweds in 1838; the wrought-iron staircase leads to the formal, second-floor entrance. ⊠ *616 St. Peter St., French Quarter* ☎ *504/522–2081* ⊕ *www.lepetittheatre.com.*

❺ Louisiana Supreme Court Building. The imposing Victorian building that takes up the whole block of Royal Street between St. Louis and Conti streets is the Old New Orleans Court, erected in 1908. It was later the office of the Wildlife and Fisheries agency, and locals still most often refer to the building by that designation. After years of vacancy and neglect, this magnificent edifice has been restored as the elegant home of the Louisiana Supreme Court. ⊠ *400 Royal St., French Quarter.*

★ ❷ **Madame John's Legacy.** Now a state museum, this is the only example in the French Quarter of West Indies architecture and early creole-colonial home design. The large, dark rooms of the main living space occupy the second story, and a porch (called a gallery) runs along the front and back of the house, providing ventilation during the steamy summers and protection from both sun and rain. The current building was constructed in 1789, following the 1788 fire that took out much of the Quarter. The

> **DON'T BET ON IT!**
>
> At some point during your visit to the French Quarter, you are bound to come across someone on the street who will offer you the following wager: "I bet you [insert dollar amount] I know where you got them shoes." It's a con, of course, and an old one at that. The answer is "You got them on your feet in New Orleans, Louisiana."

house has a colorful past. The first owner, Jean Pascal, a French sea captain, was killed by Natchez Indians. The name "Madame John's Legacy" was adopted in the late 1800s from a short story by New Orleans writer George Washington Cable. The popular tale was about Madame John, a "free woman of color" who, like many mulatto women at that time, became the mistress of a Frenchman. Having never married, the Frenchman, John (Jean), bequeathed his house and estate to her on his deathbed. ✉ *632 Dumaine St., French Quarter* ☎ *504/568–6968* 💵 *$3* ⊘ *Tues.–Sun. 9–5.*

❻ **Maspero's Exchange.** This restaurant, now known as Original Pierre Maspero's, was once a slave auction house and for many years thereafter the Exchange Coffeehouse, where the city's notable Creoles gathered. From the outside, the building appears to have only two floors, whereas inside, a middle floor, called an entresol, is in the area above the window arch. This low middle floor was used for storage. ✉ *440 Chartres St., French Quarter.*

❽ **Michalopoulos Galleries.** One of New Orleans's most beloved artists, James Michalopoulos, exhibits his expressionistic visions of New Orleans architecture in this small gallery. Michalopoulos's palette-knife technique of applying thick waves of paint invariably brings Van Gogh to mind—but his vision of New Orleans, where no line is truly straight and every building appears to have a soul, is uniquely his own. Michalopoulos was commissioned to create the official poster of the New Orleans Jazz and Heritage Festival in 1998, 2001, 2003, and 2006, bringing a new perspective to some of New Orleans's greatest musicians: Mahalia Jackson, Louis Armstrong, Dr. John, and Fats Domino. ✉ *617 Bienville St., French Quarter* ☎ *504/558–0505* ⊕ *www.michalopoulos.com* ⊘ *Mon.–Sat. 10–5:30, Sun. noon–5.*

❷⁹ **Miltenberger Houses.** The widow Amelie Miltenberger built this row of three brick town houses in the 1830s for her three sons. Two generations later, her daughter Alice Heine became famous for wedding Prince Albert of Monaco. Although the marriage ended childless and in divorce, Princess Alice was a sensation in New Orleans. ✉ *900, 906, and 910 Royal St., French Quarter.*

2

① Musée Conti Wax Museum. The history of New Orleans and Louisiana unfolds in colorful vignettes in this fun museum. Local legends are captured life size at seminal moments: Madame Lalaurie discovered torturing her slaves; Napoléon leaping out of the bathtub at news of the Louisiana Purchase; Marie Laveau selling gris-gris to downtown customers; the Duke and Duchess of Windsor attending a Mardi Gras ball. Written and audio explanations supplement the visual scenes. A miniature Mardi Gras parade fills one corridor. The museum is an enjoyable way to acquaint yourself and your children with New Orleans history, although the history depicted here tends toward the sensational and the occasionally unsubstantiated. ✉ *917 Conti St., French Quarter* ☎ *504/581–1993 or 800/233–5405* ⊕ *www.get-waxed. com* ✉ *$6.75* ⏰ *Call for hours.*

> **TALK OF THE TOWN**
>
> Although it's just two blocks away from Bourbon Street in the French Quarter, Burgundy Street is not pronounced like the wine (New Orleanians say "bur-GUN-dee" instead). And if you trot out your high-school French to ask for directions to Chartres Street, a bemused local will probably ask if you mean "CHAW-tuhs." Farther uptown, the streets named for the muses offer more challenges: Calliope ("CAL-ee-ope") and Melpomene ("MELL-pa-meen").

NEED A BREAK?

Napoleon House Bar and Café (✉ *500 Chartres St., French Quarter* ☎ *504/524–9752* ⊕ *www.napoleonhouse.com*) is a favorite gathering place for local characters, who favor such romantic drinks as the Pimm's Cup (a refreshing mixture of lemonade and Pimm's, a light gin-based liquor) and the Sazerac (the original New Orleans cocktail, a mixture of rye whiskey, simple sugars, Herbsaint, and bitters). Snack on a muffuletta sandwich (ham, salami, mozzarella, and olive salad on seeded bread) in the lush courtyard or find respite from the heat in the cool, darkened interior with its time-worn plaster walls and dignified operatic sound track. The building was the residence of Nicholas Girod, mayor of New Orleans from 1812 to 1815. Like many New Orleanians of the period, Girod was a staunch supporter of the French empire, and when he heard that Napoléon had escaped from his island exile, Girod declared his home ready to receive the emperor, should he make his way to America. Napoléon never crossed the Atlantic, but this bit of historical intrigue, amplified by legend, adds to the restaurant's allure.

㉚ New Orleans Historic Voodoo Museum. A large collection of artifacts and information on voodoo as it was—and still is—practiced in New Orleans is here in a two-room, rather homegrown museum. Items on display include portraits by and of voodoo legends, African artifacts believed to have influenced the development of the religion, and lots of gris-gris (bundles with magical ingredients). The gift shop sells customized gris-gris, potions, and voodoo dolls. ✉ *724 Dumaine St., French Quarter* ☎ *504/680–0128* ✉ *Museum $5* ⏰ *Mon.–Thurs. 10–6, Fri.–Sun. 10–7:30.*

❼ New Orleans Pharmacy Museum. This building was the apothecary shop and residence of Louis J. Dufilho, America's first licensed pharmacist with his own shop, in the 1820s. His botanical and herbal gardens are still cultivated in the courtyard. To tour the musty shop is to step back into 19th-century medicine. Even the window display, with its enormous leech jar and other antiquated paraphernalia, is fascinating. Watch for free 19th-century seasonal health tips posted in the front window. ✉ *514 Chartres St., French Quarter* ☎ *504/565–8027* 💲 *$5* 🕓 *Tues. and Thurs. 10–2; Wed., Fri., and Sat. 10–5.*

WHISTLING "DIXIE"

One popular theory for the origin of the term "Dixie" points back to Citizens Bank of New Orleans, which issued bilingual 10-dollar bank notes bearing the French word "dix" (10) on the reverse. The notes thus became known as "dixies," and the term eventually became synonymous with Louisiana, and then with the entire South. Historians are still debating this etymology . . . but it's a good story nonetheless.

★ **㊴ Old Mint.** Minting began in 1838 in this ambitious Ionic structure, a project of President Andrew Jackson. The New Orleans mint was to provide currency for the South and the West, which it did until the Confederacy began minting its own currency here in 1861. When supplies ran out, the building served as a barracks, then a prison, for Confederate soldiers; the production of U.S. coins recommenced only in 1879. It stopped again, for good, in 1909. After years of neglect, the federal government handed the Old Mint over to Louisiana in 1966; the state now uses the quarters to exhibit collections of the Louisiana State Museum. At the Barracks Street entrance, notice the one remaining sample of the mint's old walls—it'll give you an idea of the building's deterioration before its restoration. Hurricane Katrina ripped away a large section of the copper roof, and for months the twisted metal remained on the ground here, one of the most dramatic reminders of the storm in the French Quarter. Repairs to the building have begun in earnest, but the museum's reopening date remains in question. A lack of museum guards has left this and other Louisiana State Museum properties shuttered since Katrina.

At the foot of Esplanade Avenue, notice the memorial to the French rebels against early Spanish rule, the first instance of a New World rebellion against a European power. The rebel leaders were executed on this spot and give nearby Frenchmen Street its name. The principal exhibit here is the **New Orleans Jazz Collection,** a brief but evocative tour through the history of traditional New Orleans jazz. In addition to informative written explanations, a wealth of artifacts movingly tells the story of the emergent art form. Among the gems are the soprano saxophone owned by Sidney Bechet, the trumpets of Pops Celestin and Dizzy Gillespie, and the cornet given to Louis Armstrong at the juvenile home where he spent much of his youth. Sheet music, biographies, personal effects, and photos round out the displays. Across the hall from the jazz exhibit are a few rooms filled with the beautiful and locally treasured Newcomb pottery. This school of pottery was developed by teachers and students at Newcomb Women's College in Uptown New Orleans during the late 19th and early 20th centuries, and it subtly reflects the art-nouveau movement. The **Louisiana Historical Center,** which holds the French and Spanish Louisiana archives, is open free to researchers by appointment. ✉ *400 Esplanade Ave., French Quarter* ☎ *504/568–6968.*

�',, **Old Ursuline Convent.** The Ursulines were the first of many orders of religious women who came to New Orleans and founded schools, orphanages, and asylums and ministered to the needs of the poor. Their original convent was built in 1734 and is now the oldest French-colonial building in the Mississippi Valley, having survived the disastrous 18th-century fires that destroyed the rest of the Quarter. **St. Mary's Church,** adjoining the convent, was added in 1845. The original tract of land for a convent, school, and gardens covered several French Quarter blocks. Now an archive for the archdiocese, the convent was used by the Ursulines for 90 years. The convent roof was significantly damaged by Katrina's winds, and a temporary patch is clearly visible on the Chartres Street side. The Ursuline Academy, the convent's girls' school founded in 1727, is now Uptown on State Street, where the newer convent and chapel were built. The academy is the oldest girls' school in the country. It's open to the public Tuesday through Sunday, but hours may be limited depending on the season; please call for more information. ✉ *1100 Chartres St., French Quarter* ☎ *504/529–2651* 🎟 *$5.*

🈄 **Quadroon Ballroom.** In the early 1800s the wooden-rail balcony extending over Orleans Street was linked to a ballroom where free women of color met their French suitors, as Madame John of **Madame John's Legacy** is said to have done. The quadroons (technically, people whose racial makeup was one-quarter African) who met here were young unmarried women of legendary beauty. A gentleman would select a favorite beauty and, with her mother's approval, buy her a house and support her as his mistress. The sons of these unions, which were generally maintained in addition to legal marriages with French women, were often sent to France to be educated. This practice, known as plaçage, was unique to New Orleans at the time. The Quadroon Ballroom later became part of a convent and school for the Sisters of the Holy Family, a religious order founded in New Orleans in 1842 by the daughter of a quadroon to educate and care for African-American women. The ballroom itself is not open to visitors, but a view of the balcony from across the street is enough to set the historical stage. ✉ *Bourbon Orleans Hotel, 717 Orleans St., 2nd fl., French Quarter.*

🈃 **Rodrigue Studio.** Cajun artist George Rodrigue started painting blue dogs in 1984, inspired by the spirit of his deceased pet Tiffany. Since then, the blue dog has found thousands of manifestations in various settings in the cult artist's paintings. Of late, Rodrigue has ventured a few non-blue-dog works, which after nearly two decades of singular focus seems like a radical move. Rodrigue's principal gallery, a single room rather eerily lined almost entirely with paintings of the blue dog (and her evil red twin), sits directly behind St. Louis Cathedral. Rodrigue has contributed a series of post-Katrina blue-dog prints as the George Rodrigue Art Campaign for Recovery, a fund-raising effort for the rebuilding process. Among the titles is *Throw Me Something F.E.M.A.*, a whimsical play on the cry of Mardi Gras–parade attendees: "Throw me something, mister!" ⊠ *721 Royal St., French Quarter* ☎ *504/581–4244* ⊕ *www.georgerodrigue.com* ⊙ *Daily 10–6, though hrs may vary; call ahead to confirm.*

FAUBOURG MARIGNY & BYWATER

The Faubourg Marigny (pronounced FOE-berg MAR-ah-Nee), across Esplanade Avenue from the French Quarter, was developed in the early 1800s by wealthy planter Bernard de Marigny, the Creole bon vivant who made the dice game craps popular in America. Several of New Orleans's most-distinctive street names owe their origin to de Marigny, and it is here that the visitor will find Desire Street just a block away from Piety Street. But some of the streets he named, such as Good Children, Love, and Craps, no longer bear the evocative names de Marigny bestowed upon them.

With architectural styles ranging from classic creole cottage to Victorian mansion, the Marigny is in effect a residential extension of the Quarter. The streets are more peaceful and the residents more bohemian—what the French Quarter used to be like 20 years ago. Like the French Quarter, the Marigny rests on some of the city's highest ground, and it was mostly spared from the flooding of Hurricane Katrina (with the exception of a few houses near the St. Claude Avenue border). Several of the old corner town houses were significantly damaged by Katrina's winds, and a few scars of the storm remain here. In addition, a number of fires following the storm consumed blocks of riverfront warehouses as well as several historic dwellings within the Marigny. Undeterred, Marigny dwellers have returned. Frenchmen Street, the Marigny's main strip, is lined with music clubs, coffee shops, and restaurants. The nightlife here has returned in full, with music lovers spilling into the streets on most weekend nights. Many of the streets intersect at odd angles; look for street names in inlaid tiles at corners.

The Bywater, a crumbling yet beautiful old neighborhood across the train tracks at Press Street, is a haven to those musicians and artists who find the Marigny too expensive and overrun. The New Orleans Center for Creative Arts (NOCCA) occupies a beautiful campus of renovated warehouses

---

HUBIG'S PIES

One local culinary delight that is almost unknown outside the city are the fried fruit turnovers made by Hubig's Pies on Dauphine Street in the Marigny. Simon Hubig founded the bakery in Ft. Worth, Texas, and the New Orleans plant was just one of the chain. Forced by the Depression to close the other locations, Hubig held on to the New Orleans plant alone and brought on the current proprietors as partners. The pies are available in corner groceries around town.

at its edge. The Mississippi runs the length of its boundary. The bars and coffee shops scattered around this neighborhood combine elements of its working-class roots and more-recent hipster influx for a lively and distinctly local experience. Although you won't find the head-swiveling density of sights here that you will in the French Quarter, a tour through the Faubourg Marigny and especially the Bywater gives you a feel for New Orleans as it lives day to day, in a colorful, overgrown, slightly sleepy cityscape reminiscent of island communities and tinged with a sense of perpetual decay.

Numbers in the margin correspond to numbers on the French Quarter and Faubourg Marigny map.

WHAT TO SEE

④ **American Aquatic Gardens.** A commercial nursery and boutique gift shop, this small but wonderfully relaxing garden invites walks past grasses, reeds, flowers, and sculptures. Trees and fences that once shadowed some of the displays were lost during Katrina, but the sound of water still surrounds the visitor, and these grounds remain a tranquil retreat from the city for gardening enthusiasts and backyard snoozers alike. ✉ *621 Elysian Fields, Faubourg Marigny* ☎ *504/944–0410* ⊕ *www. americanaquaticgardens.com* ⊗ *Daily 9–5.*

④ **Christopher Porché-West Galerie.** This working studio and exhibit space holds the assemblages and other creations of Porché-West and, occasionally, other local artists. The atmosphere depends on the current vigor of Porché-West's activities: sometimes it is more work-oriented, sometimes more formally set up for exhibits. The gallery occupies an old pharmacy storefront, and it is open whenever the artist happens to be in, or by appointment. ✉ *3201 Burgundy St., Bywater* ☎ *504/947–3880* ⊕ *www.porche-west.com.*

④ **Dr. Bob.** This small compound of artists' and furniture-makers' studios includes the headquarters of Dr. Bob, beloved local folk artist. Dr. Bob remained in his shop during the storm until the riverfront fires across the street forced him out. The compound was damaged but has reopened, and his shop remains chock-full of original furniture, colorful signs, and unidentifiable objects of artistic fancy. The grounds still bear warning signs to potential looters and may be a bit forbidding to the first-time visitor, but once inside you'll be greeted pleasantly and left free to peruse. The sign outside advertises the open hours: BY CHANCE OR APPOINTMENT. ✉ *3027 Chartres St., Bywater* ☎ *504/945–2225.*

OFF THE BEATEN PATH

Jelly Roll Morton House. Jazz enthusiasts will want to follow Frenchmen Street beyond the borders of the Marigny to pay homage to Jelly Roll Morton at the pianist and composer's modest former home, now a private residence with nary a plaque to suggest its import. Morton was a Creole of color (free African-American of mixed race), a clear distinction from darker blacks in those days; Morton himself always explained his roots as French. Though rather affluent when Morton lived here, the neighborhood has since declined. Although some neighbors have returned since Katrina, the streets remain sparsely populated and can be intimidating—plan to take a car or taxi here. ✉*1443 Frenchmen St., Seventh Ward.*

45 Mercury Injection Studio Arts. Glassworks, mirrors, and paintings fill this tiny studio of artist Michael Cain. Don't be discouraged if the doors are closed: knock, and if Michael is around you're in for a show as he blows his fanciful pieces into existence. Visits by appointment are also available. ✉*727 Louisa St., Bywater* ☎*504/723–6397* ⊕*www.michaelcainarts.com* ✉*Free.*

43 New Orleans Center for Creative Arts (NOCCA). Many of New Orleans's
Fodor'sChoice most talented young musicians, artists, and writers pass through this
★ high-school arts program, where the faculty includes professional artists from around the country. Although the school covers all major artistic disciplines, the music program has been particularly successful: well-known alums include Donald Harrison, Terence Blanchard, Harry Connick Jr., and the Marsalis brothers. Following Hurricane Katrina, NOCCA became a combination National Guard barracks and command center for fire and rescue vehicles. Classes resumed in 2006, and the school is once again hosting its celebrated performing arts events. ✉*2800 Chartres St., Faubourg Marigny* ☎*504/940–2800* ⊕*www.nocca.com.*

46 Studio Inferno Glassworks. This working studio gives demonstrations of glassblowing and glass casting and sells the results in its gallery. The whole operation occupies a spacious red warehouse in the heart of the Bywater. ✉*3000 Royal St., Bywater* ☎*504/945–1878* ✉*Free* ☉*Weekdays 9–5, Sat. 10–5.*

44 Venusian Gardens and Art Gallery. This former 19th-century historic church building now serves as Eric Ehlenberger's art studio and gallery, displaying his luminous sculptures and dioramas. ✉*2601 Chartres St., Faubourg Marigny* ☎*504/943–7446* ⊕*http://venusiangardens.com* ☉*Weekdays 10–4; appointments preferred.*

40 Washington Square Park. This park provides a large green space in which to play Frisbee or catch some sun. During the recovery period following the storm, relief groups created a campground here, offering free food and music. The far side of the park borders Elysian Fields, named for Paris's Champs-Élysées. Though it never achieved the grandeur of its French counterpart, Elysian Fields is a major thoroughfare. Small-scale festivals or events sometimes take place in Washington Square, which is the only city public space with a French-style double alley of oaks. ✉*Bordered by Royal, Dauphine, and Frenchmen Sts. and Elysian Fields, Faubourg Marigny.*

NEED A BREAK?

Café Rose Nicaud (✉**634 Frenchmen St., Faubourg Marigny** ☎**504/949– 3300** ☉**Daily 7–3**) is a neighborhood hangout that serves hot and iced coffee or tea, sandwiches, salads, and pastries. The café is named for the free woman of color who was the originator of the New Orleans coffee stands, and its walls often feature artwork celebrating African-American culture in

THE NINTH WARD

The Ninth Ward is the largest of New Orleans's wards, or legislative districts, traditionally one of the most colorful, and since Hurricane Katrina one of the most recognized. Few can forget the television news images in the days after the storm of rooftop rescues of Ninth Ward residents while the area sat under more than 9 feet of water. Sadly, today, little progress has been made in rebuilding and repopulating the Ninth Ward. A majority of homes and businesses still stand empty and in various stages of destruction; in some areas, entire neighborhoods have been cleared, leaving empty, eerie desolation. For this reason, many tourists want to visit the area to truly understand the damage Katrina wrought. Though it was always a low- to middle-income area, the Ninth Ward had the highest rate of home ownership in the city. It is now sparsely populated, and is not safe to visit alone, outside a car, or after dark. One bus tour, offered by **Grayline Tours** (☎ *504/569–1401 or 800/535–7786*), is a safe and informative way to learn about Hurricane Katrina's effect on the city, including the Ninth Ward. If you'd like to help make things better here and elsewhere in the city, go to the New Orleans tourism bureau's Web site (www.neworleanscvb.com) and click on the voluntourism link.

New Orleans. The sidewalk tables are excellent vantage points for early-afternoon people-watching.

TREMÉ

Across Rampart Street from the French Quarter, the neighborhood of Tremé (pronounced truh-MAY) claims to be the oldest African-American neighborhood in the country. Once the site of the Claude Tremé plantation, it became home to many free people of color during the late 18th and early 19th centuries. Although most of the neighborhood did not see significant flooding from Katrina, the winds wreaked havoc on its historic structures. A vibrant and developing area before the storm, Tremé has struggled to come back since Katrina. Residents are slowly trickling back, however, and more and more of these brightly colored historic homes are being repaired. Never a highly touristed area, the Tremé now offers an even more quiet and reflective experience (unless, of course, you happen upon a second-line parade!). ■TIP➜**Like many New Orleans neighborhoods beyond the French Quarter, the Tremé has had problems with crime. Visit this area during the day, and enjoy having its rich, small museums to yourself.**

WHAT TO SEE

48 ★ **Backstreet Cultural Museum.** Local photographer and self-made historian Sylvester Francis is an enthusiastic guide through his own rich collection of Mardi Gras Indian costumes and other musical artifacts tied to the street traditions of New Orleans. Sylvester is also an excellent source for current musical goings-on in Tremé and throughout town. The museum has been renovated since Katrina and celebrated its grand reopening in early 2007. ✉*1116 St. Claude St., Tremé* ☎*504/522–4806* ✍*$5* ⊘*Tues.–Sat. 10–5.*

51 **J&M Music Shop.** A plaque on this 1835 building marks it as the former site of the recording studio that launched the rock-and-roll careers of such greats as Fats Domino, Jerry Lee Lewis, Little Richard, and Ray Charles. Although the patrons of the Laundromat that now resides in this space probably don't pay it much heed, this is one of the most significant musical landmarks in New Orleans. Owned by Cosimo Matassa, the studio operated from 1945 to 1955. ✉*840 N. Rampart St., Tremé.*

52 **Louis Armstrong Park.** This large park with its grassy knolls and lagoons is named for native son and world-famous musician Louis Armstrong (1900–71), whose statue by Elizabeth Catlett is near the brightly lighted entrance on the outer boundary of the French Quarter. To the left inside the park is **Congo Square,** marked by an inlaid-stone space where slaves in the 18th and early 19th centuries gathered on Sundays, the only time they were permitted to play their music openly. The weekly meetings held here have been immortalized in the travelogues of visitors, leaving invaluable insight into the earliest stages of free musical practices by Africans in America and African-Americans. Neighborhood musicians still congregate here at times for percussion jams, and it is difficult not to think of the musical spirit of ancestors hovering over them. Marie Laveau, the greatly feared and respected voodoo queen of antebellum New Orleans, had her home a block away on St. Ann Street, and is reported to have held voodoo rituals here regularly.

Behind Congo Square is a large gray building, the **Morris F.X. Jeff Municipal Auditorium;** to the right, behind the auditorium, is the **Mahalia Jackson Center for the Performing Arts.** The St. Philip Street side of the park houses the **Jazz National Historical Park,** anchored by **Perseverance Hall,** the oldest Masonic temple in the state. After several years of temporary residence at its visitor center in the French Quarter, this cultural preserve was scheduled to move to this permanent location in the summer of 2008. With its program of lectures, free performances, and films, the park provides a wonderful introduction to the city's musical heritage. ■TIP→**Armstrong Park is patrolled by a security detail, but be very careful when wandering, and do not visit after dark.** ✉*N. Rampart St. between St. Philip and St. Peter Sts., Tremé* ⊘*Auditorium and performing arts center open by event; check local newspapers for listings.*

50 **New Orleans African-American Museum.** Set in a historic villa surrounded by a lovely small park, this museum is a prime example of the West Indies–style, French-colonial architecture that used to fill much of the French Quarter. It was built in 1829 by Simon Meilleur, a prosperous brick maker: the main house was constructed with Meilleur's bricks, and the brick patio behind it bears imprints identifying the original manufacturer. Inside, temporary exhibits spotlight African and Afri-

CLOSE UP

A Music History Tour

The Birthplace of Jazz is a banner New Orleans wears with pride, and it's hard to visit the city without seeing and hearing signs of the rich musical heritage. The following list combines sights both on and off the beaten track.

Backstreet Cultural Museum. This tiny but fabulous museum brings together artifacts from the Mardi Gras Indian, brass band, and second-line traditions. ✉ *1116 St. Claude Ave., Tremé* ☎ *504/522–4806.*

Buddy Bolden's House. Cornetist Buddy Bolden is the legendary originator of the "hot" sound that came to be associated with jazz. He lived and played across St. Charles Avenue from the Garden District. ✉ *2309 and 2527 1st St., Uptown.*

Congo Square. Louis Armstrong Park, on the northern edge of the French Quarter, contains the original Congo Square site, marked with a plaque. During the 1700s and 1800s, Congo Square was reserved on Sunday for slaves seeking entertainment on their day off. Sharing a common language of music, rhythm, and dance, they helped link African tribal drumming rituals to jazz. ✉ *N. Rampart St. between St. Philip and St. Peter Sts., Tremé.*

Danny Barker's Birthplace. Songwriter, vocalist, banjoist and guitarist, storyteller, and jazz historian Danny Barker was a vital intergenerational link for New Orleans jazz musicians. Barker organized the Fairview Baptist Church Brass Band, whose alumni include Wynton and Branford Marsalis, Anthony "Tuba Fats" Lacen, and Charles and Kirk Joseph of the Dirty Dozen Brass Band. He worked through the 1970s as assistant curator of the New Orleans Jazz Museum led his

Onward Brass Band. ✉ *1027–1029 Chartres St., French Quarter.*

George Vitale "Papa Jack" Laine's House. One of the most successful and influential bandleaders to emerge from the early period of jazz, Laine was also a pioneer drummer. ✉ *2405 and 2422–2424 Chartres St., Marigny.*

Jazz National Historical Park. Appointed guardians of New Orleans's jazz heritage, the uniformed rangers of this unique national park are also expert musicians, compelling teachers, and affable guides to the city's music. ✉ *Armstrong Park, N. Rampart St. between St. Philip and St. Peter Sts.; visitor center: 916 N. Peters St., Tremé/French Quarter* ☎ *504/589–4841 or 504/589–4806.* JAN 2007

Jelly Roll Morton's House. The legendary pianist, who blurred the line between ragtime and jazz, lived in a mixed-race neighborhood. A "Creole of color," Morton always described his roots as French. ✉ *1443 Frenchmen St..*

Louis Armstrong's birthplace. The man who would bring jazz to the world was born in the poorest of circumstances, in a neighborhood now consumed by the Orleans Parish Prison and associated buildings. The house itself was demolished, but the legendary address still draws fans and historians to the area where it once stood. ✉ *723 Jane Alley, Mid-City.*

Jazz is still alive and well in New Orleans today. Stroll down Frenchmen Street in the Faubourg Marigny any evening, and you'll hear jazz pouring from clubs such as the Spotted Cat, d.b.a., and Snug Harbor. In the French Quarter, best bets include Preservation Hall and the Palm Court Jazz Café.

can-diaspora art and artists. The fence surrounding the complex was completely destroyed by Katrina, and some of the buildings within were damaged as well. The museum reopened in 2006, and additional improvements are planned. ✉ *1418 Governor Nicholls St., Tremé* ☎ *504/565–7497* ⊕ *www.neworleansmuseums.com* ✉ *$5* ⊘ *Tues.– Fri. 9–5, Sat. 10–4.*

❸ Our Lady of Guadalupe, International Shrine of St. Jude (Old Mortuary Chapel). Constructed in 1826 to house funerals for victims of the city's yellow-fever epidemics, this chapel is the oldest church building in New Orleans. It was a house of worship for the city's Italian immigrant population in the late 19th and early 20th centuries. In 1935, parishoners began a devotion to St. Jude Thaddeus, patron saint of lost causes; today, the church serves as the International Shrine of St. Jude. The faithful make offerings and prayers at St. Jude's statue, which is set in a nook to the left of the altar. In the rear of the chapel, to the right of the entrance, stands the statue of St. Expedite, the only such statue in a North American Church, whose devotees claim he is the saint to petition for quick fixes for problems or cures against procrastination. An old (apocryphal) story holds that the nuns of the parish received a crate from Rome that containing the statue—no identifying information for the saint it depicts. The word "expedite" was stamped on the shipping crate, so the sisters promptly erected the statue to St. Expedite. ✉ *311 N. Rampart St., Tremé* ☎ *504/525–1551.*

❹ St. Augustine Catholic Church. Ursuline nuns donated the land for this church in 1841. Upon its completion in 1842, St. Augustine's became an integrated place of worship; slaves were relegated to the side pews, but free blacks claimed just as much right to center pews as whites did. The architect, J. N. B. de Pouilly, attended the École des Beaux-Arts in Paris and was known for his idiosyncratic style, which borrowed freely from a variety of traditions and resisted classification. Some of the ornamentation in his original drawings was eliminated when money ran out, but effusive pink-and-gold paint inside brightens the austere structure. The church grounds now also house the Tomb of the Unknown Slave, a monument dedicated in 2004 to the slaves buried in unmarked graves in the church grounds and surrounding areas. Following Katrina, the Archdiocese of New Orleans planned to close seven churches in the city, including St. Augustine. Public outcry, the church's historical significance, and parishoners' dedication saved the parish, and its 10 AM Sunday gospel-jazz services continue. ✉ *1210 Governor Nicholls St., Tremé* ☎ *504/525–5934.*

Storyville. The busy red-light district that lasted from 1897 to 1917 has been destroyed, and in its place stands a public-housing project. Storyville spawned splendid Victorian homes that served as brothels and provided a venue for the raw sounds of ragtime and early jazz; an extremely young Louis Armstrong cut his teeth in some of the clubs here. The world's first electrically lighted saloon, Tom Anderson's House of Diamonds, was at the corner of Basin and Bienville streets, and the whole area has been the subject of many novels, songs, and films. In 1917, after several incidents involving naval officers, the government ordered the district shut down. Some buildings were razed almost overnight; the housing project was built in the 1930s. Only three structures from the Storyville area remain, the former sites of three saloons: Lulu White's Saloon (237 Basin Street), Joe Victor's Saloon (St. Louis and Villere streets), and "My Place" Saloon (1214 Bienville Street). Currently, a historical marker on the "neutral ground" (median) of Basin Street is the only visible connection to Alderman Sidney Story's experiment in legalized prostitution. ✉ *Basin St. next to St. Louis Cemetery No. 1, Tremé.*

CBD & WAREHOUSE DISTRICT

Bordered by the river, St. Charles Avenue, Poydras Street, and the I–10 expressway and filled with former factories and cotton warehouses, the Warehouse District began its renaissance when the city hosted the World's Fair here in 1984. Old abandoned buildings were renovated to host the fair and its events, setting the scene for future development. Structures that housed the international pavilions during the fair now make up the Ernest N. Morial Convention Center and a number of hotels, restaurants, bars, and music clubs. New Orleanians remain sensitive to the plight of Hurricane Katrina evacuees who flocked to the Convention Center in the hopes of rescue. But the images of suffering broadcast nationally from that site in 2005 began to fade after the Convention Center underwent an extensive renovation, and the surrounding neighborhood has regained its former charm and vibrancy. Today, the Warehouse District remains one of the hottest residential and arts-and-nightlife areas of the city, dotted with modern renovations of historic buildings, upscale loft residences, excellent eateries, and a number of bars and music clubs. (In fact, the area is sometimes referred to as the Arts District.) Part of Harrah's property, Fulton Street Mall, is a one-block pedestrian promenade actively developing as a stroller's destination for restaurants, clubs, and high-end shops. Stretching from the river to Carrollton Avenue, Julia Street is lined with upscale contemporary art galleries and artist studios. The Warehouse District is also a museum hub, home to the National World War II Museum, the Ogden Museum of Southern Art, the Contemporary Arts Center, the Louisiana Children's Museum, and the Memorial Hall Confederate Museum—all within a three-square-block radius.

The Central Business District (CBD) covers the ground between Canal Street and Poydras Avenue, with some spillover into the Warehouse District's official territory. The neighborhood includes many iconic sights, including the Louisiana Superdome, the New Orleans Arena, the World Trade Center, and Harrah's Casino. Canal Street is the CBD's main artery and the official dividing line between the business district and the French Quarter; street names change from American to French as they cross Canal. Newly planted with palm trees and again served by the Canal Street streetcar, the grand avenue is slowly beginning to regain some of its former elegance. Though lower Canal Street sustained severe flooding during Hurricane Katrina, most of the

CBD & Warehouse District

Iberville St.

Bienville St.

N. Rampart St.

S. Rampart St.

University Pl.

Burgundy St.

O'Keefe St.

Common St.

Dauphine St.

Poydras St.

Penn St.

Union St.

Gravier St.

14

Bourbon St.

Girod St.

Lafayette Mall

Carroll St.

Peldido St.

St. Charles
Stop

Royal St.

Julia St.

Baronne St.

Exchange Pl.

Carondelet St.

Chartres St.

Camp St.

13

Commercial St.

Dorsiere St.

Lafayette
Square

Natchez St.

Decatur St.

Howard Ave.

St. Joseph
Stop

Church St.

N. Maestri St.

S. Maestri St.

Clinton St.

N. Peters St.

Lee
Circle

Julia St.

9

Lafayette Mall

Camp St.

Clay St.

N. Front St.

2 **1**

Camp St.

8

Constance St.

Tchoupitoulas St.

3

7

Girod St.

Harrah's
New Orleans

Canal St.

4

Magazine St.

Notre Dame St.

10

6

Lafayette St.

11

World Trade
Center

5

Commerce St.

Riverwalk
Marketplace

12

Constance St.

Sylvia
Schmidt
Gallery

S. Peters St.

Poydras
Street
Wharf

Andrew Higgens Dr.

Fulton St.

Annunciation St.

Convention Center Blvd. (Front St.)

Girod
Street
Wharf

Tchoupitoulas St.

Water St.

Mississippi River

St. Joseph St.

Diamond N.
Diamond S.

Pilie St.

Triangle
St.

KEY

Streetcar

Morial
Convention
Center

Julia
Street
Wharf

0   1/2 mi

0   1/2 km

American-Italian
Renaissance Foundation
Museum and Library **11**

Arthur Roger Gallery **6**

Contemporary
Arts Center **3**

Gallier Hall **13**

John Minor Wisdom
United States Court of
Appeals Building **9**

Louisiana Children's
Museum **5**

Memorial Hall
Confederate
Museum **2**

Louisiana Superdome **14**

National World War II
Museum **4**

New Orleans School of
Glassworks and
Printmaking Studio **7**

Ogden Museum of
Southern Art **1**

Piazza d'Italia **10**

St. Patrick's Church **8**

Spanish Plaza **12**

street's tourist sights, including the Ritz-Carlton Hotel and the Shops at Canal Place, are restored and thriving. Stop in Palace Café, in the lovely former Werlein Music Building at 605 Canal Street, before 7 for a prix-fixe early dinner of New Orleans classics such as gumbo, grilled gulf fish, and white-chocolate bread pudding. Or, take in some of the beautiful old government and office buildings, especially those around Lafayette Square.

Numbers in the margin correspond to numbers on the CBD & Warehouse District map.

WHAT TO SEE

⑪ **American-Italian Renaissance Foundation Museum and Library.** Italian–New Orleans customs are explained and artifacts exhibited in this small, thoughtful museum. The research library includes records of the large local Italian immigrant community. ⊠*537 S. Peters St., Warehouse District* ☎*504/522–7294* ⊕*www.airf.org* ⊠*Free* ⊘*Wed.–Fri. 10–3, Sat. 10–2.*

❻ **Arthur Roger Gallery.** A highlight among Julia Street galleries, this gallery showcases quality contemporary art, primarily by local and regional artists. There is also a satellite gallery at 730 Tchoupitoulas in the Renaissance Arts Hotel, two blocks from the main gallery. ⊠*432 Julia St., Warehouse District* ☎*504/522–1999* ⊘*Tues.–Sat. 10–5.*

❸ **Contemporary Arts Center.** Founded in 1976, the center has endured long, hard years of economic and cultural stagnation; however, it takes great satisfaction in the Warehouse District gallery scene it has helped to spawn. The center sustained some damage during Katrina but has recovered to again host cutting-edge exhibits, often featuring local or regional artists but also welcoming the work of national and international talent. The CAC theater presents experimental and conventional concerts, jazz productions, films, dance, plays, and lectures, including a new series added in 2006, the Music of New Orleans. Hours vary during concerts, performances, lectures, and special events; call or check the Web site for details. ⊠*900 Camp St., Warehouse District* ☎*504/528–3805, 504/528–3800 theater box office* ⊕*www.cacno.org* ⊠*Gallery admission free* ⊘*Thurs.–Sun. 11–4.*

⑬ **Gallier Hall.** This Greek Revival building, modeled on the Erectheum of Athens, was built in 1845 by architect James Gallier Sr. It served as City Hall in the mid-20th century. Today it hosts special events and is the mayor's official perch during Mardi Gras parades; the kings and queens of many parades stop here to be toasted by the mayor and dignitaries and to receive the key to the city. The grand rooms inside the hall are adorned with portraits and decorative details ordered by Gallier from Paris. ⊠*545 St. Charles Ave. (entrance on the side at 705 Lafayette St.), CBD* ☎*504/565–7457, 504/658–3623 for appointment* ⊘*Weekdays 9–5; visits by appointment.*

Harrah's New Orleans. The only land-based casino in the New Orleans area, Harrah's contains 175,000 square feet of space divided into five areas, each with a New Orleans theme: Jazz Court, Court of Good Fortune, Smugglers Court, Mardi Gras Court, and Court of the Mansion. Harrah's features 100 table games, 2,100+ slots, and live entertainment at Masquerade, which includes a new bar, lounge, video tower and dancing show. Check the Web site for seasonal productions, including music, theater, and comedy. Dining and libation choices include the extensive Harrah's buffet, Cafés on Canal food court, Besch Steak House,

Bamboo Court, Gordon Biersch, Grand Isle, and Riche (the last three are part of Harrah's newly developed Fulton Street Mall, a one-block pedestrian promenade that attracts casual strollers, club goers, diners, and shoppers). ⊠8 Canal St., CBD ☎504/533–6000 or 800/427–7247 ⊕www.harrahs.com ◷Daily 24 hrs.

🕘 **John Minor Wisdom United States Court of Appeals Building.** New York architect James Gamble Rogers was summoned to design this three-story granite structure as a post office and court building in 1909. By the 1960s the post office had moved to larger digs, and McDonough No. 35 High School found refuge here after Hurricane Betsy in 1965. Today the Renaissance Revival building houses the Fifth Circuit Court of Appeals in an elaborately paneled and ornamented series of courtrooms. The dark, cool corridors of the ground floor have an arcaded, bronzed ceiling. As you enter the building and pass security, turn left and continue around the corner to find the library, where you can pick up information on the courthouse. Outside, a repeating sculpture of four women stands on each corner of the building: the four ladies represent History, Agriculture, Industry, and the Arts. The building is named for Judge John Minor Wisdom, the New Orleans native who was instrumental in dismantling the segregation laws of the South. Judge Wisdom received the Presidential Medal of Freedom in 1993. ⊠600 Camp St., CBD ☎504/310–7777 ◷Weekdays 8–5.

Julia Street. Contemporary art dealers have adopted this strip in the Warehouse District as their own. The street is lined with galleries, specialty shops, and modern apartment buildings. The first Saturday evening of each month gallery owners throw open their doors to show off new exhibits, to the accompaniment of wine, music, and general merriment. White Linen Night in August and Art for Art's Sake in October also find the galleries welcoming visitors with artist receptions and live entertainment.

Lee Circle. At the northern edge of the Warehouse District, a bronze statue of Civil War general Robert E. Lee stands high above the city on a white marble column in a traffic circle. Lee faces due north, as he has since 1884. Recent extensive renovation and new construction have greatly improved the area immediately around the circle, which now includes the **Contemporary Arts Center,** the **Ogden Museum of Southern Art,** the **National World War II Museum,** and the **Memorial Hall Confederate Museum.**

🖐 ❺ **Louisiana Children's Museum.** An invaluable resource for anyone traveling with kids, the top-notch Children's Museum is 30,000 square feet of hands-on educational fun. Favorite activities include a mini–grocery store (with both carts and registers manned by visitors), Mr. Rogers's Neighborhood, and a giant bubble station. A welcoming environment is provided for children with disabilities: most exhibits are accessible, and some are aimed directly at increasing children's awareness of the disabilities of others. Art teachers lead classes daily; theatrical storytelling takes place every morning and afternoon; and special activities such as jewelry making, face painting, and scavenger hunts are held each week. An indoor playground is reserved for toddlers ages three and under, and Toddler Time activities are held at 10 AM on Tuesday and Thursday. There's also a mini–fitness center with a kid-size stationary bicycle and rock-climbing wall. ✉*420 Julia St., Warehouse District* ☎*504/523–1357* ⊕*www.lcm.org* 💲*$7* ⊙*Tues.–Sat. 9:30–4:30, Sun. noon–4:30 (last ticket sold at 4).*

⓮ **Louisiana Superdome.** Home to the NFL's New Orleans Saints, the Louisiana Superdome has been the site of many Sugar Bowls, several NCAA Final Four basketball tournaments, and the BCS championship game, a record nine Super Bowls, and countless concerts, trade shows, and special events. The Superdome was badly damaged during Katrina and in its aftermath, when it served as a refuge of last resort for evacuees; the stadium underwent extensive renovations in the year that followed. The Superdome reopened for football in September 2006, when the Saints beat the Atlanta Falcons in front of the largest audience in ESPN history.

Built in 1975, the Superdome seats up to 100,000 people, has a 166,000-square-foot playing field, and a roof that covers almost 8 acres at a height of 27 stories. The bronze statue on the Poydras Street side is the Vietnam Veterans Memorial. The **New Orleans Arena,** behind the Superdome, is home to the NBA New Orleans Hornets and Tulane University's basketball team. Across from the Superdome on Poydras Street is a large abstract sculpture called the *Krewe of Poydras.* The sculptor, Ida Kohlmeyer, meant to evoke the frivolity and zany spirit of Mardi Gras. A couple of blocks down Poydras St. from the Superdome is the Bloch Cancer Survivors Monument, a block-long walkway of whimsical columns, figures, and a triumphal arch in the median of Loyola Avenue. ■TIP➡**The streets around the Superdome and Arena are usually busy during business hours, but at night and on weekends, except during a game, this area should not be explored alone.** ✉*1 Sugar Bowl Dr., CBD 70112* ☎*504/587–3663* ⊕*www.superdome.com.*

NEED A BREAK?

The brightly decorated bar and dining room inside Lucy's Retired Surfers Restaurant and Bar (✉*701 Tchoupitoulas St., Warehouse District* ☎*504/523– 8995* ⊕*www.lucysretiredsurfers.com*), open from 11 AM until late (kitchen closes at 10 pm), provide a nice spot for a margarita, a cup of coffee, or a Southwestern-style snack. During happy hour the bar fills up with young lawyers and paralegals who work in the area.

2 Memorial Hall Confederate Museum. This ponderous stone building at Lee Circle was built in 1891 to house a collection of artifacts from the Civil War, making it the oldest museum in the state. The displays include uniforms, flags, and soldiers' personal effects. The museum's collection survived Hurricane Katrina intact, but at this writing the museum was still operating with abbreviated hours. Call or check its Web site for updates. ✉929 Camp St., Warehouse District ☎504/523–4522 ⊕www.confederatemuseum.com ☞$7 ⊗Wed.–Sat. 10–4.

> **SECOND TO NONE**
>
> If you're lucky, you'll get swept up in a jazz street parade during your New Orleans visit. The parades themselves are often referred to as "second lines," a term that originated in the city's jazz funerals. Traditionally, a brass band accompanies a New Orleans funeral procession to the grave site, playing dirges along the way. On the return from the grave, however, the music becomes upbeat, celebrating the departed's passage to heaven. Behind the family, friends, and recognized mourners, a second group often gathers, taking part in the free entertainment and dancing—hence, the "second line."

4 National World War II Museum. The former National D-Day Museum
Fodor'sChoice was renamed in 2006 to reflect the full scope of its exhibits, which take
★ visitors from the Normandy invasion to the sands of Pacific Islands and the Home Front. The brainchild of historian and writer Dr. Stephen Ambrose, who taught for many years at the University of New Orleans until his death in 2002, this moving, well-executed examination of World War II covers far more ground than simply D-Day. The seminal moments are re-created through propaganda posters and radio clips from the period; biographical sketches of the military personnel involved; a number of short documentary films (including one bitterly sad film on the Holocaust, featuring interviews with survivors); and collections of weapons, personal items, and other artifacts from the war. The exhibits occupy a series of galleries spread through the interior of a huge warehouse space. One spotlighted exhibit, in a large, open portion of the warehouse near the entrance, is a replica of the Higgins boat troop landing craft, which were manufactured in New Orleans. In 2005 the museum announced a $300 million expansion plan to quadruple the size of the facility in several phases. Across the street from the current facility, construction has begun on an advanced-format theater, USO Experience, and Canteen. This is the first of six new pavilions proposed for the expanded campus, due to be completed in 2014. Check the Web site for updates on the expansion and a list of current movies, lectures, events, and programs. ✉925 Magazine St. (main entrance on Andrew Higgins Dr.), Warehouse District ☎504/527–6012 ⊕www.nationalww2museum.org ☞$14 ⊗Tues.–Sun. 9–5.

☕ ❼ **New Orleans School of Glassworks and Printmaking Studio.** A fun family stop, the School of Glassworks gives demonstrations of all stages of glassmaking and design, printmaking, and silver alchemy in a large warehouse space. Call ahead to check artist schedules. A shop and gallery up front displays and sells the finished products. ⊠*727 Magazine St., Warehouse District* ☎*504/529–7277* ⊕*www.neworleansglassworks. com* ☉*June–Aug., weekdays 11–5; Sept.–May, Mon.–Sat. 10–5:30.*

★ ❶ **Ogden Museum of Southern Art.** Art by Southerners, art made in the South, art about the South, artistic explorations into Southern themes, and more fill this elegant building with a glass atrium. More than 1,200 works collected by local developer Roger Ogden since the 1960s are on permanent display, along with featured exhibits. A central stair hall filters natural light through the series of galleries, and a rooftop patio affords lovely views of the surrounding area. The gift shop sells crafts by local artists. A Smithsonian affiliate, the museum sustained no damage from Hurricane Katrina and opened a couple of months after the storm. Although it's operating with abbreviated hours, Thursday nights still come alive with "Ogden After Hours," featuring live music, artist interviews, refreshments, and special gallery exhibits. ⊠*925 Camp St., Warehouse District* ☎*504/539–9600* ⊕*www.ogdenmuseum.org* ☞*$10* ☉*Wed.–Sun. 11–4 (Thurs. 6–8 with live music).*

❿ **Piazza d'Italia.** This modern plaza by architect Charles Moore is a gathering place for the large Italian community on St. Joseph's Day and Columbus Day. Its postmodern style is reminiscent of a Roman ruin. On the South Peters Street side of the piazza is the **American-Italian Museum.**

Riverwalk Marketplace. This three-block-long center of chain retail stores and local specialty shops and eateries is laid out in three tiers and lined in places by a promenade along the river's edge. Plaques along the walkway relate bits of the Mississippi River's history and folklore. Nearby at the Poydras Street streetcar stop is a grand splash of color on the flood wall, a 200-foot-long mural in tropical motifs by Julio Quintanilla. The mural was a gift to New Orleans from Mérida, Mexico, the artist's native city. Various cruise ships leave from the Julia Street Wharf slightly upriver; you can often see them from the front of the Riverwalk. Though directly on the river, the mall didn't sustain significant damage from Katrina and within a couple of months afterward was open for business, albeit with slightly reduced hours of operation. ⊠*1 Poydras St., Warehouse District* ☎*504/522–1555* ⊕*www.river walkmarketplace.com* ☉*Mon.–Sat. 10–7, Sun. noon–6.*

❽ **St. Patrick's Church.** A stark exterior gives way to a far more ornate, richly painted interior in this first church built in the American sector of New Orleans, intended to provide the city's Irish Catholics with a place of worship as distinguished as the French St. Louis Cathedral. The vaulted interior was completed in 1838 by local architect James Gallier, who moved here from Ireland in 1834 in order to work on the cathedral. High stained-glass windows and huge murals, painted in 1841, enrich the interior. ⊠*724 Camp St., Warehouse District* ☎*504/525–4413.*

NEED A
BREAK?
P. J.'s Coffee and Teas (✉*644 Camp St., CBD* ☎*504/529–3658* ⊕*www. pjscoffee.com*), a local chain serving delicious, cold-brewed iced coffee, has a small but pleasant location just off Lafayette Square.

⑫ Spanish Plaza. For a terrific view of the river and a place to relax, go behind the **World Trade Center** at 2 Canal Street to Spanish Plaza, a large, sunken space with beautiful inlaid tiles and a magnificent fountain. The plaza was a gift from Spain in the mid-1970s; you can hear occasional live music played here and you can purchase tickets for riverboat cruises in the offices that face the river.

World Trade Center. Once occupied by foreign consulates and businesses involved in international trade, the World Trade Center has lost tenants over the past decade, sustained severe damage during Katrina, and now sits largely empty. Atop the center, the Plimsoll Club's spectacular views make it a popular venue for receptions and events. The city's approval of a long-term lease has given a New York developer the go-ahead to build residential units, a four-star hotel, and a cultural museum inside the iconic building on the river at the foot of Canal Street. Walking around outside the trade center, you can visit statues and plazas: Winston Churchill is memorialized in a bronze statue in **British Park Place,** also known as Winston's Circle, where the stone-inlaid street curves in front of the Riverfront Hilton to the right; and a bronze equestrian statue of Bernardo de Galvez, Spanish governor of Louisiana in the 1780s, guards the entrance of the **Spanish Plaza** behind the World Trade Center. ✉*2 Canal St., CBD* ☎*504/529–1601.*

GARDEN DISTRICT

With its beautifully landscaped gardens surrounding elegant antebellum homes, the Garden District lives up to its name. Although very few buildings in the neighborhood are open to the public on a regular basis, enjoying the sights from outside the cast-iron fences surrounding their magnificent estates is well worth the visit. The Garden District sits on one of the city's higher ridges and escaped the post-Katrina flooding that affected lower-lying areas on the opposite side of St. Charles Avenue. Along with the Warehouse District, CBD, and Algiers Point, the Garden District was one of the first neighborhoods to reopen after the hurricane. It has since been fully repopulated by its

CREOLE VS. CAJUN

The terms "creole" and "Cajun" are used almost interchangeably outside Louisiana to refer to the region's cuisine, but a local would never confuse the two. Originally, the term "Creole" was used to refer to people born in the colonies. In New Orleans today, it is often used to refer to people of mixed European and African heritage with long family traditions in the city. The term "Cajun," short for "Acadian," refers to the descendants of French residents of Nova Scotia, Canada, who sought refuge in Louisiana after being banished by the British in the 18th century.

Adams
House **10**

Bradish-Johnson
House **8**

Brevard
House **5**

Briggs-Staub
House **14**

Buckner
Mansion **7**

Colonel
Short's
Villa **15**

Lonsdale
House **13**

Maddox
House **12**

Musson
House **3**

Payne House **6**

The Rink **1**

Robinson
House **2**

Schlesinger
House **4**

Toby-Westfeldt
House **9**

Women's Guild of
the New Orleans
Opera Association
House **11**

proud residents, many of whom represent fourth- or fifth-generation New Orleans families.

Originally the vast Livaudais Plantation, the Garden District was laid out in streets and blocks in the late 1820s. It remained part of the separate city of Lafayette until incorporated into New Orleans in 1852. The district attracted wealthy Americans who were not welcome in the creole sections of the city. Here they constructed homes in three basic architectural styles: the three-bay, London-parlor, Greek Revival design; the center-hall, columnar Greek Revival; and the raised cottage. Surrounding the houses were English-style landscaped gardens. As the Americans developed their own social life, the raised cottage and Greek Revival prototypes were more elaborately expanded to provide for entertainment and ostentation.

The Garden District is divided into two sections by Jackson Avenue. Upriver from Jackson is the wealthy **Upper Garden District,** where the homes are meticulously kept up. Below Jackson, the Lower Garden District is rougher in areas, though the homes here are often structurally just as beautiful and are increasingly being restored. Still, the streets are less well patrolled and best toured during the day. Magazine Street, lined with antiques shops, boutiques, restaurants, and coffeehouses, serves as a southern border to the Garden District. As part of the "high ground" of the city, it, too, escaped flooding from Katrina and reopened quickly following the storm; its charm and vivacity is well worth a visit. St. Charles Avenue forms the northern border. Although the **Magazine Street bus** or **St. Charles Avenue bus** lines can get you here from downtown, take the historic streetcar if you can—it's a fun and leisurely way to see the sights along the avenue. A number of companies also offer walking tours (⇨*Day Tours & Guides in New Orleans Essentials*).

Numbers in the margin correspond to numbers in the box and on the Garden District map.

UPPER GARDEN DISTRICT

WHAT TO SEE

❿ Adams House. The curved gallery on the left side of this circa-1860 house is a twist on the raised cottage theme. Greek Revival influence is evident in the columns and the windows. ⊠*2423 Prytania St., Garden District.*

❽ Bradish-Johnson House. A private girls' school since 1929, this regal building served as a residence when it was built in 1872. Though based on the common five-bay Garden District plan, this was the first house in the district to embrace the French Second Empire style, visible in the mansard roof and superficial ornamental details. ⊠*2343 Prytania St., Garden District.*

❺ Brevard House. Though Anne Rice moved out of the elegant Garden District home in 2004, the famous novelist's fans still flock to see the house that inspired the Mayfair Manor in her series *Lives of the Mayfair Witches*. The house is a three-bay Greek Revival, extended over a luxurious side yard and surrounded by a fence of cast-iron rosettes that earned the estate's historical name, Rosegate. ⊠*1239 1st St., Garden District.*

⓮ Briggs-Staub House. The only Gothic Revival house in the district was built around 1849 and has undergone several restorations. Garden District Americans typically shunned the Gothic Revival style as linked to creole-Catholic tradition, but Londoner Charles Briggs ignored decorum and had James Gallier Sr. design this anomaly, described at the time as a "Gothic cottage." The interior departed from a strict Gothic breakup of rooms, thus becoming better suited for entertaining, but Gothic detailing is prevalent both inside and out. ⊠*2605 Prytania St., Garden District.*

❼ Buckner Mansion. This 1856 home was built by cotton factor Henry S.

STAR SEARCH

The two-story 1850 corner house at 2417 Coliseum Street is home to actor John Goodman and his wife, Annabeth Hartzog. They bought the 5,000-square-foot home in 2005 from Trent Reznor, founder of the rock group Nine Inch Rails. Annabeth also owns a children's store, Pippen Lane, on nearby Magazine Street.

A GOOD WALK

One block from the streetcar stop at the intersection of Washington Avenue and Prytania Street is the **Rink ❶**, a small shopping complex that was once a roller-skating rink. Walk down Washington Avenue toward Coliseum Street: the 1600 block, on your right, is taken up by the white-walled **Lafayette Cemetery No. 1**. One of the grandest restaurants in New Orleans is Commander's Palace, across from the cemetery. On the opposite corner is the small gallery of botanical sculptor and jewelry maker **Joey Bonhage**.

A stroll down Coliseum Street toward Jackson Avenue takes you past some of the most beautiful and historic homes in the South. On your right, the 2700 block of Coliseum Street is lined with the five once-identical houses of Freret's Folly. At Coliseum and 3rd streets are the extravagant, white-columned **Robinson House ❷**, thought to be the first house in New Orleans with indoor plumbing, and the intricate iron-balconied **Musson House ❸**. Also featuring elaborate ironwork, the **Schlesinger House ❹**, to your left at 2nd Street, is a classic Greek Revival. Continuing along Coliseum, turn right and walk down 1st Street to see the Italianate Morris House and on the next corner the Carroll House, where the classic *Toys In the Attic* was filmed, both on your left. Across Chestnut Street is the transitional **Brevard House ❺**,

home to author Anne Rice from 1989 to 2004, and one block farther on the right is the **Payne House ❻**, where Confederate president Jefferson Davis died. Returning to Coliseum Street, look toward Jackson Avenue to glimpse the Seven Sisters Houses and the triple ballroom of the **Buckner Mansion ❼**.

The blocks along both Philip and 1st streets, between Prytania and Coliseum, have many noteworthy homes. At 1st and Prytania streets you will find both the regal **Bradish-Johnson House ❽**, now a private girls' school, and the relatively modest raised **Toby-Westfeldt House ❾**. At the corner of 2nd and Prytania is the predominantly Greek Revival **Adams House ❿**, as well as the hybrid **Women's Guild of the New Orleans Opera Association House ⓫**, with its distinctive octagonal turret. The **Maddox House ⓬**, across the street, is an excellent example of the five-bay expansion of the basic Greek Revival model. Venture to your left down Prytania Street, the main artery of the district. No expense was spared in the construction of the **Lonsdale House ⓭**, at Prytania and 3rd streets. Across 3rd, the **Briggs-Staub House ⓮** is one of the few Gothic Revival houses in the city. Cross Prytania Street at the corner of 4th Street to **Colonel Short's Villa ⓯**, best known for its cornstalk fence.

Buckner in overt competition with the famous Stanton Hall in Natchez, built by Buckner's former partner. Among the luxurious details are 48 fluted cypress columns and a rare honeysuckle-design cast-iron fence. The generously proportioned triple ballroom, visible from Coliseum Street, answered 19th-century New Orleans's entertaining needs and until recently was used by debutantes practicing their walks and curtsies. Now privately owned, the house served as the campus of Soulé College from 1923 to 1975. ✉*1410 Jackson Ave., Garden District.*

Carroll House. This grand Italianate home and its neighbor at 1331 1st Street, both designed by Samuel Jamison, have identical ornate cast-iron galleries. An original carriage house still stands on the large property. ⊠*1315 1st St., Garden District.*

⑮ Colonel Short's Villa. A dining-room wing is tacked onto the Greek Revival layout of this home; the two-story galleries around the wing, railed with cast iron rather than wood, were influential in the ornamental use of cast iron throughout the neighborhood. The cast-iron fence, with a pattern of morning glories intertwining with cornstalks, was ordered from a Philadelphia catalog and is certainly the most famous example of cast iron in the Garden District. Legend has it that Colonel Short purchased the fence for his wife, who was homesick for Kentucky. Another cornstalk fence similar to this one appears in the French Quarter at 915 Royal Street. ⊠*1448 4th St., Garden District.*

Freret's Folly. These once-identical Greek Revival houses were built by the son of New Orleans Mayor William Freret as a speculative project. In the wake of the Civil War, the venture failed financially, earning its name. ⊠*2700 Coliseum St., Garden District.*

House of Broel's Victorian Mansion and Dollhouse Museum. Antique furnishings fill this restored antebellum home. The dollhouse collection, owned by Bonnie Broel, includes beautiful miniatures of Victorian, Tudor, and plantation-style houses. The home also houses a wedding store; several of the rooms are devoted to gowns and other wedding necessities. Tours of the house and museum are available by appointment. ⊠*2220 St. Charles Ave., Garden District* ☎*504/522–2220 or 800/827–4325* ⊕*www.houseofbroel.com* ⊠*Mansion and museum tour $10* ⊙*Mon.–Sat. 10–5.*

Joey Bonhage Gallery. Joey Bonhage makes his beautiful metal botanical sculptures and jewelry in a dusty little gallery kitty-corner to Commander's Palace. If you're lucky, you'll catch him working on a new piece, but you can always expect a warm welcome and friendly banter. On warm days (and sometimes evenings) his door stays open to welcome in neighbors, tourists, Commander's Palace diners, and just about any passerby who wants to swap stories. ⊠*1332 Washington Ave., Garden District* ⊙*Mon.–Sat. 11–5.*

⑬ Lonsdale House. As a 16-year-old immigrant working in the New Orleans shipyards, Henry Lonsdale noticed how many damaged goods were arriving from upriver. Spotting a need for more-protective shipping materials, Lonsdale developed the burlap bag (clued in by his parents, who had picked up a sample in India). He made a fortune in burlap, only to lose it all in the 1837 depression. Lonsdale next turned to coffee importing, an industry that ran into problems during the Civil War: the Union blocked imports from Brazil, the major supplier of coffee to New Orleans. Lonsdale hit upon the fateful idea of cutting the limited coffee grinds with chicory, a bitter root, and New Orleanians have been drinking the coffee-and-chicory blend ever since. The house, built with his entrepreneurial dollars, displays many fine details, including the intricate cast-iron work on the galleries and the marble entrance hall. The statue of Our Mother of Perpetual Help in the front yard is a remnant of the house's more than 70 years as an active Catholic chapel, which ended with its controversial sale to novelist Anne Rice in 1996. Actor Nicholas Cage purchased the house in 2005. ⊠*2523 Prytania St., Garden District.*

12 **Maddox House.** Built in 1852, this house exemplifies the five-bay, center-hall extension of the Greek Revival style—notice the Ionic and Corinthian columns that support the broadened galleries. Inside is a magnificent gold ballroom decorated by a Viennese artist for the original owners. ⊠*2507 Prytania St., Garden District.*

Morris House. By the end of the 1850s, Garden District tastes began to evolve from the Greek Revival style to more-elaborate and fanciful designs. The Morris house is an excellent example of the Italianate style that became the new architectural vogue. ⊠*1331 1st St., Garden District.*

3 **Musson House.** This Italianate house was built by impressionist painter Edgar Degas's maternal uncle, Michel Musson—a rare Creole inhabitant of the predominantly American Garden District. A later owner added the famous "lace" galleries, named for their elaborate cast-iron work. ⊠*1331 3rd St., Garden District.*

6 **Payne House.** Confederate president Jefferson Davis died here on December 6, 1889; a monument out front outlines his active political and military careers. The two-story galleries overlook the side yard. Cast-iron ornaments the capitals of the Ionic columns, each embossed with the date (1848) and place (New York) of manufacture. ⊠*1134 1st St., Garden District.*

1 **The Rink.** This small collection of specialty shops was once the location of South's first roller-skating rink, built in the 1880s. Locals can be found here browsing in the **Garden District Book Shop,** which stocks regional, rare, and old books. ⊠*Washington Ave. and Prytania St., Garden District.*

NEED A BREAK?

A pleasant place to relax is outdoors on the deck of Still Perkin' (⊠*2727 Prytania St., Garden District* ☎*504/899–0335)* at the Rink. Gourmet coffees and teas and baked goods are served.

2 **Robinson House.** Styled after an Italian villa, this home built in the late 1850s is one of the largest in the district. Doric and Corinthian columns support the rounded galleries. It is believed to be the first house in New Orleans with "waterworks," as indoor plumbing was called then. Years of extensive renovation based on the original plans culminated with

New Orleans Cemeteries

New Orleans's "cities of the dead," with rows of crypts like little houses and streets organized with signs, are some of the city's most enduring images. Of the metropolitan area's 42 cemeteries, 15 are examples of the aboveground burial practices of the French and Spanish. This method was adopted in New Orleans in the early 1800s because the high water table made it difficult to bury bodies underground without having the coffin float to the surface after the first hard rain. Wealthier families could afford to build ornate individual crypts, while a more-economical option was burial inside the cemetery walls, in slots called "ovens." In the subtropical climate, bodies decomposed rapidly. After a year, the bones were swept out of the tomb, which was then ready for its next occupant. Modern-day burial methods permit underground interment, but many people prefer these ornate family tombs and vaults for their sanitation, efficiency, and mysterious beauty. The most notable of these cemeteries, listed below, are open to the public. However, several are in dangerous areas of the city, where organized group tours are the only rational way to visit. There are many good private tours, some more historical and others more theatrical. Good options are the detailed and accurate tours of St. Louis Cemetery No. 1 and Lafayette Cemetery No. 1 offered by nonprofit group **Save Our Cemeteries** (☎504/525–3377).

Lafayette Cemetery No. 1. Begun around 1833, this was the first planned cemetery in the city, with symmetrical rows, roadways for funeral vehicles, and lavish aboveground vaults and tombs for the wealthy families who built the sur-

rounding mansions. In 1852, 2,000 yellow-fever victims were buried here. Movies such as Interview with the Vampire and Easy Rider have used this walled cemetery for its eerie beauty. The cemetery is open to the public, and you can wander the grounds on your own or take an organized tour. ✉1400 block of Washington Ave., Garden District ☎Cemetery free, tour $6 ⊙Weekdays 7–2:30, Sat. 7–noon; Save Our Cemeteries tours Mon., Wed., Fri., and Sat. at 10:30.

Lake Lawn Metairie Cemetery. The largest cemetery in the metropolitan area, known to locals simply as Metairie Cemetery, is the final resting place of nine Louisiana governors, seven New Orleans mayors, three Confederate generals, and musician Louis Prima. Many of New Orleans's noted families are also interred here in elaborate monuments ranging from Gothic crypts to Romanesque mausoleums to Egyptian pyramids. Walk the grounds or drive along named streets to see them. In the mid-1800s, the cemetery was the site of the Metairie Racetrack and Jockey Club. According to legend, American millionaire Charles Howard was denied admission to the clubhouse because he was not a Creole. He vowed to buy and bury the track and the club. In 1872, the site became a cemetery, and when Howard died in 1885, it became his eternal resting place. His ornate mausoleum features a statue of a man with his finger to his lips. ✉5100 Pontchartrain Blvd., Metairie ⊙Daily 8–5.

St. Louis Cemetery No. 1. Buried here, in the city's oldest cemetery, are such notables as Etienne Boré, father of the sugar industry; Daniel Clar, financial supporter of the American Revolution; Homer Plessy of the

Plessy vs. Ferguson 1892 U.S. Supreme Court decision establishing the separate but equal "Jim Crow" laws for African-Americans and whites in the South; Paul Morphy, world-famous chess champion; former mayor Ernest "Dutch" Morial; and Marie Laveau, voodoo queen. Her tomb is marked with Xs freshly chalked by those who still believe in her supernatural powers. There are also magnificent tombs of the French, Italian, Portuguese, and Spanish Societies. St. Louis No. 1 abuts what used to be public housing projects; you can get a feel for the cemetery during daylight by exploring the first few rows of tombs, but avoid venturing too deep inside without a tour, as muggings are common. Many group tours visit this cemetery, including one by Save Our Cemeteries and even a couple guided by local Voodoo priestesses. ✉*bounded by Basin, Conti, Tremé, and St. Louis Sts., Tremé* 🖼*Cemetery free, tour $12* 🕙*Weekdays 9–3, Sun. 9–noon; Save Our Cemeteries tours Sun. at 10.*

St. Louis Cemetery No. 2. St. Louis No. 2, established in 1823, includes the tomb of a second Marie Laveau, believed to be her daughter. A number of notable local musicians are buried here, including Danny Barker and Ernie K. Doe. Also entombed here are Dominique You, a notorious pirate, and Andre Cailloux, African-American hero of the American Civil War. On Claiborne Avenue four blocks beyond St. Louis Cemetery No. 1, it, too, is in a dangerous area of town—so only visit as part of a guided group tour. ✉*N. Claiborne Ave. between Iberville and St. Louis Sts., Bayou St. John* 🕙*Weekdays 9–3, Sun. 9–noon.*

St. Louis Cemetery No. 3. Established in 1854, the St. Louis No. 3 is one block from the entrance to City Park, at the end of Esplanade Avenue. It is well paved and lined with elaborate aboveground crypts, mausoleums, and carved stone angels. Brochures are available in the office at the entrance, and crime is less of a concern at this location than at St. Louis Nos. 1 and 2. Still, a group tour is the more-prudent alternative to exploring alone. ✉*3428 Esplanade Ave., Bayou St. John.*

a re-landscaping in 2005. ✉*1415 3rd St., Garden District.*

❹ Schlesinger House. The columns and the simple lines in the framing of doors and windows stand out here. This house is a classic example of the Greek Revival style popular in the 1850s, which was used in many plantation homes upriver, as well. Its lovely ironwork was added to the front gallery in the 1930s. ✉*1427 2nd St., Garden District.*

Seven Sisters Houses. Legend has it that the seven nearly identical shotgun houses occupying the 2300 block of Coliseum Street were built for seven sisters. In fact they were the first speculation houses in the city, and some of the first in the United States. Though renovations have blurred the family resemblance, the homes are structurally distinguished only by the front galleries: some are Greek Revival, some Italianate. ✉*2300 Coliseum St., Garden District.*

❾ Toby-Westfeldt House. Dating from the 1830s, this unpretentious French-colonial home sits amid a large, plantation-like garden, surrounded by a copy of the original white picket fence. Thomas Toby, a Philadelphia businessman, moved to New Orleans and had this house built well above the ground to protect it from flooding. The house is thought to be the oldest in this part of the Garden District. ✉*2340 Prytania St., Garden District.*

⓫ Women's Guild of the New Orleans Opera Association House. This fundamentally Greek Revival house, built in 1858, has a distinctive Italianate octagonal turret, added in the late 19th century. The last private owner, Nettie Seebold, willed the estate to the Women's Guild of the New Orleans Opera upon her death in 1955. Furnished with period pieces, the house underwent extensive renovations in 2008 and is once again being used for receptions and private parties. ✉*2504 Prytania St., Garden District* ☎*504/899–1945.*

LOWER GARDEN DISTRICT

WHAT TO SEE

Derby Pottery. Fragments of wrought ironwork and other architectural details form the inspiration for many of Mark Derby's beautiful mugs, vases, and handmade Victorian reproduction tiles. His clocks and plaques, fashioned from reproductions of New Orleans's historic art-deco water-meter covers, have earned cult popularity. ✉*2029 Maga-*

DESTINATION WEDDING

An intrepid Texas couple chose Lafayette Cemetery as the site of their wedding (on a Friday the 13th, no less). The bride, groom, and guests all dressed in black, and four black limousines took the wedding party to the cemetery. The ceremony was held in one of the aisles between the graves, while a lone trumpet played "Summertime." The bride and groom, both of whom had been previously married, told the graveyard superintendent they had come to bury the past and begin their future together.

zine St., Lower Garden District ☎*504/586–9003* ⊕*www.derbypottery. com* ☉*Mon.–Sat. 10–5.*

Eiffel Tower Building. This building, one of the more unusual in the city, occupies the intersection of Josephine Street and St. Charles Avenue. Each piece of the original restaurant inside the Eiffel Tower in Paris was shipped here and carefully reassembled in 1986. Today, it houses the Cricket Club, a supper club–style event venue run by the Culinary Institute of New Orleans, whose students man the kitchen. The club hosts group cooking demonstrations by appointment and can be rented for special events. ⊠*2040 St. Charles Ave., Lower Garden District* ☎*504/304–9467* ⊕*www.cricketclubevents.com.*

Elleone Gallery. Elleone, the name local artist Lionel Milton used grow- ing up as a graffiti painter, is an acronym for Every Living Legend Excels On Natural Energy. That energy is evident in Milton's vibrant, soulful, and downright funky art, which drew national attention when it was used to decorate the house for MTV's Real World season in New Orleans. Milton has also earned a cult following from the five Voodoo Music Experience posters he has designed. Elleone Gallery juxtaposes the urban edge of Milton's art against the old-world architecture of its row-house building. ⊠*2001 Magazine St., Lower Garden District* ☎*504/592–4550* ⊕*www.elleonegallery.com* ☉*Tues.–Sat. 11–6.*

Goodrich-Stanley House. This restored creole cottage is an excellent example of the modest prototype for much of the far more elaborate architecture of the surrounding Garden District. The scale of the cre- ole cottage, derived from the climate-conscious design prevalent in the West Indies, made it easily adaptable to the higher pretensions of the Greek Revival look, as well as the slightly more reserved Colo- nial Revival. Built in 1837, the house has had one famous occupant: John Rowlands, who was adopted by Henry Hope Stanley, owner of the house. Rowlands changed his name to Henry Morton Stanley and became a renowned explorer of Africa and founder of the Congo Free States. Perhaps most notoriously, he uttered the phrase "Dr. Living- stone, I presume" upon encountering the long-lost Scottish missionary. ⊠*1729 Coliseum St., Lower Garden District.*

NEED A BREAK? One block from Coliseum Square, at the corner of Magazine and Race streets, is Mojo Coffee House (⊠*1500 Magazine St., Lower Garden Dis- trict* ☎*504/525–2244* ☉*Weekdays 6:30–midnight, weekends 7–midnight*), where you can have a seat, sip a cup of java, and relax before perusing the shops and galleries along lower Magazine.

New Orleans Metropolitan Convention and Visitors Bureau. The CVB is the main organization responsible for promoting, managing, and serv- ing New Orleans's tourism industry. In the bureau's lobby, the visi- tor center has computer stations, brochure racks, and helpful staff to answer questions about area accommodations, restaurants, events, services, and attractions. ⊠*2020 St. Charles Ave., Lower Garden Dis- trict* ☎*504/566–5011 or 800/672–6124* ⊕*www.neworleanscvb.com* ☉*Weekdays 8:30–5.*

St. Alphonsus Art and Cultural Center. Though no longer an active church, this lovely building dates from the mid-19th century and is sometimes open to visitors. It was founded for the Irish sector of Redemptorist Parish; the church across the street served the German community, and a third church down the street (no longer standing) served the French community. The frescoed, weathered interior has been preserved in its original form; admission includes a cassette tour. For an additional $2, you can take a guided tour (by appointment). A small museum displays artifacts and memorabilia from the area, including personal effects of local bishops, scrapbooks, and yearbooks. A block toward the river from Magazine, St. Alphonsus is in a high-crime area; use caution if you plan to walk here. ✉2045 Constance St., Lower Garden District ☎504/524–8116 ⌦$3, $5 with guided tour ⊘Tues., Thurs., and Sat. 10–2.; guided tours by appointment.

St. Vincent's Guesthouse. This large, brick structure was once an orphanage and home for unwed mothers. Today most of St. Vincent's has been converted into guest rooms, but you may be able to view the lobby and courtyard if you knock on the door. ✉1507 Magazine St., Lower Garden District ☎504/523–3411.

Thomas Mann Gallery I/O. Known for his imaginative jewelry and sculptural forays he calls "techno-romantic" design, Thomas Mann also showcases contemporary American crafts by other local artists in his Magazine Street gallery. ✉1812 Magazine St., Lower Garden District ☎504/581–2113 ⊕www.thomasmann.com ⊘Mon.–Sat. 11–6.

UPTOWN

Lying west of the Garden District, Uptown is the residential area on both sides of St. Charles Avenue along the streetcar route, upriver from Louisiana Avenue. It includes many mansions as sumptuous as those in the Garden District, as well as Loyola and Tulane universities and a large urban park named for John James Audubon. Traveling along the avenue from downtown to uptown provides something of a historical narrative: the city's development unfolded upriver, and the houses grow discernibly more modern the farther uptown you go.

Post-Katrina recovery has been spotty across this broad area; generally, homes and businesses on the river side of St. Charles did not flood and were more quickly repopulated, whereas many of those to the lake side of St. Charles (particularly in the area north of Freret Street that locals call Broadmoor) sat in 2 to 8 feet of floodwaters for weeks following the hurricane. You can still see water lines marking the flood height on some steps, walls, and siding. As in other flooded areas of the city, there is ongoing demolition and renovation.

The best way to see the restored or unscathed parts of this neighborhood is by traveling down St. Charles Avenue.

Fodor'sChoice **The St. Charles Avenue streetcar,** which runs down the length of the ave-
★ nue, from Canal Street to the Carrollton Riverbend, provides a won-

derful way to take in the neighborhood. In the early 1900s streetcars were the most prominent mode of public transit and ran on many streets. Today, they operate along the riverfront, Canal Street, and St. Charles Avenue. ■ TIP→**Avoid rush hours—from 7 to 9 and 3 to 6—or you may have to stand still much of the way and will not be able to enjoy the scenery.**

Another main artery, Magazine Street, traverses the Uptown area with miles of antiques shops, clothing boutiques, specialty stores, restaurants, and cafés. The Magazine Street bus can take you up and down the length of the street, which culminates at Audubon Park, a lush stretch of green that encompasses a running track, playfields, a wonderful zoo, and a golf course.

Numbers in the margin correspond to numbers on the St. Charles Avenue Uptown map.

TIMING   St. Charles Streetcar service runs every 10–15 minutes, with stops every few blocks, so expect the ride from Washington Avenue (in the center of the Garden District) or Louisiana Avenue to the Carrollton Riverbend to take about 45 minutes (considerably more during rush hour). Plan a half day minimum for visiting the Audubon Zoo and enjoying the park that surrounds it.

WHAT TO SEE

㉓ **Anthemion.** A fashion for Colonial Revival architecture in the late 19th century indicated local weariness with the excesses of the Greek Revival craze that had dominated the mid-century. Anthemion, built in 1896 and the headquarters of the Japanese consulate from 1938 to 1941, is an excellent example of this return to simplicity. ✉*4631 St. Charles Ave., Uptown.*

▌ **NEED A BREAK?**   Stop for a cup of coffee, a pastry, or a variety of lunch choices at La Madeleine (✉*601 Carrollton Ave., Uptown* ☎*504/861-8662* ⊕*www.lamad eleine.com*), a French bakery with seasonal outdoor seating at the corner where St. Charles turns into Carrollton.

☙ ★ ㊳ **Audubon Park.** Formerly the plantation of Etienne de Boré, the father of the granulated sugar industry in Louisiana, **Audubon Park** is a large, lush stretch of green between St. Charles Avenue and Magazine Street, continuing across Magazine Street to the river. Designed by John Charles Olmsted, nephew of Frederick Law Olmsted (who laid out New York City's Central Park), it contains the world-class **Audubon Zoo**; a 1.7-mi track for running, walking, or biking; picnic and play areas; Audubon Park Golf Course; a tennis court; horse stables; and a river view. Calm lagoons wind through the park, harboring egrets, catfish, and other indigenous species. The park and zoo were named for the famous ornithologist and painter John James Audubon, who spent many years working in and around New Orleans. None of the original buildings from its former plantation days remain; in fact, none of the buildings that housed the 1884–85 World's Industrial and Cot-

St. Charles Avenue Uptown

See Garden District detail map ◆

House of Broel's Victorian Mansion and Doll House Museum ◆

Mississippi River

KEY

Streetcar

TO AUDUBON ZOO →

Anthemion	23	Castles House **32**
Audubon Park **38**		Christ Church
Benjamin House **28**		Cathedral **16**
Brown House **24**		Columns Hotel **19**
Buttman Funeral		Doll House **36**
Home **18**		Elms Mansion **17**
Camelback Houses **37**		Loyola University **33**

McCarthy House **29**	Sacred Heart
Middle American Research	Academy **21**
Institute and Gallery **34**	Smith House **22**
Milton H. Latter	Sully House **20**
Memorial Library **27**	Tara **30**
Orleans Club **26**	Tulane University **35**
Rosenberg House **25**	Wedding Cake House..... **31**

0 1 mile
0 1 2 km

ton Centennial Exposition, which was held on these acres and gave New Orleans its first international publicity after the Civil War, have survived. The only reminder of this important event in New Orleans's history is Exposition Boulevard, the street address assigned to houses that front the park along the downtown side.

If time permits, you may want to venture beyond the zoo, cross the railroad tracks, and stroll along **Riverview Drive,** a long stretch of land behind the zoo that is part of Audubon Park, on the levee overlooking the Mississippi River. This area is referred to as "The Fly" by locals, after a butterfly-shape building that was torn down here some years ago, and it is a popular place for picnics and pickup sports. ✉*6500 Magazine St., Uptown* ⊕*www.auduboninstitute.org* ⊠*Free.*

> **CHEAP TREAT**
>
> As you explore Uptown, especially around Audubon Park, keep an eye out for a red-and-white wagon pulled by a white mule named Patsy. This is the Roman Candy Man, a New Orleans institution that has satisfied generations of sweet teeth with long, chewy taffy delights. Choose from vanilla, strawberry or chocolate, just 75 cents a stick.

Overlooking the Audubon Park Golf Course is the **Audubon Park Club-house** (✉*6500 Magazine St., Uptown* ☎*504/212–5285*), where you can eat breakfast or lunch in the airy dining room, or relax with a refreshing drink on the oak-tree-shaded veranda. The clubhouse, designed to resemble an Acadian cottage, is on the interior end of the parking lot accessed from Magazine Street. The golf course is public and open seven days a week.

Audubon Park Golf Course (✉, *Uptown* ☎*504/212–5285, 504/212–5290 for course tee times* ⊠*$30 weekdays, $40 weekends; green fees include cart and sales tax* ☉*Daily 7–dusk*) is the only public golf course to reopen in New Orleans since Katrina. Audubon is a par-62, 4,220-yard Denis Griffiths–designed course among Tif Eagle greens, lagoons, and sprawling oaks at the center of the park.

� ★ **Audubon Zoo.** Animals roam and frolic in natural-habitat settings at this excellent zoo in **Audubon Park.** It's home to lions, tigers, bears, sea lions, and a number of exotic species, including a family of extremely rare white (albino) alligators. The Louisiana Swamp exhibit re-creates the natural habitat of alligators, nutria (large swamp rodents), and catfish; alligator-feeding time is always well attended. Other highlights include the reptile encounter and Komodo dragon exhibit, a Sumatran Orangutan family, and white Bengal tigers. Several new attractions are available for additional ticket fees: a zoo train tour departs every 30 minutes from the swamp exhibit; the children's zoo area features a rock-climbing wall and Endangered Species Carousel; and the Safari Simulator Ride alternates five different themed experiences. You can walk here from the St. Charles Avenue streetcar or bus (No. 12), which stop across Audubon Park (allow a half hour). The Magazine Street bus also stops right at the zoo and can take you to and from Canal Street.

✉6500 Magazine St., Uptown ☎504/581–4629 ⊕www.audubon
institute.org 🔖$12.50; combination ticket for zoo and Aquarium
of the Americas $25.50; combination ticket for zoo, aquarium, and
IMAX Theater $28.50 ⊙Tues.–Fri. 10–4, weekends 10–5.

㉘ **Benjamin House.** This beaux-arts beauty, built in 1912 for cotton factor Emanuel Benjamin, shares the block with Danneel Park. It was
constructed of expensive limestone, leaving Benjamin with a bill of
$30,000—an outrageous sum at the time. ✉5531 St. Charles Ave.,
Uptown.

㉔ **Brown House.** Completed in 1904, the Brown House is the largest mansion on St. Charles Avenue. Its solid monumental look, Syrian arches,
and steep gables make it a choice example of Romanesque Revival
style. ✉4717 St. Charles Ave., Uptown.

⑱ **Bultman Funeral Home.** This huge white mansion with an enclosed garden
was one of the most elegant funeral homes in the South until it closed
shortly after Hurricane Katrina. A balcony bears a wrought-iron motif
of downward crossed arrows, a symbol of death. Tennessee Williams set
his play *Suddenly Last Summer* here in the solarium. The building was
bought by Borders in 2007 and is currently undergoing renovation to be
reborn as a bookstore. ✉3338 St. Charles Ave., Garden District

�37 **Camelback Houses.** When these were built in the late 1800s, houses were
taxed by the width and height of their facades: working-class homes
were usually narrow and long. Sometimes a second floor was added
to the back half of the house, giving it the architectural designation of
"camelback." The camelback and the gingerbread-type decoration on
porches were popular details at the turn of the 20th century. ✉7628–
7630, 7632–7634, and 7820–7822 St. Charles Ave., Uptown.

㉜ **Castles House.** Local architect Thomas Sully designed this 1896 Colonial
Revival house after the Longfellow House in Cambridge, Massachu-
setts. The interior has often appeared in the pages of design magazines.
✉6000 St. Charles Ave., Uptown.

⑯ **Christ Church Cathedral.** This beautiful Gothic Revival Episcopal church
completed in 1887 has steeply pitched gables, an architectural detail
that was a precursor to the New Orleans Victorian style. The cathedral
is the oldest non–Roman Catholic church in the Louisiana Purchase:
the congregation was established in 1805, and this is the third building
erected on the same site. It is the diocesan headquarters of the Episcopal Church in Louisiana. ✉2919 St. Charles Ave., Garden District.

⑲ **Columns Hotel.** In recent years this elegant white hotel, built in 1884
as a private home, has been the scene of TV ads, movies, and plenty
of weddings. The interior scenes of Louis Malle's *Pretty Baby* were
filmed here. The Colonial Revival hotel has a popular bar and a grand
veranda for sipping cocktails; there's live music some nights and during Sunday brunch. The grand rooms of the first floor are open to the
public; note the stained-glass skylight topping the mahogany stairwell.
✉3811 St. Charles Ave., Uptown ☎504/899–9308 or 800/445–9308
⊕www.thecolumns.com.

36 Doll House. Designed in the same Tudor style as the main house beside it for the daughter of a former owner, this is the smallest house in New Orleans to have its own postal address. ☒*7209 St. Charles Ave., Uptown.*

17 Elms Mansion. Built in 1869, this elegant home with marble fireplaces and stained-glass windows saw the Confederate president Jefferson Davis as a frequent guest. The house, which has been meticulously maintained and furnished with period pieces, is the site of many receptions. Tours of the interior are conducted on weekdays by appointment only. Highlights include a fantastic carved oak staircase and mantelpiece and 24-karat gilt moldings and sconces. ☒*3029 St. Charles Ave., Garden District* ☎*504/895–9200* ☒*Tours $5 per person* ☾*Weekdays by appointment.*

> **PERFECT PICNIC**
>
> Spicy seafood to go makes for the perfect New Orleans picnic. For seasonal boiled specialties—crawfish, crabs, shrimp, andouille sausage, corn, potatoes, and garlic—stop by the Big Fisherman (3301 Magazine Street) on your way to Audubon Park. Ask if they have fresh crawfish pies available. And don't forget the paper towels at the supermarket next door.

33 Loyola University. The Jesuits built this complex facing the avenue in 1914. The modernistic Gothic-style building on the corner is the **Louis J. Roussel Building,** which houses the music department. The campus, with its dorms, recreational center, and library, extends for two blocks behind the **Church of the Holy Name of Jesus,** a masterfully constructed Gothic and Tudor edifice. The fourth floor of the neo-Gothic **library** holds a gallery with changing exhibits by students, faculty, and other regional artists. ☒*6363 St. Charles Ave., Uptown.*

29 McCarthy House. A deep front lawn emphasizes the perfect symmetry of this classic Colonial Revival, constructed in 1903. The brick veneer and Ionic columns are emblematic of the style. ☒*5603 St. Charles Ave., Uptown.*

34 Middle American Research Institute and Gallery. Way up on the fourth floor of a musty old academic building, this research institute and gallery at **Tulane University** has exhibits of pre-Columbian and Central and South American culture. Established in 1924, the institute has an extensive collection of pre-Columbian Mayan artifacts and one of the largest collections of Guatemalan textiles in the nation. Tulane's main library has an extensive collection of books on Latin American culture associated with the research institute. ☒*Dinwiddie Hall, 4th fl., Tulane University Uptown* ☎*504/865–5110* ☒*Free* ☾*Weekdays 8:30–5.*

27 Milton H. Latter Memorial Library. A former private home now serves as the most elegant public library in New Orleans. Built in 1907 and ornamenting its own beautifully landscaped block, this Italianate–beaux-arts mansion was once the home of silent-screen star Marguerite Clark, who lived here in the 1940s. It was then purchased by the Latter family and given to the city as a library in 1948 in memory of their son, who was killed in World War II. You can sit a spell and leaf through a copy of Walker Percy's *The Moviegoer* or Anne Rice's *The Vampire Lestat* (two popular novels set in New Orleans), or just relax in a wicker chair on the solarium. This is one of the few mansions on St. Charles Avenue open to the public. Local artisans contributed the murals and carved mantels. ⊠*5120 St. Charles Ave., Uptown* ☎*504/596–2625* ⊕*www. nutrias.org* ⊗*Mon. and Wed. 9–8, Tues. and Thurs. 9–6, Sat. 10–5.*

㉖ **Orleans Club.** This sumptuous mansion was built in 1868 as a wedding gift from Colonel William Lewis Wynn to his daughter. The dormer windows, typical of French Empire style, were added during a remodeling in 1909. The side building, on the uptown side of the main building, is an auditorium added in the 1950s. The house is closed to the public but serves as headquarters to a ladies' social club and hosts many debutante teas and wedding receptions. ⊠*5005 St. Charles Ave., Uptown.*

㉕ **Rosenberg House.** The brick facade and Corinthian columns on this stately 1911 house mark it as Colonial Revival. Behind these traits, a modern, Craftsman-style interior (not open to the public) suggests the progressive tastes of the Rosenbergs. The Stirling House, next door at number 4930, provides an interesting contrast, embodying as it does the Classical Revival characteristics of a clean, white exterior and simple Doric columns. ⊠*4920 St. Charles Ave., Uptown.*

㉑ **Sacred Heart Academy.** Unusual aspects of this building, a Catholic girls' school built in 1899, include wide, wraparound balconies (or galleries) and colonnades facing a large garden. The academy is exceptionally beautiful during the December holidays, when the galleries are decked with wreaths and garlands. ⊠*4521 St. Charles Ave., Uptown.*

㉒ **Smith House.** This bucolic Mediterranean villa was built in 1906 for William Smith, president of the New Orleans Cotton Exchange. Smith himself planted the three live oak trees that have now grown to shade the expansive yard. The front porch is anchored by stone columns with capitals in the Greek honeysuckle-and-palmette pattern. ⊠*4534 St. Charles Ave., Uptown.*

㉚ **Sully House.** This was the family home of local architect Thomas Sully, who designed it around 1890. Sully was known for his use of deep shades of color and varied textures. Similar gables, towers, and gingerbread appear on many other homes in the vicinity. ⊠*4010 St. Charles Ave., Uptown.*

㉚ **Tara.** A replica built from the plans of the movie set of *Gone with the Wind,* Tara seems almost dwarfed here by far more-sumptuous houses. ⊠*5705 St. Charles Ave., Uptown.*

㉟ **Tulane University.** The venerable university sits next to Loyola University on St. Charles Avenue. Three original buildings face the avenue: **Tilton Hall** (1901) on the left, **Gibson Hall** (1894) in the middle, and **Dinwiddie Hall** (1936) on the right. The Romanesque style, with its massive stone look and arched windows and doors, is repeated in the several buildings around a large quad behind these. Modern campus buildings extend another three blocks to the rear. Tulane is well known for its medical school, law school, and fine main library. The **Sophie**

H. Newcomb College for Women was the coordinate women's college of Tulane University until it was dissolved in 2006 as part of a post-Katrina renewal plan. The college's memorial institute maintains the **Newcomb College Center for Research on Women**, a fine women's resource center that brings in speakers, writers, and academics throughout the school year. Also on the Tulane campus is the **Middle American Research Institute**. ✉ *6823 St. Charles Ave., Uptown.*

③ **Wedding Cake House.** A portico and decorative balconies help this house outshine most other mansions on the avenue. Its key beauty is the beveled leaded glass in its front door, one of the most beautiful entryways in the city. ✉ *5809 St. Charles Ave., Uptown.*

> **QUICK COOL DOWN**
>
> When the weather heats up in the spring and summer months, snowballs become the favorite way to cool down in New Orleans. Locals line up at seasonal stands tucked throughout Uptown for finely ground ice flavored with everything from chocolate to cherry to bubble-gum syrup. Some perennial favorites include Hansen's Sno-Bliz at 4801 Tchoupitoulas, Plum Street Snowball at 1300 Burdette, and SnoWizard at 4001 Magazine.

BAYOU ST. JOHN & MID-CITY

Above the French Quarter and below the lakefront, neither Uptown nor quite downtown, Mid-City is an amorphous yet proud territory embracing everything from the massive, lush City Park to gritty storefronts along Carrollton Avenue. It is a neighborhood of tremendous ethnic and economic diversity. Here you'll find great restaurants, cultural landmarks such as Mid-City Bowling Lanes, restored former plantation homes, and crumbling inner-city neighborhoods. Actual sights are few and far between in Mid-City, and the neighborhood suffered heavily from flooding during Hurricane Katrina, but the area is recovering. The neighborhood around Bayou St. John near City Park is still one of the more picturesque in town and is fruitful for walks.

Numbers in the margin correspond to numbers on the Lakefront and City Park map.

WHAT TO SEE

❽ **Alcee Fortier Park.** This tiny sliver of a park was named for philanthropist Alcee Fortier, who owned much of the surrounding area in the 19th century and founded a public school Uptown. It forms a focal point of the Bayou St. John neighborhood, surrounded by hip restaurants and shops. ✉ *Esplanade Ave. and Ponce de Leon Blvd., Bayou St. John.*

❶ **Bayou St. John.** A bayou is an inlet, a still, narrow waterway that emerges from the swamp at one end and normally joins a larger body of water at the other. This bayou—the only remaining bayou in New Orleans—borders City Park on the east and extends about 7 mi from Lake Pontchartrain to just past Orleans Avenue. It is named for John the Baptist,

Alcee Fortier
Park 8

Bayou
St. John 1

Benachi-Torre
House 5

Cabrini High
School &
Mother Cabrini
Shrine 9

Carousel
Gardens 14

City Park 15

Edgar Degas
House 3

Fair Grounds
Race Course 6

House on
Bayou Road 4

Longue Vue
House &
Gardens 16

Luling
Mansion 7

New Orleans
Botanical
Garden 12

New Orleans
Museum of Art
(NOMA) 10

Pitot House 2

Ralph's on
the Park 11

Storyland 13

Lakefront
& City Park

Lake
Pontchartrain

Lakeshore Dr.

Robert E. Lee Blvd.

Robert E. Lee Blvd.

Prentiss Ave.

Paris Ave.

St. John

Fillmore Ave.

Fillmore Ave.

Canal Blvd.

Argonne Blvd.

Orleans Ave.

Marconi Dr.

Lane St.

Mirabeau Ave.

Bayou

Harrison Ave.

City
Park

St. Bernard Ave.

Harrison Ave.

Polk Ave.

TO
PONTCHARTRAIN
CAUSEWAY

610

15

Milton St.

Wisner Blvd.

DeSaix Blvd.

St. Louis
Cemetery No. 3

14   13   12

10

Dreyfous Dr.

Fair
Grounds

City Park Ave.

11

9

7

16

Canal St.

8

6

Gentilly Blvd.

2

Moss St.

Esplanade Ave.

10

Carrollton Ave.

1

5

Orleans Ave.

N. Broad St.

3   4

0   1 mile

0   1 km

Palmetto St.

Tulane Ave.

S. Jeff Davis Pkwy.

2

whose nativity (St. John's Eve, June 23), the most important day in the year for voodoo practitioners, was notoriously celebrated on the bayou's banks in the 1800s. The first European settlers in the area, believed to have been trappers, coexisted with Native Americans here beginning in 1704. Graceful old homes join more-modern houses on picturesque **Moss Street,** along the section of the bayou nearest downtown. The small streets branching off from Moss Street make for scenic walks.

⑤ Benachi-Torre House. This elegant Greek Revival mansion was built in 1859 for the Greek consul in New Orleans. It earned the nickname "Rendezvous des Chasseurs" (meeting place of hunters) during the 19th century. The house is not open to the public. ✉*2257 Bayou Rd., at Tonti St., Bayou St. John.*

⑨ Cabrini High School and Mother Cabrini Shrine. Mother Frances Cabrini, the first American-citizen saint (she was canonized in 1946), purchased the land between Esplanade Avenue and Bayou St. John near City Park in 1905 and built the Sacred Heart Orphan Asylum here. She stayed in the Pitot House, which was on her property until she gave it to the city during construction of the orphanage. In 1959 the institution was converted to a girls' high school in St. Cabrini's name. Her bedroom has been preserved as it was when she lived here, filled with personal effects and maintained as a shrine. Call ahead to arrange a tour, which includes the bedroom and the chapel where she prayed. ✉*3400 Esplanade Ave., Bayou St. John* ☎*504/483–8690.*

🐾 ⑭ Carousel Gardens. This small amusement park, open seasonally, has a New Orleans treasure as its centerpiece—a carousel from 1906 that is on the National Register of Historic Places. The carousel and other park rides were heavily damaged in Katrina, but restoration became a focus of a number of local and visiting volunteer groups, who helped the amusement park reopen and the Carousel return to service. Although at this writing there were plans for a larger Ferris wheel, the rides here are geared to younger children, not thrill-seekers. But adults and kids alike enjoy the miniature train that takes passengers on a gentle sightseeing tour through City Park. ✉*Victory Ave., City Park, Bayou St. John* ☎*504/482–4888* ⊕*www.neworleanscitypark.com* 💲*$3* ✆ *Mar.–May and Sept.–Nov., weekends 10–4; June–Aug., daily 10–4; During Celebration in the Oaks (holiday season), 5:30–10:30 PM.*

NEED A BREAK? Just off Mystery Park, at the intersection of Mystery Street, Ponce de Leon Street, and Esplanade Avenue, is Fair Grinds Coffeehouse (✉*3133 Ponce de Leon St., Bayou St. John* ☎*504/913-9072* ⊕*www.fairgrinds.com*). Neighbors, musicians, and artists gather here for coffee, tea, and small snacks—including vegan treats—and a wide variety of community meetings, activities, and performances. Check the Web site for a calendar of events.

🐾💲⑮ City Park. City Park, a 150-year-old, 1,500-acre expanse of moss-draped oaks and gentle lagoons 2 mi from the French Quarter, suffered mightily in Hurricane Katrina's winds and flooding. The storm felled or damaged more than 1,000 trees, destroyed an 18-hole golf course, ravaged vegetation, and forced the park to lay off 90% of its staff. Nevertheless,

Fodor'sChoice
★

the park is rebuilding with the help of hundreds of local and visiting volunteers and even in its recovering state is a great place to walk or jog, play tennis, feed the ducks, visit one of its reopened attractions, or simply relax. Just beyond the main entrance at the end of Esplanade Avenue stands the **New Orleans Museum of Art** and an adjacent sculpture garden; tucked elsewhere in the sprawling park are tennis courts, a sports stadium and running track, baseball diamonds and playgrounds, along with miles of meandering walking paths and gentle lagoons rife with waterfowl. The park's art-deco benches, fountains, bridges, and ironwork are remnants of a 1930s Works Progress Administration refurbishment, and whimsical sculptures by renowned New Orleans artist Enrique Alferez dot the **New Orleans Botanical Garden**, which, although open, was severely damaged by Katrina floodwaters. The train garden here, operating on weekends only, is still a fun stop for the kids. Other children's favorites, Storyland and Carousel Gardens, are also open seasonally on weekends. Most attractions are clustered near the museum; the **Timken Center** snack bar and the golf course were still closed at this writing. But the tennis courts and the golf course's driving range are open, and families are once again staking claims on picnic tables for weekend barbecues. A popular drive-through Christmas holiday light display had to be scaled down after Katrina, but a walking tour of the botanical garden ($5) packs in holiday revelers. Call ahead or check the park's Web site for revised hours and available activities. ⊠*Bordered by City Park Ave., Robert E. Lee Blvd., Marconi Dr., and Bayou St. John* ☎*504/482–4888* ⊕*www.neworleanscitypark.com.*

❸ **Edgar Degas House.** Impressionist painter Edgar Degas stayed with his Musson cousins in this house during an 1872 visit to New Orleans, producing more than 70 works while here. Degas's mother and grandmother were both born in New Orleans, and local lore makes much of the connection. Today this is a B&B, though public tours, which include watching a film on Degas's family and their sojourn in New Orleans and a discussion of the historic neighborhood, are provided by appointment. ⊠*2306 Esplanade Ave., Bayou St. John* ☎*504/821–5009* ⊕*www.degashouse.com* ☜*$10 suggested donation* ⊙*Tours by appointment.*

❻ **Fair Grounds Race Course.** The third-oldest racetrack in the country, and one of the few remaining independent tracks, sits just off Esplanade Avenue, among the houses of Mid-City. Fire destroyed the historic old grandstand in the mid-1990s and Hurricane Katrina dealt the grounds a blow in 2005; but the newly renovated facility is modern and comfortable, complete with clubhouse restaurant and concession/snack bars. Pick up a serving of the corned beef hash, the house specialty. This is a fun place to spend a sunny afternoon on the bleachers or a rainy afternoon inside the grandstand. Reservations and proper attire (collared shirts, closed shoes, no shorts) are required for the clubhouse. ⊠*1751 Gentilly Blvd., Bayou St. John* ☎*504/943–2200 for box and restaurant reservations, 504/944–5515 for general information* ⊕*www.fairgroundsracecourse.com* ☜*Grandstand free, clubhouse $5* ⊙*Thanksgiving–Mar., check Web site for days and times.*

4 **House on Bayou Road.** This West Indies creole–style house served as the main house to an indigo plantation. It was built in 1798 by Domingo Fleitas, who was originally from the Canary Islands. Today, it houses a B&B and the New Orleans Cooking Experience, a cooking school in residence. Call a couple of weeks in advance to book a cooking class. ⊠*2275 Bayou Rd., Bayou St. John* ☎*504/945–0992* ⊕*www.house onbayouroad.com.*

7 **Luling Mansion.** The massive three-story Italianate Luling Mansion was designed by architect James Gallier Jr., and built in 1865 for Florence A. Luling. When the Louisiana Jockey Club took over the Creole Race Course (now the Fair Grounds) in 1871, it purchased this nearby mansion. For the next 20-odd years, it served as the racing organization's clubhouse. It is not open to the public. ⊠*1436–1438 Leda St., Bayou St. John.*

12 **New Orleans Botanical Garden.** Though reopened to the public, the botanical garden suffered severe damage to much of its indigenous flora due to Hurricane Katrina floodwaters and related loss of electricity, which killed most of the garden's collection of containerized plants. Still, you can stroll the peaceful 10-acre garden and its tropical conservatory and enjoy statuary by noted local artist Enrique Alferez. In the Train Garden, open on weekends, baguette-size cars roll through a miniature New Orleans village. ⊠*Victory Ave., City Park, Bayou St. John* ☎*504/483–9386* ⊕*www.neworleanscitypark.com* ☑*$6* ☉*Tues.–Sun. 10–4:30.*

★ **10** **New Orleans Museum of Art (NOMA).** Gracing the main entrance to City Park is this traditional fine arts museum, built in 1911. Modern wings, added to the original structure in the 1990s, bring light and space into the grand old building, which has an elegant central staircase and many formal rooms used as galleries. The jeweled treasures, particularly some of the famous eggs by Peter Carl Fabergé, are a favorite exhibit, along with European and American paintings, sculpture, drawings, prints, and photography. The museum holds one of the largest glass collections in the country and has developed a unique Art of the Americas collection that includes a range of Latin American and Native American works. Several period room installations feature 18th- and 19th-century American furniture and decorative arts. The comprehensive Asian art wing includes a good selection of Japanese paintings of the Edo period; African, Oceanic, pre-Columbian, and Louisiana art are also represented. Temporary exhibits often favor local topics, such as Louis Armstrong or Edgar Degas (Degas's mother's family was from New Orleans, and Degas visited and painted here). NOMA escaped serious damage during Katrina, but at this writing, the Courtyard Café was still closed. ⊠*1 Collins Diboll Circle, City Park, Bayou St. John* ☎*504/658–4100* ⊕*www.noma.org* ☑*$8; free to Louisiana residents* ☉*Wed.–Sun. 10–4:30.*

2 **Pitot House.** One of the few surviving houses that lined the bayou in the FodorśChoice late 1700s, and the only creole-colonial style house in the city open ★ to the public, Pitot House is named for James Pitot, who bought the property in 1810 as a country home for his family. Pitot built one of

Voluntourism

Tourism is the driving force behind New Orleans's economy, and visitors' dollars are helping the city rebuild. But if you want to have a more-direct impact on the Crescent City's reconstruction, grab a hammer. The groups listed below will put you to work. All sorts of jobs are available—everything from gutting homes, landscaping, and installing drywall to clerical assistance in warehouses and offices.

REBUILDING HOPE IN NEW ORLEANS (RHINO)

RHINO, a program run by the St. Charles Avenue Presbyterian Church, has been gutting homes since 1995.

■ Volunteers must be at least 16 years old.

■ Hours change depending on season.

■ Water and most tools are supplied; bring your own lunch.

■ For more information: ☎ 504/897–0101 Ext. 11 ⊕ www.spapc.org.

HABITAT FOR HUMANITY

Habitat's mission is to eliminate homelessness and make housing affordable. The organization is building new homes in Orleans and St. Bernard parishes; the most-prominent project is Musicians' Village in the Upper Ninth Ward.

■ Volunteers work from 7:15 AM to 2 PM.

■ Volunteers must be at least 16 years old.

■ For more information: ☎ 504/861–2077 ⊕ www.habitat-nola.org.

OPERATION NOAH

This program, run by the North American Board of the Southern Baptist Convention, accepts individuals and groups. There is limited supervision, so having experience helps.

■ Volunteers must be at least 15 years old to gut homes (though younger children can paint and do yard work).

■ Youth groups must have one adult for every five teens (who all must have completed the ninth grade).

■ Tools are provided (though it's recommended that you bring your own).

■ Lodging (for out-of-town groups) and meals are available.

■ For more information: ☎ 877/934–0808 ⊕ www.operationnoah.net.

OPERATION HELPING HANDS

The Catholic Charities Archdiocese of New Orleans program gutted and cleaned its 1,000th home in November 2006—but there are still 1,400 more on its waiting list.

■ Tools are provided, and there is a work-site supervisor.

■ Lodging (for out-of-town groups) and meals are available.

■ Volunteers must be at least seniors in high school to gut homes (other jobs are available for younger volunteers).

■ Volunteers should wear long pants and work boots—steel-toed, if possible.

■ The workday is 8 AM to 4 pm, with a lunch break.

■ Water and lunch are provided.

■ For more information: ☎ 504/310–6960 ⊕ www.ccano.org.

–Sue Strachan

the first cotton presses in New Orleans and served as the city's mayor from 1804 to 1805 and later as parish court judge. The Pitot House was restored and moved a block to its current location in the 1960s to make way for the expansion of Cabrini High School. It is noteworthy for its stucco-covered brick-between-post construction, an example of which is exposed on the second floor. The house is typical of the West Indies style brought to Louisiana by early planters, with galleries around the house that protect the interior from both rain and sunshine. There aren't any interior halls to stifle ventilation, and opposing doors encourage a cross breeze. The house is furnished with period antiques from the United States, and particularly Louisiana. ⊠*1440 Moss St., Bayou St. John* ☎*504/482–0312* ⌦*$5* ☉*Wed.–Sat. 10–3 or by appointment; last tour at 2.*

⓫ **Ralph's on the Park.** In 1860 Jean-Marie Saux opened a coffeehouse just outside the entrance to City Park, selling cold lemonades to the thirsty aristocrats who would venture out here from the French Quarter for the day. When Union troops set up camp in City Park during the Civil War, General Butler frequented Saux's establishment. Saux operated his coffee shop for 33 years before selling it to the Alciatore family, who also owned and operated Antoine's restaurant in the French Quarter (and still do). Since that time, the property has changed hands repeatedly, at one point serving as a favorite eatery among the prostitutes of Storyville. Now owned by famed local restaurateur Ralph Brennan, it is open for dinner daily, lunch on Friday, and Sunday brunch; a full dinner menu is also served at the bar. Sunset prix fixe dinner menus are available from 5:30 to 7. ⊠*900 City Park Ave., Bayou St. John* ☎*504/488–1000* ⊕*www.ralphsonthepark.com.*

☾ ⓭ **Storyland.** This whimsical park adjacent to the botanical garden has been a favorite romping ground for generations of New Orleans kids. The park's life-size figures, culled from children's literature, were created by some of the city's premiere Mardi Gras float builders and feature plenty of nooks and passageways for toddlers and young children to explore. ⊠*Victory Ave., City Park, Bayou St. John* ☎*504/482–4888* ⊕*www.neworleanscitypark.com* ⌦*$3* ☉*Weekends 10–5.*

Sydney and Walda Besthoff Sculpture Garden. Henry Moore's handsome Reclining Mother and Child greets visitors at the entrance of this peaceful, shady garden in the shadow of the New Orleans Museum of Art. Most of the garden's 57 sculptures, representing some of the biggest names in modern art, were donated by local pharmacy magnate and avid collector Sydney Besthoff. After Katrina, the garden suspended its daily guided tours, but you don't really need one to enjoy the collection, which includes major pieces by Jacques Lipchitz, Barbara Hepworth, and Joel Shapiro, or a stroll along the indigenously landscaped bayou that meanders through the park. ⊠*City Park, beside the New Orleans Museum of Art, Bayou St. John* ☎*504/658–4100* ⊕*www.noma.org* ⌦*Free* ☉*Wed.–Sun. 10–4:30.*

METAIRIE & THE LAKEFRONT

The neighborhood of Old Metairie is part of Orleans Parish and feels like much of Uptown. The historic **Longue Vue House and Gardens,** tucked along what seems like a country road, and the New Orleans Country Club are in the center of a particularly attractive area. Carving out several acres in the middle of Old Metairie, the elaborate tombs of the Lake Lawn Metairie Cemetery, the city's largest, are visible from the I–10 Expressway. Outside of old Metairie, however, the area has a more-modern, suburban feel. The newer sections of Metairie extend to the lakefront, much of which was heavily damaged by Hurricane Katrina. Although renovation and rebuilding continue in

various degrees in many pockets, some houses and buildings remain empty and untended, with high floodwater lines still marking their exteriors. Still, a stroll, drive or picnic along Lakeshore Drive on a sunny day is a pleasant way to take in **Lake Pontchartrain** and all its water-sports activity.

WHAT TO SEE

Lake Pontchartrain. This is a popular spot for fishing and boating: in good weather you may see lots of sailboats and windsurfers. Swimming, once very common, is slowly coming back into fashion thanks to pollution cleanup efforts. Lakeshore Drive, a road along Lake Pontchartrain, has many park and picnic areas that are popular on warm weekends and holidays. Many parking bays encourage you to stop and take a walk or sit on the seawall, the cement steps bordering the lake. The wall is a 5.5-mi levee and seawall protection system, built by the Orleans Levee Board in the 1930s and leased to the U.S. government for a hospital and for Army and Navy installations during and after World War II. A Navy air station at Elysian Fields and Lakeshore Drive once stood at the present site of the University of New Orleans. The land around the seawall area (Lake Vista) was turned into private residential districts in the 1930s. This area is relatively safe during the day because of frequent police patrols. It's best, however, not to linger after sunset.

 ⑯ Longue Vue House and Gardens. Eight acres of gardens embellished with fountains surround this city estate fashioned in the 1940s after the great country houses of England. The villa-style mansion is decorated with its original furnishings of English and American antiques, priceless tapestries, modern art, porcelain, and pottery. The fine millwork, special-ordered from New York, is mahogany and birch. You must

Algiers Point
Library **2**

Blaine Kern's
Mardi Gras
World **1**

Holy Name
of Mary Church ..**3**

Algiers Point

visit the house by tour (given hourly Wednesday–Sunday), but the gardens are open for independent exploration daily. They have various themes: the formal Spanish court, for instance, is modeled after a 14th-century Spanish garden, while a Discovery Garden introduces kids to the intricacies of horticulture. The gardens are in an ongoing state of restoration after Hurricane Katrina, which caused some tree and larger plant losses. ✉ *7 Bamboo Rd., Metairie* ☎ *504/488–5488* ⊕ *www.longuevue.com* 💲 *$10* 🕐 *Garden Mon.–Sat. 10–5, Sun. 1–5; shop Mon.–Sun. 10–4; house tours Wed–Sat. 10–5, Sun. 1–5 or by appointment; last tour at 4.*

ALGIERS POINT

Directly across the Mississippi River from the French Quarter and Canal Street, extending out into the river's curve, is the sleepy, historic neighborhood of Algiers Point. Settled at the turn of the 20th century, the community has quiet, tree-lined streets, quaint shops, and renovated Victorian houses, and has managed to remain somewhat isolated. In the early days of New Orleans, Algiers, named for the North African slave port, was a holding area for African slaves. The slaves were eventually ferried across the river to the French Quarter, where they were auctioned.

Algiers Point is best experienced by walking along its quiet streets, admiring the architecture, and savoring its small-town feel. However, because it is primarily residential and separated from the main part of the city by the river, it is isolated; you should take the usual precautions for personal safety. The big attraction here is Blaine Kern's Mardi Gras World, where many Mardi Gras floats are made.

Numbers in the text correspond to numbers on the Algiers Point map.

WHAT TO SEE

2 Algiers Point Library. This lovely Italianate library was built in 1907, a gift of Andrew Carnegie. A kiosk out front has a wealth of information on Algiers, including maps designating where various jazz artists, many of whom lived in Algiers, had homes. ⊠*725 Pelican Ave., Algiers Point* ☎*504/596–2640.*

Fodor$Choice
★

1 Blaine Kern's Mardi Gras World. Blaine Kern has for many years been the best-known artist and creator of Mardi Gras floats; he often personally conducts tours through this one-of-a-kind facility. You can watch the artists and builders at work, view a film about Mardi Gras, and buy Carnival memorabilia in the gift shop. A photo of you with one of the giant figures used on the floats makes a terrific souvenir, and there's a chest full of costumes for children to try on. A free shuttle van takes you from the ferry to Mardi Gras World; otherwise, an enjoyable 10-minute walk along the levee gets you here. ⊠*233 Newton St., Algiers Point* ☎*504/362–8211* ⊕*www.mardigrasworld.com* ☜*$17 includes cake and coffee* ⊙*Daily 9:30–4:30.*

NEED A BREAK?

Just across from the ferry landing at the corner of Delaronde and Bouny streets, Dry Dock Café & Bar (⊠*133 Delaronde St., Algiers Point* ☎*504/361–8240* ⊕*www.thedrydockcafe.com*), open from 11 AM until late (kitchen closes at 10 pm), is a nice spot for a beer, a cup of coffee, or a casual meal.

3 Holy Name of Mary Church. The largest church in Algiers, this redbrick building was constructed in 1929 to replace a former church from 1871. It is designed in English Gothic style and dominates the 400 block of Verret Street. ⊠*Verret and Alix Sts.; church office at 500 Eliza St., Algiers Point* ☎*504/362–5511.*

Mardi Gras & Jazz Fest

WORD OF MOUTH

"GO!! You will not regret [Jazz Fest]. There is no other festival like it. Mind-blowing music. It is an incredible piece of Americana and fun, fun, fun. Can be crowded, but not insane like Mardi Gras. And while you are there, buy one of the festival's official lithographs. They are stunning."

—emd

"The parades on Mardi Gras weekend are VERY popular, and the crowds at street level can be extremely thick. IF you really want to be able to 'see' the parade, grandstands are the way to go. However, there is something to be said for the experience of being in the crowd and grabbing for beads."

—NO_Native

IF YOU BELIEVE YOU'VE PARTIED WITH THE BEST, but you haven't experienced New Orleans's two major annual celebrations, Mardi Gras and Jazz Fest, it's time to expand your revelry repertoire. Just before Lent and again just before the summer heat, New Orleanians step out of their own reality and into the streets for the grandest parties of all. If it is your first trip to the Crescent City, plan carefully and do some research before you arrive. The city will welcome you, pamper you, and teach you the fine art of stepping lively.

So why is it that New Orleans is so comfortable in the party mode? Some have their theories: it's the port, the sub-sea-level elevation, or the mosquitoes that give them the fever. New Orleanians don't look for explanations or justifications—they just roll with the party.

MARDI GRAS

By Sue
Strachan

Mardi Gras (French for "Fat Tuesday") is the final day of Carnival, an entire Christian holiday season that begins on the 12th Night of Christmas (January 6) and comes crashing to a halt on Ash Wednesday, the first day of Lent. Though Mardi Gras is technically merely one day within the season, the term is used interchangeably with Carnival, especially as the season builds toward the big day. As sometimes befalls the Christmas holiday, the religious associations of Carnival serve mainly as a pretext for weeks of indulgence. Also, like Christmas, Carnival claims elaborately developed traditions of food, drink, and music, as well as a blend of public celebration (the parades) and more-exclusive festivities, which take the form of elaborate private balls.

On Mardi Gras day, many New Orleanians don costumes, face paint, and masks, and then take to the streets for the final bash-of-a-celebration before Lent. It's an official city holiday, with just about everyone but the police and bartenders taking the day off. People roam the streets, drinking Bloody Marys for breakfast and switching to beer in the afternoon, and admiring one another's finery. Ragtag bands ramble about with horns and drums, Mardi Gras anthems pour from boom boxes, and king cakes (ring-shape cakes topped with purple, green, and gold sugar) are everywhere. The Zulu, Rex, and the "trucks" parades roll Uptown to downtown with large floats carrying riders who throw plastic beads and trinkets to onlookers. They call it America's largest street party, and that seems about right.

Don't be smug: if you visit, you'll catch the fervor. After a few moments of astonished gaping, you'll yell for throws, too, draping layers of beads around your neck, sipping from a plastic cup as you prance along the street, bebopping with the marching bands, and having a grand old time.

It is never too early to begin planning your trip for Mardi Gras. Mark your calendar—Mardi Gras falls on February 24, 2009 (in 2010, Mardi Gras falls on February 16).

Mardi Gras Lingo

Krewe: A term used by all Carnival organizations to describe themselves, as in Krewe of Iris.

"Throw me somethin' mister": Phrase shouted at float riders to get their attention so they will throw beads.

"Show your": What float riders may ask women to do to get beads. Not recommended unless you want to end up on the next installment of *Girls Gone Wild!*.

Throw: Anything thrown off a float, such as beads, plastic cups, doubloons (fake metal coins), or stuffed animals.

Coconuts: Usually decorated; a prized throw only given out by riders in the Zulu parade.

Debutante: Young women, usually college sophomores or juniors, who are presented into society at Carnival balls and parties.

Carnival balls: Many krewes have black-tie balls to present debutantes. Alas, you can't buy a ticket—you have to be invited.

Rex, King of Carnival: There has to be a King, right? And this King and his krewe roll on Fat Tuesday.

Purple, green, and gold: The official colors of Mardi Gras (purple repre-

sents justice, green signifies faith, and gold stands for power), chosen by the first Rex in 1872.

King cake: An oval-shape cake that has a plastic baby hidden inside. King cakes are eaten from January 6—"Twelfth Night"—until Mardi Gras; whoever gets the baby has to buy the next cake. King cakes are often decorated with purple, green, and gold sugar or icing.

Lundi Gras: French for "Fat Monday," the day before Mardi Gras; celebrated by the arrival of Rex, King of Carnival, via boat to the riverfront. Today, the event also includes the King of Zulu, who greets Rex, and a festival with bands and food.

Mardi Gras: "Fat Tuesday" in French; the day before Ash Wednesday and the culmination of the festivities surrounding Carnival season.

Mardi Gras Indians: Groups of black men who are dressed in elaborate costumes—or "suits"—to resemble Native Americans. Most men are in "tribes" that march on Mardi Gras, in addition to St. Joseph's day and Super Sunday. This custom started in the late 19th century in response to blacks being excluded from white Mardi Gras parades and organizations.

HISTORY

No one is absolutely sure how Mardi Gras celebrations started. The history of early Louisiana Carnival celebrations isn't really documented until the 1800s, when private balls were held by the descendants of French and Spanish settlers. There were also raucous street processions, where young men wore masks and costumes and sometimes dumped flour on passersby. Then on February 24, 1857, Mardi Gras changed.

At 9 PM, 60 or so men dressed like demons paraded through the streets with two floats in a torch-lighted cavalcade. The group called itself the Mistick Krewe of Comus, after the Greek god of revelry. The krewe

CARNIVAL ROYALTY

So how do you become king or queen of a Mardi Gras parade or ball? It depends on the krewe. The hierarchy is a parody of royalty—there is a king, queen, dukes, knights, and captains, though it varies per krewe. In older-society krewes, the king is chosen by the members; other krewes rely on random drawings. Rex, King of Carnival, is chosen by the inner circle of the Rex krewe, called the School of Design; the honoree is always a prominent philanthropist and member of the New Orleans business community. Krewes like Bacchus and Endymion pick celebrity kings or grand marshals. Becoming a Queen also varies per krewe: a debutante has to find the golden bean in a faux king cake to become Queen of the Twelfth Night Revelers; other krewes put the matter to a vote. The Queen and her court don't necessarily have to be debutantes—again, it depends on the krewe.

was started by men from both New Orleans and Mobile, Alabama, where Mardi Gras parades had begun a few years earlier. Wanting to observe the holiday more fully, these men formed a secret society and sent 3,000 invitations to a ball held at New Orleans's Gaiety Theater. They had begun a tradition. As time passed (with lapses during the Civil War), invitations to the Comus ball became so coveted that one year the krewe captain advertised a $2,000 reward for two missing invitations. Comus crowned Robert E. Lee's daughter, Mildred Lee, its first queen in 1884. Though Comus no longer parades, the krewe still holds its annual ball, one of the city's most exclusive.

Through the years, other groups of men organized Carnival krewes, each with its own distinctive character. In 1872, 40 businessmen founded the School of Design, a new krewe whose ruler would be dubbed Rex, and sponsored a daytime parade for the Mardi Gras visit of His Imperial Highness the Grand Duke Alexis of Russia. They created a banner of green for faith, gold for power, and purple for justice—these remain the official Carnival colors. The first Rex parade was thrown together quickly with borrowed costumes, and there was no ball. The first reception was not until the next year, when a queen was chosen on the spot at a public ball. Eventually invitations and formal dress became required. Rex still parades on Mardi Gras morning, featuring some of the loveliest floats of Mardi Gras, and holds its lavish ball Mardi Gras night. Rex and his queen are considered the monarchs of the entire Carnival celebration. Their identities are kept secret until Mardi Gras morning, when their pictures claim the front page of the newspaper.

For many decades, krewes were strictly segregated by race; even Jews and Italians were banned from guest lists of the exclusive older balls (known as the old-line krewes). So other segments of society started clubs of their own. A black butler and dance instructor from Chicago started the Illinois Club in 1895. Though this club split into two krewes—the Original Illinois Club and the Young Men's Illinois Club—

the debutantes who serve on the courts still perform the founder's dance, the Chicago Glide, in parallel galas. The Illinois clubs don't sponsor parades, but the Zulu Social Aid and Pleasure Club, organized in 1909 by working-class black men, does. The Zulu parade precedes Rex down St. Charles Avenue on Mardi Gras day. Zulu was one of the first krewes to inte-

> ## SATCHMO'S REIGN
>
> "There's a thing I've dreamed of all my life, and I'll be damned if it don't look like it's about to come true—to be King of the Zulu's parade. After that, I'll be ready to die." –Louis Armstrong, *Time*, Feb. 21, 1949

grate, and today members span the racial and economic spectrums. These days, the elaborately decorated coconuts that Zulu float riders offer the crowd are among the most coveted of Mardi Gras throws.

After the Depression and World War II, Carnival krewes started popping up everywhere. Some were for doctors, others for businessmen, some for residents of certain neighborhoods, for women, for military men, or for gay men. The gay balls are splendid extravaganzas, with court members dressed in drag and bearing enormous, fantastical headdresses.

Parade standards changed in 1969, when a group of businessmen looking to entertain tourists the Sunday before Mardi Gras founded the Krewe of Bacchus, named after the god of wine. The sassy group stunned the city by setting new rules and strutting out with a stupendous show that dwarfed the old-line parades. The Bacchus floats (designed by Blaine Kern, who creates many other Carnival floats) were bigger than any seen before, and the king was Danny Kaye, not a homegrown humanitarian but a famous entertainer. The party following the parade was in the old Rivergate Convention Center, not in the Municipal Auditorium or a hotel ballroom, where the other balls were held. There was no queen and no court, and the party was called a rendezvous, not a ball. All guests could dance, not just members and their wives as was the custom in old-line balls, where nonmembers merely watched the proceedings. The floats rode right into the Rivergate, and you didn't have to be socially prominent—or even white—to join. The crowds have loved Bacchus from day one, and guessing which celebrities will follow the likes of Nicholas Cage, Elijah Wood, and James Gandolfini as monarch has become as popular as wondering about the identity of Rex. The arrival of Bacchus ushered in an era of new krewes with open memberships, including the Krewe of Endymion, and today many of the parades are held by these younger groups.

PARADES

Carnival parades begin in earnest two weekends before Mardi Gras, with parades day and night on weekends; there are parades each night starting the Wednesday before Mardi Gras. These parades are not the spectator activities that the term "parade" often signifies. The give-and-take between the riders on the floats and parade goers is what defines these events. The communication medium here is the "throws," or gifts the riders throw or hand to spectators. The most common throws are plastic beads, the most elaborate of which are worn like trophies by proud receivers. Other favorites include doubloons, or oversize aluminum coins, first introduced by Rex as His Majesty's official currency; plastic cups with the date and theme of the parade; medallion beads with the individual krewe's insignia; and stuffed animals.

Almost all Carnival krewes, or organizations, select a different theme each year for their parade. Themes range from whimsical to hard-edged political, though always with a tendency toward irreverence and satire. The politically incorrect is part and parcel of the subversiveness that characterizes Carnival, and stabs at government officials, racist or sexist jokes, and the glorification of gluttony are only a few of the offenses that all New Orleanians giggle at gleefully during Mardi Gras. The throws from a given float or parade will sometimes reflect that year's theme, one reason why locals dive for doubloons and plastic cups imprinted with the date and logo.

> ### MUST-SEE PARADES
>
> ■ **Bacchus:** Flashy. Be on the lookout for the immense Bacchagator and other oversize floats depicting jungle creatures.
>
> ■ **Endymion:** Even flashier. Its members are known for generous throws.
>
> ■ **Muses:** It's girls gone wild for this all-woman krewe.
>
> ■ **Rex:** Living up to its name, this truly is the king of parades.
>
> ■ **Tucks:** Like a rowdy little brother, Tucks is full of bawdy humor and mischief.
>
> ■ **Zulu:** Unique for its decorated coconut throws.

The floats and bands make up the bulk of the parades, with the odd walking "club," dance troupe, or convertible car tossed in here and there. During night parades, an extra ingredient is the flambeaux, torchbearing dancers who historically lighted the way for the parades. These days they provide little more than nostalgia and some fancy stepping to the bands, but they still earn tips along the route for their efforts.

Though parades used to roll through the French Quarter, these days the most-popular ones start Uptown at Magazine Street and Napoleon Avenue, continuing down St. Charles Avenue to Canal Street, and following Canal to their finish. Though it's chaotic all along the route, heading downtown, parade goers become more numerous: Lee Circle is particularly lively. The real action, though, is along Canal Street itself, where raucous downtowners and tourists converge. Many of the marching bands save their best energy for the turn onto Canal, where the riders generously unload their throws.

In the weeks before Mardi Gras, two quirky parades run through the Quarter. The **Krewe du Vieux** hits the street two Saturdays before Mardi Gras. Nearly every brass band in town participates, and the small floats are decorated along satirical, often off-color themes, and are pulled by donkeys, not by tractors as in other parades. One week later, on the Sunday afternoon one week before Mardi Gras, the **Krewe**

3

of **Barkus** rolls along a winding route through the Quarter in the vicinity of St. Ann Street, featuring thousands of elaborately costumed canines and their proud owners, often in coordinated attire. This is one of the most fun afternoons of the entire year in New Orleans.

MARDI GRAS WEEKEND

Although changes sometimes occur, the following parades are staples of Mardi Gras weekend.

Friday. **Hermes,** one of the oldest parading krewes, rolls first, in the early evening (usually around 6). They're followed by **Krewe d'Etat,** a relatively young krewe formed by local business leaders with a taste for satire. The Krewe d'Etat has a Dictator in place of the usual King and a Revolution instead of a ball (the sort of revolution that is by invitation only). The krewe prides itself on new and imaginative throws, such as a small stuffed jester that changes outfits annually and, when squeezed, drops such pearls of wisdom as "Live to ride—ride to live!," "Hail to the Dictator!," and "Krewe d'Etat rules!" Following Krewe d'Etat is **Morpheus,** which was founded in 2000 by a group of Carnival veterans. Their love of tradition shows in their old-school floats, but the group is also cutting-edge since it is open to both men and women.

Saturday. Saturday spotlights the largest women's krewe, **Iris,** which was formed in 1922 and began parading in 1959. Ordinarily pristine members of Uptown garden clubs let loose from behind their long masks and white gloves, flirting with the men along the route and tossing flowers to young hunks. Iris starts at 11, and is immediately followed by **Tucks,** a young, fun parade founded some 38 years ago by Loyola University students who would tour through a few Uptown streets on the way to their favorite bar, Friar Tucks. The theme is always tongue-in-cheek, and the throws are beautifully coordinated with the decor of the individual floats. A Friar Tuck doll is a must-catch from this parade.

Following Tucks, a several-hour break occurs before **Endymion,** one of the blockbuster parades of the season. In 2008 Endymion returned to its traditional Mid-City route after two years on the St. Charles Avenue route. Many parade goers head to Mid-City instead of seeing the Uptown parades because the festivities start at noon at the Orleans Avenue neutral ground. Bands, food, and other entertainment await. It's also a good idea to secure a place to stand because spectators at this parade have a tendency to be territorial about their spots. Endymion is notorious for delays; despite the afternoon starting time, it regularly reaches Canal Street late in the evening. Endymion finishes by rolling straight into the Superdome for the Extravaganza, a party attended by upwards of 14,000 people. The lineup for 2008 included the Go-Gos, the Doobie Brothers, and others; the Grand Marshal was actor Kevin Costner.

SATIRICAL PARADES

Since the beginning of Mardi Gras in New Orleans, krewes have used satire as a "safe" way to poke fun at politicians and others. Here is a list of some of the most risqué:

- Krewe d'Etat
- Krewe de Vieux
- Morpheus
- Muses

Sunday. Thoth is a daytime parade with a heartwarming peculiarity: it has designed an anomalous route that passes numerous nursing homes and hospitals, including Children's Hospital, at Tchoupitoulas and Henry Clay Avenue, by Audubon Park. The only Mardi Gras parade to follow Magazine Street, it eventually turns onto Napoleon Avenue and rejoins the usual St. Charles–Canal route. The other daytime Sunday parades are **Okeanos** and **Mid-City,** named for the neighborhood they originally rolled through.

> ### REX'S ROYAL ROOTS
>
> In 1872, Russian Grand Duke Alexis Romanoff visited New Orleans during Mardi Gras. Local businessmen wanted to entertain the duke, so they held a daytime parade—and Rex was born.

FodorsChoice ★ One of the great Mardi Gras parades, **Bacchus** takes the St. Charles–Canal route Sunday night. The floats are spectacular, including some regular favorites like the endless Bacchagator and the mammoth King Kong, as well as some new floats each year; the Budweiser Clydesdales are another crowd-pleaser. The monarch is always a celebrity ('80s wrestling icon Hulk Hogan reigned in 2008). Marching bands are at their horn-swinging best for Bacchus, and the throws pour plentifully from the floats.

★ **Monday.** There are no day parades Monday, but **Lundi Gras,** or the Monday before Mardi Gras, has become a major event downtown, especially at Spanish Plaza by the Riverwalk. Zulu, then Rex *(⇨ Mardi Gras Day)* arrive by boat along the Mississippi River and formally greet one another and their subjects at the Spanish Plaza dock. A large stage at Spanish Plaza hosts live music throughout the day. Monday night brings one of the oldest krewes and one of the youngest end to end. **Proteus,** formed in 1882, pays tribute to the sea god with beautiful floats in the old wagon style. **Orpheus,** meanwhile, always has the latest in parade technology, such as confetti blowers and automatic plastic-cup dispensers. The krewe is Harry Connick Jr.'s project, and the charming crooner's own float is one of the highlights.

MARDI GRAS DAY

On Mardi Gras day it seems that every street in the city sees a piece of a procession at one point or another. One of the following krewes is sure to meet your styles and tastes.

Early on Mardi Gras morning, you can catch **Zulu,** the oldest African-American parade. If you are not prepared, the black-faced riders, some of them in mock African dress, can seem in shockingly bad taste, but these parodies of minstrelsy are the long-standing traditions of the krewe. Zulu rolls down Jackson Avenue, turning onto St. Charles ahead of Rex, and reaches Canal Street around 11 AM, though in keeping with their mischievous customs, this timing can vary dramatically. **Rex,** traditionally regarded as king of Carnival, greets his subjects following Zulu. His floats are intricate, old-fashioned affairs, one of the visual high points of Mardi Gras day. Behind Rex are the truck parades: more than 200 flatbed trucks, each rented and decorated by an independent group, carrying some 7,000 riders in all. The trucks roll one after another for hours, without bands or walking groups between them.

Mardi Gras day also brings the appearances of the **Mardi Gras Indians** and the **walking clubs**. The walking clubs zigzag all over town, stopping in bars and swapping paper flowers and beads for kisses. One of the more-regular clubs, the **Krewe of St. Ann**, is named after the main gay strip of the French Quarter, where the parade winds up. The parade begins in the Bywater District and works its way through Faubourg Marigny before entering the Quarter. This is your best chance to see the Mardi Gras strutting of some of the city's most elaborately designed costumes.

Predating most of the major parades, the **Mardi Gras Indians** hold their own rituals in the backstreets on Mardi Gras morning. The Indians are members of African-American organizations who dress in intricately beaded costumes that often take all year to create (traditional Indians do not wear the same suit two years in a row). The Indians parade through backstreets, chanting songs from the Mardi Gras Indian repertory. The Indian tribes fall into two major categories: Uptown and downtown. To seek out the Uptown tribes on Mardi Gras morning, venture into the streets across St. Charles Avenue from the Garden District, between Jackson and Washington avenues. The downtown tribes generally revolve around Tremé. To find them, head away from the French Quarter on Ursulines Street.

WHERE TO WATCH

Where to watch parades is an important decision. **Uptown** is more of a family zone, which is not to say it is not crowded and frenzied. Most activity, though, is focused around the parades; outside parade hours, the streets revert to relative normalcy. Particularly good places to catch the parades include the vicinity of the Columns Hotel (3811 St. Charles Avenue, between Peniston and General Taylor streets), which charges a fee for access to its bar and bathrooms. The expansive front porch provides a good vantage point for those who don't need to catch any more beads. The corner of Napoleon and St. Charles avenues is a crowded but exciting place to watch, as the floats and bands turn onto St. Charles Avenue. The Garden District, particularly around 3rd and 4th streets, is reasonably family-friendly. Between Jackson Avenue and Lee Circle is a more-crowded and energetic (sometimes rowdy) place to watch, and a number of bars and stores on this strip can keep you lubricated and fed. On Mardi Gras day, costuming begins very early on St. Charles Avenue, and the street is fairly crowded by 8 AM. If you plan to spend time Uptown, it is worth getting up and out early (try to get there by 7) to share in the excitement of anticipation. The day begins with various walking clubs and makeshift bands strolling by, followed by the Zulu parade, with Rex close on its heels.

A week or so before Mardi Gras, things heat up **downtown** and along Bourbon Street and throughout the French Quarter. By Mardi Gras

> **MARDI GRAS ROYALTY**
>
> In 1956, the Duke and Duchess of Windsor attended the balls for Rex and Comus—and actually bowed to the make-believe monarchs.

weekend the crowds are so thick it is difficult to walk down Bourbon. Drinking, exchanging beads, and exhibitionism are popular activities along Bourbon, where lines form to enter the bars and drink prices go through the roof. The side streets offer some degree of refuge while still sustaining a high party pitch. At some point, most parades roll down Canal Street, which marks one boundary of the French Quarter, and the crowds shift over accordingly to bounce to the marching bands and catch some beads before ducking back into the bars or the street scene. Unlike Uptown, where parades are the focal point, downtown the parades seem merely a blip on the screen of general frenzy.

In deference to the religious pretext for this holiday, Mardi Gras "ends" with the arrival of Ash Wednesday and the Lenten season. At midnight on Tuesday night, downtown streets are cleared, and police officers on foot, in cars, and on horses cruise through the French Quarter blaring from their loudspeakers "Mardi Gras is over. Go home."

MARDI GRAS SAFETY

Whether you choose to watch the parades or to give yourself over to the madness of the mass party on Bourbon Street and throughout the Quarter, use common sense, dress comfortably, and leave your valuables safely locked up at home or in safe-deposit boxes at your hotel. Don't carry excessive amounts of cash and don't wear tempting jewelry. Travel with one or more people rather than alone if possible, and set a permanent meeting spot where your family or group will convene at preset times throughout the day.

The police increase surveillance during the chaotic Carnival season. It is legal to carry alcoholic beverages (but not glass bottles) in the streets, but excessive public drunkenness might draw the attention of the cops. Do not throw anything at the floats or bands of parades, a ticketable and truly hazardous act. On the other hand, throwing change to the flambeaux, or torch carriers, who historically light the way for night parades, is customary.

WOMEN AT
MARDI GRAS
More women than you would imagine flash as barter for good beads; if you feel tempted to follow suit, be aware that the personal videos shot on Bourbon Street often wind up on the Internet or on DVDs like *Girls Gone Wild!* Also be aware that New Orleans police do crack down on public indecency during Carnival. And if you are groped or feel threatened in any way, be assured that a police officer will probably be in your sight range.

CHILDREN AT
MARDI GRAS
In many respects Mardi Gras seems designed for kids. Floats, parades, whimsical gifts, costumes, street vendors with tasty snacks and exciting toys mark the season and revelry carries the day. The daytime parades are most suitable for family-rated fun. If you want to bring children to the evening parades, the Garden District around 3rd Street is a good option, though no spot is immune from the raucous and the bawdy.

> ### A FEST TO DIET FOR
>
> It takes 6 tons of rotini pasta and 4 tons of crawfish to make enough Crawfish Monica to feed festival crowds. Chefs go through 3 tons of pork to make a fest's worth of cochon de lait po'boys, and 3 tons of crawfish and 6 tons of cheese for the ever-popular crawfish bread.

Children are especially vulnerable during Mardi Gras and must be carefully watched. ■ TIP➡**Each year accidents occur when children (or adults) venture too near the wheels of floats. If you have kids with you, pick a spot some way back from the rolling parade.** Keep a trained eye on little hands and running feet. Many parents take the added precaution of having each child carry a note in their pocket with the parents' names, contact phone numbers, and local address.

JAZZ & HERITAGE FESTIVAL

By Russell
McCulley

Don't let the four-letter word at the center of its name intimidate you—one need not be a jazz fanatic to love the New Orleans Jazz and Heritage Festival. This is no stuffy, high-toned event for music scholars; Jazz Fest, as it's known to locals, is a sprawling, rollicking, celebration of Louisiana music, food, and culture held the last weekend in April and the first weekend in May. It takes place at the city's historic Fair Grounds Race Course, which reverberates with the sounds of rock, Cajun, zydeco, gospel, rhythm and blues, hip-hop, folk, world music, country, Latin, and, yes, traditional and modern jazz. Throw in world-class arts and crafts, exhibitions and lectures, and an astounding range of Louisiana-made food—reason enough alone for many Jazz Fest fans to make the trek—and you've got a festival worthy of America's premiere party town. Over the years, Jazz Fest lineups have come to include internationally known performers—Billy Joel and Stevie Wonder topped the bill in 2007—but at its heart the festival is about the hundreds of Louisiana musicians who live, work, and cut their chops in the Crescent City. A lot of New Orleans musicians were hit hard by Hurricane Katrina, and the Jazz and Heritage Festival is their chance to show a huge, international audience that the music survives—and the foundation that the festival benefits works to restore their lives and livelihoods.

HISTORY

Veterans of the first Jazz and Heritage Festival talk about that event, which took place in 1970 in what's now Armstrong Park, with the same awe and swagger of those who saw the Beatles' first U.S. tour or rolled in the mud at Woodstock in 1969. No wonder: the initial lineup included such legendary performers as Mahalia Jackson, Duke Ellington, Pete Fountain, Al Hirt, Fats Domino, The Meters, and the Olympia Brass Band, along with scores of other musicians and parading Mardi Gras Indian tribes. It was hardly an instant success; an oft-repeated anecdote has it that around 350 people attended the first Jazz Fest, about half the number of performers on hand.

> ### LONG RUNS
>
> The Meters, the Preservation Hall Jazz Band, Pete Fountain, the Dukes of Dixieland, the Original Tuxedo Jazz Band, Olympia Brass Band, and Lars Edegran & the New Orleans Ragtime Orchestra all performed at the first Jazz Fest in 1970—and were back at the fest in 2006.

Since then, Jazz Fest has grown in size and stature; in 2006, the first post-Katrina festival drew some 350,000 people over its two weekends and showcased the talents of some 6,000 performers, artisans, and chefs. Diehard fans travel from all over the country, even the world, to mix it up with locals, indulge in Creole and Cajun food, and take in as much music as time and stamina allow. At night, the party extends into the early-morning hours at bars and nightclubs throughout the city.

WHAT GOES ON

Most of the action takes place inside the track at the Fair Grounds Race Course in Mid-City, from 11 AM to sundown Friday through Sunday of the first weekend, and Thursday through Sunday of the second weekend. Three main stages evenly spaced around the track are reserved for the biggest draws, with a half dozen or so smaller performances and lecture spaces scattered across the grounds or in the horse-racing track's grandstand.

MUSIC & HERITAGE

For an event dedicated to an improvisational genre of music, Jazz Fest is a remarkably structured affair, with performers granted somewhere between 45 and 75 minutes to strut their stuff. Even musicians notorious for starting late and playing long are expected to stick to the tight schedule. Some stages have a specific musical bent: the Congo Square stage, for example, hosts African and African diaspora music, and the Fais-Do-Do Stage specializes in Cajun and zydeco performers. Fans of traditional jazz head for the Heritage Stage, and just about everyone spends at least a few minutes in the Gospel Tent, seeking refuge from the relentless New Orleans sun while soaking up the exuberant testimony from the likes of the Unstoppable Gospel Singers and the Greater St. Stephen Mass Choir. In 2007 the Jazz and Heritage Festival reinstated a Thursday event, which had been missing since Hurricane Katrina, to the second weekend lineup. Crowds tend to be lighter (and ticket prices a bit lower) that day, but the talent is no less impressive. The crowd-averse should also consider arriving early on any given day, when it's easier to browse the handsome arts and crafts on display and mill about the grounds without having to jostle for space. Organizers tend to schedule each festival day with the marquee stars appearing last—and the crowds inevitably build as the afternoon goes on.

> ### GET INTO THE SPIRIT
>
> If you're hanging out in the Gospel Tent—and you should—don't be too alarmed if you see over-zealous performers being led off-stage by a group of attendants in white. Choir members who get a little overcome with the spirit are led to a grassy area behind the tent, where they can recover.

With its wealth of talent (and the constant lure of amazing food), Jazz Fest presents a logistical planning challenge to the attendee. A schedule and map are essential. Don't stress out trying to catch all the big names, however; inevitably, it's the obscure bluesman, anonymous gospel shouter, or up-and-coming brass band that provides the most-indelible Jazz Fest memory.

Festival regulars make good use of the fairgrounds' stately grandstand, which hosts exhibits, panel discussions on New Orleans music and culture, cooking demonstrations (often with free samples) by local chefs, and interviews with musicians, artists, and writers. This multifloor, partially enclosed facility also provides an air-conditioned respite from the sun and heat, which can be intense in late spring. Most importantly, there are restrooms with hot water and actual plumbing on every floor for those who have an aversion to the portable toilets scattered around the racetrack's perimeter.

Full schedules and ticket information are available on the Jazz Fest Web site (⊕ *www.nojazzfest.com*). The artist lineup for 2009 will be released in February 2009.

FOOD

Two words: arrive hungry. Jazz Fest's food is almost as revered as its music, and rightly so. Behind the food booths' delightfully low-tech plywood facades, which resemble stage sets in a cheap Western film, an army of cooks from all over Louisiana are hard at work, turning out dishes both familiar (shrimp po'boys and jambalaya) and exotic (alligator sausage, anyone?). It's all delicious, and not a bad deal, with even the most-generous platters dished out for under $10. Some perennial favorites include breads stuffed with crawfish and cheese, soft-shell-crab po'boys, and Crawfish Monica, a creamy pasta dish. Vegetarians have plenty to choose from, too, especially at the food booths near Congo Square, where a plate of jama-jama (sautéed and seasoned spinach) and fried plantains provide fuel for a day of stage-hopping. Cool down with a tall cup of strawberry lemonade or chilled fruit salad dusted with shaved coconut. The festival, like the city itself, has broadened its culinary repertoire in recent years, and now includes sushi, Central American, and other international options. But the focus is still Creole-Cajun, as demonstrated by the sheer number of people

The Second Line

One of the great joys of the Jazz Fest is the odd parade that occasionally takes over the pedestrian paths, bursting through the center of the fairgrounds with an explosion of color, sun-brellas, horns, feathers, and fancy footwork. This apparently chaotic event is called a second line.

The second line is a type of parade historically associated with jazz funerals; the term "second line" is often thought originally to have referred to the secondary group of participants in such a parade, behind the band and the family. "Second line" is also used to refer to the distinctive dance moves that can be glimpsed during New Orleans street parades of all sorts.

During the early 20th century, the New Orleans second line served an important community function. At that time, African-Americans were not allowed to buy insurance, so they formed mutual-aid societies—called Social Aid and Pleasure Clubs—to help members through tough times. When a member's house burned down, or when someone died and their family lacked the funds for a proper funeral, the club would step in to help. Live bands and second-lining become integral parts of the fund-raising efforts. Combined with the city's long-standing penchant for a parade, these activities led to the current "second-line" brass-band parade tradition.

Sylvester Francis has spent the better part of a lifetime documenting second-line parades and jazz funerals; his **Backstreet Cultural Museum** (✉ *1116 St. Claude Ave., Tremé* ☎ *504/522–4806*) is a repository of Mardi Gras Indian costumes, second-line mementos, and tons of photographs. Francis also mans a Backstreet Museum booth at Jazz Fest, and will fill you in, cheerfully and at length, on the finer points of one of the city's most distinctive traditions. If you get wind of an authentic second line taking place in the city, go, but use caution. Stick to the safer-looking streets, and be prepared to make an exit if things start to get edgy.

chowing down on oyster po'boys and baskets of boiled crawfish. Keep in mind that outside food and beverages, other than bottled water, are not allowed inside the gates. Cold beer is widely available at tents on the festival grounds, but hard liquor is not served or permitted.

SHOPPING

The competition for crafts booths is nearly as fierce as that for food stalls. Unlike the cooks, however, the artists represented at Jazz Fest hail from not only Louisiana but from all over the United States. Craft areas include Contemporary Crafts, near the Gospel Tent, which sells wares from nationwide artists and artisans; the Louisiana Marketplace, near the Fais-Do-Do Stage and Louisiana Folklife Village, which showcases folk art from the city and the region; and a Native American Village, which spotlights performances and crafts related to Native American culture. Surrounding the Congo Square stage are stands with African and African-influenced artifacts, clothing, and accessories. ■TIP➔ Many of the artists have a spot for only one of the two weekends; ask about their schedule before putting off that purchase until the following week. A tent not far from the main gate sells CDs by musicians playing the festival, as well as music by other New Orleans and Louisiana artists; a nearby tent sports festival-approved shirts and accessories, along with the official, limited-edition Jazz Fest posters, which range in price from about $70 for a numbered silkscreen to several hundred dollars for a signed and numbered remarque print. ■TIP→ **It is not necessary to bring large amounts of cash to the festival. ATM machines are located throughout the site.**

FESTIVAL BASICS

PLANNING

Depending on the weather, Jazz Fest crowds tend to peak on Saturday and Sunday from mid-afternoon to closing, with the second weekend typically drawing the largest numbers. Thursday and Friday crowds are a little lighter.

Families and groups will often stake out a patch of ground near one stage, spread a blanket, and use it as a gathering spot for the day. Longtime fest goers bring plastic poles topped with a flag or silly hat to let friends know where they are encamped, or where the party has migrated, although festival security has lately become stricter about prohibiting such props. A traditional meeting-up place is the tall, conspicuous flagpole at the center of the track, but the area can become too crowded to navigate at peak times; consider arranging to meet at a quieter spot in or near the grandstand. Most important, try not to set too ambitious an agenda, and be ready to ditch plans when the mood strikes or the mix of heat, food, and swirling crowds starts to overwhelm. Duck into a shady tent for a sit and a chance to regroup; odds are, you'll discover some little-known but incredibly talented musician playing to an intimate, enthusiastic audience.

You can purchase a full program once you arrive at the festival, which includes detailed schedules and maps, as well as feature pieces. Locals usually simply tear each day's schedule and a map of the fairgrounds from the *Gambit* weekly or *OffBeat* monthly magazine. The daily *Times-Picayune* also publishes maps and schedules in its Friday "Lagniappe" section.

For advance listings of artists to be featured and other information about the Jazz Fest, you can contact the **New Orleans Jazz & Heritage Foundation** (☎*504/522–4786* ⊕*www.nojazzfest.com*), which sponsors the festival.

TICKETS Tickets are no longer available by mail order; instead, you can purchase them in advance at any Ticketmaster outlet (☎ 800/488–5252) or online at www.ticketmaster.com. If you are in town a few days before the festival, you'll get the best price by picking them up yourself at the Jazz Fest box office in the New Orleans Arena (1501 Girod Street)

A BITE OF HEAVEN

If you come across a Jazz Fest vendor selling crawfish beignets (think conch fritters, but infinitely better), get an order immediately. Trust us. It may change your life.

or at the adjacent Superdome's box office (1500 Poydras Street), which is open weekdays from 9 to 4:30. In 2008, advance tickets good for one day's admission were $40 (plus a few dollars for service fees); tickets for the Thursday event were $30. Expect to pay $10 more (and possibly endure long lines) if you wait to pay at the festival entrance.

> **APPRECIATING ART**
>
> The first official Jazz Fest poster, a three-color art nouveau image of a second-line parade marshal from 1975, sold for $3.95 at the fair. Today, it fetches around $2,000.

Children 2–11 pay $5 in advance or at the gate. Tickets are nonrefundable, and are sold by the weekend—in other words, a ticket purchased for the first weekend will get you in the first Friday, Saturday, or Sunday of the festival, but is not valid the second weekend. The festival also offers a pair of luxury packages called the Big Chief VIP Experience and the Grand Marshal VIP Pass; the premium passes, which range from $450 to $1,000, include admission (and reentry privileges) good for an entire weekend, access to shaded and strategically placed viewing stands at the three main stages, refreshments served in a private hospitality lounge, and other perks. The most expensive options include reserved, on-site parking.

WHAT TO WEAR & BRING

Jazz Fest is no place to fret about fashion; although there are tents, the grandstand, and a few trees for shade, you'll likely spend most of the day in full sun, so cool and breathable fabrics, along with a wide-brim hat, are your best bets. The quintessential Jazz Fest outfit is shorts and a well-worn concert T-shirt for men, light cotton sundress for women, with a good number of festival goers stripping down to much less. If rain threatens, bring a cap and poncho. Sunscreen and sunglasses are crucial, and pack some hand sanitizer to wash up before—and after—that mayo-oozing po'boy. Wear comfortable shoes, and ones that can get dirty. It's a racetrack, after all, and no matter how groomed it looks at the outset, by the end of Jazz Fest the ground cover is a mix of dust, straw, mud, and crawfish shells. Cameras, tarps, and blankets are allowed, but not recording equipment or video cameras. Hard-shell coolers are prohibited, but empty collapsible coolers are allowed.

CHILDREN AT JAZZ FEST

Locals grew up going to Jazz Fest; you'll see many of them carrying on the family tradition, pushing strollers and herding young ones of their own. An area just inside the infield from the grandstand is devoted to children, with music, crafts, and storytelling geared toward kids. A bulletin board in the same area posts schedules and general advice for negotiating the festival with children; nearby, it is possible to "register" your children and create identification tags for them to wear at the festival. The lawn in this kids' area is generally less populated than elsewhere on the fairgrounds, making it easier to keep an eye on children as they run about. The Kids' Tent, meanwhile, provides shade with your music. The grandstand is another great place for a cool-off, and the generally relaxed atmosphere creates a kid-friendly zone.

SAFETY

Jazz Fest itself is safe, but the neighborhood around the fairgrounds can be dodgy, especially after dark. If you are walking to a car or bus stop after the festival ends, try to go in a group and be aware of your surroundings.

MARDI GRAS & JAZZ FEST ESSENTIALS

To research prices, get advice from other travelers, and book travel arrangements, visit www.fodors.com.

BIKE TRAVEL

Renting bicycles (and locks) is a good way to sidestep the heavy street traffic and parking difficulties that Mardi Gras and Jazz Fest bring. New Orleans is small and flat, and the bike ride from the Garden District to the French Quarter takes about 15 minutes.

If you're biking to Jazz Fest, just follow Esplanade Avenue away from the river, and veer right onto Bayou Road (where everyone else is headed) just before Broad Street. There are supervised bike lots near each festival entrance, though you must bring your own lock.

BUS TRAVEL

Gray Line Tours offers continuous Jazz Fest Express shuttle service, starting at 10:30 AM, between the fairgrounds and three pick-up points: the Sheraton Hotel at 500 Canal Street; the "lighthouse" at the Toulouse Street Wharf, next to Jax Brewery; and the parking area at Marconi Meadows in City Park. Round-trip fare is $16 ($14, including parking, from the City Park location). Shuttle tickets can be picked up at the concierge desks in the Marriott Hotel (555 Canal Street) and the New Orleans Hilton Riverside (Poydras Street at the Mississippi River), a kiosk at the Toulouse Street Wharf, and at the Marconi Meadows parking lot.

A budget option is to take a Regional Transit Authority bus ($1.25 one way, $1.50 with a transfer). The Jackson–Esplanade bus (Number 91) stops along North Rampart Street before turning onto Esplanade Avenue; ask the driver where you should get off, or just follow the Jazz Fest crowd. It's a four-block walk from the bus stop to the fairgrounds. You can also buy an RTA VisiTour pass, which gives you unlimited rides for three days for $12.

INFORMATION **Festival shuttles** Gray Line Tours ☎*504/569–1401 or 800/535–7786* ⊕*www. graylineneworleans.com/jazzfest.html.* Regional Transit Authority ☎*504/248– 3900, 504/242–2600 automated information* ⊕*www.norta.com.*

CAR TRAVEL

PARKING Parking is at a premium during Mardi Gras and Jazz Fest seasons. It's best to use your hotel's facilities, even if it means extra walking to the parade route. During the final

---

COOL TALKING HEADS

Check out the exhibits, lectures, and interviews in the fairgrounds grandstand. They're often quite interesting, and the air-conditioned building provides welcome relief from the hot New Orleans sun.

weekend of Carnival the French Quarter is closed to automobile traffic; scope out a lot or a spot in the CBD. It is also impossible to cross the parade route at any point in a car, and many bus routes are disrupted. If possible, leave the car behind and take a taxi, the streetcar, or a bike—or just walk.

At Jazz Fest, parking at the fairgrounds is expensive and extremely limited; it is best to find another way to get here. If you must drive, you will have to come early for the privilege of paying $35 for a spot at the fairgrounds; otherwise, join the rest of the caravan making ever-wider circles beyond the fest in search of street parking, which is free (but zoned for two-hour maximum parking for nonresidents in many places). Parking-control officers can be aggressive about ticketing, or in some cases towing, cars that exceed the time limit or are parked too close to corners, driveways, or fire hydrants.

> ### KNOW THE RULES
>
> Jazz Fest security can be tight; read the rules before you arrive (available on the Jazz Fest Web site), and don't try to sneak any booze through the gates. Same goes for video cameras: still photos are allowed, but no filming or audio recording.

DISABILITIES & ACCESSIBILITY

Because Mardi Gras is a street party, visitors with disabilities will be able to access almost all areas; only the private grandstands are not wheelchair accessible. That being said, be aware that street and sidewalk quality can vary, and some street curbs do not have ramps. Be sure to map out accessible restrooms ahead of time.

At Jazz Fest, the festival does its best to assist visitors with disabilities, from providing wheelchairs and special viewing locations and convenient restrooms to doing snack runs to a favorite food booth. However, this is a huge event held mainly on a dirt-and-grass field, and disabled visitors must be ready for a challenge. Service information for people with disabilities is available at the Access Center just inside the grandstand. People with mobility limitations should use the Gentilly Boulevard Vehicular Gate for accessible parking or the Gentilly Boulevard Pedestrian Gate when arriving or leaving by taxi. Reinforced surfaces crossing the track and paved pathways on the infield facilitate wheelchair passage. Telephones are mounted at wheelchair height. The Paralyzed Vets of America operate a booth immediately inside the Gentilly Boulevard entrance where you can borrow a conventional wheelchair.

Wheelchair-accessible shuttle-bus service is available at New Orleans Tours' designated pickup and drop-off points. All grandstand stages have reserved wheelchair spaces and accessible restrooms, and there are wheelchair-accessible portable toilets spaced throughout the fairgrounds; the Access Center has passkeys. Access assistance is available at food booths, and the access center can help arrange text-telephone service and assistive-listening devices for the hearing impaired. Braille and large-print programming information is available at all information booths and the Access Center, which also has recorded program information.

INFORMATION The Jazz and Heritage Festival Web site ⊕ *www.nojazzfest.com* has information for people with disabilities. Advocacy Center for the Elderly and Disabled ✉ *1010 Common St., Suite 2600,* ☎ *504/522-2337 (also TTY), 800/960-7705 (also TTY) www.advocacyla.org.* Jazz Fest Access Center ☎ *504/522-4786.* New Orleans Tours ☎ *504/212-5925* ⊕ *www.notours.com.*

EMERGENCIES

During Mardi Gras, the police are out in full force. If there's a problem, there should be police or paramedics somewhere along the parade route, especially near major intersections. For medical problems, familiarize yourself with local hospitals—not all have reopened since Hurricane Katrina. The nearest hospital to the parade route is Touro Infirmary, which is just off on Prytania Street, between Louisiana Avenue and Delachaise Street.

At Jazz Fest, a first-aid station inside the track in front of the grand-stand, as well as two outposts in the infield, stock bandages, salves, and other basic medical needs. In case of problems more serious than a sunburn or a scrape, full medical facilities are available.

LODGING

Mardi Gras and Jazz Fest draw millions of people from the world over. Make room reservations as soon as possible—a year in advance is not too early. Space can become available off and on as reservations are released leading up to the event. A hotel may have no rooms available one day but 10 the next. Keep trying. Minimum-stay requirements are often in effect at area hotels. Many area hotels have special four-night-stay package rates. Consider bed-and-breakfasts Uptown or on Esplanade Avenue.

MARDI GRAS LINKS

You'll find parade routes, schedules, and all things Mardi Gras on the following sites.

INFORMATION Arthur Hardy's Mardi Gras Guide ⊕ *www. mardigrasguide.com.* Everything New Orleans ⊕ *www.nola.com.* MardiGras.com ⊕ *www.mardigras.com.* New Orleans Convention and Visitors Bureau ⊕ *www.neworleanscvb.com.*

RESTROOMS

It can be tricky to gain access to a bathroom during Mardi Gras, so you may find yourself using a "Port-o-Let" most of the time. If you are staying at a hotel, it should give you a pass so you can come and go at your leisure. Most grandstands have portable toilets, and most restaurants and bars allow patrons to use their facilities. At certain intersections, such as Napoleon and St. Charles avenues, there are public Port-o-Lets—however, these are far and few between. Public urination is against the law and the police department will not hesitate to arrest someone for doing just that.

At Jazz Fest, the best bathroom spots are on the upper floors of the grandstand. This is well worth the walk; the bathrooms are air-conditioned and clean, and you can wash your hands. Otherwise, portable toilets are clustered in several locations outside the racetrack perimeter.

TAXIS

Cabs cruise the French Quarter and CBD but rarely beyond. Reliable companies with 24-hour service are United Cabs and Yellow-Checker Cabs. The metered fare is $3.50 at the flag drop, $1.60 per mile, and $1 for each additional passenger. During special events such as Jazz Fest and Mardi Gras, many cabbies charge a flat fee of $4 or $5 per passenger or the metered rate, whichever is higher. A metered taxi fare from the French Quarter to Jazz Fest should run about $10 to $12.

INFORMATION   United Cabs ☎ *504/522–9771 or 524–9606.* Yellow-Checker Cabs ☎ *504/525–3311.*

VISITOR INFORMATION

INFORMATION   New Orleans Convention and Visitors Bureau ✉ *2020 St. Charles Ave., Garden District,* ☎ *504/566–5011 or 800/672–6124* 🖷 *504/566–5021* ⊕ *www.neworleanscvb.com.* New Orleans Welcome Center ✉ *529 St. Ann St., on Jackson Sq., French Quarter,* ☎ *504/568–5661.*

Where to Eat

WORD OF MOUTH

"Just got back from a trip to NoLa and if you go to Acme Oyster Bar, sit at the bar, and talk to the shuckers and eat, eat, eat. We had the oysters (raw) every day for a week here."

—John

"The flavors at Herbsaint are delicious, layered, and complex. The waiters make excellent wine recommendations and do a wonderful job of taking care of customers. We loved the shrimp and grits!"

—Nicole

By Paul A.
Greenberg

NEW ORLEANS IS KNOWN AS MUCH FOR ITS SENSORY expression as it is for its joie de vivre, and nowhere is this more evident than in the stellar cuisine offered at local restaurants. Visitors who limit their scope to traditional Louisiana dishes, such as jambalaya, red beans and rice, gumbo, and étouffée, will just be scratching the surface. All of that is readily available, but the delectable surprise of dining in New Orleans is the diversity of dishes and cuisines that are available in the city, not to mention the culinary ingenuity on display.

Old or new, the menus at New Orleans's restaurants reflect three centuries of multiple cultures constantly contributing to the always-simmering culinary gumbo pot. What influences can you expect to taste? The list is long, but it's easy to find dashes of Spanish, French, Italian, German, African, Caribbean, and Croatian flavor—and increasingly, Asian and Latin influences. The result is a city that can literally feed the masses—and do so in a style that will remind everyone of their home base.

Menus are often works in progress, constantly evolving. At ONE, Chef Scott Snodgrass's Uptown restaurant, the menu changes seasonally. Come in on a cold winter night, and you're likely to find ale-braised rabbit with stoned ground grits. Downtown at 7 on Fulton, you might opt for seared scallops with smoked tomatoes and almonds with hollandaise sauce. Or go traditional at the world-renowned Commander's Palace with Chef Tory McPhail's crispy soft-shell crab with pinched herbs and shaved sweet onions. And there has rarely been an appetite that could not be satisfied with a serving of Chef Raymond Toups's wild mushroom bisque with jumbo lump crabmeat and just a hint of cognac at Restaurant Anatole's. Still, if you have any lingering doubts about the imaginative spirit of New Orleans culinary wizards, take a bite of the sweetbreads with capers and souffléed potatoes at Arnaud's. Case closed.

With such precious food, a visit to New Orleans calls for planning meal stops as carefully as sightseeing trips. Come hungry.

WHAT IT COSTS				
	$$$$	$$$	$$	$	¢
AT DINNER	over $35	$26–$35	$17–$25	$9–$16	under $9

Restaurant prices are for a main course at dinner, excluding sales tax of 9.5%.

FRENCH QUARTER

AFRICAN

$ ✕ **Bennachin.** New Orleans's creole cuisine borrows ingredients and techniques from the African diaspora, but Bennachin, which highlights the cooking of Gambia and Cameroon, is one of the city's few truly African restaurants. Beef stews are superb here, specifically one with a tart, gingery, ground-melon-seed sauce. All stews come with rice or mashed yams, which you traditionally eat with your hands.

Vegetarian options include black-eyed-pea fritters, and spicy sautéed spinach served with plantains and coconut rice. Exposed brick walls and African wall hangings surround about a dozen tables and a small open kitchen. Service is adequate. ⊠*1212 Royal St., French Quarter* ☎*504/522–1230* ▭*AE, D, MC, V* ⛾ *BYOB.*

AMERICAN

★ **$$–$$$** ✕**Peristyle.** Chef Tom Wolfe has taken this venerable French Quarter eatery to new heights since assuming ownership in 2004. An excellent starter is the crispy veal sweetbreads, followed by a Louisiana crabmeat and roasted beet salad. The excellent cinnamon-smoked tenderloin is served with apple pecan streusel, and wild game lovers should try the confit rabbit with goat cheese ravioli. The main dining room is lined with sleek tufted banquettes, exhibiting the laid-back elegance of a fine French bistro. ⊠*1041 Dumaine St., French Quarter* ☎*504/593–9535* ▭*AE, D, MC, V* ☉*Closed Sun. and Mon. No lunch Tues.–Thurs. and Sat.*

★ **¢–$$** ✕**Port of Call.** People wait for an hour-plus outside Port of Call every night, in the heavy heat of July and the downpours of September, for fist-thick burgers made from freshly ground beef, grilled to order and served with baked potatoes (no fries here) that are always perfectly fluffy. For the definitive experience, drink a Monsoon while you wait (Port of Call's mind-bending take on the Hurricane), and order your potato "loaded" (with mushrooms, cheddar cheese, sour cream, butter, chives, and bacon bits). Stellar muffuletta pizza and juicy filet mignon are also available. The dark, smoky barroom isn't suitable for small children. ⊠*838 Esplanade Ave., French Quarter* ☎*504/523–0120* ⌚*Reservations not accepted* ▭*AE, MC, V.*

CAFÉS & COFFEEHOUSES

¢ ✕**Café du Monde.** No trip to New Orleans is complete without a cup

Fodor'sChoice of chicory-laced café au lait and addictive sugar-dusted beignets in
★ this venerable creole institution. The tables under the green-and-white striped awning are jammed at every hour with locals and tourists feasting on powdery doughnuts and views of Jackson Square. The magical time to go is just before dawn, when the bustle subsides and you can hear the birds in the crepe myrtles across the way. Four satellite locations (Riverwalk Marketplace in the CBD, Lakeside Shopping Center in Metairie, Esplanade Mall in Kenner, Oakwood Mall, in Gretna, and 4700 Veterans Blvd. in Metairie) are convenient but lack the character of the original. ⊠*800 Decatur St., French Quarter* ☎*504/525–4544* ▭*No credit cards.*

CAJUN

$$–$$$$ ✕**K-Paul's Louisiana Kitchen.** In this comfortable French Quarter café of glossy wooden floors and exposed brick, chef Paul Prudhomme started the blackening craze and added "Cajun" to America's culinary vocabulary. Two decades later, thousands still consider a visit to New Orleans partly wasted without a visit to K-Paul's for his inventive gumbos, fried crawfish tails, blackened tuna, roast duck with rice dressing, and sweet potato–pecan pie. Prices are steep, but servings are generous. And although you can make reservations these days, it's still tradition

KNOW HOW

New Orleans's centuries-old preoccupation with food often appeals more to the palate and the heart than to the eye or the intellect. The most artfully prepared restaurant dish has a short shelf life if the flavor doesn't live up to the presentation.

Today, New Orleans's dining culture is infinitely more diverse than in the days when po'boy sandwiches and elegant French-creole sauces dominated the culinary spotlight. Asian, Latin American, and Mediterranean cuisines coexist with the traditional creole-Acadian dishes.

The restaurants we list are the cream of the crop in each price category. It's difficult to get a bad meal in this town, so read up on your cuisine options and savor every bite.

BRUNCH

Upscale restaurants on the tourist track often serve very reasonable, fixed-price brunch menus, many of them buffet style. A jazz group often supplies live music. Sunday, from late morning to early afternoon, is the prime time for brunch, although a few restaurants serve brunch on other days, too.

Among the more-reliable spots for these brunches are Commander's Palace, Palace Café, and Ralph's on the Park, all for the festive atmosphere and food quality; Arnaud's, for the glittery main dining room; and Elizabeth's, for the down-home Southern cooking and attitude on Saturday.

DRESS

If you're eating in a luxury restaurant or in one of the old-line, conservative creole places, dress appropriately. If you don't know whether jackets are required or jeans are frowned upon, telephoning to find out is a simple matter. You'll probably be more comfortable, and so will the restaurant's other customers. Also, you may avoid being turned away at the door (though some formal restaurants do keep loaner jackets on hand).

Unless otherwise noted, restaurants listed in this book allow casual dress. Reviews mention dress only when men are required to wear a jacket or a jacket and tie.

MEALTIMES

White-tablecloth restaurants in New Orleans adhere to traditional service hours—11 or 11:30 AM to about 2 PM for lunch, and about 6 to 10 PM for dinner. Sunday and Monday are the most-frequent closing days for full-service restaurants. A Saturday lunch, even in a popular upscale restaurant, can be tough to find outside the Quarter.

Unless otherwise noted, the restaurants listed in this guide are open daily for lunch and dinner.

RESERVATIONS

Most restaurants in New Orleans accept reservations, and many of the very popular places become quickly booked, especially on Friday and Saturday nights. Reservations are always a good idea: we mention them only when they're essential or not accepted. The best strategy is to reserve as soon as you decide where and when you'd like to go; **several weeks ahead of time is not too far in advance to reserve for trips during Mardi Gras, Jazz Fest, or other special events.** Reconfirm as soon as you arrive. If you must cancel, let the reservations desk know immediately.

TIPPING

The standard for tipping in New Orleans is no different from that in the rest of the country—at least 15% or 20%. Sales taxes for restaurants are 9.5%, which means that doubling the tax is a widespread practice. This applies not only to fine-dining establishments but also casual places with table service. Rarely is the maître d' tipped, since gratuities are generally pooled among the service staff. Most menus contain a notice that a service charge is automatically added to the bill for groups of eight or more.

WHAT IT COSTS

The cost of a meal in the city's more-upscale restaurants—with their smart decor, expensive ingredients, and carefully selected wines—is about what you'd expect to pay in other U.S. cities. The bargains are found in the more-casual full-service restaurants, where a simple lunch or dinner can frequently be had for much less than $25. However, even the more-expensive restaurants offer fixed-price menus of three or four courses for substantially less than what an à la carte meal costs, and coffee or tea is usually included.

As a rule, serving sizes are more than generous—some would say unmanageable for the average eater—so many diners order two appetizers rather than a starter and a main course, which can make ordering dessert more practical.

If you are watching your budget, be sure to ask the price of daily specials recited by the waiter or captain. The charge for specials at some restaurants is noticeably out of line with the other prices on the menu. Always review your bill. Even on computerized checks, mistakes do occur. No matter whose favor the mistake is in, it is a courtesy to bring it to your server's attention.

Also consider the fixed-price, early-evening specials offered at so many mid-range and upscale restaurants. Eating early can cut your bill in half, and the food quality generally doesn't suffer.

Our restaurant reviews indicate what credit cards are accepted (or not) at each establishment, but if you plan to use a credit card it is a good idea to double-check its acceptability when making reservations or before sitting down to eat.

4

to line up along Chartres Street before the doors open. ⊠*416 Chartres St., French Quarter* ☏*504/524–7394* ⚜*Reservations essential* ▭*AE, D, DC, MC, V* ☽*Closed Sun.*

CARIBBEAN

$$–$$$ ✕**Dominique's.** Dominique Macquet's island sensibilities bear testament to his upbringing on Mauritius. There's farm-raised conch all over his menu: baby conch ceviche, baby conch–and–white bean chowder, and sautéed farm-raised cracked conch on smothered corn risotto. Dominique's light touch keeps even the most-complex combinations from careening over the top. The meal begins best with Louisiana blue crab and coconut soup, and every meal ends whimsically with complimentary cotton candy. The wine list is well conceived and covers all bases. ⊠*1001 Toulouse St., French Quarter* ☏*504/586–8000* ▭*AE, D, DC, MC, V* ☽*No lunch.*

CREOLE

$$–$$$$ ✕**Antoine's.** If Antoine's wasn't already a culinary deity, Frances Parkinson Keyes made it one with her 1948 novel *Dinner at Antoine's*. Though some people believe Antoine's heyday passed before the turn of the 20th century, others wouldn't leave New Orleans without at least one order of oysters Rockefeller, a dish invented here. Other notables on the bilingual menu include *pommes de terre soufflées* (fried potato puffs), pompano *en papillote* (baked in parchment paper), and baked Alaska. Tourists generally sit in the front room, but walking through the grand labyrinth is a must. Be prepared for lackluster service. A jacket is required. ⊠*713 St. Louis St., French Quarter* ☏*504/581–4422* ⚜*Reservations essential* ▭*AE, DC, MC, V* ☽*Closed Sun.*

$$–$$$$ ✕**Arnaud's.** This grande dame of classic creole restaurants still sparkles. In the main dining room, ornate etched glass reflects light from charming old chandeliers while the late founder, Arnaud Cazenave, gazes from an oil portrait. The overflow spills into a labyrinth of plush banquet rooms and bars. The ambitious menu includes classic dishes as well as more-contemporary ones. Always reliable are Shrimp Arnaud—cold shrimp in a superb rémoulade—and oyster stew, as well as the fish in crawfish sauce, beef Wellington, and crème brûlée. Jackets are requested in the main dining room. Be sure to visit the Mardi Gras museum upstairs. ⊠*813 Bienville St., French Quarter* ☏*504/523–5433* ⚜*Reservations essential* ▭*AE, D, DC, MC, V* ☽*No lunch Sat.*

★ $$$–$$$$ ✕**Bistro at Maison de Ville.** Forget everything you thought you knew about hotel restaurants. "The Bistro," as locals refer to it, defies convention with its charming, European-inspired decor, intimate dining room that seats 44, and a kitchen so tiny it would fit in the average utility closet. Still, Chef Greg Picolo's dishes, like fine sautéed Louisiana gulf fish, osso bucco, bouillabaisse, and bacon-wrapped filet mignon, are so well conceived that one might picture an operation much larger and more sophisticated. The wine list is legendary in these parts, and the ambience is as well suited to a marriage proposal as it is to a power lunch. The Bistro may just be the best-kept secret in the French Quarter. ⊠*727 Toulouse St, French Quarter* ☏*504/561–5858* ▭*AE, D, DC, MC, V* .

Where to Eat in the French Quarter & Faubourg Marigny

Acme Oyster and
Seafood Restaurant 2
Antoine's 13
Arnaud's 8
Bayona 11
Bennachin 29
Bistro at Maison
de Ville 19

Bourbon House 4
Brennan's 12
Broussard's 10
Café du Monde 23
Café Maspero 17
Central Grocery 24

Croissant d'Or
Patisserie 28
Dickie Brennan's
Steakhouse 3
Dominique's 20
Fiorella's Café 27
Galatoire's 6
Gumbo Shop 18

GW Fins 7
Irene's Cuisine 25
Johnny's Po'boys 16
K-Paul's
Louisiana Kitchen 14
Mona's Café & Deli 32
Mona Lisa 30

Mr. B's Bistro 5
Muriel's Jackson
Square 22
Nola 15
Pelican Club 1
Peristyle 21
Port of Call 31

Praline Connection 33
Rémoulade 9
Stella! 26
Sukho Thai 34
Wasabi 35

4

$$–$$$ ✕**Bourbon House.** Perched on one of the French Quarter's busiest corners, this is Dickie Brennan's biggest and flashiest restaurant yet (he also owns Palace Café and Dickie Brennan's Steakhouse); it's a solid hit with seafood aficionados. If it weren't for the noisy adjacent sports bar, the raw bar would be prime real estate, with its sterling oysters on the half shell; chilled seafood platters; and antique, decorative oyster plates. Glistening beneath the golden glow of bulbous hanging lamps, the main dining room is a more-appropriate place for digging into the creole catalog—andouille sausage stuffed crab, oysters Bienville, and gulf fish pecan. Take your frozen bourbon-milk punch in a go-cup. Why? Because you can. ⊠*144 Bourbon St., French Quarter* ☏*504/522–0111* ▤*AE, D, DC, MC, V.*

★ **$$$–$$$$**   ✕**Brennan's.** Lavish <u>breakfasts</u> are what first put Brennan's on the map. They're still a big draw from morning to night on two floors of luxuriously appointed dining rooms in a gorgeous 19th-century building. The best seats include views of the lush courtyard and fountain. For breakfast, eye-opening cocktails flow freely, followed by poached eggs sandwiched between such treats as hollandaise, creamed spinach, artichoke bottoms, and Canadian bacon; all are listed with suggested wines. Headliners at lunch or dinner include textbook versions of oysters Rockefeller and seafood gumbo, and bananas Foster, which was created here. Looking for consistency? Chef Lazone Randolph has been creating culinary delights in Brennan's kitchen for more than 40 years. The wine list is a stunner, both in quantity and quality. ⊠*417 Royal St., French Quarter* ☏*504/525–9711* ⌖*Reservations essential* ▤*AE, D, MC, V.*

$$–$$$ ✕**Broussard's.** If local restaurants were judged solely by the beauty of their courtyards, Broussard's would be a standout—but if you have the pleasure of dining here, you'll also enjoy consistently outstanding cuisine. From the chef's crab cakes with olive muffuletta relish and caper shallot mayonnaise; to a hearty corn, shrimp, and sweet potato bisque; to tender roasted pork medallions with goat cheese and wild rice, Brousard's provides a meal you won't forget anytime soon. Fight the good fight for an outdoor table, and ask about the selection of savory sauces to accompany your entrée. The praline crème brûlée is perfection. ⊠*., French Quarter* ☏*504/581–3866* ⌖▤*AE, D, DC, MC, V* ☾*Closed Sun.*

$$–$$$ ✕**Galatoire's.** Galatoire's has always epitomized the old-style French-
FodorśChoice   creole bistro. Many of the recipes date to 1905. Fried oysters and
★   bacon en brochette are worth every calorie, and the brick-red rémoulade sauce sets a high standard. Other winners include veal chops in béarnaise sauce, and seafood-stuffed eggplant. The setting downstairs is a single, narrow dining room lighted with glistening brass chandeliers; bentwood chairs and white tablecloths add to its timelessness. You may reserve a table in the renovated upstairs rooms, though the action is on the first floor, where partying regulars inhibit conversation but add good people-watching entertainment value. Friday lunch starts early and continues well into early evening. A jacket is required. ⊠*209 Bourbon St., French Quarter* ☏*504/525–2021* ▤*AE, D, DC, MC, V* ☾*Closed Mon.*

¢–$$ ✕**Gumbo Shop.** Even given a few modern touches—like the vegetarian gumbo offered daily—this place evokes a sense of old New Orleans. The menu is chock-full of regional culinary anchors: jambalaya, shrimp creole and rémoulade, red beans and rice, bread pudding, and seafood and chicken-and-sausage gumbos, heavily flavored with tradition but easy on your wallet. The patina on the ancient painting covering one wall seems to deepen by the week, and the red-and-white-check tablecloths and bentwood chairs are taking on the aspect of museum pieces. ⊠ *630 St. Peter St., French Quarter* ☎ *504/525–1486* ⚐ *Reservations not accepted* ▭ *AE, D, DC, MC, V.*

$$–$$$ ✕**Mr. B's Bistro.** Those who wonder if there really is a New Orleans restaurant that can properly cater to both tourists and locals need look no further than Mr. B's. Situated on one of the busiest French Quarter corners, this bistro never disappoints when it comes to consistency, culinary innovation, and full flavors. Using as many ingredients and products indigenous to Louisiana as possible, the chef offers a standout pepper cured duck risotto, an irresistible honey-ginger-glazed pork chop, and one of the best barbecued shrimp dishes in the city. First-timers must try the "Gumbo Ya-Ya," and no meal here can end without the hot buttered pecan pie. Upscale yet accessible, Mr. B's is still on the map because of its just-right seasonings, its windows on the French Quarter world, and its dedication to service. ⊠ *201 Royal St., French Quarter* ☎ *504/523–2078* ▭ *AE, D, DC, MC, V.*

Fodor's Choice
★

$$–$$$ ✕**Muriel's Jackson Square.** Among Jackson Square's many dining spots, Muriel's is easily the most ambitious, in both atmosphere and menu. In the large downstairs rooms, quaint prints and architectural relics evoke the city's colorful past, while diners in comfy chairs indulge in hearty updated renderings of old creole favorites. Occasionally, the faint sounds of freelance jazz waft inside. Chef Guy D. Sockrider is one of fewer than 500 Certified Executive Chefs worldwide; he excels with seafood, exemplified by his wood-grilled tuna and redfish. Sauces are flavorful, but never overpowering, and local ingredients populate the menu in dishes such as crawfish mashed potatoes, or the perfectly textured jumbo lump crabmeat that completes the Veal Oscar. Be sure to fight the good fight for a balcony table with a panoramic view of Jackson Square. ⊠ *801 Chartres St., French Quarter* ☎ *504/568–1885* ▭ *AE, DC, MC, V.*

$$–$$$ ✕**Nola.** Fans of Emeril Lagasse will want to grab a seat at the food bar overlooking the open kitchen in the chef's French Quarter restaurant. One of the few see-and-be-seen spots in the Quarter, Nola has freewheeling appetizers, the standout being "Miss Hay's stuffed chicken wings" with hoisin dipping sauce. Entrées, like the grilled pork porterhouse with sugar-glazed sweet potatoes, are heavy but delicious. Be warned, after a few bites of the buttermilk fried chicken with bourbon mashed sweet potatoes, you may start looking for property here. Leave room in your tummy, and heart, for the white-chocolate bananas-Foster bread pudding. The space is arty and bright, but too many hard surfaces makes the noise bounce around, which can create a loud environment. ⊠ *534 St. Louis St., French Quarter* ☎ *504/522–6652* ⚐ *Reservations essential* ▭ *AE, D, DC, MC, V* ⊗ *No lunch Sun. –Fri..*

4

¢–$$ ✕**Rémoulade.** Operated by the owners of the posh Arnaud's, Rémoulade is more laid back and less pricey. It serves the same Caesar salad and pecan pie, as well as a few of the signature starters: shrimp Arnaud in rémoulade sauce, baked oysters, turtle soup, and shrimp bisque. The marble-counter oyster bar and mahogany cocktail bar date from the 1870s; a dozen oysters shucked here, paired with a cold beer, can easily turn into two dozen, maybe three. Tile floors, mirrors, a pressed-tin ceiling, and brass lights create an old-time New Orleans environment. It's open daily until midnight. ⊠*309 Bourbon St., French Quarter* ☎*504/523–0377* ▤*AE, D, DC, MC, V.*

DESSERT

¢ ✕**Croissant d'Or Patisserie.** Locals compete with visitors for a table in this colorful, pristine pastry shop, which serves excellent and authentic French croissants, pies, tarts, and custards, as well as an imaginative selection of soups, salads, and sandwiches. Wash them down with real French breakfast coffee, cappuccino, or espresso. Grab a table during breakfast hours for great people-watching. Hours are 7 AM to 4:30 PM. ⊠*617 Ursulines St., French Quarter* ☎*504/524–4663* ▤*AE, MC, V* ☉*Closed Tues.*

ECLECTIC

$$–$$$ ✕**Pelican Club.** Chef Richard Hughes's chic restaurant was once called "understated hip with a festive flip." Sassy New York flourishes permeate the menu of this smartly decorated but eminently comfortable place in the heart of the French Quarter. Still, evidence of Hughes's Louisiana origins keeps popping up. He turns out what may be the best crab cakes in the city (infused with fresh gulf shrimp) but with the surprise addition of pineapple-jalapeño chutney, served over fried green tomatoes. Tender, flaky yellowfin tuna is accented with roasted red pepper brandy cream sauce, and the Australian rack of lamb with rosemary-pesto crust is almost a spiritual experience. ⊠*312 Exchange Pl., French Quarter* ☎*504/523–1504* ▤*AE, D, DC, MC, V* ☉*Closed Mon. No lunch.*

$$–$$$ ✕**Stella!** Chef Scott Boswell has evolved into one of the city's most
FodorsChoice innovative and daring culinarians. Try Canadian lobster, blue foot,
★ and chanterelle mushroom risotto for starters. The almond- and herb-crusted boneless Australian rack of lamb is strictly upscale comfort food, the perfect prelude to chocolate cake with hot buttered lemonade. Stella! now sits comfortably among New Orleans's best fine-dining restaurants. ⊠*1032 Chartres St., French Quarter* ☎*504/587–0091* ▤*AE, D, DC, MC, V* ☉*No lunch.*

ITALIAN

★ $–$$ ✕**Irene's Cuisine.** Its walls are festooned with enough snapshots, garlic braids, and crockery for at least two more restaurants, but it all just adds to the charm of this cozy Italian-creole eatery. From Irene DiPietro's kitchen come succulent roasted chicken brushed with olive oil, rosemary, and garlic; original, velvety soups; and fresh shrimp, aggressively seasoned and grilled before joining linguine glistening with herbed olive oil. Waits here can stretch to the 90-minute mark during peak dinner hours, which is just enough time for a bottle of wine (or two) in the convivial little piano bar. It's easily the friendliest service personnel in the French Quarter. ✉ *539 St. Philip St., French Quarter* ☎ *504/529–8811* ⚑ *Reservations not accepted* ☰ *AE, MC, V* ⊘ *No lunch.*

★ **$–$$** ✕ **Mona Lisa.** Ask a New Orleanian where to find the best pizza in the city, and you'll probably be directed to Mona Lisa, where the food has remained consistently mouthwatering for decades. The salads and sandwiches are outstanding, but you'll rarely see a table without a pizza on it. All of the usual ingredients are available, but there's also an imaginative selection of specialty pizzas, most notably the Hawaiian and the Mediterranean. The wine list has steadily improved over the years, and the tiramisu is one of the French Quarter's best-kept sweet secrets. Hundreds of versions of the Mona Lisa adorn the walls (Mona with a cigar? Check.) in a relaxed setting. ✉ *1212 Royal St., French Quarter* ☎ *504/522–6746* ⚑ *Reservations not accepted* ☰ *AE, MC, V.*

PO'BOYS & OTHER SANDWICHES

¢–$ ✕ **Café Maspero.** The low prices, big portions, and neighborhood camaraderie at the bar keep people coming back. Pastrami and corned beef are local favorites; the half-pound hamburger (with cheese, chili, or both) is long on bulk but short on taste. Arched doors and windows give the vast brick dining room a little character. Service is perfunctory, and, most days, be prepared to wait outside in line for up to half an hour. ✉ *601 Decatur St., French Quarter* ☎ *504/523–6250* ⚑ *Reservations not accepted* ☰ *No credit cards.*

¢–$ ✕ **Central Grocery.** This old-fashioned Italian grocery store produces
Fodor's Choice authentic muffulettas, one of the gastronomic gifts of the city's Italian
★ immigrants. Good enough to challenge the po'boy as the local sandwich champs, they're made by filling round loaves of seeded bread with ham, salami, mozzarella, and a salad of marinated green olives. Sandwiches, about 10 inches in diameter, are sold in wholes and halves. You can eat your muffuletta at a counter, or get it to go and dine on a bench on Jackson Square or the Moon Walk along the Mississippi riverfront. The Grocery closes at 5:30 PM. ✉ *923 Decatur St., French Quarter* ☎ *504/523–1620* ☰ *D, MC, V. No dinner.*

$–$$ ✕ **Fiorella's Café.** Steps away from the hubbub of the French Quarter's flea market is this casual and friendly bar and eatery, which specializes in classic po'boys, New Orleans–style plate lunches, and some of the best fried chicken in town. Red beans and rice show up on Monday, meat loaf takes the spotlight on Tuesday, and Thursday is butter bean day; hearty breakfasts are an everyday feature. Space is tight, but the food and the prices are easy to swallow. ✉ *45 French Market Pl. (another entrance at 1136 Decatur St.), French Quarter* ☎ *504/528–9566* ☰ *AE, D, MC, V.*

☪ ¢–$ ✕ **Johnny's Po'boys.** Strangely enough, good po'boys are hard to find in the French Quarter. Johnny's compensates for the scarcity with a cornucopia of them, even though the quality is anything but consistent, and the prices are somewhat inflated for the tourist trade. Inside the soft-crust French bread come the classic fillings, including lean boiled ham, well-done roast beef in garlicky gravy, and crisply fried oysters or shrimp. The chili may not cut it in San Antonio, but the red beans and rice are the real deal. The surroundings are rudimentary. It's open until

Food Glossary

Andouille (pronounced ahn-*dooey*). A mildly spiced Acadian smoked sausage of lean pork, it often flavors gumbos, red beans and rice, and jambalayas.

Barbecue shrimp. The shrimp are not barbecued but baked in their shells in a blend of olive oil, butter, or margarine and usually seasoned with bay leaf, garlic, and other herbs and spices.

Béarnaise (pronounced bare-*nayz*). This sauce of egg yolk and butter with shallots, wine, and vinegar is used on meat and fish.

Beignet (pronounced ben-*yay*). Although a beignet was originally a rectangular puff of fried dough sprinkled with powdered sugar, the term can also refer to fritters or crullers containing fish or seafood.

Bisque. A thick, heartily seasoned soup, bisque is most often made with crawfish, crab, or shrimp. Cream appears in some versions.

Boudin. A seasoned pork-and-rice sausage.

Bouillabaisse (pronounced *booey-yah-base*). A creole bouillabaisse is a stew of various fish and shellfish in a broth seasoned with saffron and often more-assertive spices.

Boulette (pronounced *boo-*let). This is minced, chopped, or pureed meat or fish shaped into balls and fried.

Bread pudding. In the traditional version, stale French bread is soaked in a custard mix, combined with raisins, and baked, then served with a hot sugary sauce flavored with whiskey or rum.

Café au lait. This hot drink is a blend, often half and half, of strong coffee and scalded milk.

Café brûlot (pronounced broo-*loh*). Cinnamon, lemon, clove, orange, and sugar are steeped with strong coffee, then flambéed with brandy and served in special pedestaled cups.

Chicory coffee. The ground and roasted root of a European variety of chicory is added to ground coffee in varying proportions. Originally used for reasons of economy, coffee with chicory is now favored by many New Orleanians. It lends an added bitterness to the taste.

Crème brûlée (pronounced broo-*lay*). Literally, this means "burned cream." It's a custard with a brittle crust of browned sugar.

Dirty rice. In this cousin of jambalaya, bits of meat, such as giblets or sausage, and seasonings are added to white rice before cooking.

Dressed. A po'boy "dressed" contains lettuce, tomato, pickles, and mayonnaise or mustard.

Étouffée (pronounced ay-too-*fay*). Literally, "smothered," the term is used most often for a thick stew of crawfish tails cooked in a roux-based liquid with crawfish, fat, garlic, and green seasonings.

Gumbo. From an African word for okra, it can refer to any number of stewlike soups made with seafood or meat and flavored with okra or ground sassafras and myriad other seasonings. Frequent main ingredients are combinations of shrimp, oysters, crab, chicken, andouille, duck, and turkey. A definitive gumbo is served over white rice.

Jambalaya (pronounced jam-buh-*lie*-uh). Rice is the indispensable ingredient in this relative of Spain's paella. The rice is cooked with a mix of diced meat and seafood in tomato and other seasonings. Shrimp and ham make frequent appearances, as do sausage, green pepper, and celery.

Meunière (pronounced muhn-*yehr*). This method of preparing fish or soft-shell crab entails dusting it with seasoned flour, sautéing it in brown butter, and using the butter with lemon juice as a sauce. Some restaurants add a dash of Worcestershire sauce.

Mirliton (pronounced merl-i-*tawn*). A pale green member of the squash family, a mirliton is usually identified as a vegetable pear or chayote. The standard preparation is to scrape the pulp from halved mirlitons, fill them with shrimp and seasoned bread crumbs, and bake them.

Muffuletta. The city's southern Italian grocers created this round-loaf sandwich traditionally filled with ham, salami, mozzarella, and a layer of chopped, marinated green olives. Muffulettas are sold whole and in halves or quarters.

Oysters Bienville (pronounced byen-*veel*). In this dish, oysters are lightly baked in their shells under a cream sauce flavored with bits of shrimp, mushroom, and green seasonings. Some chefs also use garlic or mustard.

Oysters en brochette (pronounced awn-bro-*shet*). Whole oysters and bits of bacon are dusted with seasoned flour, skewered, and deep-fried. Traditionally, they're served on toast with lemon and brown butter.

Oysters Rockefeller. This dish, baked oysters on the half shell in a sauce of pureed aromatic greens laced with anise liqueur, was created at Antoine's, which keeps its recipe a secret. Most other restaurants make do with spinach.

Panéed veal (pronounced pan-*aid*). Breaded veal cutlets are sautéed in butter.

Po'boy. A hefty sandwich, the po'boy is made with the local French bread and any number of fillings: roast beef, fried shrimp, oysters, ham, meatballs in tomato sauce, and cheese are common. A po'boy "dressed" contains lettuce, tomato, pickles, and mayonnaise or mustard.

Praline (pronounced *prah*-leen). A sweet patty-shape confection made of pecans, brown sugar, butter, and vanilla.

Ravigote (pronounced rah-vee-*gote*). In creole usage, this is a piquant mayonnaise—usually made with capers—used to moisten blue crabmeat.

Rémoulade (pronounced ray-moo-*lahd*). The classic creole rémoulade is a brick-red whipped mixture of olive oil with mustard, scallions, cayenne, lemon, paprika, and parsley. It's served on cold peeled shrimp or lumps of back-fin crabmeat.

Souffléed potatoes. These thin, hollow puffs of deep-fried potato are produced by two fryings at different temperatures.

Tasso (pronounced *tah*-so). Acadian cooks developed this lean, intensely seasoned ham. It's used sparingly to flavor sauces and gumbos.

around 4 PM daily. ✉*511 St. Louis St., French Quarter* ☎*504/524–8129* ▤*No credit cards* ☽*No dinner.*

SEAFOOD

★ ☾ ¢ – $ ✕**Acme Oyster and Seafood Restaurant.** A rough-edge classic in every way, this no-nonsense eatery at the entrance to the French Quarter is a prime source for cool and salty raw oysters on the half shell; shrimp, oyster, and roast-beef po'boys; and tender, expertly seasoned red beans and rice. Table service, once confined to the main dining room out front, is now provided in the rear room as well. Expect rather lengthy lines at the marble-top oyster bar (trust us though, it's worth it). Crowds lighten in the late afternoon. ✉*724 Iberville St., French Quarter* ☎*504/525–1160* ⌕*Reservations not accepted* ▤*AE, D, DC, MC, V.*

$$–$$$ ✕**GW Fins.** Seafood is the quarry of many a New Orleans visitor, and
Fodor'sChoice   GW Fins meets the demand with variety and quality, ranging from
★   gumbos to New Bedford sea scallops. A bounty of fish species from around the world is among the menu's lures. Chef Tenney Flynn's menu changes daily, depending on what fresh seafood is delivered, but typical dishes have included a luscious Canadian sea bass, Hawaiian big-eye tuna, and sautéed rainbow trout with spinach, oysters, and shiitake mushrooms, fired up with tasso. For dessert, try the baked-to-order deep-dish apple pie. The spacious dining room's attractive modern decor and the enthusiastic service make this a relaxing refuge from the French Quarter's crowds. ✉*808 Bienville St., French Quarter* ☎*504/581–3467* ▤*AE, D, DC, MC, V* ☽*No lunch.*

SOUTHERN

$–$$$ ✕**Bayona.** "New World" is the label Louisiana native Susan Spicer
Fodor'sChoice   applies to her cooking style, which results in such signature dishes
★   as the goat cheese crouton with mushrooms in Madeira cream, and crispy, fried smoked quail served on a salad with bourbon-molasses vinaigrette. The bouillabaisse with shrimp, mussels, and snapper is about as authentic as Louisiana cooking can be, while the grilled duck breast with a pepper jelly glaze is Southern with a capital "S." These and other imaginative dishes are served in an early-19th-century creole cottage that glows with flower arrangements, elegant photographs, and trompe l'oeil murals suggesting Mediterranean landscapes. Don't skip pastry chef Christy Phebus's sweets, such as a dark chocolate banana torte with espresso crème caramel. ✉*430 Dauphine St., French Quarter* ☎*504/525–4455* ⌕*Reservations essential* ▤*AE, DC, MC, V* ☽*Closed Sun. No lunch Mon. or Tues.*

STEAK

$$–$$$$ ✕**Dickie Brennan's Steakhouse.** "Straightforward steaks with a New Orleans touch" is the axiom at this clubby and luxurious red-meat specialist, the creation of a younger member of the Brennan family of restaurateurs. After stellar martinis in the dark cherry-lined lounge, walk the drugstore-tile floor to the cavernous dining room and dig into classic, expensive cuts of top-quality beef and seafood. The standard beefsteak treatment is light seasoning and a brush of butter. Among the several other toppers are five buttery sauces. The expansive oyster bar has become a classic corner gathering place for tourists and locals.

✉ *716 Iberville St., French Quarter* ☎ *504/522–2467* ⊟ *AE, D, DC, MC, V* ⊘ *No lunch weekends.*

FAUBOURG MARIGNY

CREOLE

☺ $–$$ ✕**Praline Connection.** Down-home cooking in the southern-creole style is the forte of this *very Southern* restaurant a couple of blocks from the French Quarter. The fried or stewed chicken, smothered pork chops, fried chicken livers, and collard greens are definitively done, and the soulful filé gumbo, peas with okra, and sweet-potato pie are welcome in a neighborhood otherwise in short supply of soul food. Add a congenial staff and a comfortable dining room, and the end result is a fine place to enjoy relaxing mealtime. The adjacent sweetshop holds such delights as sweet-potato cookies and creole pralines. ✉ *542 Frenchmen St., Faubourg Marigny* ☎ *504/943–3934* ⊟ *AE, D, DC, MC, V.*

JAPANESE

★ $–$$ ✕**Wasabi.** If it weren't for the smidgen of a sign jutting from the side of Wasabi's windowless building, you'd never guess at the bright, clean goings-on inside. The restaurant splits into two rooms; you wait in the neighborhoody bar area if the dining space is crowded (it usually is). The fish and rice are fresh as can be, and a Japanese kitchen turns out succulent beef dishes and great udon noodle soups. The wasabi-honey shrimp entrée combines three unlikely ingredients, but so many approve that it has become a signature. It's open until 2 AM Friday and Saturday. ✉ *900 Frenchmen St., Faubourg Marigny* ☎ *504/943–9433* ⚠ *Reservations not accepted* ⊟ *AE, D, DC, MC, V* ⊘ *Closed Sun. No lunch Sat.*

MIDDLE EASTERN

¢–$ ✕**Mona's Café & Deli.** The modest and spotless spaces at Mona's are not the most colorful in town. But inside this rather bare and simple place you'll find some of the best, basic eastern-Mediterranean cooking. Cut open a ball of crunchy fried *kibbe* and the reward is superbly seasoned beef and lamb. The tabouleh here, made with lots of parsley and mint, is more than just seasoned bulgur wheat. Gyro sandwiches are meaty, and the falafel are flavorful, too. The Lebanese iced tea is eminently refreshing, as is the friendly laid-back service. ✉ *504 Frenchmen St., Faubourg Marigny* ☎ *504/949–4115* ⊟ *AE, MC, V.*

THAI

$–$$ ✕**Sukho Thai.** Certainly the most prolific Thai restaurant in the area, Sukho Thai fits snugly into its arty neighborhood with servers wearing all black, an art gallery approach to decorating, and brightly colored dishes. Dry and wet curries are so vibrant that the pastes seem made to order. Whole steamed fish brushed with spicy chili sauce gains a citrusy perfume from lemongrass and Kaffir lime leaf. Creative house-made desserts take the form of barely sweetened coconut custard and black-rice pudding. The most-imaginative and extensive tea menu in the area compensates for the lack of a liquor license. ✉ *1913 Royal*

Fodor's Choice ★

St., Faubourg Marigny ☎*504/948–9309* ▭*AE, D, MC, V* ⬚ *BYOB* ⊘ *Closed Mon. No lunch weekends.*

CBD & WAREHOUSE DISTRICT

AMERICAN

$$–$$$$ ✕ **New Orleans Grill.** The British furnishings span several centuries in these dazzling dining spaces, with body-hugging chairs and canvases depicting aspects of upper-class England. The equally dazzling menus change frequently, and are filled with a smart combination of Louisiana specialties and Continental delicacies. The variety is exemplified by a succulent barbecued shrimp pie that precedes a grilled redfish with cracked-black-peppered blue crab fingers, and Vidalia onions. Just when you think the best is behind, out comes the city's best cheese plate, followed by soothing cordials. The wine cellar, with its collection of vintage Bordeaux reds, remains awesome. The bountiful daily buffet lunch has become *the* power lunch spot in town. A jacket is required. ✉ *Windsor Court Hotel, 2nd level, 300 Gravier St., CBD* ☎*504/522–1992* ⌚*Reservations essential* ▭*AE, D, DC, MC, V.*

CAJUN

$$–$$$$ ✕ **Bon Ton Café.** The Bon Ton's opening in 1953 marked the first appearance of a significant Cajun restaurant in New Orleans, and its crawfish dishes, gumbo, jambalaya, and oyster omelet have retained their strong following ever since. The bustle in the dining room peaks at lunchtime on weekdays, when businesspeople from nearby offices come in droves for baked eggplant with shrimp, fried catfish, turtle soup, and warm, sugary bread pudding. If you can sacrifice the afternoon for pleasure, try a Rum Ramsey cocktail. The veteran servers are knowledgeable and fleet-footed. ✉ *401 Magazine St., CBD* ☎*504/524–3386* ▭*AE, DC, MC, V* ⊘*Closed weekends.*

$–$$ ✕ **Cochon.** Chef-owned restaurants are common in New Orleans, but this one builds on the owner's family heritage. Chef Donald Link prepares Cajun dishes he learned to cook at his grandfather's knee. The interior may be a bit too rustic and noisy for some patrons, but the food will make up for it. Try the fried boudin with pickled peppers—trust us on this one. Then move on to black-eyed pea and pork gumbo, and a hearty Louisiana cochon (pork) with turnips, cracklings, and cabbage. If you want to experience true regional cuisine, this is the place. ✉*930 Tchoupitoulas St., Warehouse* ☎*504/588–2123* ⌚*Reservations not accepted* ▭*AE, MC, V.*

$$–$$$$ ✕ **Grand Isle.** This Louisiana fish camp–theme restaurant gave a significant boost to the emerging entertainment district surrounding the Fulton Street corridor and Harrah's Casino. All of the seafood served here comes directly off the coast of Grand Isle, Louisiana, and everything is fresh (never frozen). The rustic interior, reminiscent of 1920s and '30s Louisiana, is the perfect backdrop for turtle stew, spicy boiled shrimp, lobster with roasted shrimp sauce, fresh gulf fish, and a lemon icebox pie that will make you fall in love with New Orleans all over again. They don't take reservations, and the place is generally packed, but it's worth the wait (which also gives you an excuse to spend some

time at the elegant mahogany bar). *575 Convention Center Blvd., CBD* ☎*504/520–8530* ⊕*www.grandislerestaurant.com* ⚑*Reservations not accepted* ▭ *AE, D, DC, MC, V.*

$$–$$$ ╳ **Lüke.** Chef John Besh's Lüke is a love letter to the old brasseries that once reigned in New Orleans; dine here, and you'll feel as if you've traveled back to a time when rattan bistro chairs, blackboard specials, and newspaper racks were de rigueur. Start your meal with a Sazerac (a local cocktail of whiskey, bitters, and absinthe) or mint julep, and work your way into rabbit and duck liver pâté, followed by a fried oyster, bacon, and avocado salad. French and old-world German influences produce some distinctive entrées, including a cochon de lait (roast pork) sandwich, redfish court-bouillon, and a Louisiana speckled trout almandine that will remind you why New Orleans is so revered as a culinary destination. ⊠ *333 St. Charles Ave., CBD* ☎*504/378–2840* ⊕*www.lukeneworleans.com* ⚑▭ *AE, D, DC, MC, V* ⊗*Closed Sun.*

$$–$$$$ ╳ **MiLa.** Chefs Slade Rushing and Allison Vines-Rushing, from Mississippi and Louisiana respectively, merged the names and cuisines of their home states to produce MiLa. The restaurant defines a new Southern elegance with its comfy/chic atmosphere and its culinary tributes to each chef's childhood memories of Southern cooking. The results are dishes like pan-roasted sweetbreads with black truffle grits, and roasted grouper with creamed mustard greens. All of the produce comes from a working farm in Mount Hermon, Louisiana. Insider's tip: Take a seat at the bar, and try the hot deer sausage and cheddar biscuits. ⊠ *817 Common St., CBD* ☎*504/412–2580* ⊕*http://milaneworleans.com* ▭ *AE, D, DC, MC, V* ⊗*No lunch Sat.*

CREOLE

$$–$$$$ ╳ **Anatole's.** Chef Raymond Toups's long history in New Orleans includes extended stints at some of the most highly regarded eateries in town. When he opened his own restaurant in a high-profile downtown block, expectations ran high, and he has yet to disappoint. A tempting array of seafood appetizers (try the gulf shrimp sautéed in cognac) leads easily into a fine selection of steaks. The generously portioned filet mignon is flamed table-side and coated in crushed peppercorns. After your last bite of house-made mango sorbet, ask about the unique selection of dessert cocktails, and enjoy one in the elegant, clubby adjacent lounge. ⊠ *600 St. Charles Ave., CBD* ☎*504/274–0105* ▭ *AE, D, DC, MC, V.*

$$$–$$$$ ╳*Emeril's.* Celebrity chef Emeril Lagasse's urban-chic flagship restaurant is always jammed. A wood ceiling in a basket-weave pattern muffles much of the clatter and chatter. The ambitious menu gives equal emphasis to creole and modern American cooking—try the barbecue shrimp here for one of the darkest, richest versions of the local specialty. Desserts, such as the renowned banana cream pie, verge on the gargantuan. Service is meticulous, and the wine list's depth and range should soothe even the most persnickety imbiber. ⊠*800 Tchoupitoulas St., Warehouse District* ☎*504/528–9393* ⚑*Reservations essential* ▭*AE, D, DC, MC, V* ⊗*No lunch weekends.*

Where to Eat in CBD & the Warehouse District

Louisiana Superdome

KEY

🚋 Streetcar

St. Charles Stop

St. Charles Stop

St. Joseph Stop

Lafayette Sq.

Mississippi River

200 yards

200 meters

Anatole's **19**
August **12**
Bon Ton Café **15**
Cochon **3**
Cuvée **14**
Drago's **9**
Eleven 79 .... **2**
Emeril's **4**

Emeril's Delmonico **1**
Grand Isle **8**
Herbsaint **20**
Lüke **18**
MiLa **17**
Mother's **13**
New Orleans Grill **11**
Palace Café **16**

Riche **10**
Rio Mar **6**
7 on Fulton **7**
Tommy's Cuisine **5**

$$$–$$$$　✕**Emeril's Delmonico.** Chef Emeril Lagasse bought the traditional, unpretentious, century-old Delmonico and converted it into a large, extravagantly appointed restaurant with the most-ambitious revamping of classic creole dishes in town. The high-ceiling dining spaces are swathed in upholstered walls and superthick window fabrics. Local oyster preparations are a reliable option, as are New Orleans–style barbecue shrimp, crab cakes, and sautéed fish meunière. Prime dry-aged steaks with traditional sauces have emerged as a specialty in recent years, but the menu gets more ambitious by the month. Plush and polish are the bywords here, and the service can be exemplary. ⊠ *1300 St. Charles Ave., CBD* ☎ *504/525–4937* ⚐ *Reservations essential* ☰ *AE, D, DC, MC, V* ⊗ *No lunch Sat.*

$$–$$$　✕**Palace Café.** Crafted from what used to be New Orleans's oldest music store, this Dickie Brennan stalwart is a convivial spot to try some of the more-imaginative contemporary creole dishes, such as crabmeat cheesecake, stuffed rabbit, and seafood pastas. Desserts, especially the white-chocolate bread pudding and the house-made ice creams, are luscious. Drugstore-tile floors, stained-cherry booths, and soothing beige walls set the mood. The wraparound mezzanine is lined with a large mural, populated by the city's famous musicians. Take a seat at the outdoor sidewalk café for small plates and wine. The Sunday jazz brunch is New Orleans all the way. ⊠ *605 Canal St., CBD* ☎ *504/523–1661* ⚐ *Reservations essential* ☰ *AE, D, DC, MC, V.*

ECLECTIC

$$–$$$　✕**7 on Fulton.** Restaurateur Vicky Bayley wowed the masses in the '90s with Mike's on the Avenue. Now she's back with this chic, sleek eatery just down the street from the Morial Convention Center. Rich entrées, such as the bacon-wrapped pork tenderloin with braised celery and mustard sauce, and duck breast à la orange, win over even the most skeptical diners. The favorite dessert, chocolate doberge, will brighten your whole day, and don't miss the warm crab-and-gnocchi appetizer with lemon beurre blanc. ⊠ *701 Convention Center Blvd., CBD* ☎ *504/525–7555* ⚐ *Reservations essential* ☰ *AE, MC, V.*

FRENCH

$$$–$$$$　✕**Riche.** Every town needs a classic, authentic French restaurant, and Riche fills that role in New Orleans. The interior combines old-world elegance and architectural elements with contemporary fabrics and an airy ambience; French doors open to a patio with additional seating. The big draw is the chef's French onion soup, featuring seven types of onions. The Plateaux de Fruits de Mer features an abundance of oysters, shrimp, and littleneck clams. Take a seat at the raw bar to see the dynamic kitchen staff in action. After dinner, spend some time in "528," featuring live jazz nightly. ⊠ *Harrah's New Orleans Hotel, lobby level, 228 Poydras St., CBD* ☎ *504/522–0787* ⚐ *Reservations essential* ☰ *AE, D, DC, MC, V.*

ITALIAN

$$–$$$$　✕ **Drago's.** For almost 40 years the Cvitanovich family restaurant has been a fixture in Metairie, just a short drive from downtown New Orleans. When it was revealed the family would open a second location

inside the Hilton Riverside hotel, locals knew to expect good things. The Italian dishes and oyster-heavy menu that has satisfied the masses for decades were simply duplicated at the hotel, but on a larger scale. Best known for its charbroiled oysters, authentic Italian pasta recipes, live main lobster dishes, and fried seafood entrées, Drago's is a true local institution. Families love the place—especially because of the kids' menu—and the warm apple cobbler is the sweet stuff legends are made of. ⊠ *2 Poydras St., CBD* ☎*504/584–3911* ⊟ *AE, D, DC, MC, V.*

★ **$$–$$$** ✕**Eleven 79.** If the Rat Pack boys were alive today, they'd grab a corner table in this tiny, softly lighted Italian eatery, where garlic rules and red wine is revered. Dean Martin music adds a soft ambience, while candlelit tables serve as the perfect platform for tender pastas bathed in perfectly seasoned sauces. Start every meal with the house Italian salad, and be good to yourself with *panéed* veal with asparagus, buffalo mozzarella, roasted red peppers, and lemon sauce. Every dish is full of flavor, and the chef has an even hand with seasonings. There is no such thing as a bad meal at Eleven 79. ⊠*1179 Annunciation St., Warehouse District* ☎*504/229–1179* ⌖*Reservations essential* ⊟*AE, D, DC, MC, V* ⊘*No lunch.*

★**$$** ✕**Tommy's Cuisine.** The dining rooms here are clubby and festive, and the crowd is always interesting. Don't overlook the *panéed* oysters; the lamb chops blanketed with béarnaise sauce; or the roasted half chicken saturated with the flavors of rosemary and garlic. Service is gentlemanly, the chef's dinner specials are imaginative, and the wines span all of Italy. After dinner, head next door to the cushy Tommy's Wine Bar. ⊠*746 Tchoupitoulas St., Warehouse District* ☎*504/581–1103* ⌖*Reservations essential* ⊟*AE, D, DC, MC, V* ⊘*No lunch.*

PO'BOYS & OTHER SANDWICHES

¢–**$$** ✕**Mother's.** Tourists line up for down-home eats at this island of blue-collar sincerity amid downtown's glittery hotels. Mother's dispenses delicious baked ham and roast-beef po'boys (ask for "debris" on the beef sandwich and the bread will be slathered with meat juices and shreds of meat), home-style biscuits and jambalaya, and a very good chicken gumbo in a couple of bare-bones—yet charming—dining rooms. Breakfast service is a bit slow, but that doesn't seem to repel the hordes fighting for seats at peak mealtimes. Service is cafeteria style, with a counter or two augmenting the tables. ⊠*401 Poydras St., CBD* ☎*504/523–9656* ⌖*Reservations not accepted* ⊟*AE, MC, V.*

SEAFOOD

★ **$$** ✕**Rio Mar.** Chef Adolfo Garcia's largely seafood menu reflects his Spanish style and Panamanian heritage. Each of his several ceviches has its own distinct marinade and combination of superfresh seafood. For entrées, try the stewlike zarzuela of seafood, with chunks of fish and shellfish in a peppery red broth. It's all tapas at lunch, when you tick off your selections on a small menu card: salty serrano ham, roasted peppers, Manchego cheese, marinated seafood. The dining room's low ceiling and tiled floor don't make for great acoustics, but the gold-hue walls with their rustic iron ornamentation would not be misplaced in

Barcelona. ⊠ *800 S. Peters St., Warehouse District* ☎ *504/525–3474* ▤ *AE, D, DC, MC, V* ⊗ *Closed Sun. No lunch Sat.*

SOUTHERN

$$$–$$$$
Fodor'sChoice
★

✕**August.** If the Gilded Age is long gone, someone forgot to tell the folks at August, whose main dining room shimmers with masses of chandelier prisms, thick brocade fabrics, and glossy woods. Service is anything but stuffy, however, and chef John Besh's modern technique adorns every plate. Nothing is mundane here: handmade gnocchi with blue crab and winter truffle shares menu space with slow-cooked pork belly and butter-poached main lobster with black truffles. Expect the unexpected—like slow-roasted Kobe beef short ribs with Jerusalem artichokes. The sommelier is happy to confer with you on the surprisingly affordable wine list. ⊠ *301 Tchoupitoulas St., CBD* ☎ *504/299–9777* ⚏ *Reservations essential* ▤ *AE, MC, V* ⊗ *Closed Sun. No lunch Sat.*

★ **$$–$$$$**

✕**Cuvée.** With a name that refers to a blend of wines, this restaurant divides its inspirations between France's Champagne region and south Louisiana. The menu rests on a firm French foundation, but the flavors are often distinctively New Orleans. Talented chef Robert Iacovone sometimes seems unstoppable, like when he fashions the city's most-elegant cane-syrup smoked-duck breast paired with walnut blue-cheese risotto, or when he presents his pork tenderloin with juniper and Gruyère apple streudel. Main courses are gutsy and inspired, as is the wine list. All are decanted in a space defined by exposed brick and gilt-framed paintings. ⊠ *322 Magazine St., CBD* ☎ *504/587–9001* ⚏ *Reservations essential* ▤ *AE, DC, MC, V* ⊗ *Closed Sun. No lunch Sat.*

$$–$$$
Fodor'sChoice
★

✕**Herbsaint.** Upscale food and moderate prices are among Herbsaint's assets. Chef Donald Link turns out food that sparkles with robust flavors and top-grade ingredients. "Small plates" and side dishes such as charcuterie, a knock-'em-dead shrimp bisque, house-made pasta, and cheese- or nut-studded salads are mainstays. Don't overlook the rich and flavorful shrimp and green-chili grits cakes with *tasso* cream sauce. More-substantial choices include Dijon crusted lamb shoulder with baked white beans. For dessert, the crème fraîche panna cotta with Louisiana strawberries and almond biscotti will ensure future return trips. The plates provide most of the color in the lighthearted, often noisy, rooms. The wine list is expertly compiled and reasonably priced. ⊠ *701 St. Charles Ave., CBD* ☎ *504/524–4114* ⚏ *Reservations essential* ▤ *AE, D, DC, MC, V* ⊗ *Closed Sun. No lunch Sat.*

GARDEN DISTRICT/UPTOWN

AMERICAN

$$–$$$

✕**La Petite Grocery.** Flower shops often morph into intimate fine-dining establishments in New Orleans. This one, in soft creams and reds with just-bright-enough lighting and a sturdy, mahogany bar, has caught on in a big way with the locals. Chef-owner Anton Schulte draws on contemporary American tastes, using Louisiana raw materials when he can. A seemingly ordinary pan–roasted chicken is enlivened with mushroom bread pudding, while a Berkshire pork shank is served over stoned ground grits and strictly Southern greens. Rich, sticky sauces

Where to Eat Outside the Downtown Area

See French Quarter detail map

See CBD and Warehouse District detail map

Louisiana Superdome

Angelo Brocato's **16**
Basil Leaf **12**
Brigtsen's **9**
Café Degas **21**
Casamento's **31**
Clancy's **37**

Clementine's
Belgian Bistrot **25**
Commander's Palace ... **28**
Crabby Jack's **7**
Dakota **6**
Dante's Kitchen **8**
Elizabeth's **23**

Franky & Johnny's **36**
Jacques-Imo's Café **13**
The Joint **24**
Kyoto **33**
La Crêpe Nanou **34**
La Madeline **11**
Le Parvenu **3**

La Petite Grocery **30**
La Provence **4**
La Vita **20**
Lilette **29**
Liuzza's by the Track ... **22**
Mandina's **15**
Martinique **35**

Mosca's **1**
ONE **10**
Parkway Bakery
& Tavern **18**
Pascal's Manale **32**
Ralph's on the Park **17**
Restaurant des Familles ... **2**

Tan Dinh **26**
Two Sister's Kitchen **19**
Vega Tapas Bar **5**
Vizard's on the Avenue ... **27**
Ye Olde College Inn **14**

in the French tradition are a major specialty—few dishes are without one. ⊠*4238 Magazine St., Uptown* ☎*504/891–3377* ⚓*Reservations essential* ☰*AE, MC, V* ⊘*Closed Sun and Mon. No lunch.*

$$–$$$ ✕**Lilette.** Proprietor-chef John Harris uses New Orleans and French Fodor'sChoice culinary traditions as springboards for Lilette's inspired dishes. Look ★ for pan-roasted Alaskan cod with mushrooms and roasted potatoes, or roasted Muscovy breast of duck with creamed potatoes and fennel. For dessert, the goat cheese quenelles with lavender honey are as light as sorbet but more satisfying. The thoughtful wine list is boutique oriented, and the unique cocktail selection holds even more surprises. Framed mirrors hang along the maroon walls of the intimate front dining room–cum–bar. A few more tables fill out a second room and patio. ⊠*3637 Magazine St., Uptown* ☎*504/895–1636* ⚓*Reservations essential* ☰*AE, D, DC, MC, V* ⊘*Closed Sun. and Mon.*

CAFÉ

$ ✕**La Madeleine.** The lines are ever present in this French-theme bakery-café, which is part of a chain. The huge selection of pastries includes napoleons, cheesecakes, and éclairs, as well as brioches and breads from the wood-burning oven. Salads, hearty soups (the tomato basil is fantastic), overstuffed sandwiches, and light entrées are also available. Surprisingly, the kitchen excels with pasta dishes. It closes at 9 PM daily. ⊠*601 S. Carrollton Ave., Uptown* ☎*504/861–8662* ☰*AE, D, MC, V.*

CAJUN/CREOLE

$–$$ ✕**Jacques-Imo's Cafe.** Oak Street might look like any other sleepy urban Fodor'sChoice thoroughfare by day, but once the sun sets, the half-block stretch con- ★ taining Jacques-Imo's Cafe feels like the center of the universe. Prepare for lengthy, but festive waits in the crowded bar for a table in the boisterous, swamp-theme dining rooms (fortunately, the bartenders are skilled). The modest-looking but innovative food is worth it: deep-fried roast beef po'boys, alligator sausage cheesecake, Cajun bouillabaisse, and smothered rabbit over grits are among the excellent only-at-Jacques-Imo's specialties. All main courses come with salad and corn muffins. Reservations are accepted for parties of five or more. ⊠*8324 Oak St., Uptown* ☎*504/861–0886* ☰*AE, D, DC, MC, V* ⊘*Closed Sun. No lunch.*

CARIBBEAN

$$–$$$ ✕**Martinique.** The name suggests more Caribbean influence than is actually present in this one-room restaurant and its tropical courtyard. The French emphasis is Martinique's calling card, shining through in such items as French onion gratiné, escargot with exotic mushrooms, pulled duck confit, braised meat, chèvre, and demi-glace-based sauces. Still, regulars demand the Louisiana touch; try the blue crab cake with mango, lime, and chipotle vinaigrette. Budget for wine; the irresistible list is continually updated. Dinner menus change every eight weeks. The corner table in Martinique's courtyard is a popular marriage-pro-posal spot. ⊠*5908 Magazine St., Uptown* ☎*504/891–8495* ⚓*Reservations essential* ☰*AE, MC, V* ⊘*No lunch.*

CREOLE

★ **$$–$$$** ✕**Brigtsen's.** Chef Frank Brigtsen's fusion of creole refinement and Acadian earthiness reflects his years as a protégé of Paul Prudhomme. His dishes represent some of the best south Louisiana cooking you'll find anywhere. Everything is fresh and filled with deep, complex tastes. The butternut shrimp bisque defines comfort food. Rabbit and chicken dishes, usually presented in rich sauces and gravies, are full of robust flavor. The roux-based gumbos are thick and intense, and the warm bread pudding is worth every calorie. Trompe l'oeil murals add whimsy to the intimate spaces of this turn-of-the-20th-century frame cottage. Ask for a table on the enclosed front sun porch. ☒*723 Dante St., Uptown* ☎*504/861–7610* ⌖*Reservations essential* ▭*AE, DC, MC, V* ◷*Closed Sun. and Mon. No lunch.*

$$–$$$ ✕**Clancy's.** Understatement defines the mood at locally beloved Clancy's. The decor is neutral, with gray walls and a few ceiling fans above bentwood chairs and white linen cloths. The small bar is usually filled with regulars who know one another (and tourists who wish they were regulars). Most of the dishes are imaginative treatments of New Orleans's favorites. Some specialties, like the fresh sautéed fish in cream sauce flavored with crawfish stock and herbs, are exceptional. Other signs of an inventive chef are the expertly fried oysters matched with warm Brie, and a peppermint ice-cream pie. On more-festive nights you may yearn for earplugs. ☒*6100 Annunciation St., Uptown* ☎*504/895– 1111* ⌖*Reservations essential* ▭*AE, D, DC, MC, V* ◷*Closed Sun. No lunch Mon. and Sat.*

$$$–$$$$ ✕**Commander's Palace.** No restaurant captures New Orleans's gastronomic heritage and celebratory spirit as well as this one, long considered the grande dame of New Orleans's fine dining. The recent renovation has added new life, especially upstairs, where the Garden Room's glass walls have marvelous views of the giant oak trees on the patio below; other rooms promote conviviality with their bright pastels. The menu's classics include panéed Mississippi rabbit ; a spicy and meaty turtle soup; terrific grilled veal chops with grits; and a wonderful sautéed gulf fish coated with crunchy pecans. Among the addictive desserts is the bread-pudding soufflé. Weekend brunches are a New Orleans tradition. Jackets are preferred at dinner. ☒*1403 Washington Ave., Garden District* ☎*504/899–8221* ⌖*Reservations essential* ▭*AE, D, DC, MC, V.*

Fodor'sChoice
★

$$–$$$ ✕**Vizard's on the Avenue.** Chef Kevin Vizard has been steaming up New Orleans kitchens for years now, but his St. Charles Avenue eatery is the culmination of years of experimentation and creativity at places like Commander's Palace and Café Adelaide. Vizard excels at unlikely combinations like duck breast with sauerkraut, and imaginative preparations like citrus and spice-rubbed pork tenderloin. The fried-oyster bruschetta with foie gras mousse appetizer is second only to the chef's gumbo. All of this happens in minimalist surroundings, with stunning artwork and a stellar window view of the nonstop activity on the avenue. ☒*2203 St. Charles Ave., Garden District* ☎*504/529–9912* ▭*AE, D, DC, MC, V.*

Fodor'sChoice
★

4

FRENCH

$–$$ ✕**La Crêpe Nanou.** French chic for the budget-minded is the style in this welcoming little neighborhood bistro, where, during peak hours, there might be a half-hour wait for a table. Left Bank Paris is evoked by the woven café chairs out on the sidewalk and awnings that resemble metro-station architecture. The Gallic focus is evident in the filet mignon, which is served with one of several classic French sauces. Other reliable standbys are the pâté maison, hearty lentil soup, and lavish dessert crepes. Space is a little tight in the oddly configured dining areas, but the whimsical paintings and profuse greenery combine to create an inviting room. ✉*1410 Robert St., Uptown* ☎*504/899–2670* ✍*Reservations not accepted* ▭*AE, DC, MC, V* ◎*No lunch.*

ITALIAN

$–$$$ ✕**Pascal's Manale.** This restaurant is closely identified with a regional anomaly: barbecue shrimp (which involves neither a barbecue nor barbecue sauce). The original recipe, introduced a half century ago, remains unchanged: jumbo shrimp, still in the shell, are cooked in a buttery pool enhanced with just the right amount of creole spice and pepper. The rest of the menu, mostly seafood and Italian-style creations, is uneven. Turtle soup, fried eggplant, and raw oysters are good starters. The atmospheric old bar and the two dining rooms were recently restored and refreshed, breathing new life into the venerable eatery. Bartenders mix proper Sazeracs. ✉*1838 Napoleon Ave., Uptown* ☎*504/895–4877* ✍*Reservations essential* ▭*AE, D, DC, MC, V* ◎*Closed Sun. No lunch.*

JAPANESE

¢–$$ ✕**Kyoto.** Part of a three-block commercial pocket of residential Uptown, Kyoto is as much a neighborhood restaurant as it is a destination for fresh fish and slightly Americanized sushi preparations. Behind the sushi bar in the front room, sushi chefs oversee the creation of off-menu rolls (the Steve Roll contains tuna, snow crab, salmon, and avocado); ask the chefs what special rolls are available. The tuna *tataki*, perhaps Kyoto's most frequently ordered item, is a masterpiece of ruby-red tuna, avocado, and a soy sauce tarted up with lime juice. Full of wooden tables and college students, the two dining rooms are bright and relaxed. ✉*4920 Prytania St., Uptown* ☎*504/891–3644* ▭*AE, D, MC, V* ◎*Closed Sun.*

SEAFOOD

¢–$$ ✕**Casamento's.** Tiled in gleaming white and cream-color ceramic, FodorśChoice Casamento's has been a haven for Uptown seafood lovers since 1919. ★ Family members still wait tables and staff the immaculate kitchen out back, while a reliable handful of oyster shuckers ensure that plenty of cold ones are available for the standing-room-only oyster bar. Specialties from the diminutive menu include oysters lightly poached in seasoned milk; fried shrimp, trout, and soft-shell-crab platters; and fried oysters, impeccably fresh and greaseless, served between thick slices of white toast. Everything is clean, and nothing is superfluous. Even the houseplants have a just-polished look. ✉*4330 Magazine St.,*

Uptown ☎*504/895–9761* ⚱*Reservations not accepted* ▤*No credit cards* ⊘*Closed Sun., Mon., and early June–late Aug.*

¢–$ ✕**Franky & Johnny's.** If you're trying to find the quintessential New Orleans neighborhood restaurant, look no further. Team pennants, posters, and football jerseys vie for space on the paneled walls of the low-ceiling bar and dining room, while a jukebox blares beneath them. From the kitchen's steaming cauldrons come freshly boiled shrimp, crabs, and crawfish, piled high and ready to be washed down with ice-cold beer. The daily po'boy roster might feature fried crawfish tails or oysters, meatballs in tomato sauce, or roast beef with gravy, but the fried-shrimp po'boy is Franky & Johnny's calling card. Table service is efficient. ⊠*321 Arabella St., Uptown* ☎*504/899–9146* ⚱*Reservations not accepted* ▤*AE, D, MC, V.*

SOUTHERN

$$ ✕**Dante's Kitchen.** Ask local chefs where they dine on their day off, and chances are a good number of them will mention Dante's Kitchen. Chef Emmanuel Loubier, a nine-year veteran of Commander's Palace, prepares seasonal menus for those with a sense of adventure. Duck breast is served with root beer–candied sweet potatoes, pork loin is tangerine-glazed, and beef tenderloin is topped with pork "debris." Desserts, such as the sweet-potato-and-white-chocolate pie, are homey and hearty. An outdoor patio is especially welcoming on cooler nights and during weekend brunches. ⊠*736 Dante St., Uptown* ☎*504/861–3121* ▤*AE, D, DC, MC, V.*

$$$–$$$$ ✕ **ONE.** Intimate, neighborhoody, and chic all at once, ONE is to neighborhood eateries as boutique hotels are to big-box hotels. The interior is sleek and sophisticated, while the kitchen is wide open. Guests can even request a seat at the food bar, where the chef cooks the food before your eyes. Chef Scott Snodgrass and co-owner Lee McCullough are the perfect hosts, and seem to love every minute of it. Typical of Snodgrass's creations are stewed country ribs in a red wine demi glace, or a grilled beef tenderloin with warm beef shoulder rillete and Stilton cheese. This is a place to dine slowly and linger over a good brandy. ⊠ 8132 Hampson St., *Uptown* ☎504/301–9061 ▤ *AE, D, DC, MC, V.*

THAI

$–$$ ✕**Basil Leaf.** Familiar Thai standbys—spring rolls, pad Thai, chicken-and-coconut soup, and the like—get a new lease on life in the kitchen of chef-proprietor Siam Tiparwat. These expertly prepared traditional dishes are backed up by a slew of thoroughly original creations served in the crisp, simple dining room, which is enlivened by a mural depicting a Buddhist temple. Gently flavored green and red Thai curries, especially those with chicken or shrimp, are prepared with the instinctual talent of a Thai native, as are the firm yet tender dumplings filled with bits of scallop. The sautéed calamari in basil red curry sauce is addictive. ⊠*1438 S. Carrollton Ave., Uptown* ☎*504/862–9001* ▤*AE, D, MC, V* ⊘*No lunch weekends.*

MID-CITY

CAJUN/CREOLE

¢–$ ✕**Liuzza's by the Track.** Fried-oyster po'boys drenched in garlic butter, milky bowls of sweet-corn-and-crawfish bisque, and grilled Reuben sandwiches with succulent corned beef are some of the reasons you might decide to tolerate the poor ventilation in this barroom near the racetrack and Jazz Fest grounds. The seafood gumbo is always different and always good—thin on body, but heavy on spice. The pièce de résistance here is a barbecue-shrimp po'boy, for which the shrimp are cooked in a bracing lemon-pepper butter with enough garlic to cure a cold. ✉ *1518 N. Lopez St., Mid-City* ☎ *504/943–8667* ⚑ *Reservations not accepted* ═ *AE, D, MC, V* ☾ *Closed Sun.*

Fodor'sChoice
★

$–$$ ✕ **Mandina's.** Although New Orleans boasts many nationally known restaurants, locals here are most attracted to the city's neighborhood corner restaurant. Mandina's has been a fixture on Canal Street for decades, serving just the right combination of expected favorites, including étouffée, jambalaya, po-boys, fried seafood, and perfect pastas. A recent full renovation has done nothing to dampen locals' love for this place, nor has it diminished the full flavors of the house shrimp rémoulade, crawfish cakes, turtle soup, or tender red beans with Italian sausage. If you are looking for the ideal bar and restaurant to spend a football Sunday, this is your place, complete with flat-screen TVs and the iciest brewskis in town. ✉ *3900 Canal St., Mid-City* ☎ *504/482–9179* ═ *AE, D, DC, MC, V.*

♺ ¢–$$ ✕**Ye Olde College Inn.** A stalwart neighborhood joint, the College Inn now occupies a brand-new building, after decades in the older structure next door. Although the menu remains largely untouched, it is a bit more limited. The flat, greasy burgers are still among the best in town, particularly when ordered with fresh-cut French fries and a hot-pink nectar cream soda. The fried-green-tomato-and-shrimp rémoulade po-boy is one of the most delightfully indulgent sandwiches in town. A seat at the horseshoe-shape oyster bar is arguably one of the best in town, but locals miss the aged ambience of the old location. ✉ *3016 S. Carrollton Ave., Mid-City* ☎ *504/866–3683* ═ *AE, D, MC, V* ☾ *No dinner Sun. and Mon.*

CREOLE

★ $$–$$$ ✕**Ralph's on the Park.** Seasoned restaurateur Ralph Brennan conceived this beautifully renovated historic building to provide a menu that mixes contemporary creole regulars with innovative new ideas. Chef Gus Martin excels with full-flavored seafood dishes like blackened redfish served with a peppery crab cake, or gulf shrimp with creole tasso in roasted garlic sauce. By all means, try the pan-seared foie gras appetizer over a sweet-potato pancake. For Sunday brunch, the veal grillades and thyme goat cheese grits will remind you that you are way down South. Vegetarians and produce-lovers are treated to an entire vegetarian menu, and the solid wine list is always evolving. ✉ *900 City Park Ave., Mid-City* ☎ *504/488–1000* ⚑ *Reservations essential* ═ *AE, MC, V* ☾ *Closed Mon. No dinner Sun.*

10 Places to Eat for Under $10

Angeli on Decatur. This corner restaurant has huge windows, perfect for watching the parade of Decatur Street's pierced, tattooed, and woozy nightlife while you nosh on pizza, burgers, or Middle Eastern appetizers. The kitchen stays open late on weekends. ✉ *1141 Decatur St., French Quarter* ☎ *504/566–0077.*

Balcony Bar & Café. The kitchen at this popular Uptown bar stays open as late—sometimes as late as 4 AM on weekends. The menu includes burgers, pizza, and various fried objects; a stiff margarita washes it all down. ✉ *3201 Magazine St., Uptown* ☎ *504/895–1600.*

Café du Monde. At the end of some nights, only a mouthful of sugary fried dough will do. Café du Monde is ready with beignets and coffee or hot chocolate. They pride themselves on never closing. ✉ *800 Decatur St., French Quarter* ☎ *504/525–4544.*

Clover Grill. As much a scene as a restaurant, this classic diner in the heart of the Quarter's gay section serves up waffles, omelets, and hamburgers grilled under abandoned hubcaps to devoted locals and the post-disco set. ✉ *900 Bourbon St., French Quarter* ☎ *504/598–1010.*

The Joint. While you may be hard-pressed to find good barbecue in New Orleans, the tiny nondescript "joint" is the exception to the rule. The only item higher than $10 is a rack of ribs for $10.95. Try the signature beer or lemonade with hot sauce. Really. ✉ *801 Poland Ave., Bywater* ☎ *504/949–3232.*

Juan's Flying Burrito. You may have to wait a half hour for a table, but the jerk chicken burritos and spicy shrimp quesadillas are worth it. The margaritas are powerful, and the bill is easy on your wallet. ✉ *4724 S. Carrollton Ave., Mid-City* ☎ *504/486–9950* ✉ *2018 Magazine St., Uptown* ☎ *504/569–0000..*

La Peniche. A cult classic and a short stroll from the music clubs of Frenchmen Street, La Peniche is the post-party kitchen of choice among musicians and various hipsters. Pancakes, omelets, and burgers, along with local specialties like red beans and rice, are the standard fare. They're closed Tuesday night through Thursday morning. ✉ *1940 Dauphine St., Faubourg Marigny* ☎ *504/943–1460.*

Mimi's. This hip, friendly bar serves up a delicious menu of hot and cold tapas such as mushroom Manchego toast, grilled pork tenderloin with guava sauce, and salmon with saffron aioli. You can nosh on a cheese and olive plate or serrano ham and chorizo plate. Mimi's serves tapas until 2 AM on weekdays and 4 AM on weekends. ✉ *2601 Royal St., Bywater* ☎ *504/942–0690.*

Parkway Bakery & Tavern. Whether it's a sloppy, fully dressed roast beef po'boy; a thick, oversize burger; or a hot dog with perfectly seasoned chili, it all comes in under 10 bucks. Half of the fun here is perusing the 20th-Century New Orleans memorabilia on the walls. ✉ *538 N. Hagan St., Mid-City* ☎ *504/482–3047.*

Trolley Stop Cafe. The exterior of this former gas station has been artfully transformed into a replica of a New Orleans streetcar. Inside, the lengthy menu features every conceivable breakfast dish and a full selection of sandwiches, salads, and soups. ✉ *1923 St. Charles Ave., Garden District* ☎ *504/523–0090.*

¢–$ ✗ **Two Sister's Kitchen.** A bona fide creole soul experience awaits at this family-owned eatery. Think fried chicken with macaroni and cheese; shrimp-and-okra stew; and deep, dark, oily kitchen-sink gumbo. Chitterlings, smothered rabbit, and stewed hen also roll out of the kitchen in record time, as steam tables keep most of the prepared food warm during the hectic lunch rushes. As you dine, you're likely to overhear musicians recapping the previous evening's jazz performance. With its vinyl-topped tables and television, the dining room is far from spotless—but it's the epitome of homey. The kitchen closes by 4 PM. ⊠223 N. Derbigny St., Mid-City ☎504/524–0056 ⚞Reservations not accepted ⊟No credit cards ⊘Closed Sun. No dinner.

DESSERT

¢–$ ✗ **Angelo Brocato's.** Traditional Sicilian fruit sherbets, ice creams, pastries, and candies are the attractions at this quaint little sweetshop that harks back to the time when the French Quarter was peopled mostly by Italian immigrants. The shop has since moved to the Mid-City area, but the biscotti, cannoli, and the lemon and strawberry ices haven't lost their status as local favorites. The shop closes at 10 PM weekdays (except Monday), 10:30 PM weekends. ⊠214 N. Carrollton Ave., Mid-City ☎504/488–1465 ⊟D, MC, V. ⊘Closed Mon.

Fodor'sChoice ★

FRENCH

$–$$ ✗ **Café Degas.** Dining at Café Degas is like dining at a sidewalk café in Paris, even though the restaurant is completely covered. There's a tree growing through the center of the dining room, and the front windows overlook picturesque Esplanade Avenue. Employees are matter-of-fact, in a relaxing European way. The regular fare here—pâté, onion soup, steamed mussels, duck in orange sauce, steaks, dessert crepes—is a mixture of French-bistro cooking and what you might find at a countryside inn. Daily specials, such as a perfectly chilled, creamy vichyssoise, are always creative and ingenious. ⊠3127 Esplanade Ave., Mid-City ☎504/945–5635 ⊟AE, D, DC, MC, V ⊘Closed Mon. and Tues.

PO'BOYS & OTHER SANDWICHES

$–$$ ✗ **La Vita.** This tiny, oddly shaped building has been home to several failed restaurants, but the neighborhood seems to have latched on to its most-recent occupant. That probably has a lot to do with La Vita's authentic Italian cuisine. Sauces are slow cooked, and full of flavor. Pizzas are baked in a specially designed wood-burning oven that produces a perfect crust, and salads are fresh and generously portioned—especially the Caprese salad with fresh mozzarella and locally grown creole cherry tomatoes. If you're in the mood for pasta, you can't go wrong with the Manicotti Quatro Formagio, with tomato basil sauce. ⊠3201 Esplanade Ave., Mid-City ☎504/943–0990 ⊛www.lavitapizza.com ⚞Reservations not accepted ⊟AE, D, DC, MC, V ⊘Closed Sun.

★ $ ✗ **Parkway Bakery & Tavern.** Contractor-by-trade Jay Nix resurrected more than just a dilapidated building when he reopened Parkway: he also brought back to life a dormant community spirit. You can find neighbors and regulars from other parts of the city sinking into Parkway's roast beef and grilled-ham po'boys; some simply wander in for a hot dog and beer at the bar, and to glance around at the New Orleans nostalgia decorating the walls. Local favorite Hubig's fried pies are the only desserts—you can chart the seasons by the available flavors. As it's near the fairgrounds, Parkway jumps during Jazz Fest. ✉ *538 Hagan Ave., Mid-City* ☎*504/482–3047* ⌨*Reservations not accepted* ▭*AE, D, MC, V.*

BYWATER

BARBECUE

¢–$$ ✕**The Joint.** The owners couldn't have chosen a more-appropriate name for this canary-yellow cinder-block building pressed up against the railroad tracks. If the color doesn't draw you in, the smell of meat—pork shoulder, pork ribs, beef brisket—cooking in the custom-made smoker out back will. Side dishes go above and beyond in concept and execution, particularly the sweet-and-sour baked beans, and the crispy-on-the-outside mac and cheese. Lemon pound cake is a fitting country dessert. Order takeout if comfort is a priority, as picnic tables and a jukebox set a spartan stage in the cool dining room. ✉*801 Poland Ave., Bywater<ZIP>70119* ☎*504/949–3232* ⌨*Reservations not accepted* ▭*MC, V* ☉*Closed Tues. and Wed.*

SOUTHERN

☾ ¢–$ ✕**Elizabeth's.** "Real food, done real good" is the motto at Elizabeth's, a real down-home Southern joint where the vinyl-print tablecloths look just like grandma's, and where breakfast is the most important meal of the day. The menu offers everything from traditional po'boys (try the "Big Ass Hamburger"), to a stellar braised lamb shank with roasted garlic, to crispy fried chicken livers with pepper jelly. The fried seafood platters are huge and moderately priced, and the fried-oyster po'boy is irresistible. Work off your breakfast upstairs with a game of pool. The staff is spunky, and so is the Bywater neighborhood clientele. ✉*601 Gallier St., Bywater* ☎*504/944–9272* ⌨*Reservations not accepted* ▭*MC, V* ☉*Closed Mon. and Tues. No dinner Sun.*

Fodor'sChoice
★

OUTSIDE CITY LIMITS

BELGIAN

$–$$ ✕**Clementine's Belgian Bistrot.** Affordable Belgian home cooking, more pleasing to the palate than to the eye, is in great abundance at this tucked-away suburban bistro. Beef stew made with Belgian ale, veal meatballs in red sauce, and mussels steamed in variously seasoned white-wine broths all come with freshly cut Belgian fries. Only the most-disciplined diners can keep to just one order. Savory and sweet crepes, made-to-order and thicker than the French variety, are the greatest bargains. A fine selection of Belgian beers encourages lingering in the lodgelike environs. Call for directions. ✉*2505 Whitney Ave., Gretna* ☎*504/366–3995* ▭*D, MC, V* ☉*Closed Sun. and Mon.*

CAJUN/CREOLE

★ ☾ ¢–$ ✕**Crabby Jack's.** Panéed rabbit po'boys, fried-green-tomato-and-shrimp rémoulade salads, and fried chicken draw legions of urban New Orleanians out to Jefferson. Crabby Jack's is a down-home, boxy joint; it's not exactly comfortable, but since the food is too good to wait for, most people eat here. Smoky red beans, muffulettas, and jambalaya are all first rate and cheap, though the creative fresh-fish specials provide a more-definitive experience. This is also the site of a seafood wholesaler, and the seasonal boiled seafood couldn't get any fresher. ⊠*428 Jefferson Hwy., Jefferson* ☎*504/833–2722* ▤*AE, D, MC, V* ☾*Closed Sun. No dinner.*

☾ $–$$$ ✕**Restaurant des Familles.** No time for a trip to Cajun country? This restaurant, about a half-hour's drive from central New Orleans, is the next best thing (although you'd better ask for directions when reserving a table). Just a few yards from the vast windows are the slow-moving waters of Bayou des Familles, providing a primeval tableau. Dramatically illuminated at night, the huge Acadian-style raised cottage has a kitchen that produces familiar, and locally beloved, seafood in the creole style—shrimp rémoulade, crawfish étouffée, turtle soup, redfish meunière, and fried oysters and bacon en brochette. The oyster-and-artichoke soup is one of the best around. ⊠*Rte. 3134, north of the intersection with Rte. 45, Crown Point* ☎*504/689–7834* ⌖*Reservations essential* ▤*AE, D, MC, V* ☾*Closed Mon. and Tues.*

CREOLE

★ $$–$$$$ ✕**Dakota.** Warm colors, lustrous woods, and floral accents set the scene at Dakota, the most successfully ambitious restaurant on the north shore. Owner-chef Kim Kringlie's inspirations may be multicultural, but his seasonal menus are solidly grounded in south Louisiana. A crackly soft-shell crab is stuffed with a variety of expertly seasoned shellfish. Oysters are char-grilled with Parmesan cheese, herbs, and truffle oil. Pork tenderloin is smoked and glazed with cane syrup before it's brushed with bourbon-barbecue butter. ⊠*629 U.S. 190, Covington* ☎*985/892–3712* ▤*AE, DC, MC, V* ☾*Closed Sun. No lunch Sat.*

FRENCH

$$–$$$ ✕**La Provence.** It's almost an hour's drive from central New Orleans, but the glorious French-provincial food and relaxing atmosphere of this exceptional restaurant are well worth the trip. Braised local rabbit with fennel, tomatoes, and garlic are exceptional, and the house-made ricotta dumplings with jumbo lump crabmeat and fresh herbs are the answer to a cold winter's night. Separating the two dining rooms, hung with pleasant Provençal landscape paintings, is a hearth that welcomes you on damp winter days. In warmer seasons, the tree-shaded deck is almost as congenial. ⊠*U.S. 190, 7 mi from the Lake Pontchartrain Causeway, Lacombe* ☎*985/626–7662* ⌖*Reservations essential* ▤*AE, MC, V* ☾*Closed Mon. and Tues. No lunch Wed.–Sat.*

$$–$$$$ ✕**Le Parvenu.** Inside a cozy little cottage, Le Parvenu's homey mood is reinforced by pastel-hue dining rooms lined with flouncy drapery and unobtrusive prints. "Classic" is the word that comes to mind time and again with the authentic French-creole menus. Breaded lobster tails join

lumps of first-quality crabmeat, crawfish, and shrimp in a sauce tinged with cognac. The sweet edge of a plum sauce moderates the earthy flavor of a rack of pink and juicy lamb chops. Cream soups are a specialty, and the best may be a bisque of mirliton dotted with bits of shrimp and crab. ⊠ *509 Williams Blvd., Kenner* ☎ *504/471–0534* ⚠ *Reservations essential* ⊟ *AE, DC, MC, V.*

ITALIAN

$–$$$
Fodor's Choice
★

✕ **Mosca's.** The food here—combining Louisiana ingredients and Italian ingenuity—is good enough to lure city folk to isolation about 30 minutes from the city. Baked oysters with bread crumbs, olive oil, garlic, and herbs approach the summit of Italian-creole cuisine. The Italian shrimp are cooked in an herbed mix of olive oil and spices, the roasted chicken with rosemary is luscious, and the house-made Italian sausage is full of peppery goodness. Getting a table usually means waiting at the bar, even if you have made reservations (not accepted Saturday). ⊠ *4137 U.S. Hwy. 90, Avondale* ☎ *504/436–9942* ⚠ *Reservations essential* ⊟ *No credit cards* ☉ *Closed Sun. and Mon. No lunch.*

MEDITERRANEAN

$–$$$

✕ **Vega Tapas Café.** The word *tapas* in the name is deceptive, since the serving sizes at Vega are closer to those of appetizers, with prices correspondingly lower. The high success rate of the dishes, mostly Mediterranean-inspired, enhances the adventure. If there is a calling card here, it's the chef's "lamb lollipops," glazed with sherry and served with violet-grape mustard. There is an educated selection of wines, many of them Spanish, and specialty cocktails. Everything is served in a large, minimally decorated room lined with hard surfaces, which ups the noise level a couple of notches. ⊠ *2051 Metairie Rd., Metairie* ☎ *504/836–2007* ⊟ *AE, D, DC, MC, V* ☉ *No lunch.*

VIETNAMESE

¢–$
Fodor's Choice
★

✕ **Tan Dinh.** Serving arguably the best Vietnamese food in the area, Tan Dinh is a 20-minute drive from downtown New Orleans, but a world away in flavor. Goat stew with bean curd, roasted quail with sticky rice cakes, steamed flour cakes topped with dried shrimp, and jellyfish salad are among the more-exotic menu items. Spring rolls, noodle soups, and sandwiches, all equally good, might be safer bets for Vietnamese newcomers. With cherry-stained chairs and faux-marble tabletops, the restaurant exhibits a convincing polish. ⊠ *1705 Lafayette St., Gretna* ☎ *504/361–8008* ⚠ *Reservations not accepted* ⊟ *No credit cards* ☉ *Closed Tues.*

Where to Stay

WORD OF MOUTH

"We've stayed at the Soniat House for the past two years and wouldn't consider staying anywhere else when visiting New Orleans! Beautiful rooms, perfect locations, charming staff and oh my lord those biscuits . . ."

—Chrissy

"When we checked into our room [at Loft 523], I was in awe—it was simply beautiful. The furnishings were all modern and simple, but luxurious and exquisite."

—Becky

"[Windsor Court Hotel] is superb in every aspect—especially in service. The staff would die for you! I have nothing to complain about!"

—Matt

By Paul A.
Greenberg

DECIDING WHERE TO STAY IN New Orleans has everything to do with what you want from your visit. To soak up the local color and experience the city's rich culture, a French Quarter hotel or bed-and-breakfast is your best choice. For a quieter, more-serene experience in close proximity to major attractions, head to comfortable properties Uptown, in the Garden District, and in surrounding areas like the Faubourg Marigny. Business travelers will find the elegant, well-appointed Central Business District (CBD) hotels convenient, comfortable, and designed with business in mind. And if you appreciate the contemporary chic ambience of historic warehouses and commercial buildings that have been refashioned into elegant hotels, head to the Warehouse District, where massive spaces with exposed brick walls add distinctive atmosphere to both moderately priced and upscale hotels.

New Orleans honors its European heritage with facilities and services tailored for international travelers, and it attracts families with its diverse collection of tourist attractions. Many hotels are within walking distance of such area attractions as the Riverwalk shopping complex and Harrah's New Orleans Casino. New Orleans, much like New York, is a "walking city." If you are visiting for the first time, try to book one of the hotels that is centrally located and within walking distance of major attractions. Lodging descriptions in this chapter frequently indicate centrally located properties. Many hotels are also located near the city's streetcar lines, which runs the entire length of the city.

When you book, remember to check the hotel's Web site for detailed descriptions or call local reservation services for lists of facilities that meet your price and location needs. Be aware that many hotels run Internet-only specials, and you may find price breaks by hotel shopping online. With respect to physically challenged travelers, all large hotels are in compliance with the Americans with Disabilities Act. Some guesthouses and B&B inns in 19th-century structures are still not fully equipped for people with disabilities.

If you plan to visit the city more than once, try to create a different lodging experience each time. For your first visit, try a large, bustling, downtown hotel; for your next visit, perhaps a romantic getaway in an outlying guesthouse, where old-world charm and atmosphere are so proudly preserved.

WHAT IT COSTS				
$$$$	**$$$**	**$$**	**$**	**¢**
2 PEOPLE	over $275	$200–$275	$150–$199	$100–$149	under $100

Prices are for two people in a standard double room in high season, excluding 13% city and state taxes.

KNOW-HOW

RESERVATIONS

Book your room as far in advance as possible—up to a year ahead for Mardi Gras, Jazz Fest, or other special events.

SERVICES

Most hotels have private baths, central heating, air-conditioning, and private phones. More and more major hotels have added Wi-Fi or in-room broadband Internet service. Most major hotels also have video or high-speed checkout capability and can arrange babysitting. Smaller B&Bs and hotels may not have all of these amenities; ask before you book your room.

Some major hotels have pools; those that do not may have working agreements with nearby health clubs or other facilities to allow guests to use club facilities for a nominal fee.

Most hotels have parking available, but this can run you as much as $30 a day. Valet parking is usually available at the major hotels. If you park on the street, keep in mind that New Orleans meter maids are relentless, and ticketing is imminent for illegally parked vehicles. You can save time and headaches by taking cabs from one part of the city to another.

WHAT IT COSTS

Properties are assigned price categories based on a range from least-expensive standard double rooms at high season (excluding holidays) to most expensive. We list all facilities available, but we do not specify whether they cost extra. When making accommodation inquiries, always ask what is included in the rate.

The lodgings we list are the most desirable in each price category, but these rates are subject to updating and change. Use Fodors.com to shop around for rooms before booking. Many major hotels occasionally offer Internet special rates. Be aware that room rates may be higher in October (considered peak-Convention season) and during the July 4 weekend (due to the annual Essence Music Festival). Rates are also high at the end of April and beginning of May during Jazz Fest.

FRENCH QUARTER/FAUBOURG MARIGNY

Although much of the Quarter is commercially oriented toward tourism, elegant but comfortable hotels and B&Bs or guesthouses are tucked away in remote residential pockets, and a number of grand imposing lodgings are scattered throughout. If you're staying in a busy part of the Quarter, you may want to request a room away from the side of the building that faces the street. In larger hotels, be sure to ask for a room with a balcony or view.

HOTELS

$$$–$$$$ **Astor Crowne Plaza.** Located on the edge of the French Quarter on bustling Canal Street, this property features a rooftop pool with spectacular city views. Dickie Brennan's Bourbon House Restaurant, with the best raw seafood bar in the city, is on the lobby level. All guest rooms have extra-large televisions, Wi-Fi, and elegant, comfy furniture. The hotel is in an artfully restored downtown office building, within walking distance of everything that counts in the Quarter and down-

Where to Stay
in Downtown
New Orleans

Louis Armstrong Park

57

N. Rampart St.

Burgundy St.

Dumaine St.

St. Philip St.

Ursulines St.

Gov. Nicholls St.

56 Barracks

Dauphine St.

47

48

55 St.

Bourbon St.

St. Peter St.

Orleans St.

St. Ann St.

46

Royal St.

50 **51**

52

54

Chartres St.

53

Jackson Square

Madison St.

49

Moon Walk

0 ——— 1/4 mi

0 ——— 1/4 km

5

Ambassador Hotel **18**
Astor Crowne Plaza **32**
Bienville House Hotel **36**
Bon Maison Guest House **47**
Bourbon Orleans Hotel **46**
Chateau Sonesta **31**
Claiborne Mansion **54**
Courtyard by Marriott **27**
Dauphine Orleans **41**
Depot House at Madame Julia's **1**
Doubletree Hotel **20**
Embassy Suites **8**
Garlands Guest House
& Creole Cottages **57**
Hampton Inn **22**
Hampton Inn and Suites—
Convention Center **10**
Harrah's New Orleans Hotel **13**
Holiday Inn–Chateau Le Moyne **40**
Holiday Inn French Quarter **33**
Homewood Suites **2**
Hotel InterContinental **7**
Hotel Maison de Ville **44**
Hotel New Orleans **11**
Hotel Provincial **49**
Hotel Royal **51**
Hotel Villa Convento **50**
International House **26**
La Quinta Inn and Suites
Downtown **24**
Lafayette Hotel **5**
Lafitte Guest House **48**
Le Pavillon Hotel **3**
Le Richelieu in the French Quarter ...**53**
Loews New Orleans Hotel **14**
Loft 523 ....**28**
Maison Dupuy **45**
Melrose Mansion **56**
Monteleone Hotel **38**
New Orleans Hilton Riverside **12**
New Orleans Marriott Hotel **34**
Omni Royal Orleans Hotel **43**
Parc St. Charles **6**
Pelham Hotel **21**
Queen & Crescent Hotel **23**
Ramada Plaza Inn
on Bourbon Street **42**
Renaissance Arts Hotel **9**
Renaissance Pere Marquette **29**
The Ritz Carlton New Orleans **30**
Royal Sonesta Hotel **39**
Sheraton New Orleans **25**
Soniat House **52**
Staybridge Suites New Orleans **15**
St. James Hotel **19**
Vieux Carré Palms **55**
W Hotel New Orleans **17**
W Hotel New Orleans
French Quarter **37**
Westin Canal Place **35**
The Whitney **4**
Windsor Court Hotel **16**

town. **Pros:** Within walking distance of all of the local attractions that matter, large guest rooms. **Cons:** Unimaginative decor, main entrance opens on to the busiest corner of the busiest street in the city. ✉*739 Canal St., French Quarter,* ☎*504/962–0500 or 800/684–1127* ⊕*www. astorcrowneplaza.com* ↩*707 rooms, 25 suites* ⚐*In-room: Wi-Fi. In-hotel: restaurant, room service, bar, pool* ▤*AE, D, DC, MC, V.*

$$–$$$$ ▣**Bienville House Hotel.** Small and intimate, this is the place for travelers searching for the ambience of gracious old New Orleans. The property was renovated in 2007, and is in an exciting area of the Quarter, with colorful shops, restaurants, and entertainment venues nearby. Lovely guest rooms are furnished with antiques and reproduction pieces; some have balconies overlooking one of the most beautiful courtyards in the city. The hotel is within walking distance of some of the best restaurants in the Quarter, but has no restaurant of its own. **Pros:** Close to French Quarter attractions, downtown restaurants, riverfront, and Harrah's Casino. **Cons:** A bit pricey, noise carries inside at night from the street. ✉*320 Decatur St., French Quarter,* ☎*504/529–2345* ⊕*www.bien villehouse.com* ↩*80 rooms, 3 suites* ⚐*In-room: Wi-Fi. In-hotel: restaurant, bar, pool, laundry service, parking (fee)* ▤*AE, D, MC, V.*

$$–$$$$ ▣**Bourbon Orleans Hotel.** Located in the absolute center of the French Quarter, this property has been exquisitely renovated. The lobby level exudes turn-of-the-20th-century New Orleans glamour, and includes the consistently outstanding Paillard's Restaurant. Guest rooms are spacious and well appointed, but those that face the street are a bit hard on the ears, due to all of the nightly activity on Bourbon Street. Business travelers will appreciate ergonomic office chairs and in-room Wi-Fi. The Lobby-level Bourbon Oh! bar is a quiet place to have cocktails and people-watch through wall-to-wall windows, and Napoleon's Itch bar is great for late-night Bourbon Street fun. **Pros:** Recent renovation was very meticulous. **Cons:** Lobby level is often crowded and noisy with curious passers-by; hotel is steps from loud, 24-hour Bourbon Street bars. ✉*717 Orleans Ave., French Quarter,* ☎*504/523–2222* ⊕*www. bourbonorleans.com* ↩*346 rooms, 16 suites* ⚐*In-room: Wi-Fi. In-hotel: restaurant, bars, gym, parking (fee)* ▤*AE, D, DC, MC.*

$$–$$$$ ▣**Chateau Sonesta.** John Kennedy Toole's comic masterpiece, *A Confederacy of Dunces,* begins under the clock of D.H. Holmes department store on Canal Street, now this well-maintained upscale hotel. In Toole's honor, the clock and a statue of the novel's antihero, Ignatius J. Reilly, remain. Rooms at the hotel are large, with high ceilings and neutral decor; some have columns and beams, remnants of the original building. Balcony rooms overlook Bourbon Street, Dauphine Street, or one of two interior courtyards. Three suites with whirlpool baths surround an atrium. The hotel dining room, Tiempo, is open only for breakfast. **Pros:** Within walking distance of all French Quarter attractions, Red Fish Grille is adjacent to the hotel. **Cons:** Hotel dining room serves breakfast only, high-traffic intersection located just outside the main entrance. ✉*800 Iberville St., French Quarter,* ☎*504/586–0800 or 800/766–3782* ⊕*www.chateausonesta.com* ↩*251 rooms, 11 suites* ⚐*In-room: Wi-Fi. In-hotel: restaurant, room service, bar, pool, gym, parking (fee)* ▤*AE, D, DC, MC, V.*

$–$$$ 🏨 **Dauphine Orleans.** This French Quarter property is comfortable but not exceptional. The average-size rooms have good-quality fabrics; each has an iron and ironing board, a hair dryer, and two bathrobes. Rooms and suites are located in the main building, in a smaller building, and in cottages. The lounge is an erstwhile 19th-century bordello, and the exercise room is a small 19th-century creole cottage just off the pool. **Pros:** Minutes from Bourbon Street—but far enough away that it's quiet. **Con:** Utilitarian decor. ✉*415 Dauphine St., French Quarter,* ☎*504/586–1800 or 800/521–7111* ⊕*www.dauphineorleans.com* ⬅*104 rooms, 7 suites* ♿*In-room: Ethernet. In-hotel: bar, pool, gym, public Wi-Fi, parking (fee)* ▤*AE, D, DC, MC, V.*

★ $–$$$ 🏨 **Holiday Inn–Chateau Le Moyne.** This quiet hotel one block off Bourbon Street exudes old-world atmosphere with its traditional New Orleans architecture and period furnishings. Eight suites are in creole cottages off a tropical courtyard; all rooms are furnished with antiques and reproductions and have coffeemakers, hair dryers, and irons and ironing boards. **Pros:** Great location, affordable rates. **Cons:** Chain property. ✉*301 Dauphine St., French Quarter,* ☎*504/581–1303 or 800/465–4329* ⊕*www.holiday-inn.com* ⬅*160 rooms, 11 suites* ♿*In-room: Wi-Fi. In-hotel: restaurant, bar, pool, parking (fee)* ▤*AE, D, DC, MC, V.*

$$–$$$$ 🏨 **Holiday Inn French Quarter.** Although this could be a Holiday Inn in Anytown, USA, the advantage here is the location. This clean, busy, centrally located property is within walking distance of all the major French Quarter restaurants and the Central Business District. It's a good place to stay with kids (there are on-site laundry facilities). A nice indoor pool makes up for the lack of luxury. **Pros:** Moderately priced by French Quarter standards, adjacent to Checkered Parrot theme restaurant. **Cons:** Utilitarian accommodations, slow elevators. ✉*124 Royal St., French Quarter,* ☎*504/529–7211 or 800/448–2296* ⊕*www.holiday-inn.com* ⬅*374 rooms* ♿*In-room: Ethernet. In-hotel: restaurant, room service, bar, pool* ▤*AE, D, DC, MC, V.*

$$–$$$$ 🏨 **Hotel Maison de Ville.** Delightfully secluded amid the hustle and bustle **Fodor'sChoice** of the French Quarter, this property oozes refined elegance and romance. **★** Tapestry-covered chairs, a gas fire burning in the sitting room, and antiques-furnished rooms all contribute to a 19th-century atmosphere. Some rooms are in former slave quarters in the courtyard; others are on the upper floors of the main house. Breakfast is served on a silver tray, and port and sherry are available in the afternoon. For a special hideaway, book one of the hotel's Audubon Cottages. The Bistro at Maison de Ville is one of the best-kept culinary secrets in the French Quarter. **Pros:** Unique rooms, personal and consistently above-average service. **Con:** Tough to get a reservation. ✉*727 Toulouse St., French Quarter,* ☎*504/561–5858 or 800/634–1600* ⊕*www.maisondeville.com* ⬅*14 rooms, 2 suites, 7 cottages* ♿*In-room: Wi-Fi. In-hotel: pool, parking (fee), no kids under 12* ▤*AE, D, DC, MC, V* ⧦*CP.*

$$–$$$$ 🏨 **Hotel Provincial.** The next time you want to stay in a "real New Orleans hotel," consider this one. The interiors have 19th-century touches, with exposed brick walls, a lush courtyard with iron grillwork, and buildings that date back to the French Quarter's earliest years. The bright rooms are a good size, and many overlook the courtyard. It's like stepping back in time—but with all the modern conveniences. A big plus at this hotel is Stella!, Chef Scott Boswell's fine-dining restaurant. One of the best dining spots in the city, it's a bit pricey, but totally worth it. **Pros:** Quaint atmosphere, quiet surroundings (in a residential section of the French Quarter). **Cons:** Rates can be on the pricey side. ✉*1024 Chartres St., French Quarter,* ☎*504/581–4995 or 800/535–7922* ⊕*www.hotelprovincial.com* ✍*93 rooms, 6 suites* ⌂*In-room: Ethernet. In-hotel: restaurant, bar, pool, parking (fee)* ⊟*AE, D, DC, MC, V.*

★ **$–$$$**   🏠**Le Richelieu in the French Quarter.** Close to the Old Ursuline Convent and the French Market, Le Richelieu combines the friendly personal charm of a small hotel with luxe touches (upscale toiletries, hair dryers)—at a moderate rate. Some rooms have mirrored walls and large walk-in closets, and all have brass ceiling fans, irons, and ironing boards. A recent renovation has significantly freshened the place up. Balcony rooms have the same rates as standard rooms (you can request a balcony when you reserve, but the hotel will not guarantee one). An intimate bar and café is off the courtyard, with tables on the terrace by the pool. Many regular customers wouldn't stay anywhere else. **Pros:** Great value, excellent service, some rooms have balconies. **Cons:** Not all rooms have balconies. ✉*1234 Chartres St., French Quarter,* ☎*504/529–2492 or 800/535–9653* ⊕*www.lerichelieuhotel.com* ✍*69 rooms, 17 suites* ⌂*In-room: refrigerator, Wi-Fi. In-hotel: restaurant, bar, pool, concierge, parking (no fee)* ⊟*AE, D, DC, MC, V.*

$–$$$ 🏠**Maison Dupuy.** Seven restored 19th-century town houses surround one of the Quarter's prettiest courtyards, anchored by a spectacular fountain. Lush tropical greenery and palm trees provide a serene setting for meals and cocktails, and soft lighting and comfortable seating add to the courtyard's attraction. Most rooms are fairly large, and some have balconies. Chef Dominique Macquet is the guiding force at Dominique, the hotel's stellar restaurant, which specializes in Louisiana and Caribbean cuisine (dinner only). For more-casual dining, the adjacent French Quarter Bistro serves breakfast, lunch, and dinner. The hotel is two blocks from Bourbon Street. **Pros:** Close to the heart of the French Quarter, excellent hotel restaurant. **Cons:** Not all rooms have balconies. ✉*1001 Toulouse St., French Quarter,* ☎*504/586–8000 or 800/535–9177* ⊕*www.maisondupuy.com* ✍*187 rooms, 13 suites* ⌂*In-room: Wi-Fi. In-hotel: restaurant, pool, gym, parking (fee)* ⊟*AE, D, DC, MC, V.*

$$$–$$$$ 🏠**Monteleone Hotel.** The grande dame of French Quarter hotels—with its ornate baroque facade, liveried doormen, and shimmering lobby chandeliers—was built in 1886 and renovated in 2004. A stellar addition is the full-service Spa Aria. Rooms are extra large and luxurious, with rich fabrics and a mix of four-poster beds, brass beds, and beds with traditional headboards. Junior suites are spacious; sumptuous VIP suites come with extra pampering. The slowly revolving Carousel piano bar (⇨*Nightlife*) in the lobby is a local landmark, and the first-rate dinner in the hotel's Hunt Room Grill is one of the city's best-kept secrets. There's live jazz every night in the lounge. **Pros:** Ideal central location offering access to French Quarter and downtown locations; civilized, old New Orleans feel; recently reno-

FodorśChoice
★

vated. **Con:** While the Hunt Room Grill is very nice, the hotel's more-casual restaurant offers mediocre food and poor service. ⊠*214 Royal St., French Quarter,* ☎*504/523–3341 or 800/535–9595* ⊕*www.hotelmonteleone.com* ⊸*600 rooms, 55 suites* ⬧*In-room: Wi-Fi. In-hotel: 3 restaurants, bar, pool, gym, spa, concierge, public Wi-Fi*⊟*AE, D, DC, MC, V.*

HAUNTED HOTEL

Generations of guests at the Monteleone have experienced paranormal events. A locked restaurant door opens and closes almost every evening, and an elevator occasionally stops on the wrong floor—leading guests down a hallway that grows chilly; some claim to have seen ghostly images of children playing. In March 2003, the International Society of Paranormal Research investigated and made contact with more than a dozen earthbound entities. Among them were several former employees and a man who died inside the hotel.

$$$–$$$$ 🖼**New Orleans Marriott Hotel.** The Marriott has a fabulous view of the Quarter, the CBD, and the river. It's an easy walk from the Canal Place mall, the Riverwalk, and the Convention Center. Rooms are comfortable, service is friendly (if uneven), and nightly jazz enlivens the lobby—but the hotel lacks New Orleans charm. The Canal Street streetcar line provides convenient access to most parts of the city. Keep in mind that this high-rise convention hotel is located on Canal Street, the busiest street in the downtown area. **Pros:** Good location, very clean. **Cons:** Typical chain hotel, inconsistent service. ⊠*555 Canal St., French Quarter,* ☎*504/581–1000 or 800/228–9290* ⊕*www.neworleansmarriott.com* ⊸*1,290 rooms, 54 suites* ⬧*In-room: Ethernet. In-hotel: restaurant, bar, pool, gym, public Wi-Fi, parking (fee)*⊟*AE, D, DC, MC, V.*

$$$–$$$$ 🖼**Omni Royal Orleans Hotel.** This elegant white-marble hotel built in

Fodor's Choice 1960 is a replica of the grand St. Louis Hotel of the 1800s. Sconce-

★ enhanced columns, gilt mirrors, fan windows, and three magnificent chandeliers re-create the atmosphere of old New Orleans. Some rooms have marble baths and marble-top dressers and tables; others have balconies. The lobby level Rib Room has been one of the city's culinary showpieces for more than 40 years. The rooftop pool has the city's best overhead view of the French Quarter. **Pros:** Old-world elegance, sparkling cleanliness throughout, central location. **Cons:** Some rooms need updating, pool area can get crowded. ⊠*621 St. Louis St., French Quarter,* ☎*504/529–5333 or 800/843–6664* ⊕*www.omnihotels.com* ⊸*346 rooms, 16 suites* ⬧*In-room: Wi-Fi. In-hotel: restaurant, pool, gym, parking (fee)*⊟*AE, D, DC, MC.*

$$$–$$$$ 🖼**Ramada Plaza Inn on Bourbon Street.** Located on the site of New Orleans's original French opera house, this property is not one of the city's most-elegant lodgings—but it is well kept and affordable. Rooms facing the courtyard are quieter, but the 32 with Bourbon Street balconies are coveted during Mardi Gras. The hotel is on one of the busiest blocks of Bourbon Street, so be prepared for 24-hour activity—both outside and in. **Pros:** Good value, ideal for those who want to be in the heart of the French Quarter. **Cons:** Lackluster decor, utilitarian

5

accommodations, slow service. ✉ *541 Bourbon St., French Quarter*, ☎*504/524–7611 or 800/535–7891* ⊕*www.innonbourbon.com* 🛏*186 rooms, 2 suites* ⚴*In-room: Wi-Fi. In-hotel: pool, parking (fee)* ▤*AE, DC, MC, V.*

$$$$ 🖼**Ritz-Carlton New Orleans.** The
Fodor's Choice Ritz occupies the artfully con-
★ verted, historic Maison Blanche department store building with a luxurious hotel reminiscent of old New Orleans. Rooms are furnished with local antiques, and feature oversize marble bathrooms and plush linens. The Club Floor has 75 rooms, including one suite, with a concierge and a private lounge. The expansive lobby, adorned in carefully selected fine art and upscale furnishings found in traditional New Orleans homes, opens onto a luxurious courtyard. The hotel's dining room, Mélange, offers re-creations of signature dishes from high-profile restaurants throughout the city (though the quality of the food is inconsistent). The hotel, within walking distance of most attractions and minutes from the Convention Center, borders the French Quarter and faces the CBD. **Pros:** Luxurious rooms and suites, excellent live evening entertainment, great lobby lounge, world-class spa. **Cons:** Service is uneven and inconsistent service, property has a chain hotel feel. ✉*921 Canal St., French Quarter*, ☎*504/524–1331* ⊕*www.ritzcarlton.com* 🛏*527 rooms, 38 suites* ⚴ *In-hotel: restaurant, bars, spa, parking (fee)* ▤*AE, D, DC, MC, V.*

$$–$$$$ 🖼**Royal Sonesta Hotel.** Step from the revelry of Bourbon Street into
Fodor's Choice the marble elegance of this renowned hotel's lobby, where lush plants
★ enhance a cool, serene atmosphere. Most guest rooms are of average size, furnished with light-color reproduction antiques: many have French doors that open onto balconies or patios. Rooms facing Bourbon Street are noisy, but most are sufficiently soundproof. Begue's Restaurant is locally beloved and presents one of the city's best Sunday buffet brunches; the charming Desire Oyster Bar, on the lobby level, faces Bourbon Street and serves local seafood delicacies. **Pros:** Outstanding service; bustling, cavernous lobby; great balcony views of the Quarter. **Con:** Consistent high occupancy can lead to slow elevator service. ✉*300 Bourbon St., French Quarter*, ☎*504/586–0300 or 800/766–3782* ⊕*www.royalsonestano.com* 🛏*500 rooms, 32 suites* ⚴*In-room: Wi-Fi. In-hotel: 2 restaurants, bar, pool, gym, concierge, parking (fee)* ▤*AE, D, DC, MC, V.*

$$$$ 🖼**W Hotel New Orleans French Quarter.** This sleekly renovated modern hotel has one of the best locations in the Quarter. Most rooms are in the main building, and many have balconies that overlook either the courtyard or Chartres Street. Some have French doors that open

---

CLIMBERS BEWARE!

One of the best Mardi Gras parade viewing spots in town is the Royal Sonesta Hotel balcony. To keep revelers from climbing up from the street below, the staff greases all the support poles with petroleum jelly. The media turns out in droves, and the hotel turns the event into a party. For many New Orleanians, this odd event signifies the true beginning to Mardi Gras weekend. Festivities start at 10 AM the Friday before Mardi Gras; after the poles are greased, many attendees flood into the hotel for a lavish seafood buffet.

directly onto a sundeck. Two of the four carriage-house suites share a cheery sundeck; others overlook the courtyard. The hotel is adjacent to Bacco, a contemporary Italian eatery operated by renowned restaurateur Ralph Brennan. The hotel also provides a "Whatever, whenever" policy—24-hour concierges will find those barbecued ribs you're craving at 3 AM, arrange a deep-tissue massage—even track down a last-minute gown for a Mardi Gras ball. Pros: Well-kept rooms and public areas, great restaurant. Con: A bit too "hip" for the French Quarter—the place feels more like SoHo than New Orleans. ⊠ *316 Chartres St., French Quarter,* ☎ *504/581–1200 or 800/448–4927* ⊕ *www.whotels. com* ⬢ *98 rooms, 4 suites* ⬙ *In-room: Wi-Fi. In-hotel: restaurant, bar, pool, parking (fee)* ▭ *AE, D, DC, MC, V.*

$$$–$$$$ ☷ **Westin Canal Place.** The Westin was designed with great views in mind. The huge, rose, Carrara-marble lobby, with European antiques, jardinieres, and grand piano, is on the 11th floor of the Canal Place shopping mall; tea is served daily in the lobby or the River 127 Restaurant, which has one of the few upscale bars in the city. Two-story arched lobby windows overlook the French Quarter and the great bend in the Mississippi River. Rooms have marble foyers and baths. Perks on the two executive floors include complimentary continental breakfast and afternoon hors d'oeuvres. Pros: Luxurious, sparkling rooms and suites; fabulous views of the Mississippi River and French Quarter. Con: Lobby is located on the 11th floor—and can be a bit cumbersome to access. ⊠ *100 Iberville St., French Quarter,* ☎ *504/566–7006 or 800/996–3426* ⊕ *www.westin. com* ⬢ *438 rooms, 41 suites* ⬙ *In-room: Wi-Fi. In-hotel: restaurant, room service, bar, pool* ▭ *AE, D, DC, MC, V.*

GUESTHOUSES & BED-AND-BREAKFASTS

¢–$$ ☷ **Bon Maison Guest House.** Quaint accommodations lie within the gates of this 1833 town house, on the relatively quiet end of Bourbon Street. Rooms in the former slave quarters, off the lush brick patio with tropical plants, are pleasantly (if not elaborately) furnished and have ceiling fans. Two large suites with kitchenettes are in the main house. Be prepared for lots of stair climbing if your room is on one of the upper floors (the house doesn't have an elevator). All rooms have private entrances, kitchenettes, and baths. The quiet ambience will make you feel like you're staying in a private home. Pros: Within walking distance of all French Quarter attractions, just a block or two from several major restaurants. Con: Uninspired room decor. ⊠ *835 Bourbon St., French Quarter,* ☎ *504/561–8498* ⊕ *www.bonmaison. com* ⬢ *3 rooms, 2 suites* ⬙ *In-room: Wi-Fi, refrigerator. In-hotel: no elevator* ▭ *MC, V.*

$–$$$$ ☷ **Claiborne Mansion.** Enormous rooms with high ceilings, canopy or four-poster beds, polished hardwood floors, and rich fabrics embellish this handsome 1859 mansion in the Faubourg Marigny, on the fringe of the French Quarter. The house overlooks Washington Square Park and has a lush, dramatically lighted rear courtyard and pool. Although it's spacious and elegant, the charming house still feels intimate. Celebrities regularly book it for the privacy, but families appreciate its suites with separate bedrooms. Think of the mansion as an authentic mid-19th-century home—with cable and air-conditioning.

Pros: Elegant alternative to hotels and B&Bs, within walking distance of several great restaurants and jazz clubs. Con: Street parking only. ✉ *2111 Dauphine St., Faubourg Marigny,* ☎ *504/949–7327* ⊕ *www. claibornemansion.com* ⇆ *2 rooms, 5 suites* ⬙ *In-room: VCR. In-hotel: pool, no elevator* ⊟ *AE, MC, V* ⫶◎⫶ *BP.*

★ **$–$$$$**   ⬙ **Garlands Guest House & Creole Cottages.** This charming 1926 guest-house is located in historic Tremé, within walking distance of the French Quarter (although walking here at night is not recommended). Free-standing creole cottages and elegant suites are decorated with antiques and reproductions, and the gardens are meticulously maintained. The daily breakfast is exquisite, featuring local favorites like stuffed French toast and homemade biscuits with Southern gravy. The property has a secure, secluded feel; it's a quiet alternative to the French Quarter. **Pros:** Not widely known, even among frequent New Orleans visitors; quaint, intimate surroundings. **Con:** The neighborhood is a bit dicey—not a good place to walk around after dark. ✉ *1129 St. Phillip St., Tremé,* ☎ *504/523–1372 or 800/523–1060* ⊕ *www.historicgarlands.com* ⇆ *10 rooms* ⬙ *In-room: refrigerator, Ethernet. In-hotel: no elevator* ⊟ *AE, MC, V.*

¢**–$$$$**   ⬙ **Hotel Royal.** Think of the coolest SoHo boutique hotel and mix in some authentic New Orleans traditional elegance, and you'll this is your place. Many rooms in this circa-1830 home are pleasantly over-size; four have wet bars and balconies overlooking Royal Street, and two have hot tubs. Distinctly modern amenities complement high ceil-ings and antebellum furnishings. A recent renovation yielded comfort-able and attractive updates, including classic modern lobby furnishings and elegantly constructed marble bathrooms. The complimentary con-tinental breakfast comes from the nearby Croissant d'Or, the favorite bakery of French Quarter residents. (⇨ *Where to Eat, French Quar-ter).* **Pros:** Centralized French Quarter location, recent renovation. **Con:** No in-room or in-hotel Wi-Fi. ✉ *1006 Royal St., French Quarter,* ☎ *504/524–3900 or 800/776–3901* ⊕ *www.melrosegroup.com* ⇆ *30 rooms* ⬙ *In-room: Ethernet. In-hotel: no elevator, parking (fee)* ⊟ *AE, D, DC, MC, V* ⫶◎⫶ *CP.*

★ **$–$$$**   ⬙ **Hotel Villa Convento.** The Campo family provides around-the-clock service in this four-story 1848 creole town house. Although it's just blocks from the Quarter's tourist attractions, shopping, and great restaurants, this guesthouse is on a surprisingly quaint, quiet street, close to the Old Ursuline Convent. Each morning you can have crois-sants and fresh-brewed coffee on the lush patio, or just step across the street to the charming Croissant d'Or (⇨ *Where to Eat, French Quarter).* Rooms, which are furnished with reproductions of antiques, vary in price; some have balconies, chandeliers, or ceiling fans. **Pros:** Located in residential section of the French Quarter, local legend says the hotel was once a high-traffic bordello. **Cons:** Room decor and lin-ens need updating. ✉ *616 Ursulines St., French Quarter,* ☎ *504/522–1793* ⊕ *www.villaconvento.com* ⇆ *25 rooms* ⬙ *In-room: Wi-Fi.* ⊟ *AE, D, DC, MC, V* ⫶◎⫶ *CP.*

$$–$$$ ⬙ **Lafitte Guest House.** A four-story 1849 French-style manor house, the Lafitte is meticulously restored, with rooms decorated with period furnishings. Room 40 takes up the entire fourth floor and overlooks French Quarter rooftops. Room 5, the loft apartment, overlooks the beautiful courtyard. Breakfast can be brought to your room, served in the Victorian parlor, or enjoyed in the courtyard; wine and hors d'oeuvres are served each evening. **Pros:** Feels like a historic mansion, recently upgraded linens, new furnishings. **Con:** Located on a high-traffic corner of Bourbon Street. ✉*1003 Bourbon St., French Quarter,* ☎*504/581–2678 or 800/331–7971* ⊕*www.lafitteguesthouse.com* ⇋*14 rooms, 2 suites* ☐*In-room: Wi-Fi. In-hotel: concierge, no-smoking rooms* ☐*AE, D, DC, MC, V* ⦿*CP.*

$$$–$$$$ ▦**Melrose Mansion.** Down pillows and fine-milled soaps; a full breakfast served poolside, in a formal dining room, or in your room; and rooms filled with 19th-century Louisiana antiques are among the attractions of this handsome 1884 Victorian mansion. Rooms and suites are spacious, with high ceilings and polished hardwood floors. Cocktails are served each evening in the formal drawing room. Baths are sumptuous affairs; those in suites have hot tubs. All but one of the rooms have a wet bar, and one has a private patio. **Pros:** Pure luxury, very private, lots of pampering. **Cons:** Unreasonable refund policy on reservations—and full room charges must be paid in advance. ✉*937 Esplanade Ave., French Quarter,* ☎*504/944–2255* ⊕*www.melrose group.com* ⇋*8 rooms, 4 suites* ☐*In-room: Wi-Fi. In-hotel: bar, pool, no elevator* ☐*AE, D, MC, V* ⦿*BP.*

$$$–$$$$ ▦**Soniat House.** This singularly handsome property comprises three
Fodor's Choice meticulously restored town houses built in the 1830s. Polished hard-
★ wood floors, Oriental rugs, and American and European antiques are complemented by contemporary artwork. Amenities include Annick Goutal toiletries, goose-down pillows, and Egyptian cotton sheets. Some rooms and suites have hot tubs. Exotic plants fill two secluded courtyards, where afternoon cocktails and an unforgettable breakfast ($12.50 extra) of homemade biscuits and strawberry jam, fresh-squeezed orange juice, and café au lait can be enjoyed, weather permitting. An on-site antiques shop carries exquisite European furnishings. Many regular New Orleans visitors consider this is the city's finest hotel. **Pros:** Sheer, refined elegance; incomparable privacy; expert service; afternoon wine service that is as civilized as it gets. **Cons:** None come to mind, if it's in your price range. ✉*1133 Chartres St., French Quarter,* ☎*504/522–0570 or 800/544–8808* ⊕*www.soniathouse. com* ⇋*20 rooms, 13 suites* ☐*In-room: Wi-Fi. In-hotel: concierge, parking (fee)* ☐*AE, MC, V.*

$$–$$$$ ▦**Vieux Carré Palms.** In a residential neighborhood on the edge of the French Quarter, this elegantly furnished, spacious B&B provides a private, intimate setting with quick access to French Quarter attractions. You're served champagne upon arrival, and the smell of fresh French pastries fills the hallways every morning. Rooms are spacious, well appointed, and homey; some face tree-lined Esplanade Avenue. This is one of the most comfortable inns in the city—and your host is as gracious as they come. **Pros:** Residential neighborhood, private quarters. **Con:** Very few rooms, so it can be hard to get a reservation.

⊠723 *Esplanade Ave., French Quarter,* ☏504/949–2572 *or* 800/523–9091 🖷504/949–2572 ➵4 *suites* ♿ *In-hotel: no elevator*🖬*MC, V.*

CBD & WAREHOUSE DISTRICT

The CBD and Warehouse District—the latter is also referred to as the "Warehouse/Arts District" because of the proliferation of great galleries—is perfect for visitors who prefer accommodations in luxurious high-rise hotels or smaller boutique properties. Some of the hotels listed are within walking distance of the French Quarter, but shuttles, taxis, and buses are also readily available. For safety reasons, be sure to take a cab after dark if you stay here.

HOTELS

$$–$$$ 🏨 **Ambassador Hotel.** Guest rooms at this hotel bordering the CBD and Warehouse District have real character, with hardwood floors, oversize windows, and high ceilings. Four-poster iron beds, armoires, and local jazz prints are among the furnishings. Exposed brick walls and ceiling fans add to the ambience of the pre–Civil War building. This is a good alternative to the huge convention hotels; you're just steps from the major downtown attractions and the Convention Center, and Harrah's New Orleans Casino is a five-minute walk. The Diplomat Bar & Grill, located on the lobby level, serves burgers, steaks, and grilled items. **Pros:** Distinctive decor, urban/chic atmosphere. **Con:** Some first-floor rooms let in too much noise from street and lobby area. ⊠*535 Tchoupitoulas St., CBD,* ☏504/527–5271 *or* 800/455–3417⊕*www.ambassadorneworleans.com*➵*165 rooms*♿*In-room: Wi-Fi. In-hotel: restaurant, bar, parking (fee)*🖬*AE, D, DC, MC, V.*

$$$–$$$$ 🏨 **Courtyard by Marriott.** The iron trellis balcony overlooking St. Charles Avenue is just one of many nods to the Verandah Hotel, which occupied this building from 1829 to 1855. Architectural elements from the original hotel have been artfully incorporated into the current design, and the centerpiece of this property is a stunning six-story atrium. Balcony rooms overlooking St. Charles Avenue are in high demand during Mardi Gras. The dining room is open for breakfast only, but the hotel is within walking distance of restaurants and other attractions. **Pros:** Central CBD location, close to the French Quarter. **Con:** Significant street noise at all hours. ⊠*124 St. Charles Ave., CBD,* ☏504/581–9005 *or* 800/321–2211⊕*www.marriott.com*➵*140 rooms*♿*In-room: Ethernet, Wi-Fi. In-hotel: restaurant, pool, gym, parking (fee)*🖬*AE, D, DC, MC, V.*

$$–$$$ 🏨 **Doubletree Hotel.** This chain hotel is close to the river, across the street from Canal Place mall, and a block from the French Quarter. The small, comfortable lobby is adorned with floral arrangements and bowls of potpourri, along with the hotel's trademark jar of freshly baked chocolate-chip cookies. The decor is country French, and rooms have an open, airy feeling, with pastel draperies and spreads and light-color furniture. Rooms ending in 05 are larger. The hotel is adjacent to the French Quarter, close to tourist attractions and the Convention Center. **Pros:** Adjacent to French Quarter and Riverfront attractions, across the street from the upscale Canal Place shops. **Cons:** Some rooms could

use refreshing/updating, restaurant quality is average at best. ✉*300 Canal St., CBD,* ☎*504/581–1300 or 800/222–8733* ⊕*www.double tree.com* ⤳*363 rooms, 15 suites* ♿*In-room: Ethernet. In-hotel: restaurant, bar, pool, gym, laundry service, public Wi-Fi, parking (fee), no-smoking rooms* ▭*AE, D, DC, MC, V.*

$$$–$$$$ ⛨**Embassy Suites.** If your primary target is the Morial Convention Center or the Warehouse District's contemporary art galleries and museum collection, this is a great choice. The balconied high-rise sits right on Gallery Row. All suites have a bedroom and separate parlor (with three phones and a TV in each room), and coffeemaker; most have balconies. Room service

> ## BED & BREAKFASTS
>
> Bed-and-breakfasts provide an intimate alternative to hotels and motels, and New Orleans has many charming accommodations of this kind.
>
> **Bed & Breakfast.com** (✉*700 Brazos St., Austin, TX* ☎*512/322–2710 or 800/462–2632* 🖨*512/320–0883* ⊕*www. bedandbreakfast.com*). **New Orleans Bed & Breakfast and Accommodations** (✉*671 Rosa Ave., Suite 208, Metairie* ☎*504/838–0071 or 888/240–0070* 🖨*504/838–0140* ⊕*www. neworleansbandb.com*).

is available from the Sugar House restaurant. The Lofts at Embassy Suites is in a separate building just around the corner. Both properties are close to Morial Convention Center, which is about three blocks away. The hotel is also within walking distance of some of the best Warehouse/Arts District restaurants, including Emeril's and Tommy's Cuisine. **Pros:** Spacious, well-maintained rooms. **Cons:** Mediocre restaurant and room service. ✉*315 Julia St., CBD,* ☎*504/525–1993 or 800/362–2779* ⊕*www.embassyneworleans.com* ⤳*347 suites* ♿*In-room: refrigerator, Wi-Fi. In-hotel: restaurant, gym* ▭*AE, D, MC, V* ⊚*BP.*

$–$$ ⛨**Hampton Inn.** This moderately priced facility is one of several office buildings that have been converted into hotels. The lobby, with lavish furnishings and decor, is an oasis in the midst of the bustling CBD. Rooms are large and comfortable, and all bathrooms have hair dryers. Among the safety features are key-access elevators. Just a few blocks from Bourbon Street, the hotel is surrounded by great restaurants and attractions. A surprisingly lavish complimentary buffet breakfast is served daily, and complimentary beer, wine, and snacks are served in the evening Monday through Thursday. **Pros:** Particularly nice continental breakfast, convenient to French Quarter (but be careful when walking at night). **Con:** Rooms that face the street can be noisy. ✉*226 Carondelet St., CBD,* ☎*504/529–9990 or 800/426–7866* ⊕*www. neworleanshamptoninns.com* ⤳*187 rooms* ♿*In-room: refrigerator, Wi-Fi. In-hotel: restaurant, gym, concierge, parking (fee)* ▭*AE, D, DC, MC, V* ⊚*CP.*

$$$ ⛨**Hampton Inn and Suites–Convention Center.** Two century-old warehouses have been converted into a French Colonial–style hotel that is comfortable, architecturally distinctive, and moderately priced. The grand lobby has original hardwood floors and exposed brick walls, and

the lobby bar overlooks a pool and a lush garden courtyard. Rooms are large and airy, with four-poster beds and wood floors; many overlook a small park. The hotel is on the edge of the Warehouse District, directly across the street from the Convention Center; it's within walking distance of several moderately priced restaurants, including Wolfe's in the Warehouse, Rio Mar, and 7 on Fulton. **Pros:** Exquisite renovation, architecturally stunning, minutes from Convention Center. **Con:** Not a great area to walk around late at night. ⊠*1201 Convention Center Blvd., Warehouse District,* ☎*504/566–9990 or 800/292–0653* ⊕*www. neworleanshamptoninns.com* ⤶*288 rooms* ⭱*In-room: Wi-Fi. In-hotel: bar, pool, gym, parking (fee)* ▤*AE, D, DC, MC, V*⊠*CP.*

$$$$
Fodor'sChoice
★

▦ **Harrah's New Orleans Hotel.** Located directly across the street from Harrah's New Orleans Casino, this 26-story hotel is richly appointed with marble floors, exquisite chandeliers, plush furnishings, and artwork selected and installed by local gallery owner Arthur Roger. The lobby-level restaurant, Riche, features strictly French cuisine, and big-name local entertainers headline "528," an adjacent jazz club nightly. Guest rooms are larger than the local norm and have extras like refrigerators, high-definition televisions, cordless phones, and Wi-Fi. The Fulton Street Corridor, a four-block promenade featuring shops, private party spaces, and live entertainment areas, is connected to the hotel. **Pros:** Well-trained staff provides above-average service; guests without cars can easily walk to Riverfront, CBD, and French Quarter attractions. **Con:** The hustle and bustle of this part of town might not suit travelers seeking peace and quiet. ⊠*Poydras St. at Fulton St., CBD,* ☎*504/533–6000 or 800/847–5299* ⊕*www.harrahs.com* ⤶*450 rooms, 81 suites* ⭱*In-room: refrigerator, Wi-Fi. In-hotel: restaurant, bar, pool, gym, spa, laundry service, concierge* ▤*AE, D, DC, MC, V.*

☾ **$$**

▦ **Homewood Suites by Hilton.** This is one of the city's most central and spacious hotels (suites are 625 square feet). Contemporary furnishings mix easily with traditional New Orleans ambience. High ceilings, big windows, and a kid-friendly atmosphere make this a perfect pick for families. A complimentary buffet breakfast is served every morning; the manager's evening reception has beer, wine, and snacks. **Pros:** Casual atmosphere, huge apartment-size rooms. **Con:** No in-hotel restaurant—and you'll need to travel some distance from good dining choices. ⊠*901 Poydras St., CBD,* ☎*504/581–5599* ⊕*www.homewoodsuites.com* ⤶*166 suites* ⭱*In-room: kitchen, refrigerator, Ethernet, dial-up. In-hotel: pool, gym, public Wi-Fi* ▤*AE, D, DC, MC, V.*

★ **$$$–$$$$**

▦ **Hotel InterContinental.** One of the major convention hotels, the InterContinental is a modern rose-granite structure overlooking St. Charles Avenue. Public spaces include a spacious, inviting second-floor lobby and a peaceful sculpture garden. Guest rooms are large and well lighted, with matching draperies and quilted spreads; balcony rooms overlook an urban garden. The Club level contains some of the city's finest suites, featuring original artwork commissioned for the hotel and antique furnishings from around the globe. **Pros:** Superior service, elegant lobby-level cocktail lounge, club-level rooms are among the best accommodations in the city. **Con:** Off-site fitness center. ⊠*444 St. Charles Ave., CBD,* ☎*504/525–5566 or 800/445–6563* ⊕*www.*

intercontinental.com ⌖*482 rooms, 20 suites* ☂*In-room: Ethernet. In-hotel: 2 restaurants, bar, pool, gym, laundry service, public Wi-Fi, parking (fee)* ▤*AE, D, DC, MC, V.*

$$–$$$ ⚏**Hotel New Orleans.** This eight-story property, formerly a Holiday Inn, is across the street from the Convention Center. Built around a three-story atrium, it has a handsome lobby with marble floors and wood paneling. All rooms are soundproof and have irons and ironing boards, coffeemakers, and hair dryers; executive rooms and suites have two phone lines, call waiting, and speakerphones. Several noteworthy restaurants, the Riverwalk, and Harrah's New Orleans Casino are within walking distance. **Pros:** Close to Convention Center and Riverwalk shopping center. **Cons:** Typical chain hotel, no trace of New Orleans decor or ambience. ⊠*881 Convention Center Blvd., Warehouse District,* ☎*504/524–1881 or 800/465–4329* ⊕*www.hiselect.com* ⌖*168 rooms, 2 suites* ☂*In-room: Ethernet. In-hotel: restaurant, bar, gym, laundry facilities, public Wi-Fi, no-smoking rooms* ▤*AE, D, DC, MC, V* ⋈⌐*CP.*

★ **$$–$$$$** ⚏**International House.** The lobby of this boutique hotel is an architectural dream, with 23-foot-high ceilings, ornate pilasters, marble floors, and a seasonally changing decor. Fine linens and fabrics enhance the guest rooms, which, although a little too small, are attractively decorated in a contemporary New Orleans style. All rooms have CD players and black-and-white photographs of jazz greats; bathrooms, some with glass-enclosed double shower stalls, are sleek and contemporary. A recent lobby redesign by L.A. designer LM Pagano is simultaneously elegant, cutting edge, and inviting. The hotel is also home to Loa, a trendy, see-and-be-seen cocktail spot. **Pro:** Great downtown location, especially appropriate for those who like cool, sophisticated surroundings. **Con:** Lacks typical New Orleans warmth. ⊠*221 Camp St., CBD,* ☎*504/553–9550 or 800/633–5770* ⊕*www.ihhotel.com* ⌖*119 rooms, 3 suites* ☂*In-room: Wi-Fi. In-hotel: bar, gym, public Wi-Fi, parking (fee)* ▤*AE, D, MC, V.*

$ ⚏**La Quinta Inn and Suites Downtown.** Rooms here are surprisingly well appointed, if not luxurious, despite the moderate rates. Every room has an oversize desk, built-in closets, and a large bathroom with a bright tile floor. The hotel features one of the few outdoor pools downtown. **Pros:** Pet friendly; within easy walking distance of the French Quarter. **Cons:** Typical chain hotel, lacks traditional New Orleans charm. ⊠*301 Camp St., CBD,* ☎*504/598–9977* ⊕*www.laquinta.com* ⌖*166 rooms, 16 suites* ☂*In-room: Ethernet. In-hotel: pool, gym, laundry facilities, public Wi-Fi* ▤*AE, D, DC, MC, V.*

★ **$$–$$$$** ⚏**Lafayette Hotel.** This small brick building has housed the Lafayette since it was built in 1916. Handsome millwork, brass fittings, and marble baths adorn the property throughout. The tiny lobby is chic, and guest rooms are spacious and sunny. Some rooms have four-poster beds; all have cushy easy chairs and ottomans. Some second-floor rooms have floor-length windows that open onto a balcony; a number overlook Lafayette Square. Chef Raymond Toups's (formerly of Rib Room) Anatole's Restaurant, featuring authentic southern Louisiana cooking, is on the lobby level. **Pros:** Streetcar stops right outside the

5

front door, within walking distance of Riverfront and French quarter attractions, pet friendly. **Con:** Not a great area for walking late at night. ⊠ *600 St. Charles Ave., CBD,* ☎ *504/524–4441 or 800/733–4754* ⊕ *www.thelafayettehotel.com* ⟿ *24 rooms, 20 suites* ⚙ *In-room: Wi-Fi. In-hotel: restaurant, laundry service, concierge , parking (fee), no-smoking rooms* ⊟ *AE, D, DC, MC, V.*

★ $$$–$$$$ **Le Pavillon Hotel.** Magnificent chandeliers adorn the European-style lobby of this historic 1907 hotel, and a handsome collection of artwork lines the corridors; the marble railing in the clubby Gallery Lounge is originally from the Grand Hotel in Paris. Guest rooms have high ceilings and identical traditional decor; suites are particularly luxurious. The elegant Crystal Room has a huge weekday salad-and-pasta lunch buffet, as well as à la carte service. The opulent hotel bar has 30-foot ceilings, marble columns, and a magnificent mahogany bar. Locals consider it one of the most civilized spots in the city for an afternoon cocktail. **Pro:** Elegant, "Old South" ambience. **Cons:** Guest rooms could use some updating and brightening. ⊠ *833 Poydras St., CBD,* ☎ *504/581–3111 or 800/535–9095* ⊕ *www.lepavillon.com* ⟿ *219 rooms, 7 suites* ⚙ *In-room: Wi-Fi. In-hotel: restaurant, bar, pool, gym, laundry service, parking (fee), no-smoking rooms* ⊟ *AE, D, DC, MC, V.*

$$$–$$$$
Fodor's Choice
★
    Loews New Orleans Hotel. A refashioned bank building in the heart of downtown is home to this plush 21st-century hotel. The West Indies–style lobby provides a welcoming atmosphere, and bright spacious rooms are enriched with local artwork and soothing colors. The guest rooms are among the largest and most well appointed in the city. Café Adelaide and the Swizzlestick Bar, both on the lobby level, are operated by the same family that owns the legendary Commander's Palace Restaurant. This may look like a typical chain hotel on the outside—but inside it's singular in its quality and consistency. **Pros:** Well managed, accessible to everything that counts downtown, reliable in service and product. **Con:** Located on one of the busiest downtown streets in the city. ⊠ *300 Poydras St., CBD,* ☎ *504/595–5310 or 800/235–6397* ⊕ *www.loewshotels.com* ⟿ *273 rooms, 12 suites* ⚙ *In-room: Wi-Fi. In-hotel: restaurant, bar, pool, gym, spa, laundry service, concierge* ⊟ *AE, D, DC, MC, V.*

$$–$$$ **Loft 523.** This sleek, seductive loft hotel is so subtle from the outside, you may have trouble finding it among the surrounding buildings. Once inside, the atmosphere is strictly contemporary and chic—think Frank Lloyd Wright mixed with a SoHo loft. Cavernous limestone bathrooms with Aveda amenities, stone vanity tables, Frette linens, Fortuny lamps, and DVD surround-sound systems make this an adult playground. A personal assistant is assigned to you at check-in for your entire stay. **Pro:** Sexiest environment of any hotel in the city. **Con:** Some guests may find the experience a bit too trendy. ⊠ *523 Gravier St., CBD,* ☎ *504/200–6523* ⊕ *www.loft523.com* ⟿ *16 rooms* ⚙ *In-room: VCR, dial-up, Wi-Fi. In-hotel: room service, bar, gym, concierge* ⊟ *AE, D, DC, MC, V.*

$$$$ **New Orleans Hilton Riverside.** The sprawling multilevel Hilton complex sits right on the Mississippi, with superb views. Guest rooms have French-provincial furnishings, and the 180 rooms that share a concierge

have fax machines. The lavish Sunday brunch is consistently outstanding. Adjacent to Riverwalk Shopping Center, the hotel is directly across the street from Harrah's New Orleans Casino; the Riverfront streetcar stops out front. The health club is among the best in town, and the hotel has a resident golf pro and a four-hole putting green. Designed for large convention groups, this hotel is also a great choice for independent travelers. **Pros:** Well-maintained facilities, hotel runs like a well-oiled machine. **Cons:** The city's biggest hotel, typical chain service and surroundings, garage needs better lighting. ⊠*Poydras St. at the Mississippi River, CBD,* ☎*504/561–0500 or 800/445–8667* ⊕*www. neworleans.hilton.com* ◜1,600 rooms, 67 suites ◿In-room: Wi-Fi. In-hotel: 3 restaurants, tennis courts, pools, gym, parking (fee), no-smoking rooms* ⊟*AE, D, DC, MC, V.*

¢–$$$ 🎯 **Parc St. Charles.** This property is on one of the Big Easy's best Carnival corners, at the intersection of Poydras Street and St. Charles Avenue. Rooms in the intimate hotel are decorated with contemporary furniture, and large plate-glass windows provide lots of light and wide views of the CBD. The hotel's restaurant, Panasia, serves Thai cuisine. **Pros:** Possibly the best location for Mardi Gras parade viewing in the city, pet friendly. **Cons:** Room decor is lackluster and needs updating/refreshing, street noise can be a problem at night. ⊠*500 St. Charles Ave., CBD,* ☎*504/522–9000 or 888/211–3447* ⊕*www.parcstcharles.com* ◜*120 rooms, 2 suites ◿In-room: safe, Wi-Fi. In-hotel: restaurant, bar, pool, gym, parking (fee), no-smoking rooms* ⊟*AE, D, DC, MC, V.*

¢–$$$$ 🎯 **Pelham Hotel.** A restored four-story office building houses the charming Pelham, an ideal place for those who want to be in the center of the CBD—near the Riverwalk, Harrah's New Orleans Casino, and the Convention Center—but who seek a quiet alternative to the bustling convention hotels. The small lobby has a green-marble floor and fresh flowers. Rooms are small; some have four-poster beds, and all have marble baths with terry robes and English soaps. Inside rooms, though attractively furnished, have no windows. You can use the fitness center and pool at the nearby Sheraton for $10 per day. Rosie's Diner, on the lobby level, serves comfort food and diner fare 24 hours a day. **Pros:** Centrally located, but far enough away from heavily traveled tourist streets; pet friendly. **Con:** Diner food is mediocre at best. ⊠*444 Common St., CBD,* ☎*504/522–4444 or 800/659–5621* ⊕*www. thepelhamhotel.com* ◜*60 rooms ◿In-room: safe, Wi-Fi. In-hotel: restaurant, room service, laundry service, concierge, parking (fee)* ⊟*AE, D, DC, MC, V.*

$$–$$$ 🎯 **Queen & Crescent Hotel.** Intimate and tasteful, this hotel two blocks outside the French Quarter is a good alternative to the megahotels that surround it. The 1913 building retains many of its original architectural elements. Guest rooms are small, but come with in-room coffeemakers, hair dryers, and ironing boards. The hotel is a good choice for business travelers who don't want to stay in the large convention properties. **Pro:** Feels like a smaller, more-intimate property. **Cons:** No in-hotel restaurant, not advisable to walk around the nearby neighborhood late at night. ⊠*344 Camp St., CBD,* ☎*504/587–9700 or 800/975–6652* ⊕*www.queenandcrescenthotel.com* ◜*196   rooms ◿In-room:*

safe, Wi-Fi. In-hotel: gym, parking (fee), no-smoking rooms ⊟AE, D, DC, MC, V.

$$$–$$$$ 🏨**Renaissance Arts Hotel.** Art lovers looking to stay close to downtown but not in the CBD should check out this circa-1910 warehouse-turned-hotel; the huge windows now make for great views from the guest rooms. Local gallery owner Arthur Roger—who opened a second location of his nationally acclaimed gallery on the lobby level—hand-selected every piece of art in the hotel. The comfortable, spacious, well-designed rooms are furnished with a minimalist bent. La Cote Brasserie, the hotel's restaurant, has an upscale, urban feel, with an open kitchen and rotating art displays. **Pros:** Modern, well-appointed facilities; beautiful artwork. **Con:** Odd location—especially for those who want to walk downtown or to the French Quarter. ⊠*700 Tchoupitoulas St., Warehouse District,* ☎*504/613–2330 or 800/431–8634* ⊕*www.marriott.com* ➯*208 rooms, 9 suites* ⊝*In-room: safe, dial-up, Wi-Fi. In-hotel: restaurant, bar, pool, concierge* ⊟*AE, D, DC, MC, V.*

> ### HOTEL OR GALLERY?
>
> Some of the best galleries in New Orleans are located in the Warehouse/Arts District, but guests at the Renaissance Arts Hotel don't even have to leave the property to see fine works of art. The Arthur Roger Project is located lobby level at the hotel, and fine art, all selected and installed by the renowned gallery owner, adorns the hotel's public spaces, guest rooms, and sculpture garden. Most of the art is local, although internationally known artists are represented as well.

$–$$$ 🏨**Renaissance Pere Marquette Hotel.** Rooms at this historic downtown urban-chic property are generously sized and surprisingly quiet, even though the hotel sits in the middle of the CBD. Each has soothing colors, comfortable fabrics, and an oversize marble bathroom. A jazz theme is carried throughout the hotel, with each floor named after a renowned musician. **Pros:** New hotel restaurant MiLa seems promising. **Cons:** Chain property. ⊠*817 Common St., CBD,* ☎*504/525–1111 or 800/372–0482* ⊕*www.renaissancehotels.com* ➯*275 rooms, 5 suites* ⊝*In-room: safe, dial-up. In-hotel: restaurant, room service, bar, pool, gym, laundry service, concierge* ⊟*AE, D, DC, MC, V.*

$$–$$$$ 🏨**St. James Hotel.** The St. James defines privacy in the CBD. Rooms, decorated West Indies–style with tropical accents, are set far enough from busy Magazine Street to ensure quiet and solitude. Restaurant Cuvée *(⇨ Where to Eat, CBD & Warehouse District)* sits adjacent to the hotel lobby. This hotel is one of the best-kept secrets in the local hotel collection; it's a great choice for business travelers looking for proximity to the CBD and leisure travelers who want to avoid the high-energy atmosphere of the French Quarter. **Pros:** The epitome of privacy, pet friendly. **Con:** Room quality is inconsistent. ⊠*330 Magazine St., CBD,* ☎*504/304–4000* ⊕*www.saintjameshotel.com* ➯*86 rooms, 6 suites* ⊝*In-room: Wi-Fi. In-hotel: restaurant, pool, laundry service, concierge* ⊟*AE, D, MC, V.*

$$$–$$$$ 🏨**Sheraton New Orleans.** The oversize lobby of this hotel is usually bustling with conventioneers. A tropical atmosphere permeates the Pelican

Bar, which presents nightly jazz and sells a fine assortment of cigars. Chef Chris Brown offers a nice balance of creole and Cajun-style dishes in the airy second-floor Roux Bistro. Executive rooms come with many special amenities, but even regular guest rooms are spacious and well appointed. Expect top-quality service, but keep in mind that the hotel caters primarily to big convention groups. One of the great downtown eateries, the Palace Café (⇨ *Where to Eat, CBD & Warehouse District*), is right across Canal Street. **Pros:** Large hotel with lots of availability, well-established staff, great service. **Cons:** Typical corporate convention property, lacks the warmth of some of its competitors. ✉ *500 Canal St., CBD,* ☎ *504/525–2500 or 800/253–6156* ⊕ *www. sheratonneworleans.com* ⇱ *1,100 rooms, 72 suites* ⚐ *In-room: Wi-Fi. In-hotel: 3 restaurants, bar, pool, gym, parking (fee), no-smoking rooms* ▤ *AE, D, DC, MC, V.*

$$–$$$ 🖼 **Staybridge Suites New Orleans.** The emergence of the utilitarian all-suite hotel in the early 1990s has spawned numerous versions, but this one is exceptionally comfortable. Spacious guest rooms have full kitchenettes, a business work area, free Wi-Fi, and nice city views. The hotel has limited housekeeping service, on-site laundry facilities, and a good-size pool. The best feature here is the location—right across from Harrah's Casino, within walking distance of riverfront attractions and the Convention Center. **Pros:** Located directly across from Harrah's Casino, within walking distance of riverfront attractions, spacious all-suite accommodations. **Cons:** A bit generic, no in-hotel restaurant, located on one of the busiest corners in the downtown area. ✉ *502 Tchoupitoulas St., CBD,* ☎ *504/571–1818 or 800/541–4998* ⊕ *www. ichotelsgroup.com* ⇱ *182 suites* ⚐ *In-room: Wi-Fi. In-hotel: bar, gym, public Wi-Fi, parking (fee)* ▤ *AE, D, MC, V.*

★ **$$$$** 🖼 **W Hotel New Orleans.** A sleek, contemporary blend of East Coast sophistication and Southern charm gives way to inspired accommodations at the W. Rooms are decorated in red and black, with first-rate amenities such as Bliss bath products and beds with goose-down pillows and comforters; 100 are designated as home-office rooms. The lobby has a trendy upscale look, and the Rande Gerber–designed Whiskey Blue lounge is on the lobby level. **Pros:** Great for those looking for contemporary, hip quarters. **Con:** Beautifully designed, but lacking the warmth of comparable properties in the city. ✉ *333 Poydras St., CBD,* ☎ *504/525–9444 or 800/777–7372* ⊕ *www.whotels.com* ⇱ *423 rooms, 23 suites* ⚐ *In-room: Wi-Fi. In-hotel: restaurant, gym, public Wi-Fi, parking (fee)* ▤ *AE, D, DC, MC, V.*

$$ 🖼 **The Whitney, A Wyndham Historic Hotel.** The historic Whitney Bank Building has been classically restyled into a true European-style hotel. Listed on the National Register of Historic Places, this elegant property is in the middle of downtown. Rooms include comfy pillow-top mattresses, upscale toiletries and amenities, and ergonomic chairs. **Pro:** L'il Dizzy's Café—known for authentic "soul" food—is located on the lobby level. **Con:** Located at one of the busiest downtown intersections in the city. ✉ *610 Poydras St., CBD,* ☎ *504/581–4222 or 800/996–3426* ⊕ *www.wyndham.com* ⇱ *70 rooms, 23 suites* ⚐ *In-room: Ether-*

net, Wi-Fi. In-hotel: restaurant (breakfast only), bar, gym, no-smoking rooms ⊟*AE, D, MC, V.*

$$$–$$$$

Fodor'sChoice

★

🖼**Windsor Court Hotel.** Exquisite, gracious, elegant, eminently civilized…these words are frequently used to describe Windsor Court, but all fail to capture the wonderful essence of this hotel. From Le Salon's delightful afternoon tea—the city's only authentic European presentation, served daily in the lobby—to the unbelievably large rooms, this is one of *the* places to stay in New Orleans. Plush carpeting, canopy and four-poster beds, fully stocked wet bars, marble vanities, and mirrored dressing areas are just a few of the many amenities. The New Orleans Grill (⇨ *Where to Eat, CBD & Warehouse District*) is considered the premiere fine-dining room in the city, and the Polo Lounge has one of the best martini presentations to be found anywhere. The hotel is four blocks from the French Quarter. **Pros:** Old-world elegance, superior service. **Cons:** None come to mind, if it's in your price range. ⊠*300 Gravier St., CBD,* ☎*504/523–6000 or 800/262–2662* ⊕*www.windsor courthotel.com* ⬌*58 rooms, 266 suites, 2 penthouses* ⟳*In-room: Wi-Fi. In-hotel: 2 restaurants, bar, pool, gym, laundry service, parking (fee)* ⊟*AE, D, DC, MC, V.*

GUESTHOUSES & BED-AND-BREAKFASTS

¢–$

🖼**Depot House at Madame Julia's.** What once was Madame Julia's Boarding House is now a charming, no-frills collection of creole town houses dating from 1830. All rooms have shared baths, but most guests don't seem to mind. The atmosphere is family-like and friendly; Joanne, the proprietor, says it's like staying at grandmother's without a curfew. Near major attractions, this B&B is recommended for visitors on a budget who appreciate authentic local ambience. A complimentary bakery breakfast is served under the Garden Tent. **Pros:** Charming ambience, owners are hospitable and fun, room rates are among the lowest in town. **Cons:** Shared bathrooms, street noise, small rooms. ⊠*748 O'Keefe St., CBD,* ☎*504/529–2952* 🖷*504/529–1908* ⬌*15 rooms* ⟳*In-room: no phone. In-hotel: no elevator* ⊟*No credit cards.*

GARDEN DISTRICT/UPTOWN

The Garden District and Uptown are ideal areas if you don't want to stay downtown. All of the following properties are on or close to fashionable, mansion-lined St. Charles Avenue. Traffic in the Garden District and Uptown is not quite as heavy as downtown, and you're much more likely to find free or inexpensive parking—which can save you as much as $20 to $30 per night compared to CBD and French Quarter hotels. Many properties in these areas are just a short walk from the St. Charles streetcar line. Walking in this area after dark is not recommended.

HOTELS

$–$$

🖼**Avenue Plaza Resort.** A spartan lobby belies the many amenities here. Public areas include a romantic lounge with dark-wood panels from a French chalet. Spacious rooms have generous dressing areas; decor is either traditional or art deco—both are equally appealing. The health club has a Turkish steam bath, Swiss showers, and a Scandinavian sauna. The pool is in a pleasant courtyard, and a sundeck and hot tub are on the roof. If you're looking for real local charm, this is the place. Mr. John's Steakhouse, located on the lobby level, is a great place for a moderately priced steak. **Pros:** Picturesque location, delightful, private pool and patio area. **Con:** Room decor is a bit dated. ⊠*2111 St. Charles Ave., Garden District,* ☎*504/566–1212 or 800/439-6493* ⊕*www.avenueplazahotel.com* ⬎*256 suites* ⌂*In-room: kitchen, refrigerator, Wi-Fi. In-hotel: restaurant, bar, pool, gym, spa, laundry facilities, parking (fee)* ⊟*AE, D, DC, MC, V.*

$ ⌗**Best Western St. Charles Inn.** The canopied entrance to this small Uptown hotel is almost hidden from view, squeezed between a restaurant and a café. The inn has good-size rooms, each with a dressing area and cable TV. Those in the front, with St. Charles Avenue views, are best. A continental breakfast and a newspaper are brought to your room each morning, and the staff is friendly and accommodating. A great advantage of staying at this hotel is the spate of great restaurants within quick walking distance. **Pros:** Great location if you want to be on the streetcar line, close to good dining options, intimate. **Cons:** Room decor is unimaginative and dull, lots of street noise. ⊠*3636 St. Charles Ave., Garden District,* ☎*504/899–8888 or 800/489–9908* ☎*504/899–8892* ⬎*40 rooms* ⌂*In-room: Wi-Fi. In-hotel: parking (no fee)* ⊟*AE, D, DC, MC, V*¦⍉¦*CP.*

$–$$$ ⌗**Columns Hotel.** This impressive, white-columned 1883 Victorian hotel is listed on the National Register of Historic Places. The wide veranda, set with cloth-covered tables for outdoor dining or cocktails, is very inviting, as are the two parlors furnished with period pieces. Dark and intimate, the lounge is a favorite with locals and has excellent live progressive jazz Monday through Thursday; there's also a Sunday jazz brunch. One of the most impressive staircases you may ever climb leads to the large—though somewhat sparsely furnished—rooms. A recent renovation of the lobby area and third-floor rooms has brought the place back to life. If you can wangle a weekend Mardi Gras reservation here, you'll have one of the best seats on St. Charles Avenue for the nightly parades. **Pros:** Exquisite architecture, having a cocktail on the veranda is one of the city's great pleasures, perfect parade-watching spot. **Con:** Second-floor rooms feel a bit stale (try to book on the third floor). ⊠*3811 St. Charles Ave., Uptown,* ☎*504/899–9308 or 800/445–9308* ⊕*www.thecolumns. com* ⬎*20 rooms* ⌂*In-room: Wi-Fi. In-hotel: restaurant, bar* ⊟*AE, MC, V*¦⍉¦*CP.*

¢–$$$$ ⌗**Hotel Le Cirque.** This former YMCA has been artfully transformed into a stylish, contemporary boutique hotel. Rooms are extremely small but elegant, with chic minimalist decor. The hotel's extensive art collection includes Herb Ritts's black-and-white photos in public areas and Philippe Starck benches in the courtyard. It's located somewhat off the beaten path, between downtown and the Garden District. **Pros:** Streetcar stop right outside the front door, urban/chic decor. **Cons:** Exercise caution in this area if you go out after dark, limited lobby space and public areas. ⊠*2 Lee Circle, CBD,* ☎*504/962–0900* ⊕*www.hotel lecirqueneworleans.com* ⬎*137 rooms, 2 suites* ⌂*In-room: Wi-Fi. In-hotel: concierge* ⊟*AE, D, MC, V.*

Where to Stay Outside the Downtown Area

St. Charles Guest House 11
Sully Mansion 14

Maison Perrier Bed & Breakfast 19
New Orleans Airport Hilton 1
New Orleans Marriott Metairie 3
Park View Guest House 20

Four Points by Sheraton 2
Grand Victorian 15
Hotel Le Cirque 10
House on Bayou Road 7
Josephine Guest House 13

Chimes Bed and Breakfast 18
Columns Hotel 16
Days Hotel Metairie 5
Edgar Degas House 9
1896 O'Malley House 6

Ashton's Bed & Breakfast 8
Avenue Plaza Resort 12
Best Western Landmark Hotel 4
Best Western St. Charles Inn 17

GUESTHOUSES & BED-AND-BREAKFASTS

$-$$ ⊞ **1896 O'Malley House.** This house is sheer elegance. Rooms are furnished with beautiful antiques, with heavy cypress doors, hardwood floors, granite bathroom counters, and oversize windows with plush draperies. The owners have paid attention to every detail, down to the chocolates delivered with the evening turndown service—on a silver tray. Step outside and board the Canal Street streetcar for a quick ride downtown. This place is a true find. **Pros:** Surprisingly low rates, steps away from the Canal Street streetcar line. **Con:** Some distance from downtown and French Quarter attractions. ⊠ *120 S. Pierce St., Uptown,* ☎ *504/488–5896 or 866/226–1896* ⊕ *www.1896omalleyhouse.com* ✍ *8 rooms* ⟍ *In-room: Wi-Fi. In-hotel: no elevator* ⊟ *AE, MC, V* ⊺⊖⧵ *CP.*

$-$$

Fodor's Choice

★

⊞ **Chimes Bed & Breakfast.** Jill and Charles Abbyad's charming Uptown residence has rooms in the main house and a converted carriage house, with hardwood or slate floors. The Abbyads maintain a homey environment with all the conveniences of a large hotel: hair dryers, irons, stereos, coffeemakers, and private entrances. A continental breakfast is served in the airy dining room; afterward, you can relax in the butterfly garden in the courtyard. English, French, Arabic, and Spanish are spoken in the house, and children are welcome. All rooms have private entrances onto the courtyard. **Pros:** Premises and guest rooms are extremely well kept and clean. **Con:** Noise carries easily from room to room. ⊠ *1146 Constantinople St., Uptown,* ☎ *504/899–2621* ⊕ *www.chimesneworleans.com* ✍ *5 rooms* ⟍ *In-room: Wi-Fi. In-hotel: no elevator, some pets allowed, no-smoking rooms* ⊟ *AE, MC, V* ⊺⊖⧵ *CP.*

$$-$$$$

Fodor's Choice

★

⊞ **Grand Victorian Bed & Breakfast.** Just a block and a half from Commander's Palace, the Grand Victorian more than lives up to its lofty name. Each lavishly appointed room evokes old Louisiana with period pieces and distinctive private baths. The Greenwood Suite includes a hot tub, stained-glass windows, and a private balcony that extends across the front of the house and overlooks historic St. Charles Avenue. An oak-shaded common balcony on the second floor stands atop a traditional New Orleans garden. A continental breakfast is served in either the dining room or on the balcony. **Pros:** True elegance, rooms are exquisitely appointed, possibly the best B&B value in the area. **Cons:** None come to mind. ⊠ *2727 St. Charles Ave., Garden District,* ☎ *504/895–1104 or 800/977–0008* ⊕ *www.gvbb.com* ✍ *8 rooms* ⟍ *In-room: Wi-Fi. In-hotel: restaurant, no elevator* ⊟ *AE, D, MC, V.*

$-$$ ⊞ **Josephine Guest House.** This restored Italianate mansion, one block from St. Charles Avenue, was built in 1870. European antiques fill the rooms, and Oriental rugs cover the gleaming hardwood floors. There are four rooms and a parlor in the main house, and two smaller—but still spacious—rooms occupy the *garçonnière;* bathrooms are oversize and plush. A creole breakfast, complete with homemade biscuits, can be brought to your room or taken on the secluded patio. **Pros:** Some guest rooms are oversize, furnishings are authentic to the period. **Con:** Exercise caution if walking in this area after dark. ⊠ *1450 Josephine St., Garden District,* ☎ *504/524–6361 or 800/779–6361* ⊕ *www.josephine.us* ✍ *6 rooms* ⟍ *In-hotel: no elevator* ⊟ *AE, D, DC, MC, V* ⊺⊖⧵ *CP.*

5

$$–$$$$ 🖼 **Maison Perrier Bed & Breakfast.** This 1890s Victorian mansion report-edly housed a gentlemen's club, and rooms have been named after the ladies of the evening who entertained here. Comfortable, spacious rooms have high ceilings and exceptionally large, well-appointed pri-vate baths; some have private balconies and sitting rooms. The daily homemade breakfast may include waffles and praline French toast. Fresh-baked brownies and tea are served in late afternoon; compli-mentary wine, beer, and cheese are served in the charming front parlor on Friday and Saturday evening. **Pros:** Recent redecorating has truly brought the place up a notch, the lavender "Dolly's Room" is one of the most beautiful rooms in town, fantastic balconies for Mardi Gras parade watching. **Cons:** Rooms that face St. Charles Avenue can be noisy. ✉ *4117 Perrier St., Uptown,* ☎ *504/897–1807 or 888/610–1807* ⊕ *www.maisonperrier.com* 🍽 *9 rooms* ♿ *In-room: Wi-Fi. In-hotel: no elevator* ▤ *AE, D, MC, V.*

¢–$$ 🖼 **Park View Guest House.** Adjacent to beautiful Audubon Park, this Vic-torian guesthouse has graced St. Charles Avenue since 1884. Rooms on the east side have great views of the park. The general rule here is that you get either antiques or a view: brass beds and ceiling fans are found in the "view" rooms. There is a lounge with a fireplace, and breakfast is served in a bay-window dining room. **Pros:** Incomparable views of Audubon Park, easy access to St. Charles streetcar line, great restau-rants nearby. **Con:** Not convenient to downtown or French Quarter attractions. ✉ *7004 St. Charles Ave., Uptown,* ☎ *504/861–7564 or 888/533–0746* ⊕ *www.parkviewguesthouse.com* 🍽 *22 rooms, 16 with bath* ♿ *In-hotel: no elevator* ▤ *AE, D, MC, V* ⏐◎⏐ *CP.*

¢–$ 🖼 **St. Charles Guest House.** Simple and affordable, this 125-year-old European-style B&B is located in the historic Garden District, conve-nient to the St. Charles Avenue streetcar line (stop 11) and an easy ride or walk to the French Quarter (just 17 blocks away). A complimen-tary bakery breakfast is served by the pool. Telephones are available in the lobby, but books replace TVs in this low-tech, high-character guesthouse (though Internet and fax service are available in the office). The peace and quiet is often interrupted by the musicians, artists, and educators discussing the "laissez les bons temps rouler" nature of the city. Tours can be arranged at the front desk. **Pros:** Rates are among the lowest in town, within walking distance of the St. Charles streetcar line, well run by B&B veterans Joanne and Dennis Hilton. **Cons:** Spar-tan furnishings and surroundings. ✉ *1748 Prytania St., Garden Dis-trict,* ☎ *504/523–6556* ⊕ *www.stcharlesguesthouse.com* 🍽 *30 rooms, 24 with bath* ♿ *In-room: no a/c (some), no TV, Wi-Fi. In-hotel: pool, no elevator* ▤ *AE, MC, V* ⏐◎⏐ *CP.*

★ $–$$$ 🖼 **Sully Mansion.** New Orleans architect Thomas Sully built this hand-some, rambling Queen Anne–style house in 1890. In the foyer, light filters through stunning, pastel-color stained-glass windows that are original to the house. The guest rooms have high ceilings, oil paint-ings, tall windows with swagged floor-length drapes, and Victorian hand-me-downs. A neighbor to other grand mansions, the house is on a tree-lined street—just a block from St. Charles Avenue and close to Magazine Street shops. **Pros:** Old-world charm, owners are experts at paying individual attention to guests. **Cons:** None come to mind. ✉*2631 Prytania St., Garden District,* ☎*504/891–0457 or 800/364–2414* ⊕*www.sullymansion.com* ⇨*5 rooms, 2 suites* ⌂*In-room: Wi-Fi. In-hotel: no elevator* ▤*AE, D, MC, V* ❚⊙❚*CP.*

MID-CITY

GUESTHOUSES & BED-AND-BREAKFASTS

$–$$ ⛨**Ashton's Bed & Breakfast.** Few details have been missed in re-creating this sumptuous 1861 mansion, nine blocks from the French Quarter. Eight distinctively appointed guest rooms have a range of beds, including iron, Shaker, and four-poster. The full breakfast includes such treats as *pain perdu* (French toast), eggs Benedict, and crab cakes. Fresh baked goods and snacks are constantly replenished in the house. The common parlor has a selection of great books, and the backyard is intimate and quiet. Concierge services are provided. **Pros:** Exquisite, spacious room decor; nice location, not far from New Orleans City Park. **Con:** No streetcar or easy public transportation nearby. ✉*2023 Esplanade Ave., Mid-City,* ☎*504/942–7048 or 800/725–4131* ⊕*www. ashtonsbb.com* ⇨*8 rooms* ⌂*In-room: Wi-Fi. In-hotel: no elevator, concierge* ▤*AE, MC, V* ❚⊙❚*BP.*

$–$$$$ ⛨**Edgar Degas House.** Once home to French Impressionist Edgar

Fodor'sChoice Degas, this historic 1852 home retains its original floor plan and col-

★ ors. Spacious second-floor rooms have chandeliers that hang from 14-foot ceilings; one has a whirlpool bath; another has a balcony. The owners are happy to give you a private tour of the house, which has become a favorite local spot for weddings and private parties. Parlors on the first floor display reproductions of the artist's works. You can have an authentic creole breakfast in the large private rear courtyard. **Pros:** Meticulously maintained and expertly operated, designated on the U.S. National Register of Historic Places. **Cons:** None come to mind. ✉*2306 Esplanade Ave., Mid-City,* ☎*504/821–5009 or 800/755–6730* ⊕*www.degashouse. com* ⇨*9 rooms* ⌂*In-hotel: no elevator* ▤*AE, MC, V* ❚⊙❚*CP.*

★ **$$–$$$$** ⛨**House on Bayou Road.** This circa-1798 West Indies–style creole plantation home, set on 2 acres of lawns and gardens, has rooms filled with Louisiana antiques, including handsome four-poster featherbeds. Accommodations are in the main house as well as in detached cottages. The grand suite in the private cottage has a skylight over the bed, bookshelves, and a whirlpool bath. A celebrity favorite, this inn has hosted Dan Aykroyd, Alfre Woodard, Fran Drescher, and Brad Pitt.

> **DELICIOUS DIGS**
>
> The luxurious House on Bayou Road has a truly unique amenity—a cooking school. The New Orleans Cooking Experience, which offers half-day and multiday classes, is located in the 1798 inn's state-of-the-art teaching kitchen. For total immersion, sign up for the cooking school vacation program, which focuses on traditional creole and Cajun recipes; classes are taught by noted New Orleans chefs like James Beard, award-winning chef Frank Brigtsen, and New Orleans's "food diva," Poppy Tooker.

A cooking school is conducted on the premises. **Pros:** Quiet, private, a bit off the beaten path. **Cons:** Be careful about walking in this area after dark, not really convenient to restaurants. ⊠*2275 Bayou Rd., Bayou St. John,* ☎*504/945–0992, 504/949–7711, or 800/882–2968* ⊕*www. houseonbayouroad.com* ⇌*8 rooms, 1 cottage* ⌂*In-room: Wi-Fi. In-hotel: pool, no elevator* ⊟*AE, DC, MC, V* ⏀*BP.*

KENNER/AIRPORT

★ **$–$$** 🏨 **New Orleans Airport Hilton.** Located directly across from the Louis Armstrong New Orleans International Airport, this is ideal spot for travelers flying in late or departing early in the morning. The decor throughout is surprisingly upscale, with muted pastel colors that coordinate well with the soft-pink Caribbean-style exterior. The hand-woven area rugs are from England. Check out the 21-station fitness center and oversize outdoor hot tub. **Pros:** Nice amenities, Crabtree & Evelyn bath products, big emphasis on linens and bed comfort. **Con:** Not suitable for those who want to visit the French Quarter (which is 11 mi away). ⊠*901 Airline Hwy., Kenner* ☎*504/469–5000 or 800/445–8667* ⊕*www.neworleans.hilton.com* ⇌*317 rooms, 2 suites* ⌂*In-room: Wi-Fi. In-hotel: restaurant, bar, tennis court, pool, gym, airport shuttle, parking (fee)* ⊟*AE, D, DC, MC, V.*

METAIRIE

$$–$$$ 🏨 **New Orleans Marriott Metairie at Lakeway.** This Marriott features grand vistas of Lake Pontchartrain, spacious guest rooms and suites, and a state-of-the-art health club, the Lakeway Athletic Club. The Bistro 38 Restaurant serves Country French cuisine, prepared by renowned local chef Dominique Macquet. The Lobby Lounge has live entertainment several nights a week. All rooms have 30-inch flat-screen televisions. **Pros:** Room decor is as upscale and well appointed as any downtown New Orleans property, outstanding in-hotel dining. **Con:** Hotel is located in an area that requires a car. ⊠*3838 N. Causeway Blvd., Metairie* ☎*504/836-5253 or 800/522–6963* ⊕*www.neworleans lakesidehotel.com* ⇌*220 rooms, 30 suites* ⌂*In-room: Wi-Fi. In-hotel: restaurant, bar, pool, parking (fee)* ⊟*AE, D, DC, MC, V.*

Nightlife & the Arts

WORD OF MOUTH

"You haven't really experienced New Orleans until you walk down Bourbon Street after dark. It is loud and crazy, but great people-watching. You have to see it to believe it. Stay nearby but not on Bourbon Street, so you can get away from the craziness when you feel like it."

—Rhonda

By Russell
McCulley

PEOPLE COME TO EAT, LISTEN TO LIVE MUSIC, AND PARTY; and the city still delivers on all three counts. No American city places such a premium on pleasure as New Orleans. From swank hotel lounges to sweaty dance clubs, refined jazz clubs and raucous Bourbon Street bars, this city is serious about frivolity—and famous for it. Partying is more than an occasional indulgence in this city—it's a lifestyle.

The city's fabled nightlife was one of the first things to rebound from Hurricane Katrina; indeed, at least one French Quarter bar, Johnny White's, stayed open during the storm and its long aftermath, offering warm beer and companionship to a handful of shell-shocked residents and hordes of visiting journalists. Things have since stabilized; Bourbon Street is once again awash in neon and noise, and neighborhood joints throughout the city have reopened. Locals seem to be socializing more than ever, seeking camaraderie and community, and expressing a newfound appreciation for the music and culture that, in Katrina's wake, appeared more fragile and precious than ever.

Still, the city's nightlife—and to a degree its performing arts—is struggling to recover its former glory, especially those venues that relied on the tourist and convention trade for most of their business. Musicians themselves face a host of issues; many lost instruments and steady gigs, and the city's current housing shortage has all but eliminated the relatively cheap rents that enabled artists and service-industry workers to live close to their jobs. However, in the city that cradled jazz and helped birth the blues, it should be no surprise that the musical heart beats on. There are plenty of opportunities to hear live music—not just jazz and blues, but rock, hip-hop, Cajun and zydeco, folk, electronica, and homegrown New Orleans R&B.

Many establishments listed in this chapter as simply bars or lounges nonetheless host some live music—sometimes it's almost hard to get away from it. If you have never visited the city before, you should consider the following standouts, which are described in more detail later in the chapter. Famous institutions such as **Preservation Hall** and the **Palm Court Jazz Café** carry the torch of traditional jazz. Next door to Preservation Hall is the internationally known watering hole **Pat O'Brien's,** where the atmosphere is loud and lively, fueled by such colorful cocktails as the Hurricane and Purple People Eater. **Snug Harbor,** on Frenchmen Street, showcases more-formal jazz performances, both local and national. Next door, **d.b.a.** hosts an eclectic menu of local music, including Latin, funk, and blues. Also for the hip set is the **Circle Bar,** lovingly referred to as the world's smallest bar. The lineup at **Tipitina's** varies nightly, from rhythm and blues to rock, jazz, and funk, with Cajun dancing on Sunday evening. Swinging singles and happy couples alike dance to toe-tapping Cajun music and its black counterpart, zydeco, seven nights a week at **Mulate's** and frequently at the **Maple Leaf** and the **Mid-City Bowling Lanes** (known informally as the Rock 'n' Bowl). A number of Louisiana swamp pop and rhythm-and-blues musicians who had hit songs at the dawn of the rock and roll era still call the city home; if you're lucky, your visit might coincide

Practical Matters

Bars tend to open in the early afternoon and stay open well into the morning hours; live music, though, follows a more-restrained schedule. Some jazz spots and clubs in the French Quarter stage evening sets around 6 PM or 9 PM; at a few clubs, such as the Palm Court, the bands actually finish by 11 PM. But this is the exception: for the most part, gigs begin between 10 and 11 PM, and locals rarely emerge for an evening out before 10. Keep in mind that the lack of a legal closing time means that shows advertised for 11 may not start until after midnight.

It's best to bring cash to neighborhood clubs that host music or just serve drinks. Many take plastic but a few do not. In those places where you can run a tab, you'll be asked to leave your credit card with the bartender. Don't forget to collect it at the end of the night.

Dress codes are as rare as snow in New Orleans. On any given night in the French Quarter, and especially during the Carnival season, you'll see everything from tutus, fairy wings, and ball gowns to T-shirts and torn jeans.

Many bars on Bourbon Street entice visitors by presenting bands and/or strip shows with no cover charge. They make their money by imposing a two-drink minimum, with draft beer or soft drinks—served in small glasses—costing $5 to $8 apiece. Prices range from $4 to $8 a drink in hotel lounges and get cheaper as you move farther away from the Quarter. Music clubs generally charge a flat cover between $5 and $20, with the high-end prices usually reserved for national touring artists, holidays, and special occasions. A single admission covers all sets for the evening at a given club (but you might be asked to feed the kitty at more-modestly priced shows).

Check the public radio stations WWOZ at 90.7 FM, which showcases Louisiana music, and Tulane University's WTUL at 91.5 FM, for a calendar of musical happenings about town. For detailed and up-to-date listings, consult the Friday "Lagniappe" entertainment supplement of the *Times-Picayune*, or *Gambit*, the alternative weekly that appears on Sunday and is carried free in many bars, cafés, and stores. The *TP*'s daily listing also covers many clubs. The monthly *OffBeat* magazine has in-depth music coverage and listings and is available at many hotels, stores, and restaurants; by the end of the month, though, listings in *OffBeat* become less reliable. But you can check the magazine's Web site for music listings at ⊕ *www. offbeat.com*. Never be shy about calling clubs to ask what kind of music a given group plays. It's a good idea to call before going anywhere, since hours may vary from day to day and the lineup sometimes changes.

6

with an increasingly rare performance by Fats Domino or an appearance by the radiant Irma Thomas.

If you don't care for the club scene—or have kids in tow—the National Park Service sponsors free live music shows at a couple of locations in the French Quarter: the patio of its headquarters at 419 Decatur Street, and on a stage at the French Market visitor center for the New Orleans Jazz National Historical Park (919 North Peters Street)—which also has a good selection of books and compact disks. Call 504/589–4841 for a schedule. The Louisiana Music Factory (210 Decatur Street, 504/586–1094), one of the city's last record stores, hosts occasional in-store appearances by local artists; it's a great place to pick up CDs by regional musicians.

NIGHTLIFE

BARS & LOUNGES

FRENCH QUARTER

★ **Bombay Club.** A longtime favorite for the martini set, Bombay Club has become equally known for its upscale dinner menu. It's a rather swanky place for the French Quarter, with leather chairs and dark paneling, and one of the few places in the city that enforces a dress code, although it's not overly formal: no shorts, no jeans. Tucked away from the street, this bar in the Prince Conti Hotel hosts live music on many nights. ⊠ *830 Conti St., French Quarter* ☎ *504/586–0972.*

Carousel Revolving Bar. The piano bar at the Hotel Monteleone comes with a literary pedigree: Tennessee Williams, Truman Capote, and Ernest Hemingway all drank here. Grab a bar stool at the eponymous revolving carousel and mull over your own "Great American Novel." ⊠ *214 Royal St., French Quarter* ☎ *504/523–3341.*

Cat's Meow. There are many New Orleanians who rarely set foot in the French Quarter; when they do, they tend to gravitate toward this popular karaoke bar, where "American Idol" wannabes of all ages come to practice their chops. Even Louisiana export Britney Spears is said to have graced the stage at the Cat's Meow—long before she was tabloid fodder, of course. ⊠ *701 Bourbon St., French Quarter* ☎ *504/523–1157.*

Chart Room. Unpretentious even by New Orleans standards, this little bar not far from Canal Street draws a good number of locals from the Quarter and beyond. Drinks are a better value here than in many places in the neighborhood. ⊠ *300 Chartres St., French Quarter* ☎ *504/522–1708.*

Coop's Place. The kitchen at Coop's turns out some surprisingly good versions of Louisiana staples. The po'boys and gumbo are some of the best in the Quarter, and you can wash them down with a selection of 20 bottled beers (including 6 on draft) or a glass of wine from the short but respectable list. Casual dining stretches into the wee hours, when neighborhood regulars and service-industry workers gather around the bar and popular pool table. ⊠ *1109 Decatur St., French Quarter* ☎ *504/525–9053.*

Cosimo's. Few tourists make their way to this hip neighborhood bar tucked away in a far corner of the Lower Quarter. A short flight of stairs leads to a pool and dart room, and quirky chandeliers, ample windows, and a decent wine selection lend the street-level bar a touch of class. An adjacent restaurant serves Tex-Mex treats, including fish tacos and fat burritos; to order, you have to ring a bell and the chef pops his head out the kitchen door. ⊠ *1201 Burgundy St., French Quarter* ☎ *504/522–9715.*

CLOSE UP

Nightlife Around Town

The **French Quarter** and the **Faubourg Marigny** are the easiest places to hear music. Dozens of quality bands play nightly at clubs that are within walking distance of one another, and the myriad dining options make it convenient to spend a whole evening here. Frenchmen Street in the Marigny is currently the hottest music strip in town. Locals flock to this area because it's easier to park on the street and the drinks and cover charges are cheaper than in the Quarter. Much of Frenchmen's activity is within a three-block area. You can roam the streets and window-shop bars or loiter outside on the sidewalk—a popular activity on weekend nights and during peak festival seasons. Clubs along this strip charge a $5–$7 cover for music or none at all. Snug Harbor, the premiere modern jazz venue in town, is pricier, with shows usually costing $10–$20, but a seat is always guaranteed.

Uptown is rich in clubs, although they are far less concentrated, tucked instead down various residential and commercial streets. A minor hub has formed around the Riverbend area, far uptown where St. Charles Avenue and Carrollton Avenue intersect. Cooter Brown's, right at the levee, is a good stop for imported beers and local grub, served all night. Some blocks away, near Carrollton and Oak streets, the Maple Leaf hosts live music every night of the week. Around the corner you will find Carrollton Station, which has bands on the weekends, although walking the few short blocks is not a good idea. Another hub is Magazine Street in the lower Garden District, where you can sit at an outdoor table at the Bulldog or drink on the balcony at the Balcony Bar. Although driving

the two minutes from one spot to the next might seem silly, it is not safe to walk. It's best to call a taxi.

The **Warehouse District** harbors a number of good bars and clubs, some of them in renovated 19th-century warehouses that hark back to the city's cotton exporting heyday. The enormous New Orleans Convention Center runs along the edge of this district, and many spots are often filled with dazed conventioneers. The Central Business District (CBD) has a few establishments, but at night it's mostly quiet.

Perhaps the edgiest local scene is in the **Bywater** District, home to a dozen low-key bars, straight, gay, and mixed. The corner of Royal and Franklin streets forms something of a hub, with a smattering of bars catering to a varied crowd. At the far end of the Bywater, you can be sure to find one of the hippest events of the week when Kermit Ruffins plays Vaughan's every Thursday. On Sunday a mini-party takes place in the courtyard of the wine retail shop, Bacchanal.

Mid-City, the area near City Park and Bayou St. John, suffered a lot of damage in Hurricane Katrina's flooding; restaurants and the handful of bars worth visiting in the area, like the residents themselves, were slow to return. As of this writing, however, a few stalwarts were back, most notably the ever-popular Rock 'n' Bowl shows at Mid-City Bowling Lanes and Banks Street Bar, which returned to a nightly live-music schedule fairly soon after the storm. Venues are fairly spread out and parts of the neighborhood are not the safest, so a car or taxi is recommended at night.

6

Crescent City Brewhouse. This convivial brewpub makes five specialty brews on the premises and one seasonal selection. The suds pair well with oysters on the half shell and other pub grub. Jazz combos set up near the entrance most afternoons, and seating on a second-floor balcony affords a nice view of the Mississippi River and busy Decatur Street. ⊠ *527 Decatur St., French Quarter* 🕾 *504/522–0571.*

> **LIGHTS OUT**
>
> In January 2007, Louisiana enacted a law that bans smoking in restaurants and in bars where food accounts for more than 50% of total sales. Check before you light up; just because it looks like a bar doesn't mean you can enjoy that cigar.

The Dungeon. A narrow alley leads to this aptly named, skull-and-chain-theme bar, which doesn't open until 10:30 PM. Partying here is a rite of passage for many young locals, and the place has become a cult destination of sorts; the rich and famous might turn up, shaking it on the dance floor alongside the regulars. It's not to be confused with the Front of the Dungeon, a more-traditional bar next door. ⊠ *738 Toulouse St., French Quarter* 🕾 *504/523–5530.*

★ **French 75.** Sophistication awaits in the form of rich cigars and fine liquor served up in cozy French-style surroundings. The specialty here is the French 75, made with brandy and premium champagne. After a round or two, venture upstairs to the Germaine Wells Mardi Gras Museum, showcase for many ball gowns worn by the original owner's daughter. ⊠ *813 Bienville St., French Quarter* 🕾 *504/523–5433.*

Kerry Irish Pub. This comfortably well-worn Irish pub has a pool table, a jukebox stocked with the Pogues and Flogging Molly and, of course, Guinness on draft. A small stage at the back hosts singer-songwriters and R&B or jazz musicians most evenings, with no cover charge. ⊠ *331 Decatur St., French Quarter* 🕾 *504/527–5954.*

Fodor'sChoice **Lafitte's Blacksmith Shop.** Probably the most photographed building in
★ the Quarter after St. Louis Cathedral, this 18th-century cottage was, according to legend, once a blacksmith shop that served as a front for the eponymous pirate's less legitimate business ventures. Today, it's a popular and atmospheric piano bar with a rustic, candlelit interior and a small outdoor patio that has banana trees and a sculpture by the late Enrique Alferez (whose work also decorates City Park). ⊠ *941 Bourbon St., French Quarter* 🕾 *504/522–9397.*

Molly's at the Market. This stretch of Decatur Street sports a number of hangouts where bartenders and waiters from other downtown spots wind down after their shifts. Molly's also draws a lot of writers and local media types with special happy hours for journalists; during campaign season, candidates for mayor and city council serve as guest bartenders, mixing drinks for and sparring with reporters. ⊠ *1107 Decatur St., French Quarter* 🕾 *504/525–5169.*

★ **Napoleon House Bar and Cafe.** This vintage watering hole has long been popular with writers, artists, and various other free spirits; locals who wouldn't be caught dead in the French Quarter come here often. It is a living shrine to the New Orleans school of decor: faded grandeur. Chipped wall paint, diffused light, and a tiny courtyard with a trickling fountain and lush banana trees create a timeless escapist mood. The house specialty is a Pimm's Cup (Pimm's No. 1, juice, and club soda—a sort of fizzy, spiked lemonade); a menu including sandwiches, soups, salads, and cheese boards is also available. This is the perfect place for late-afternoon people-watching. ⊠*500 Chartres St., French Quarter* ☎*504/524–9752.*

Old Absinthe House. A low-key oasis in the middle of Bourbon Street's excess, the building that houses this popular watering hole has had some illustrious visitors over its 200-year history, including Oscar Wilde, Mark Twain, Franklin Roosevelt, and Frank Sinatra. Thousands of business cards stapled to the wall serve as interesting wallpaper. ⊠*240 Bourbon St., French Quarter* ☎*504/523–3181.*

Pat O'Brien's. Sure, it's touristy, but there are reasons Pat O's has been a must-stop on the New Orleans cocktail trail for so long. For one thing, there's plenty of room to spread out, from the elegant side bar and piano bar that flank the carriageway entrance to the lush (and in winter, heated) patio. Friendly staff, an easy camaraderie among patrons, and a signature drink—the pink, cloying, and extremely potent Hurricane, which comes with a souvenir glass—make this French Quarter stalwart a pleasant afternoon diversion. ⊠*718 St. Peter St., French Quarter* ☎*504/525–4823.*

FAUBOURG MARIGNY

Bacchanal Fine Wine & Spirits. Although technically it is a wineshop, Bacchanal, in the far reaches of Bywater, is also part tasting room, part neighborhood hangout. Among the wine racks in the old New Orleans building are two big round tables, as well as seating in the courtyard. You can have a bottle uncorked on the premises or order by the glass. High-end Scotches, bourbons, and rums are also on the menu. Sunday afternoons are especially fun, when a local band (and often a chef with a grill) sets up on the courtyard. ⊠*600 Poland Ave., Bywater* ☎*504/948–9111.*

Fodor'sChoice **d.b.a.** A slice of Manhattan sophistication on Frenchmen Street, d.b.a.
★ is the southern outpost of the East Village hot spot. The selection— including international beers on tap, aged Scotches, and obscure tequilas, all listed on chalkboards above the bar—is reason enough to visit. Live music most nights and the Marigny's best people-watching make it a neighborhood favorite. ⊠*616 Frenchmen St., Faubourg Marigny* ☎*504/942–3731.*

Mimi's. The big windows at this corner bar and café stay open most evenings, letting the atmosphere of the shabby-chic neighborhood drift in. Downstairs is a popular gathering spot, with bar stools and a few tables; there's more seating upstairs, along with a kitchen that turns out a respectable selection of tapas well into the early morning hours. ⊠*2601 Royal St., Faubourg Marigny* ☎*504/872–9868.*

R Bar. The owner of one of the city's more-adventurous art galleries took over this Marigny nightspot a few years back. But there's nothing especially high-toned about R Bar, where classic New Wave (and pitchers of local Abita Beer) are always on tap. The place likes to run some offbeat specials—on Monday night, for example, 10 bucks will get you a shot and a haircut—and it's the best place to catch the Krewe of St.

Downtown Nightlife

Bombay Club **18**
Bourbon Pub **31**
Bridge Lounge **3**
Café Lafitte in Exile **33**
Carousel Revolving Bar .. **15**
Cat's Meow **27**
Chart Room **14**

Checkpoint Charlie's **46**
Chris Owens Club **20**
Circle Bar **2**
Coop's Place **44**
Corner Pocket **19**
Cosimo's **40**
Cowpokes **52**

Crescent City
Brewhouse **24**
d.b.a. **48**
Donna's Bar & Grill **38**
The Dungeon **21**
Ernst Cafe **8**
528 on Fulton **11**
French 75 .... **17**

Fritzel's European
Jazz Pub **28**
Golden Lantern **41**
Good Friends **35**
Handsome Willy's **1**
House of Blues **12**
Howlin' Wolf **5**
Kerry Irish Pub **13**

Louis Armstrong Park

N. Rampart St.

Burgundy St.

Toulouse St.

Dauphine St.

Orleans Ave.

St. Peter St.

St. Ann St.

Wilk Row

Jackson Square

Madison St.

Dumaine St.

St. Philip St.

Ursulines St.

Gov. Nicholls St.

Barracks St.

Esplanade Ave.

Bourbon St.

Touro St.

Kerlerec St.

Royal St.

Frenchmen St.

Elysian Fields Ave.

Bourbon St.

Royal St.

Chartres St.

Decatur St.

French Market Pl.

N. Peters St.

◆ Café du Monde
Moon Walk

Mississippi River

0   1/4 mi
0   1/4 km

King Bolderis 39
Lafitte's Blacksmith
Shop 34
Lucy's Retired Surfer's
Bar & Restaurant 9
Margaritaville Café 42
Mimi's 51

Molly's at the Market 43
Mulate's 7
Napoleon House
Bar and Cafe 23
Napoleon's Itch 29
Ninth Circle 36
Old Absinthe House 16
One Eyed Jacks 22

Oz 30
Palm Court Jazz Café 45
Parade Disco 32
Pat O'Brien's 26
Preservation Hall 25
R Bar 47
Rawhide 37

Republic 6
Snug Harbor 49
Spotted Cat 50
Vic's Kangaroo Cafe 10
Ugly Dog Saloon 4

Bright Lights, Big Easy

One legacy of New Orleans's Caribbean cultural climate that comes as a pleasant shock to many visitors is the city's tolerant attitude toward alcohol. Most bars stay open as long as a crowd is on hand: with 24-hour liquor licenses, closing time is strictly voluntary. Revelers can leave a bar and take their drinks along. Whiskey, beer, or wine can be purchased anywhere, anytime, at such unlikely outlets as gas stations or drive-through daiquiri depots. And, beware, liquor used to mix drinks is rarely measured. New Orleans bartenders are generous people.

Many bars advertise the Hurricane—a rum-and-fruit concoction that is the signature drink at **Pat O'Brien's**, which is the best place to order one. Less Hawaiian Punch-y than the Hurricane is the light-pink Monsoon, a specialty at **Snug Harbor.**

Ann parade early Mardi Gras day, when the procession of outlandishly costumed revelers makes an extended pit stop here ✉ *1431 Royal St., Faubourg Marigny* ☎ *504/948–7499.*

CBD & WAREHOUSE DISTRICT

Bridge Lounge. Formerly a showcase for gritty punk bands, Bridge Lounge had a radical makeover a few years back; now, instead of motorcycle jackets and wild hair, it's mostly youngish professionals kicking back, many with their dogs in tow. The drinks are good, the light flattering, and the owners' oenophilia is reflected in the bar's extensive list of wines by the glass. ✉ *1201 Magazine St., Warehouse District* ☎ *504/299–1888.*

Ernst Cafe. Ernst has been operating as a bar since the first years of the 20th century, and the classic interior and upstairs balcony provide a welcome respite to conventioneers, lawyers from nearby firms, and service-industry folks finishing shifts at surrounding hotels. The menu is classic, too, heavy on bar food staples like fried seafood, wraps, and burgers. ✉ *600 S. Peters St., Warehouse District* ☎ *504/525–8544.*

Handsome Willy's. Sandwiched between a forlorn stretch of the Interstate 10 overpass and the Medical District, Handsome Willy's—named for a dapper repeat customer of the notorious brothel that used to be on the site—dubs itself "a bar and hot dog bistro." The menu has daily specials to go with the dogs, and at night there's a rotating cast of DJs, frequent (and irreverent) literary events, and the occasional live band on the outdoor patio. It's not on any tourist map, but casually hip and worth seeking out. ✉ *218 S. Robertson St., CBD* ☎ *504/525–0377.*

Lucy's Retired Surfer Bar & Restaurant. Space can get tight in this out-of-its element urban beach bar, especially when the after-work crew jams the bar in search of beer and margaritas. The other half of the place is a restaurant that serves tasty sandwiches, fish tacos, and brunch on weekends; upstairs, a secondary club hosts occasional open-mike comedy shows. ✉ *701 Tchoupitoulas St., Warehouse District* ☎ *504/523–8995.*

Ugly Dog Saloon. Sporting events blare from big-screen televisions as customers chow down on some of the Warehouse District's best barbecue at this cavernous barroom. The vibe is decidedly macho, but friendly bartenders make everybody feel welcome. ✉*401 Andrew Higgins Dr., Warehouse District* ☎*504/569–8459.*

Vic's Kangaroo Café. This narrow Aussie pub has a dartboard, a good beer selection, and a menu sprinkled with Cajun-style dishes. It's especially lively on Friday afternoons when the downtown after-five crowd hits the bars. ✉*636 Tchoupitoulas St., Warehouse District* ☎*504/524–4329.*

> ### ONE FOR THE ROAD
>
> Although bottles and glasses are officially banned on the street, New Orleans is one of the few places where it's perfectly legal to carry a drink on the street. Ready to move on? Ask the bartender for a "go-cup."

UPTOWN & THE GARDEN DISTRICT

The Bulldog. The crowd routinely spills out onto the sidewalk picnic tables at this hopping Magazine Street beer bar. The "dawg" has 50 different brews on tap and a pub-grub menu, but during crawfish season, many patrons opt for boiled mudbugs from the corner seafood market across the street. ✉*3236 Magazine St., Garden District* ☎*504/891–1516.*

Fodor'sChoice
★ **Columns Hotel.** An evening cocktail on the expansive front porch of the Columns, shaded by centuries-old oak trees and overlooking the St. Charles Avenue streetcar route, is one of the more-romantic New Orleans experiences. The Victorian Lounge, with period decor and a fireplace, and plenty of decaying elegance, draws a white-collar crowd of all ages. Live jazz combos play Monday through Wednesday evenings. ✉*3811 St. Charles Ave., Uptown* ☎*504/899–9308.*

F&M Patio Bar. For some people, an all-nighter in New Orleans isn't complete until they've danced on top of the pool table at this perpetually open hangout. There's a loud jukebox, a popular photo booth, and a late-night kitchen (it gets going around 8 PM and keeps serving until early in the morning). The tropical patio can actually be peaceful at times. You'll need a car or a taxi to get here. ✉*4841 Tchoupitoulas St., Uptown* ☎*504/895–6784.*

Fat Harry's. An enviable location at the corner of St. Charles and Napoleon avenues makes Fat Harry's a coveted spot for Mardi Gras parade watching. The rest of the year it attracts a rowdy late-night college crowd and a more-mixed group in early evenings. When the weather's nice, the sidewalk tables fill up fast. ✉*4330 St. Charles Ave., Uptown* ☎*504/895–9582.*

The Kingpin. Deep-red walls and a velvet Elvis lend this Uptown spot a touch of kitsch, but it's the friendly atmosphere, a jukebox stocked with vintage soul and modern rock, and a young, attractive crowd that draws people in nightly. Stop in on a Sunday during football season for barbecue and a chance to cheer on the beloved Saints. ✉*1307 Lyons St., Uptown* ☎*504/891–2373.*

Parasol's Restaurant & Bar. Po'boy devotees practically genuflect at the mention of this hole-in-the-wall, which has been serving the sloppy sandwiches, along with Guinness on tap, for more than 50 years. The annual St. Patrick's Day party at Parasol's spills out into the surrounding neighborhood of the Lower Garden District; it's grown so large that police have to erect barricades to keep traffic out—or keep the revelers in. ⊠*2533 Constance St., Garden District* ☎*504/897–5413.*

St. Joe's. Formerly a notorious hangout for underage college students, St. Joe's changed owners and image, and adopted a more-upscale clientele a few years back. The narrow front bar draws inspiration from Latin American churches; the back patio, strung with Chinese lanterns and decorated with statues of Asian deities, is a "Caribbean Zen temple," in the owner's words. Drinks are made with real juice, and the mojitos are especially popular. ⊠*5535 Magazine St., Uptown* ☎*504/899–3744.*

MID-CITY & BEYOND

Finn McCool's. Heavy flooding and extensive looting shut this Mid-City bar down for months post-Katrina, but the Irish owners rebuilt, even adding a fish-and-chips shop. Run by devoted soccer fans, the bar beams in European football games via live satellite feed for devout expats, who because of the time difference sometimes gather at 7 AM to hoist stouts and cheer on their team. On Monday night, there's a popular and competitive trivia quiz; prizes include sacks of potatoes. ⊠*3701 Banks St., Mid-City* ☎*504/486–9080.*

Pal's. Tucked away in a quiet Bayou St. John neighborhood, this little gem is a surprisingly hip hangout with a carefully crafted, Rat Pack–era louche vibe, right down to the pinup girl wallpaper in the men's room. Thursday is martini and manicure night, when one price gets you well groomed and well oiled. ⊠*949 N. Rendon St., Bayou St. John* ☎*504/488–7257.*

COFFEEHOUSES

Fodor'sChoice
★ **Café du Monde.** It just wouldn't be a trip to New Orleans without a stop at the French Market mainstay, which has been dishing up chicory-laced café au lait and sugar-dusted beignets since 1862. The open-air seating area, with a view of Jackson Square, makes for prime people-watching. ⊠*800 Decatur St., French Quarter* ☎*504/525–4544.*

Café Rose Nicaud. Named after a former slave who bought her freedom by selling coffee in Jackson Square, this comfortable Marigny coffee shop also has a respectable wine and beer selection, along with a café menu of soups, salads, and sandwiches. There's free wireless Internet for the lunching laptop set. ⊠*632 Frenchmen St., Faubourg Marigny* ☎*504/949–3300.*

CC's Coffeehouse. The coffee shop–retail outlet for the local Community Coffee brand, CC's offers muffins, pastries, and croissants, along with a decent cup of java. Iced coffee drinks are popular, especially during the extended New Orleans summer. ⊠*941 Royal St., French Quarter* ☎*504/581–6996* ⊠*2800 Esplanade Ave., Mid-City* ☎*504/482–9865* ⊠*900 Jefferson Ave., at Magazine St., Uptown* ☎*504/891–4969.*

P. J.'s Coffee & Tea Cafes. This chain of coffeehouses has locations throughout New Orleans. Though the decor favors a country-bumpkin shade of pink, the coffee is excellent, and the cold-brewed iced coffee—a New Orleans specialty—is the best in the city. Hours vary among locations, with the University District branch on Maple Street usually open latest. ✉ *7624 Maple St., Uptown* ☎ *504/866–7031* ✉ *5432 Magazine St., Uptown* ☎ *504/895–2202* ✉ *644 Camp St., CBD* ☎ *504/529–3658*.

Rue de la Course. When nearby universities are in session, students camp out here getting hopped up on caffeine while tapping out their theses on laptops. The comfortable surroundings and nice views of Magazine Street will make you want to linger, too. Both locations are open daily until midnight. ✉ *3121 Magazine St., Uptown* ☎ *504/899–0242* ✉ *1140 S. Carrollton Ave., Uptown* ☎ *504/861–4343*.

GAMBLING

Admission to all the casinos is free, but you must be 21 or older to enter. Harrah's New Orleans, at the foot of Canal Street, is the only land-based casino and is by far the largest and nicest. The other casinos are on boats, which remain dockside. Harrah's and Boomtown Belle are open 24 hours daily, and feature live entertainment.

Boomtown Belle Casino. On the west bank of the Mississippi River, the *Boomtown Belle* is docked at the Harvey Canal, 10 mi from New Orleans. The vessel has 30,000 square feet of gaming space and accommodates 1,600 passengers. Besides the 1,500 slots and 46 gaming tables, the casino has a café, arcade, and lounge. ✉ *4132 Peters Rd., Harvey* ☎ *504/366–7711* ⊕ *www.boomtownneworleans.com*.

Harrah's New Orleans. Commanding the foot of Canal Street, this beaux-arts-style casino is the largest such facility in the South. Its 100,000 square feet hold 2,900 slots and 120 gaming tables. The casino's dining options include an upscale steak restaurant run by local celebrity chef John Besh and the French brasserie Riche. Valet parking is available. ✉ *4 Canal St., CBD* ☎ *504/533–6000 or 800/427–7247* ⊕ *www. harrahs.com*.

Treasure Chest Casino. Seven minutes from the airport on Lake Pontchartrain, the *Treasure Chest* has more than 900 slot machines, 40 gaming tables, and a no-smoking gaming area. The lunch and dinner buffet serves Louisiana specialties; a free shuttle operates to and from nearby hotels. It's open daily from 11 AM to 3 AM, and until 5 AM on Friday and Saturday. ✉ *5050 Williams Blvd., Kenner* ☎ *504/443–8000 or 800/443–8000* ⊕ *www.treasurechestcasino.com*.

GAY & LESBIAN

New Orleans has a sizable gay-and-lesbian community and has long been a popular destination for gay travelers. Mardi Gras and Southern Decadence, which takes place Labor Day weekend in early September, are the biggest draws. Crowds are also thick at Halloween and at Easter, when a gay Easter parade rolls through the Quarter. The city celebrates Gay Pride in October, but it's a fairly low-key affair, perhaps because of the competition from the wealth of other gay gatherings.

Bars are concentrated in the French Quarter, especially near the intersection of Bourbon and St. Ann streets, and in the Faubourg Marigny, where they tend to be quieter and populated almost entirely by locals from the surrounding neighborhood. A few bars are clustered on North Rampart Street, on the Quarter's northern edge, but exercise caution when walking around here late at night. Women are welcome at most all of the establishments listed below, but there are very few bars, and none in the Quarter, that cater exclusively to lesbians. A scene of sorts has developed around **Swirl** (⊠ *3143 Ponce de Leon, Mid-City* ☎ *504/304–0635*), a wineshop just off Esplanade Avenue near City Park, where the Friday-evening wine tastings draw a throng of neighborhood denizens, including a disproportionate number of gay women.

A more-complete list of nightlife and other services can be found in the free publication *Ambush* available at most bars or at **FAB—Faubourg Marigny Art and Books** (⊠ *600 Frenchmen St., Faubourg Marigny* ☎ *504/947–3700*), which carries a selection of gay titles, works by New Orleans authors, and art.

BARS

Bourbon Pub. You can't miss this 24-hour video bar at the corner of St. Ann and Bourbon, especially in early evenings, when the doors are open and the dance crowd spills into the street. There's usually a cover charge on Friday and Saturday nights after 10 PM; Sunday afternoon is devoted to vintage videos by assorted gay icons. ⊠ *801 Bourbon St., French Quarter* ☎ *504/529–2107.*

Café Lafitte in Exile. A Bourbon Street stalwart, Lafitte attracts a somewhat older and very casual group of gay men. The bar has a second floor with a pool table and wraparound balcony with a bird's-eye view of the street scene below. Sunday afternoon, when the oldies spin and the paper-napkin confetti flies, is especially lively. ⊠ *901 Bourbon St., French Quarter* ☎ *504/522–8397.*

Corner Pocket. Filmmaker John Waters reportedly counts the Pocket as a New Orleans favorite, and with skinny, tattooed strippers on the bar and an inebriated drag queen emceeing the show, it's easy to see why. Sleazy fun on a good night, but keep your wits about you. ⊠ *940 St. Louis St., French Quarter* ☎ *504/568–9829.*

Country Club New Orleans. The clothing-optional pool at this handsome 19th-century Bywater mansion gets crowded on muggy summer weekends. Up front (and well out of eyeshot), elegant sitting rooms have been converted into an ambitious but reasonably priced restaurant. The club music cranks up after the restaurant closes. Gay neighborhood residents form the core of the Country Club's business, but all are welcome. ⊠ *634 Louisa St., Bywater* ☎ *504/945–0742.*

Cowpokes. Cowboy long before gay cowboy was cool, this Western-theme bar on the fringes of the Marigny triangle doubles as a local theater troupe's performance space. Cowpokes offers dance lessons and frequent contests; call for a schedule, and take a cab. ⊠ *2240 St. Claude Ave., Faubourg Marigny* ☎ *504/947–0505.*

Golden Lantern. The Lower Quarter has become a lot more upscale since this neighborhood gay haunt's heyday, but the Lantern soldiers on. The bartender's whims determine the music, the drinks are strong, and the 4–9 PM happy hour is one of the city's longest. The bar is best known as ground zero for the annual Southern Decadence drag parade, when a throng gathers out front for the kickoff. ✉ *1239 Royal St., French Quarter* ☎ *504/529–2860.*

> **FEED THE KITTY**
>
> Bring cash to live music clubs; many bands play for tips alone. Expect the hat (or more often, an old coffee can) to be passed around once per set.

Good Friends. With its tasteful decor and reasonable volume level, Good Friends provides a slightly more-upscale, sedate alternative to the blasting disco bars down the street. The Queen's Head Pub on the second floor, open weekends, has darts, a wraparound balcony, and respectable martinis. Brush up on your show tunes at the popular Sunday afternoon piano sing-along. ✉ *740 Dauphine St., French Quarter* ☎ *504/566–7191.*

Napoleon's Itch. The only no-smoking gay bar in New Orleans, this narrow space offers a tobacco-free alternative right in the heart of St. Ann-and-Bourbon gay central. The screeching diva dance music is pretty much the same as in the neighboring bars, but comfy sofas and handsome bartenders are a plus, and the crowd tends to be a bit dressier. ✉ *732 Bourbon St., French Quarter* ☎ *504/371–5450.*

Ninth Circle. One of the more-popular Rampart Street bars, this small joint gets jumping late with DJs and frequent drag shows. The sunrise happy hour caters to service-industry workers just coming off the night shift. ✉ *700 N. Rampart St., French Quarter* ☎ *504/524–7654.*

Rawhide. As the name indicates, this is a rowdy—and sexually charged—leather-and-Levi's bar. It's two blocks from Bourbon Street and is open around the clock. ✉ *740 Burgundy St., French Quarter* ☎ *504/525–8106.*

DANCE BARS

Oz. A spacious dance club with a demographic skewed to young gay men, Oz nevertheless draws a good number of straight men and women, largely because of the scarcity of good dance floors in the French Quarter. It's open around the clock and tends to peak very late. ✉ *800 Bourbon St., French Quarter* ☎ *504/593–9491.*

Parade Disco. High-energy disco rules at this dance club above the Bourbon Pub. If it gets to be too much, a quieter back bar and a balcony offer retreat. The crowd is mostly male and young, but women (lesbian or not) are welcome. ✉ *801 Bourbon St., above Bourbon Pub, French Quarter* ☎ *504/529–2107.*

MUSIC VENUES

First-time visitors to New Orleans are often bowled over by the amount of both musical talent the city contains and the opportunities to witness it live—in clubs, coffee shops, at festivals, even on the street. Use the following list as a starting point: the venues selected here host good bands on a regular basis, but represent just a fraction of the opportunities you'll have to hear live music.

Most of the city's live music clubs—especially those in the parts of town most frequented by visitors—have reopened. Still, music is a fickle business, even in the best of times, so call ahead before heading out to some far-flung nightclub, or check the entertainment listings in one of the city's periodicals. French Quarter—and Faubourg Marigny—jazz clubs usually get going around 8 PM; some present music in the afternoon as well, usually on weekends. The opening sets at neighborhood bars and rock clubs usually don't start until 10 PM or later.

FRENCH QUARTER

Chris Owens Club. The owner and star of this eponymous nightclub is a reluctantly aging French Quarter dancer and entertainer, whose slightly risqué act includes gams, feathers, and conga drums. The kitsch factor is high in the black-and-white tile theater, but the ebullient Ms. Owens takes it all very seriously, and her energy and dedication are admirable. ⊠ *500 Bourbon St., French Quarter* ☎ *504/523–6400.*

★ **Donna's Bar & Grill.** Donna's is a great place to hear traditional jazz, R&B, and the city's young brass bands in an informal neighborhood setting. On Monday night many of the city's top musicians stop by after their regular gigs to sit in for the diverse sets of drummer Bob French; free red beans and rice are served. ⊠ *800 N. Rampart St., French Quarter* ☎ *504/596–6914.*

Fritzel's European Jazz Pub. Although much of the Bourbon Street scene can seem crass or tawdry, this modest club, with its tattered interior and picnic table seating, feels just right. Jazz and German beer are on tap daily, and the intimate setting erases the distance between audience and band, which invariably includes seasoned, accomplished musicians. ⊠ *733 Bourbon St., French Quarter* ☎ *504/561–0432.*

★ **House of Blues.** Despite its name, blues is a relatively small component in the booking policy, which also embraces rock, jazz, country, soul, funk, world music, and more, performed by everyone from local artists to international touring acts. The adjoining restaurant has an eclectic menu, with classic Southern cuisine, served in ample portions at reasonable prices. The **Parish,** a smaller, more-intimate offshoot upstairs from the main house, hosts local and touring groups. ⊠ *225 Decatur St., French Quarter* ☎ *504/529–2583 concert line.*

Margaritaville Café. Yes, it's named after *that* song. Jimmy Buffett's devoted fans, called "parrotheads," flock to this shrine to the singer-songwriter-author that has local and regional blues, rock, and zydeco performers starting sets as early as 3 PM and going into the night. Menu items such as the "Cheeseburger in Paradise" derive from Buffett songs, and several varieties of the salt-rimmed signature drink are served. Decor consists mainly of Buffett photos, and the man himself has been known to drop in occasionally. ⊠ *1104 Decatur St., French Quarter* ☎ *504/592–2565.*

One Eyed Jack's. This former Toulouse Street theater plays host to touring modern rock acts as well as local up-and-comers. The 19th-century saloon interior provides an appropriately decadent backdrop for

The Saga of Preservation Hall

Of all the clubs that went dark after Hurricane Katrina, perhaps none was missed as sorely as Preservation Hall, the 45-year-old shrine to traditional jazz. Fans of the music rejoiced when the venerable club reopened, eight months after the storm, with a kickoff party timed to coincide with the opening of Jazz Fest 2006. The opening gala included at least one celebrity—U2's The Edge, who sat in with the house band on a funked-up version of his band's hit "Vertigo"—but the real guests of honor were the members of the Preservation Hall Jazz Band, many of whom lost homes and instruments in Katrina, and who were still scattered around the country. For them, it was a homecoming party, if only a temporary one.

"I'm trying to move back here," said banjoist Carl LeBlanc, who had been living with family in Houston since the storm. But "a lot of people are not even coming back," he said. LeBlanc, like many of his fellow musicians, had found plenty of work in his adopted hometown. But "a lot of New Orleans musicians, the ones who need this place's soul," he said, putting his hand to his heart, "they're coming back just to refuel every once in a while."

With entire neighborhoods still struggling to rebuild, many musicians are finding it easier to live elsewhere. Bassist Walter Payton landed a job

teaching music in north Louisiana, and planned to stay. "I bought a house in Tallulah. And I'm loving it, man," he said. Even though Payton's Uptown home survived the storm, uncertainty about the music industry's future in New Orleans was keeping him away, at least for a time. "There are a lot of people who are dying to come back. And they ain't got nothing to come back to," he said. "I have a house here, but if I come back, I'm going to be doing less than I'm doing now."

Fortunately, things have turned out better for Payton's former bandmates than many had feared. Private donations and grants helped keep the club open through the first, difficult post-Katrina summer of 2006. Conventioneers and leisure travelers have begun trickling back to the city, and the Preservation Hall Jazz Band has maintained a hectic tour schedule that began not long after the storm. But musicians, and the infrastructure that supports them, still face a lot of hurdles. New Orleans's tourism industry is still far below its pre-Katrina peak, and there's a shortage of affordable housing in the city. Amid all of these uncertainties, though, the music will survive. "That's my purpose in life," said trombonist Lucien Barbarin, whose family lineage includes the jazz greats Paul Barbarin and Danny Barker. "To keep this music alive."

Fleur de Tease, a resident burlesque troupe. ✉ *615 Toulouse St., French Quarter* ☎ *504/569–8361*.

Palm Court Jazz Café. Banjo player Danny Barker immortalized this restaurant in his song "Palm Court Strut." The best of traditional New Orleans jazz is presented in a classy setting with tile floors, exposed brick walls, and a handsome mahogany bar. There are decent creature comforts here; regional cuisine is served, and you can sit at the bar and rub elbows with local musicians. There's a wide selection of records, tapes, and CDs on sale here. ⊠*1204 Decatur St., French Quarter* ☎*504/525–0200.*

★ **Preservation Hall.** The jazz tradition that flowered in the 1920s is enshrined in this cultural landmark by a cadre of distinguished New Orleans musicians, most of whom were schooled by an ever-dwindling group of elder statesmen. There is limited seating on benches—many patrons end up squatting on the floor or standing in back—and no beverages are served or allowed. Nonetheless, the legions of satisfied customers regard an evening here as an essential New Orleans experience. Cover charge is $10, but can run a bit higher for special appearances. ⊠*726 St. Peter St., French Quarter* ☎*504/522–2841 or 504/523–8939.*

> **MINORS WELCOME**
>
> Bourbon Street's entertainment options are largely off-limits to children, but younger music fans need not feel excluded. Both Preservation Hall and Palm Court Jazz Café welcome underage patrons; other clubs, including Tipitina's and Howlin' Wolf, occasionally host all-ages shows. Kids are also welcome at the free shows staged by the National Park Service's New Orleans Jazz Historical Park, both at the park's visitor center (419 Decatur Street, 504/589–4841) and the Tuesday-through-Saturday afternoon shows at 916 North Peters Street, in the French Market.

OFF THE BEATEN PATH

Ernie K-Doe's Mother-in-Law Lounge. Home base for the late rhythm-and-blues singer (and self-declared Emperor of the Universe) Ernie K-Doe, the Mother-in-Law, named after K-Doe's 1960s hit song, is a singularly New Orleans experience. K-Doe's devoted widow, Ms. Antoinette, carries on the big man's eccentric tradition, including a tendency to turn over the stage to just about anyone who shows up and wants to play. K-Doe memorabilia decorates every nook, and a scarily lifelike effigy of K-Doe himself sits in one corner. Antoinette presides over it all with good cheer and some of the best free red beans and rice you're likely to find. The neighborhood is dodgy, so take a cab. And plan to stay late: the joint usually doesn't start jumping until midnight. ⊠*1500 N. Claiborne Ave., Tremé* ☎*504/947–1078.*

FAUBOURG MARIGNY & BYWATER

Checkpoint Charlie's. This bustling corner bar draws young locals who shoot pool and listen to blues and rock, whether live or from the jukebox—24 hours a day, seven days a week. There's also a paperback library and a fully functioning Laundromat. ⊠*501 Esplanade Ave., Faubourg Marigny* ☎*504/947–0979.*

★ **Snug Harbor.** This intimate club is one of the city's best rooms for soaking up modern jazz, blues, and R&B. It is the home base of such esteemed talent as vocalist Charmaine Neville and pianist-patriarch Ellis Marsalis (father of Wynton and Branford). The dining room serves good local food but is best known for its burgers. Budget-conscious types can listen to the band through speakers in the bar without paying the rather high cover charge. ⊠*626 Frenchmen St., Faubourg Marigny* ☎*504/949–0696.*

Fodor'sChoice **Spotted Cat.** Jazz, funk, and blues bands perform nearly every night,
★ with early-afternoon sets weekends, at this rustic club right in the thick
of the Frenchmen Street action. A rattan seat near the front window
makes for good people-watching. ✉ *623 Frenchmen St., Faubourg
Marigny* ☎ *504/943–3887*.

Vaughan's. Jazz trumpeter Kermit Ruffins's Thursday-night sets (served
up with free red beans and rice) are the big draw at this ramshackle
place in Bywater's farthest reaches; at other times, it's a picturesque and
exceptionally friendly neighborhood bar with live music two or three
nights a week and boiled seafood or barbecue in the back. ✉ *800 Les-
seps St., at Dauphine St., Bywater* ☎ *504/947–5562*.

CBD & WAREHOUSE DISTRICT

Circle Bar. About 10 PM, hipsters and scenesters descend on this underground rock club in an old Lee Circle town house; earlier in the evening, anything goes. If you can't squeeze into the room that holds
what must be the world's tiniest stage, you can watch the action on
a monitor over the bar. ✉ *1032 St. Charles Ave., Warehouse District*
☎ *504/588–2616*.

528 on Fulton. Across from its looming casino, Harrah's has created its
own mini-entertainment district just off Poydras Street. This upscale
jazz venue is part of it. The room is attractive, if a little sanitized, by
New Orleans music club standards, but the acoustics are good and the
entertainment top-notch. Shows take place Wednesday through Saturday. ✉ *528 Fulton St., CBD* ☎ *504/533–6117*.

Howlin' Wolf. This longtime Warehouse District music club recently relocated to a larger space across the street, but the focus is still on touring
rock bands and local hardcore, funk, Latin, and hip-hop acts. ✉ *907
S. Peters St., Warehouse District* ☎ *504/529–5844*.

Mulate's. Across the street from the Convention Center, this large restaurant seats 400, and the dance floor quickly fills with couples twirling
and two-stepping to authentic Cajun bands from the countryside. Regulars love to drag first-timers to the floor for impromptu lessons. The
home-style Cajun cuisine is quite good, and the bands play until 10:30
or 11 PM. ✉ *201 Julia St., Warehouse District* ☎ *504/522–1492*.

Republic. A newcomer to the Warehouse District music scene, this rock
venue retains the rough-timbered feel of the cotton-and-grain warehouse it used to be. The club books touring indie rock bands as well as
local acts; DJs take over the sound system late at night. ✉ *828 S. Peters
St., Warehouse District* ☎ *504/528–8282*.

UPTOWN

Carrollton Station. This cozy little neighborhood bar showcases local
roots rock acts on weekends. It's a few blocks off St. Charles Avenue,
and worth a trip to see one of Susan Cowsill's frequent performances.
✉ *8140 Willow St., Uptown* ☎ *504/865–9190*.

Le Bon Temps Roulé. Local acts from a wide range of genres—rock, jazz,
blues, or funk—take the stage nightly at this lovably ramshackle Magazine Street nightspot. The music gets started after 10 PM; pool tables
and a limited pub-grub menu keep the crowd, which includes a lot of
students from nearby Tulane and Loyola universities, entertained until
then. ✉ *4801 Magazine St., Uptown* ☎ *504/897–3448*.

Fodor'sChoice **Maple Leaf.** The phrase "New Orleans institution" gets thrown around
★ a lot, but this place deserves the title. It's wonderfully atmospheric, with
pressed-tin walls and a lush tropical patio, and one of the city's best
venues for blues, New Orleans–style R&B, funk, zydeco, and jazz. On
Sunday, the bar hosts the South's longest-running poetry reading. It's a
long haul from the French Quarter, but worth the trip, especially if combined with a visit to one of the restaurants clustered near this commercial
stretch of Oak Street. ⊠*8316 Oak St., Uptown* ☎*504/866–9359.*

★ **Tipitina's.** A bust of legendary New Orleans pianist Professor Longhair,
or "Fess," greets visitors at the door of this Uptown landmark, which
takes its name from one of his most-popular songs. As the concert
posters pinned to the walls attest, Tip's hosts a wide variety of touring
bands and local acts. The long-running Sunday-afternoon Cajun dance
still packs the floor. The Tipitina's Foundation has an office and workshop upstairs, where local musicians affected by Hurricane Katrina can
network, gain access to resources, and search for gigs. ⊠*501 Napoleon
Ave., Uptown* ☎*504/895–8477.*

MID-CITY

Banks Street Bar and Grill. Over the past few years, this Mid-City neighborhood nightspot has become one of the city's most reliable venues for
local music, with live shows—sometimes two—every night of the week.
The bill of fare tends to blues and funk, with Walter "Wolfman" Washington and the Roadmasters putting in regular appearances. ⊠*4401
Banks St., Mid-City* ☎*504/486–0258.*

★ **Mid-City Lanes Rock 'n' Bowl.** Down-home Louisiana music in a vintage
bowling alley? Go ahead, try not to have fun. The shambling strip mall
that holds this bowling alley–cum–music club sat in floodwater for
weeks, but the second floor of Rock 'n' Bowl stayed high and dry. Owner
John Blancher loves the music, whether it's blues, rockabilly, R&B, or
swamp pop, and his enthusiasm is infectious. Thursday is zydeco night,
when some of the best musicians from rural Louisiana take the stage.
⊠*4133 S. Carrollton Ave., Mid-City* ☎*504/482–3133.*

THE ARTS

For a relatively small city, New Orleans has a remarkably active and varied
performing-arts community. For current listings, check the daily calendar
in the *Times-Picayune* and its Friday "Lagniappe" section. The free alternative weekly *Gambit* also runs an extensive weekly calendar of events.

Ticket prices for theater and for concerts vary widely, from $10 for per-
formances at smaller venues to $70 for top acts at major halls. You can
purchase tickets from box offices. **Ticketmaster** (☎*504/522–5555* ⊕*www.
ticketmaster.com*) sells tickets for performances at many venues.

CLASSICAL MUSIC

Friends of Music. This organization brings superior performers from all
over the world to Tulane University's **Dixon Hall** (⊠*Tulane University,
Willow St. entrance, Uptown* ☎*504/865–5267*). Concerts take place

approximately once a month, and tickets usually cost $10 to $20. ☎504/895–0690 ⊕www.friendsofmusic.org.

Louisiana Philharmonic Orchestra. The always good, sometimes excellent LPO lost its primary performing space when the Orpheum Theater went up for sale post-Katrina. The orchestra regrouped and resumed its performance schedule, however, staging a wide range of classical concerts at Tulane and Loyola university auditoriums and at local churches. The orchestra also performs children's concerts and free concerts at parks and public spaces around the city, as well as a popular Casual Classics Series at the suburban Pontchartrain Center (E *4545 Williams Blvd., Kenner*). Tickets for most events range from $25 to $65, with discounts for students and seniors. ⊠*1010 Common St., Suite 2120, CBD* ☎504/523–6530 ⊕www.lpomusic.com.

Fodor'sChoice ★ **New Orleans Center for Creative Arts (NOCCA).** Wynton Marsalis and Harry Connick Jr. are just two of the better-known alumni of this prestigious high school. NOCCA hosts some fine student and faculty shows at its modern Faubourg Marigny campus, and its Center Stage Series presents top-notch performances by visiting jazz, classical, dance and theater artists. The focus is on emerging talent, and tickets usually sell out fast. ⊠*2800 Chartres St., Bywater* ☎504/940–2787 ⊕www.nocca.com.

DANCE

New Orleans Ballet Association. With the Mahalia Jackson Theater of the Performing Arts temporarily out of commission due to Hurricane Katrina, the city's prestigious dance organization has taken up temporary residence in several venues around town, including Tulane University's Dixon Hall. Tickets run $30 to $80, with discounts for students and seniors. ⊠*1 Lee Circle, Warehouse District* ☎504/522–0996 ⊕www.nobadance.com.

FILM

Landmark's Canal Place Cinemas. A southern branch of the art-house chain occupies a tight four-screen space in the upscale Canal Place shopping center, on the edge of the French Quarter. ⊠*Canal Pl., 333 Canal St., French Quarter* ☎504/581–5400 ⊕www.landmarktheatres.com.

New Orleans Film Festival. The New Orleans Film and Video Society presents this two-week festival in October, bringing in top international films and visits from directors and screenwriters. ☎504/309–6633 ⊕www.neworleansfilmfest.com.

Prytania Theatre. A visit to the city's last single-screen movie house, hidden in an Uptown residential area, is a reminder of the days when neighborhood movie houses offered entertainment as well as air-conditioned relief from the summer heat. The Prytania shows first-run crowd-pleasers and the occasional independent feature. ⊠*5339 Prytania St., Uptown* ☎504/891–2787.

MUSIC VENUES

Many of the city's major concert facilities are still closed due to damage from Hurricane Katrina. The **New Orleans Arena** (✉ *1501 Girod St., CBD* ☎ *504/587–3663* ⊕ *www.neworleansarena.com*) is the venue of choice for hip-hop and pop stars. It is also home to the New Orleans Hornets.

OPERA

New Orleans Opera Association. The October-through-March season generally showcases four operas; performances traditionally are held at the Mahalia Jackson Theater of the Performing Arts, which was damaged by flooding. The company has taken up temporary residence at Tulane University's McAlister Auditorium; tickets run $35 to $120 for premium seating. *1010 Common St., Suite 1820, CBD* ☎ *504/529–2278* ⊕ *www.neworleansopera.org.*

THEATER

★ **Le Chat Noir.** A classy tiled bar leads to a state-of-the-art performance space, where the night's entertainment might be a touring torch singer, a comedy revue, a campy movie spoof, or Varla Jean Merman, the gender-bending chanteuse and frequent Chat Noir guest. The Arts District cabaret is elegant and eclectic, and patrons, whether in their twenties or fifties, are appropriately urbane. ✉ *715 St. Charles Ave., Warehouse District* ☎ *504/581–5812* ⊕ *www.cabaretlechatnoir.com.*

★ **Le Petit Théâtre.** The oldest continuously running community theater in the United States occupies a historic building in the French Quarter and puts on quality plays year-round. It has children's entertainment, in addition to its usual fare of classics, musicals, and dramas, often on local themes. Events in the Tennessee Williams Festival take place here in March. ✉ *616 St. Peter St., French Quarter* ☎ *504/522–2081* ⊕ *www.lepetittheatre.com.*

★ **Southern Repertory Theater.** This well-established theater company specializes in first-rate contemporary theater productions. Southern Rep stages premieres by regional and international playwrights; Edward Albee debuted one of his plays, The Goat, or Who is Sylvia? here in 2004. ✉ *Canal Place, 3rd level, 333 Canal St., French Quarter* ☎ *504/522–6545* ⊕ *www.southernrep.com.*

Tulane University. Best known for its summer bills of fare, the university has several theater groups that stage top-notch productions. **Summer Lyric Theatre** (☎ *504/865–5269* ⊕ *www.summerlyric.tulane.edu*) produces three crowd-pleasing musicals every summer; tickets run $25 to $32, and tend to sell out fast. Tulane's **Summer Shakespeare Festival** (☎ *504/865–5105* ⊕ *www.neworleansshakespeare.com*) interprets the Bard in imaginative, high-quality productions. ✉ *Tulane University Campus, Uptown* ⊕ *www2.tulane.edu.*

Shopping

WORD OF MOUTH

"Magazine Street (my favorite street in New Orleans) is long and the shops and restaurants are scattered about. The best thing is to rent a car for a day and drive it. If you see something you like park and go in. There are blocks with lots of little shops so three or so stops could include visits to many stores."

—neworleansagogo

By Kandace
Power Graves

SHOPPING IN NEW ORLEANS IS like opening a treasure chest in which everything you want is at your fingertips, from rare antiques to novelty T-shirts, artwork, jewelry, and packaged foods that represent the city's flavors and culture.

New Orleanians have a deep love and devotion for the Crescent City and the varied ethnic components that make up its unique cultural gumbo. For shoppers, this translates into merchandise that reflects that pride, including jewelry and clothing bearing city icons such as the fleur-de-lis—a French symbol associated with the city since its early days—Mardi Gras masks, tributes to its world-class food and culture, and unique and often humorous statements about Hurricane Katrina and its effects on New Orleans (which are still deeply felt). New Orleanians also strongly support local entrepreneurs, which means shoppers can find many unique works by local artists and items produced in the city.

> ### PRIDE IN BLOOM
>
> The fleur-de-lis, historically an emblem of French royalty, has long been an icon of New Orleans. Since Hurricane Katrina, however, locals have fallen in love with it all over again, and artists have found creative and beautiful ways to use it to adorn a range of items including jewelry, T-shirts, artwork, candles, glassware, and even wrought-iron home decor. You can find many examples of the quintessential New Orleans symbol at stores all over the city.

Make sure you take home some of the city's local artwork, including the posters and artwork designed around New Orleans's special events such as Mardi Gras and the New Orleans Jazz & Heritage Festival (which often become collector's items). You also can pick up original artworks by locals, both emerging and established, which also will become collector's items. Favorite sons such as Tennessee Williams and William Faulkner are often depicted, as are historic areas of the city. The special sounds of New Orleans—Dixieland and contemporary jazz, rhythm and blues, Cajun, and zydeco—are available in music stores and live-music venues such as Preservation Hall, Snug Harbor, and House of Blues. Independent bookstores and major chains stock a plethora of local cookbooks, photography, history, and local literature and lore. Clothing stores focus on items that wear well in the subtropical heat, with styles ranging from the latest runway fashions, European designer wear, and vintage items, as well as styles from local designers.

WHAT'S WHERE

The main shopping areas in the city are the French Quarter, with narrow, picturesque streets lined with specialty, gift, fashion, and antiques shops and art galleries; the Central Business District (CBD), populated mostly with specialty and department stores; the Warehouse District, best known for contemporary arts galleries and cultural museums; Magazine Street, home to antiques shops, art galleries, home-furnishing stores, dining venues, fashion boutiques, and specialty shops; and the Riverbend/Maple Street area, which offers clothing, jewelry, and bookstores, as well as some specialty shops.

FRENCH QUARTER

Browsing through the picturesque storefronts in this compact area is as much a cultural experience as a shopping excursion, and unique treasures are waiting everywhere to be discovered. If your energy lags, plenty of cafés, coffee shops, candy shops, and bistros will provide a boost.

Jax Brewery. A historic building that once was a factory for Jax beer now holds an upscale mall filled with local shops and a few national chains such as Chico's, along with a food court and balcony that overlooks the Mississippi River. Shops in Jax provide souvenirs, fashions, books, and more, with an emphasis on New Orleans–theme items. The mall is open daily, and during hot days serves as an air-conditioned refuge. ⊠ *600 Decatur St., French Quarter* ☎ *504/566–7245* ⊕ *www. jacksonbrewery.com.*

ANTIQUES

The shops that line the French Quarter's streets are filled with an array of clothing, jewelry, novelties, works of art, and antique furniture and accessories, mostly from the 17th to 20th centuries. Tourists are the main customers for these shops, so you can expect a friendly reception and accommodating service. Ask about shipping; most will ship items to your home. The **New Orleans Tourism Marketing Corporation** (⊕ *www. neworleansonline.com*) has information about local businesses on its Web site. The **Royal Street Guild** publishes a pamphlet about French Quarter businesses; you can pick it up in shops and hotels in the neighborhood. If you want a personal guide, local art and antiques shopping consultant **Macon Riddle** (☎ *504/899–3027* ⊕ *www.neworleansantiquing. com*) conducts half- and full-day personalized shopping expeditions by appointment; they can sometimes gain access to antiques warehouses that are not normally open to the public.

Brass Monkey. Across the street from the original State Supreme Court Building, now a police headquarters, this shop is packed with Limoges boxes in a variety of forms, antique walking sticks with silver handles and other unique designs, Venetian glass, and English Staffordshire porcelain items. ⊠ *407 Royal St., French Quarter* ☎ *504/561–0688.*

★ **French Antique Shop.** One of the largest collections of European crystal and bronze chandeliers in the country glitters over gilded mirrors, authentic 18th- and 19th-century hand-carved and marble mantels, French and Continental furniture, porcelain, and objets d'art in this shop, which has operated at the same address since 1947 and is run by a third generation of the founding family. ⊠ *225 Royal St., French Quarter* ☎ *504/524–9861* ⊕ *www.gofrenchantiques.com.*

Harris of Royal. Locals as well as visitors are drawn to this shop for its four floors of 19th-century paintings, 18th- and 19th-century French and English furniture, trumeau mirrors, estate jewelry, bronze sculptures, and chandeliers. ⊠ *233 Royal St., French Quarter* ☎ *504/523–1605* ⊕ *www.harrisantiques.com.*

Keil's Antiques. Leave yourself plenty of time to browse through the three floors of 18th- and 19th-century furniture, chandeliers, estate jewelry, art, statuary, and other furnishings at this business, run by the

French Quarter Shopping

N. Rampart St.

Conti St.

St. Louis St.

Toulouse St.

St. Peter St.

Orleans St.

St. Ann St.

Dumaine St.

Louis Armstrong Park

Burgundy St.

Dauphine St.

23

Bourbon St.

39

38

4
5 6

9
8 12 10

13

20 21 22

24

Orleans St.

41

55 56
57 58

Royal St.

7 11

25 26

37 36

40

54

14
3
15 16

Chartres St.

17

Conti St.

St. Louis St.

27

42

St. Peter St.

43

St. Ann St.

53

2

Bienville St.

19
28
18

35

Wilk. Row

34
33
32

Jackson
Square

52
47
46

Madison St.

51

Dumaine St.

Decatur St.

1

Clinton St.

29 · 31

44 45

48 49

50

N. Peters St.

Moon Walk

Clay St.

N. Front St.

Mississippi River

0   1/4 mile
0   1/4 kilometer

Angela King Gallery **5**

Artist's Market **69**

Aunt Sally's
Praline Shop **45**

Bourbon French
Parfums **55**

Brass Monkey **20**

Café du Monde **44**

Cajun Clothing Co. **30**

Community
Flea Market **66**

Currents Fine Jewelry **8**

Dashka Roth Contemporary
Jewelry **17**

Dauphine Street Books **23**

Elliott Gallery **26**

Erzulie's Authentic Voudou **56**

Esoterica Occult
Goods **62**

Evan's Creole
Candy Factory **49**

French Market **67**

Faulkner House
Books **42**

Fifi Mahony's **60**

Forever New Orleans **40**

The French Antique Shop ... **6**

Galerie Rive Gauche **7**

A Gallery for Fine
Photography **3**

Great Artists' Collective ...**57**

Harouni Gallery **58**

Harris of Royal **4**

Hové Parfumeur, Ltd. **54**

The Idea Factory **51**

Jax Brewery **29**

Keil's Antiques **12**

The Kite Shop **32**

Kurt E. Schon, Ltd. **18**

La Belle Galerie & the
Black Art Collection **15**

Laura's Candies **16**

Librairie Book Shop **52**

Little Toy Shoppe **46, 63**

Louisiana
Music Factory **1**

Lucullus **35**

M.S. Rau **37**

Mask Gallery **36**

Michalopoulos **14**

Moss Antiques **22**

New Orleans School of
Cooking and Louisiana
General Store **19**

Oh Susannah **34**

The Quarter Smith **28**

Rendezvous, Inc. **33**

Rock and Roll
Collectibles and
Vieux Carre Vinyl **65**

Rodrigue Studios **41**

Rothschild's Antiques **10**

Rouge Beauty **61**

Royal Antiques **9**

Royal Cameo Glass **11**

Rumors **24**

Santa's Quarters **64**

Saving NOLA **31**

Serendipitous Masks **50**

Sigle's Historic
New Orleans
Metal Craft **59**

Sterling Silvia **68**

Sword and Pen **25**

Tobasco Country Store **47**

Trashy Diva **53**

Victoria's Shoes **27**

Vintage 429 ....**21**

Violets **43**

Waldhorn & Adler **13**

Wehmeier's
Belt Shop **38**

What's New **48**

Whisnant Galleries **2**

Yesteryear's **39**

N. Rampart St.

St. Philip St.

Ursulines St.

Gov. Nicholls St.

Burgundy St.

Dauphine St.

Bourbon St.

59

60

Royal St.

St. Philip St.

Ursulines St.

Gov. Nicholls St.

Chartres St.

64

69→

Decatur St.

N. Peters St.

French Market Pl.

68

65 - 67 →

fourth generation of the family that started it in 1899. ✉ *325 Royal St., French Quarter* ☎ *504/522–4552.*

Fodor'sChoice ★ **Lucullus.** The entire store is focused on the art of food—preparing it, serving it, and eating it—and is filled with French tables, English china, cooking and serving utensils that range from fine silver to hand-forged items, and more, mainly from the 18th and 19th centuries. The shop is owned by Patrick Dunne, author of *Epicurean Collector.* ✉ *610 Chartres St., French Quarter* ☎ *504/528–9620* ⊕ *www.lucullusneworleans.com.*

Fodor'sChoice ★ **M. S. Rau.** Historically significant items, such as furniture and other pieces from royal families, are spotlighted among 18th- and 19th-century French, American, and English furniture, sterling silver, cut glass, statuary, and jewelry in this 30,000-square-foot store, which opened in 1912. ✉ *630 Royal St., French Quarter* ☎ *504/523–5660 or 800/544–9440* ⊕ *www.rauantiques.com.*

Moss Antiques. French and English antiques from the early 19th century are the specialty, including furniture with inlaid woods, porcelain oyster plates, walking sticks, and silver services. ✉ *411 Royal St., French Quarter* ☎ *504/522–3981* ⊕ *www.mossantiques.com.*

Rothschild's Antiques. Signs that read PLEASE DO NOT TOUCH. THESE ITEMS CANNOT BE REPLACED emphasize the rarity of the 18th-, 19th-, and 20th-century French and English antique home furnishings available here. Most of the store's real business, however, is its jewelry, much of it one-of-a-kind pieces its artisans design and manufacture, as well as antique and estate pieces. ✉ *321 Royal St., French Quarter* ☎ *504/523–5816* ⊕ *www.rothschildsantiques.com.*

Royal Antiques. French, English, and Continental antique furniture, chandeliers, estate jewelry, and art from the 18th and 19th centuries are what have kept this shop in business since 1899. ✉ *309 Royal St., French Quarter* ☎ *504/524–7033* ⊕ *www.royalantiques.com.*

Waldhorn & Adler. Founded in 1881, the city's oldest antiques store specializes in French, Italian, and English furniture from the 18th, 19th, and early 20th centuries, but also has estate jewelry, and watches by Rolex, Cartier, and Patek Philippe. ✉ *343 Royal St., French Quarter* ☎ *504/581–6379* ⊕ *www.waldhornadlers.com.*

★ **Whisnant Galleries.** Antique weapons and armor are the real eye-catchers, but the shop also carries a large selection of antique gilded furniture; paintings from the 18th, 19th, and 20th centuries; African and ethnic art; religious items; objets d'art; and antique jewelry. ✉ *229 Royal St., French Quarter* ☎ *504/524–9766* ⊕ *www.whisnantgalleries.com.*

ART & CRAFTS GALLERIES

Angela King Gallery. Paintings, prints, and sculpture showcased include works by Peter Max, Ernest Trova, Leroy Neiman, M.L. Snowden, and many others. ✉ *241 Royal St., French Quarter* ☎ *504/556–8240* ⊕ *www.angelakinggallery.com.*

Artist's Market. This co-op of regional artists showcases a wide variety of works, including handmade masks, photography focusing on New Orleans personalities and scenes, ceramics, blown-glass items, paintings, wrought-iron architectural accents, prints, jewelry, beads, and more. ✉ *1228 Decatur St.,French Quarter* ☎ *504/561–0046* ⊕ *www. artistsmarketnola.com.*

Mardi Gras Shopping Blitz

New Orleans during Mardi Gras may seem chaotic, but it's actually very organized, and those locals who participate are focused on capturing their favorite prizes thrown from floats and showing off their city to visitors. Orient yourself by attending some evening parades before you jump into the all-day celebration on Fat Tuesday, and you'll soon find you can catch beads and other trinkets like a pro. Next, you'll want to find a suitable costume and mask to fully immerse yourself in the experience. You can assemble a costume easily if you keep your eyes open at such places as the **Community Flea Market** in the back part of the French Quarter. Then walk over to Royal Street for makeup, wigs, and costume jewelry at **Fifi Mahony's** before you continue on down Royal Street to the **Artists Market,** where you'll find an assortment of masks you'll want to keep long after Mardi Gras has faded into Lent. For a one-stop costume experience, travel to Magazine Street and **Funky Monkey,** where you can find handmade costumes, stockings, wigs, and accessories in one place, or the **Encore Shop,** where you can choose from affordable ball gowns, suits, and more. The important thing to remember about Mardi Gras is that it is meant to be fun for all ages. So dress the part, enjoy the sardonic humor of Carnival krewes' floats, and have a ball.

Elliott Gallery. Pioneers of modern and contemporary art are represented, with a large selection of prints and paintings by Theo Tobiasse, Max Papart, Nissan Engle, James Coignard, Garrick Yrondi, and others. ⊠ *540 Royal St., French Quarter* ☎ *504/523–3554* ⊕ *www.elliottgallery.com.*

Galerie Rive Gauche. Dedicated to original European paintings by contemporary artists, the offerings here include colorful landscapes and vibrant and moody works in both abstract and realistic styles by emerging artists (including a few from outside Europe). ⊠ *318 Royal St., French Quarter* ☎ *504/524–5623.*

Fodor'sChoice ★ **A Gallery for Fine Photography.** The rare books and photographs here include works from emerging local artists like Josephine Sacabo and Jerry N. Uelsmann; luminaries such as E.J. Bellocq, Ansel Adams, and Henri Cartier-Bresson; and more-contemporary giants, including Annie Leibovitz, Walker Evans, Helmut Newton, and local Herman Leonard. ⊠ *241 Chartres St., French Quarter* ☎ *504/568–1313* ⊕ *www.agallery.com.*

Great Artists' Collective. More than 40 artists display their works in this double-shotgun house in the middle of the French Quarter. You'll find paintings, metalwork mirrors, a vast array of earrings, blown glass, ceramics, wood sculptures, fabric handbags, Shibori clothing, hats, ironwork, masks, vignettes in oyster shells, and more. ⊠ *815 Royal St., French Quarter* ☎ *504/525–8190* ⊕ *www.greatartistscollective.com.*

Harouni Gallery. David Harouni, a favored artist among locals and businesses who decorate their walls with fine art, displays his take on neo-Expressionism in his paintings of faces, figures, and streetscapes, created in this gallery-studio space. He also sells silk screens. ⊠ *829 Royal St.,*

7

French Quarter ☎ *504/299–8900* ⊕ *www.harouni.com.*

Kurt E. Schon, Ltd. In the hushed atmosphere of an art museum, and with a well-educated staff, this gallery showcases high-end European paintings from the 18th and 19th centuries. A sister gallery at 523 Royal Street displays contemporary art. ⊠ *510 St. Louis St., French Quarter* ☎ *504/524–5462* ⊕ *www.kurteschonltd.com.*

La Belle Galerie & the Black Art Collection. African-American experiences in music, history, contemporary life, and culture are portrayed through limited-edition graphics, photographs, posters, paintings, furniture, ceramics, textiles, and sculpture. ⊠ *309 Chartres St., French Quarter* ☎ *504/529–3080.*

Michalopoulos. Local artist James Michalopoulos showcases his own, slightly slanted visions of New Orleans's architecture, street scenes, and personalities in oil paintings, lithographs, prints, posters, and serigraphs. ⊠ *617 Bienville St., French Quarter* ☎ *504/558–0505* ⊕ *www.michalopoulos.com.*

Rodrigue Studios. Louisiana artist George Rodrigue is best known for his vibrant Blue Dog series, which is collected by such celebrities as Whoopi Goldberg and Tom Brokaw. Images of the artist's Cajun ancestors in stylized, traditional Acadiana settings and his colorful impressions of hurricanes are available in original paintings and signed and numbered silk-screen prints. ⊠ *721 Royal St., French Quarter* ☎ *504/581–4244* ⊕ *www.georgerodrigue.com.*

Vintage 429. An essential stop for memorabilia collectors, the store carries items autographed by celebrities, including a pink guitar signed by Madonna; Pirates of the Caribbean memorabilia signed by Johnny Depp, Orlando Blum, and Keira Knightly; photos of TV-show casts; posters from performances; first-edition signed books; and more. New items arrive every week. ⊠ *429 Royal St., French Quarter* ☎ *504/529–2288 or 866/846-8429* ⊕ *www.vintage429.com.*

BOOKS

Literary legends like Tennessee Williams, William Faulkner, Truman Capote, and Anne Rice called New Orleans home for at least part of their lives, and a number of other modern writers work in and write about the city, its food, and its culture. Because of this heritage, bookstores give local authors optimum shelf-space exposure, and cookbooks, local history, and picture books are sold in gift shops in the Quarter; bibliophiles can also browse through the area's used-book stores.

MARDI GRAS CLOSURES

The city essentially shuts down on Lundi Gras (Monday) and Mardi Gras (Fat Tuesday), with only grocery and convenience stores, pharmacies, and restaurants left open. Most merchants close from Sunday through Tuesday (and some shut down through Ash Wednesday), since street closures for parades and festivities make conducting commerce difficult. Plus, many of the shop owners and employees are attending Mardi Gras themselves.

Dauphine Street Books. Stocking both new and used books, this store specializes in local history, the arts, modern fiction, and out-of-print titles. ✉ *410 Dauphine St., French Quarter* ☎ *504/529–2333.*

Faulkner House Books. Named for William Faulkner, who lived and wrote here in the 1920s, this bookstore specializes in rare and out-of-print books by Southern authors. It also hosts an annual Words & Music Festival that salutes Faulkner and new Southern writers and musicians. ✉ *624 Pirate's Alley, French Quarter* ☎ *504/524–2940* ⊕ *www.faulknerhousebooks.net.*

Fodor$Choice ★ **Librairie Book Shop.** Set up like a library with well-stocked shelves of old, new, and hard-to-find volumes, this spot carries the Quarter's largest selection of books, posters, and postcards of local lore. ✉ *823 Chartres St., French Quarter* ☎ *504/525–4837.*

CLOTHING & ACCESSORIES

The fashion scene in New Orleans is a curious mix of sassy, sexy, bohemian, and classic with an edge, spiked with a dose of vintage.

Cajun Clothing Co. A smaller version of the locally popular Perlis (⇨ *Magazine Street)*, this shop carries clothing for men, women, and children, with a focus on Polo shirts, boxers, and ties with crawfish logos, as well as everything from Hawaiian shirts to boxers printed with images of Tabasco products. ✉ *Jax Brewery, 600 Decatur St., Suite 104, French Quarter* ☎ *504/523–6681* ⊕ *www.perlis.com.*

Fifi Mahony's. Anyone with a love for pretty things and a flair for the dramatic will love this place, with its custom wigs, wild accessories, cosmetics for costuming or everyday enhancement, hair-care products, and creative advice. ✉ *934 Royal St., French Quarter* ☎ *504/525–4343* ⊕ *www.fifi-mahony.com.*

Fodor$Choice ★ **Trashy Diva Boutique.** Retro fashions inspired by the 1920s to the 1950s are mixed with vintage women's apparel, dresses designed by store owner Candice Gwinn, romantic jewelry, upscale shoes, and hats. The Trashy Diva Lingerie Boutique next door (831 Chartres Street) features corsets and romantic eveningwear. ✉ *829 Chartres St., French Quarter* ☎ *504/581–4555* ⊕ *www.trashydiva.com.*

Victoria's Shoes. Jimmy Choo, Giuseppe Zanotti, and Charles David are just a few of the names available at this upscale shoe emporium, which also carries handbags and jewelry. ✉ *328 Chartres St., French Quarter* ☎ *504/568–9990.*

Violets. Girly girls rule at this boutique, which caters to the softer side of females with dresses, skirts, sexy blouses, handbags, jewelry, and accessories—many that hark to the Edwardian and 1920s periods. ✉ *808 Chartres St., French Quarter* ☎ *504/569–0088.*

Wehmeier's Belt Shop. Exotic leathers—especially American alligator, lizard, and South African ostrich—become fashionable men's and women's belts, boots, shoes, handbags, wallets, briefcases, and even golf bags at this 50-year-old store. ✉ *719 Toulouse St., French Quarter* ☎ *504/525–2758 or 888/525–2758* Canal Place, ✉ *333 Canal St., CBD* ☎ *504/681–2082* ⊕ *www.wehmeiers.com.*

7

FOOD & GIFT PACKAGES

Food is an integral part of New Orleans culture and one of its favorite exports. Visitors can pack up or have shipped home most of the items they taste in local restaurants, from pralines to prepackaged mixes and spices.

Aunt Sally's Praline Shop. Satisfy your sweet tooth with an array of pralines made while you watch. The traditional version is concocted from cane sugar spiked with pecans, but newer treatments include chocolate and other ingredients. You also can buy pre-packaged tomato gravy, muffuletta mix, Bourbon Street glaze, and Italian salad dressing, as well as art and books about New Orleans. ⊠ *810 Decatur St., in the French Market, French Quarter* ☎ *504/524–3373 or 800/642–7257* ⊕ *www.auntsallys.com.*

Café du Monde. This open-air café and New Orleans landmark serves café au lait (half-coffee, half hot milk) and beignets (hole-less doughnuts sprinkled liberally with powdered sugar). Take-home products from the café include prepackaged chicory coffee and beignet mix, coffee mugs, prints, and posters depicting the spot. The café's store across the street also sells logo T-shirts, aprons, and other souvenirs. ⊠ *800 Decatur St., French Quarter* ☎ *504/525–4544* ⊕ *www.cafedumonde.com.*

Evans Creole Candy Factory. The smell of candy being made on-site will draw you in to this shop, which was established in 1900. You'll find a variety of pralines, pecan logs, and New Orleans's own Cuccia Chocolates, as well as gift baskets. ⊠ *848 Decatur St., French Quarter* ☎ *504/522–7111 or 800/637–6675* ⊕ *www.evanscreolecandy.com.*

French Market. New Orleans chefs snap up local farmers' wares and produce for their restaurants' kitchens at this covered, open-air emporium. Seasonal produce includes pecans, sugarcane, mirlitons (chayotes), creole tomatoes, strawberries, okra, and lots more. ⊠ *1008 N. Peters St., French Quarter* ☎ *504/522–2621* ⊕ *www.frenchmarket.org.*

Laura's Candies. In the candy-making business since 1913, this shop sells sweet pralines as well as chocolate specialties—including its signature Mississippi mud, made with milk or dark chocolate laced with caramel. ⊠ *331 Chartres St., French Quarter* ☎ *504/525–3880 or 800/992–9699* ⊕ *www.laurascandies.com.*

New Orleans School of Cooking and Louisiana General Store. You can learn Louisiana cooking techniques at this school (located in a renovated 1800s molasses warehouse); lessons are spiced with history and tales about the state's famous cuisine. The store also stocks all kinds of regional spices, condiments, sauces, snacks, gift baskets, and cookbooks. ⊠ *524 St. Louis St., French Quarter* ☎ *504/525–2665 or 800/237–4841* ⊕ *www.nosoc.com.*

Tabasco Country Store. Named for the famous Louisiana-produced hot sauce, the store also offers spices, cookbooks, Louisiana- and cooking-theme clothing and aprons, kitchen accoutrements, ties, posters, pewter items with New Orleans icons, and more. ⊠, *French Quarter* ☎ *504/539–7900* ⊕ *http://countrystore.tabasco.com.*

JEWELRY

Currents Fine Jewelry. Owners Terry and Sylvia Weidert create a variety of chic, art deco–inspired designs in 14- and 18-karat gold and platinum. ✉ *305 Royal St., French Quarter* ☎ *504/522–6099.*

Fodor'sChoice **Dashka Roth Contemporary Jewelry.**
★ The handmade contemporary jewelry on display here (by designer Dashka Roth and other American craftspeople) is eclectic, but the focus is mainly on Judaica, including kiddush cups, mezuzahs, menorahs, and dreidels. The store is closed for all Jewish holidays. ✉ *332 Chartres St., French Quarter* ☎ *504/523–0805 or 877/327–4523* ⊕ *www.dashkaroth.com.*

Quarter Smith. Gemologist and gold- and silversmith Ken Bowers will custom-design a special piece of jewelry for you, or you can choose from a selection of estate pieces. ✉ *535 St. Louis St., French Quarter* ☎ *504/524–9731* ⊕ *www.quartersmith.com.*

★ **Sterling Silvia.** Silvia and Juan Asturias operate this business near the French Market, where Silvia's fleur-de-lis and flower-inspired jewelry designs share space with other silver jewelry from Chile, Mexico, Indonesia, Russia, Thailand, and elsewhere. There's also jewelry made from coral beads, gift items, ceramic dolls, and more. ✉ *41 French Market Pl., French Quarter* ☎ *504/299–9225 or 504/299–9229* ⊕ *www.joangood.com.*

MASKS

Masks traditionally created to wear during Mardi Gras are great to buy as souvenirs and gifts, but also are gaining popularity as decorative works of art. There are feather masks and mass-produced ceramic versions available for about $10, but better, handcrafted, locally made masks that bear the artist's insignia are more of an investment. Cost can run as high as several thousand dollars, depending on the materials used, size, and craftsmanship.

Mask Gallery. One of the treats of visiting this shop is watching the artist Dalili fabricating the intricate but wearable masks out of leather at his workstation at the front of the store. The store also sells jewelry and glass items. ✉ *636 Royal St., French Quarter* ☎ *504/523–6664* ⊕ *www.neworleansmask.com.*

Rumors. Thirty-five artists from around the country create masks of all sizes from leather, ceramics, and feathers to wear on your face, as a lapel pin, as jewelry, or to hang on your wall as art. The shop also sells walking sticks with decorative handles and juju dolls to bring good fortune. ✉ *513 Royal St., French Quarter* ☎ *504/525–0292 or 888/278–6672* ⊕ *www.rumorsno.com.*

HEALTHY JAVA

Made from the roasted root of *Cichorium pumilum,* or wild endive, chicory has been used for centuries to stretch supplies of scarce or expensive coffee. New Orleanians believe it adds richness and smoothness to the drink, and local manufacturers like Community, French Market, Luzianne, and Café Du Monde add up to 30% chicory to the coffee they sell. Chicory is also caffeine-free and reportedly is healthful for your liver, helps control blood sugar and reduce cholesterol, and boosts bone-mineral density.

7

Crescent City to Go!

There are lots of tasty treats to sample while you're in the Big Easy—but you don't have to overeat while you're here, since many of its famous tastes come in easy-to-pack (or ship) forms. In the French Quarter you can pick up classic pralines at **Aunt Sally's Praline Shop** or **Laura's Candies,** which also sell other to-go items. Don't forget beignet mix and chicory coffee to re-create breakfast at **Café du Monde.** In the Warehouse District, **Riverwalk Marketplace** has candy shops that will make fudge and pralines while you watch, then package them for you to take home. Stores like **Creole Delicacies & Cookin' Cajun** can not only provide all the ingredients you need to create New Orleans dishes in your own kitchen, they'll even give you cooking classes to help you do it right. All the city's bookstores and many gift shops are stocked with a variety of cookbooks by local chefs and tomes about the area's foods. Uptown, stop in **Savvy Gourmet** for packaged gourmet mixes, cooking lessons, and samples of the foods you'll want to remember.

Serendipitous Masks. The layout of the shop, with masks mingled with elaborately dressed dolls, evokes the air of a ball or the playroom of royalty. The masks are made by local artists using exotic feathers, jewels, ceramics, and leather. ⊠ *831 Decatur St., French Quarter* ☎ *504/522–9158.*

Yesteryear's. Elaborate feather masks made by owner Teresa Latshaw and other artists comprise most of the inventory, but voodoo dolls and folklore objects are also available. ⊠ *626 Bourbon St., French Quarter* ☎ *504/523–6603.*

MUSIC

Though many of New Orleans's musicians haven't returned home permanently since Hurricane Katrina, those who are here keep the city's special brands of jazz, rhythm and blues, funk, and fusion alive in local clubs, on the streets, and through recordings. The latter is an easy way to take these special sounds home with you as a reminder of the city's special musical flavors.

★ **Louisiana Music Factory.** A favorite haunt for locals looking for New Orleans's and regional music—new and old—this retail store has records, tapes, CDs, DVDs, sheet music, and books as well as listening stations, music-oriented T-shirts, original art of musicians, and a stage for live concerts. ⊠ *210 Decatur St., French Quarter* ☎ *504/586–1094* ⊕ *www.louisianamusicfactory.com.*

Rock and Roll Collectibles and Vieux Carré Vinyl. Give yourself plenty of time to browse through this small shotgun-style store, which has some 30,000 vinyl records as well as tapes, CDs, and videos. The emphasis is on collectibles, with records from the 1920s and 1930s as well as choices in rock, Cajun, zydeco, rhythm and blues, country, and jazz. Although the packed racks and stuffed boxes on bookshelves and on the floor may seem overwhelming, everything is organized and clearly labeled. ⊠ *1214 Decatur St., French Quarter* ☎ *504/561–5683.*

NOVELTIES & GIFTS

Community Flea Market. Dozens of vendors set up tables inside and outside this recently renovated covered market to sell new merchandise such as jewelry, handbags, T-shirts, and curios as well as vintage and used items, clothing, and collectibles at discount prices. Vendors also set up stands outside the covered area. The market generally is open daily from about 7 AM to 8 PM, but hours can vary depending on the weather. ✉ *Governor Nicholls St., in the French Market, French Quarter* ☎ *504/596–3420* ⊕ *www.frenchmarket.org.*

Erzulie's Authentic Voudou. Stepping into this shop is like entering the mystical world of voodoo, with altars displaying good-luck charms and other ritual items, spell kits, elixirs and potions, body-care products, voodoo dolls, gris-gris bags, and gift items. Psychic-, tarot- and palm readings are available. ✉ *807 Royal St., French Quarter* ☎ *504/525–2055 or 866/286–8368* ⊕ *www.erzulies.com.*

Esoterica Occult Goods. For a hint of New Orleans's fabled past, head here to pick up potions, gris-gris, jewelry, spell kits, incense, altar and ritual items, and books on magic and the occult arts and sciences. You can make an appointments for a tarot reading, past-life regression, or an astrological consultation. ✉ *541 Dumaine St., French Quarter* ☎ *504/581–7711* ⊕ *www.onewitch.com.*

Forever New Orleans. It's all about the Crescent City in this small shop filled with New Orleans–theme items including glassware adorned with pewter fleur-de-lis, affordable jewelry that boasts local icons, stationery, tiles, clocks, ceramics, framed crosses, charms, bottle stoppers, frames, candles, and more. ✉ *700 Royal St., French Quarter* ☎ *504/586–3536.*

★ **Idea Factory.** Wood becomes art at the hands of craftspeople who carve clocks; functional items such as clipboards, boxes, and company logos; as well as more-whimsical items including toys, whirligigs, hand-carved board games, puzzle boxes, kaleidoscopes, and freestanding works of art. The shop is closed Tuesday. ✉ *838 Chartres St., French Quarter* ☎ *504/524–5195* ⊕ *www.ideafactoryneworleans.com.*

Rendezvous Inc. A throwback to romantic old New Orleans, this shop on Jackson Square has linens and lace in forms ranging from christening outfits for babies to clothing to table runners, napkins, women's handkerchiefs, and more. It also offers a charming array of antiques and reproductions such as perfume bottles, tea sets, fleur-de-lis, and crosses. ✉ *522 St. Peters St., French Quarter* ☎ *504/522–0225* ⊕ *www.rendezvouslinens.com.*

Royal Cameo Glass. Beautiful and unique items made of glass are the specialty here, with a spotlight on exclusive cameo glass and pieces by Ulla Darni and Afro Celotto, Lotton art glasses, ceiling light fixtures, lamps, vases, sculpture, jewelry, and artwork by American studio artists. ✉ *322 Royal St., French Quarter* ☎ *504/522–7840* ⊕ *www.royalcameo.com.*

Santa's Quarters. It's Christmas year-round at this shop, which displays a diverse range of traditional and novelty ornaments and decorations, Santa Clauses of all kinds, and a host of Louisiana-theme items that make great souvenirs. ✉ *1025 Decatur St., French Quarter* ☎ *504/581–5820 or 800/262–8717* ⊕ *www.santasquartersno.com.*

Saving NOLA. Dedicated to New Orleans and its recovery, this store provides an array of T-shirts that celebrate the city, jewelry featuring New Orleans icons, and other works by local artists, including small paintings, posters, picture frames, and handmade boxes. ✉ *Jax Brewery, 600 Decatur St., French Quarter.*

Sigle's Historic New Orleans Metal Craft. New Orleans's architectural elements, often used on French Quarter buildings, have been hand-crafted here since 1938. The shop has a selection of metal accents and cast-iron planters; they can also custom-design items. ✉ *935 Royal St., French Quarter* ☎ *504/522–7647.*

> **A RELAXING SCENT**
>
> Take home the scents of New Orleans with soaps, room sprays, candles, and perfumes in sweet olive or vetivert. The latter was a staple in proper creole house-holds, where it was used to keep moths away from fabrics and add a pleasant scent to bed linens and clothing stored in armoires. Oil extracted from the roots of the grassy plant is popular among aromatherapy enthusiasts, who claim the scent relieves stress and increases energy.

What's New. Everything in the store carries a New Orleans theme, making it a great place to buy souvenirs people will actually want to keep and use, including fleur-de-lis–clad flasks, decorative pillows, night-lights with shades made from photographs of city scenes, glassware, ceramics, jewelry, and other works by local artists. ✉ *824 Decatur St., French Quarter* ☎ *504/586–2095.*

PERFUMES

The exotic smells of New Orleans's subtropical climate—sweet olive, magnolia, vetivert—are bottled by the city's *parfumeurs,* who will also handcraft custom scents by request.

Bourbon French Parfums. Opened in 1843, the shop has about three dozen signature scents for men and women, including a 200-year-old formula for men's cologne. It will custom-blend perfumes for individuals based on assessments of body chemistry, personality, and scent preferences. The shop also sells perfume bottles and toiletries. ✉ *805 Royal St., French Quarter* ☎ *504/522–4480 or 800/476–0303* ⊕ *www.neworleansperfume.com.*

Fodor's Choice **Hové Parfumeur, Ltd.** Scented oils, soaps, sachets, and potpourri have
★ been made to order on-site for three generations and are sold all over the world. There are 52 fragrances for men and women, as well as bath salts, anti-aging treatments, massage and body oils, antique shaving and dressing-table accessories, new and antique perfume bottles, and bed and bath items. ✉ *824 Royal St., French Quarter* ☎ *504/525–7827* ⊕ *www.hoveparfumeur.com.*

TOYS

☾ **Kite Shop.** The ceiling is thick with hanging wind socks. Kites of all designs, including an assortment of stunt kites, line one wall; another is stocked with hand and finger puppets, marionettes, flying toys, and other fanciful playthings. ✉ *542 St. Peter St., French Quarter* ☎ *504/524–0028* ⊕ *www.kiteshopneworleans.com.*

Sword and Pen. This store stocks beautifully crafted and hand-painted miniature armies, from sword- and spear-wielding ancient Roman and Greek soldiers to World War II troopers. It also has a selection of war memorabilia, including Civil War hats and uniform insignia from a variety of conflicts. ⊠ *528 Royal St., French Quarter* ☎ *504/523–7741.*

Little Toy Shoppe. There's a mix of New Orleans souvenirs, miniature die-cast metal cars from the Model-T to the Hummer, character lunch boxes, puppets, plastic animals, costume hats, and collectible Madame Alexander dolls in a dozen different costumes at this 50-year-old business. ⊠ *900 Decatur St., French Quarter* ☎ *504/522–6588* ⊠ *513 St. Ann St., French Quarter* ☎ *504/523–1770* ⊕ *www.littletoyshoppe.com.*

Oh Susannah. Many stores in the French Quarter carry collectible dolls, but this one has one of the largest and highest-quality selections, including dolls from Annette Hinestedt and Hildegard Gunzel. ⊠ *518 St. Peter St., French Quarter* ☎ *504/586–8701.*

CBD & WAREHOUSE DISTRICT

This area between the French Quarter and the Magazine Street shopping district is filled with boutique hotels, upscale malls, locally owned and national chain department stores, and (in the Warehouse District) museums and art galleries displaying a variety of artworks and crafts from local, regional, and nationally known artists. Julia Street in particular is a cornucopia of small art galleries, many of them artist-owned.

Canal Place. This upscale shopping center focuses on national chains including Williams-Sonoma, Pottery Barn, Banana Republic, Saks Fifth Avenue, and Brooks Brothers, but also includes quality local stores like the artist co-op RHINO, Wehmeier's Belt Shop, Saint Germain shoes featuring Donald Pliner, and a selection of jewelry and accessories. Mignon Faget is a jewelry store that carries the local designer's full line of Louisiana-inspired creations. ⊠ *333 Canal St., CBD* ☎ *504/522–9200* ⊕ *www.theshopsatcanalplace.com.*

Riverwalk Marketplace. Built in what once was the International Pavilion for the 1984 World's Fair, Riverwalk Marketplace offers a plethora of souvenirs and luxury jewelry, clothing, shoes, and high-tech gadgets from stores such as Banana Republic, Gap, and Brookstone. Stores with a more-local approach include Bayou Bangles, Cookin' Cajun Cooking School, French Quarter Pens, Mardi Gras Madness, and Only in New Orleans. There's a food court with local candies, a Café du Monde, and a variety of dining choices. An outside balcony that extends much of the length of the mall overlooks the Mississippi River and provides a place for a respite from shopping. Outside the mall is Spanish Plaza, the scene of frequent outdoor concerts and special events. ⊠ *1 Poydras St., Warehouse District* ☎ *504/522–1555* ⊕ *www.riverwalkmarketplace.com.*

ART & CRAFTS GALLERIES

The city's galleries are an active and lively part of the entertainment scene, with a concentration of respected venues in this area. The local daily and weekly newspapers publish listings that detail openings of new exhibits, which generally are accompanied by wine, hors d'oeuvres, and sometimes music. Because many of the galleries are artist-owned and operated, hours and days of operation can vary. It's best to call and confirm gallery hours; many owners are also happy to set up special appointments for you to view their art. Brochures with maps of the Warehouse Arts District are available in hotels, galleries, and shops.

Ariodante. Local and national artists are represented at this gallery, which has custom-made cases that display high-end but reasonably priced contemporary crafts, including glass items, sculpture, furniture, photography, paintings, ceramics, jewelry, and decorative accessories. ✉ *535 Julia St., Warehouse District* ☎ *504/524–3233* ⊕ *www.ariodante gallery.com*

Art For The Soul. This small gallery features arts and crafts from 25 local and regional artists, including functional art, lamps, ceramics, masks, jewelry, purses, candles, and decorative arts. The gallery also sells custom furniture. ✉ *818 Howard Ave., Suite 101, Warehouse District* ☎ *504/558–7770.*

Fodor'sChoice   **Arthur Roger Gallery.** One of the most respected names among art afi-
     ★   cionados, Arthur Roger has compiled a must-see collection of local contemporary artworks by Lin Emery, Jacqueline Bishop, and Willie Birch, as well as such national names as glass artist Dale Chihuly and filmmaker-photographer John Waters. ✉ *432 Julia St., Warehouse District* ☎ *504/522–1999* ⊕ *www.arthurrogergallery.com.*

Contemporary Arts Center. Focusing on visual and performing arts by local and regional artists, the center curates innovative exhibits with all types of installations, ranging from the beautiful to the bizarre. The galleries are open Thursday through Sunday from 11 to 4. ✉ *900 Camp St., Warehouse District* ☎ *504/528–3805* ⊕ *www.cacno.org.*

George Schmidt Gallery. History, particularly New Orleans history, is the passion of artist George Schmidt. His gallery displays and sells paintings and narrative art, from small-scale monotypes to mural-size depictions of historic moments. He also sells signed and numbered prints of his work. The gallery is open Tuesday through Saturday. ✉ *626 Julia St., Warehouse District* ☎ *504/592–0206* ⊕ *www.georgeschmidt.com.*

Heriard-Cimino Gallery. The front gallery holds a changing solo exhibit, and a second gallery displays abstract and figurative paintings, sculptures, drawings, photos, and prints from contemporary artists—most based in New York, Miami, or Louisiana. The gallery is open Tuesday through Saturday. ✉ *440 Julia St., Warehouse District* ☎ *504/525–7300* ⊕ *www.heriardcimino.com.*

Jean Bragg Gallery of Southern Art. Aficionados call it the city's best source for collectible pottery from Newcomb and George Ohr, but the gallery also carries 19th- and 20th-century Louisiana paintings. Contemporary artist exhibits are presented each month. ✉ *600 Julia St., Warehouse District* ☎ *504/895–7375* ⊕ *www.jeanbragg.com.*

Jonathan Ferrara Gallery. Cutting-edge art with a message is standard at this gallery's monthly exhibits. Contemporary paintings, photography, mixed-media artworks, sculpture, and glass and metalwork by local and international artists are displayed. ✉ *400-A Julia St., Warehouse District* ☎ *504/522–5471* ⊕ *www.jonathanferraragallery.com.*

CBD & Warehouse District Shopping

KEY

🚋 Streetcar

Adler's **14**

Ariodante **6**

Art For The Soul **1**

Arthur Roger Gallery **8**

Canal Place **17**

Clock and Watch Shop **13**

Contemporary
Arts Center **11**

Creole Delicacies &
Cookin' Cajun **20**

Deville Books &
Prints **12**

George Schmidt Gallery **4**

Heriard-Cimino Gallery **7**

Jean Bragg Gallery
of Southern Art **5**

Jonathan Ferrara
Gallery **2**

LeMieux Gallery **9**

Meyer the Hatter **15**

New Orleans School of
Glassworks and
Printmaking Studio **10**

Ogden Museum of
Southern Art **3**

RHINO Contemporary
Craft Co. **18**

Riverwalk
Marketplace **19**

Rubensteins **16**

The Walking Co. **21**

Fodor's Choice ★ **LeMieux Gallery.** Gulf Coast artists from Louisiana to Florida display art and crafts here alongside work by the late New Orleans abstract artist Paul Ninas. ✉ *332 Julia St., Warehouse District* ☎ *504/522–5988* ⊕ *www.lemieuxgalleries.com.*

♻ **New Orleans School of Glassworks and Printmaking Studio.** The South's largest glassblowing and printmaking studio has a viewing room where visitors can watch glassblowers at work. The rest of the gallery displays and sells functional and decorative art in glass and metal sculptures. ✉ *727 Magazine St., Warehouse District* ☎ *504/529–7279* ⊕ *www.neworleansglassworks.org.*

Ogden Museum of Southern Art. You don't have to pay admission to enter this museum's store, where you can buy ceramics, glassworks, decorative pieces, and jewelry. The museum is filled with exhibits of Southern contemporary and folk art, photography, and more. It is open Wednesday through Sunday, with live music and after-hours events on Thursday. ✉ *925 Camp St., Warehouse District* ☎ *504/539–9600* ⊕ *www.ogdenmuseum.org.*

Fodor's Choice ★ **RHINO Contemporary Crafts.** The name stands for Right Here In New Orleans, which is where most of the artists whose arts and crafts are displayed in this co-op live and work. You'll find original paintings in varying styles, metalwork, sculpture, ceramics, glass, functional art, jewelry, fashion accessories, and artwork made from found objects. The gallery also holds art classes for children. ✉ *333 Canal St., Shops at Canal Place, CBD* ☎ *504/523–7945* ⊕ *www.rhinocrafts.com.*

BOOKS

Deville Books & Prints. A sentimental favorite among locals, this old-fashioned bookstore has lots of New Orleans and Southern literature, and a staff with exceptional knowledge about both. It also sells art prints and provides custom framing. ✉ *736 Union St., CBD* ☎ *504/525–1846.*

CLOTHING

Meyer the Hatter. One of the South's largest hat stores, Meyer the Hatter has been in operation for 113 years and is run by a third generation of the Meyer family. It's a favorite of locals seeking men's headwear and has a large selection of dress hats, fun Kangols, tweed caps, and women's fashion hats. Meyer has a faithful following of out-of-towners, too. ✉ *120 St. Charles Ave., CBD* ☎ *504/525–1048 or 800/882–4287* ⊕ *www.meyerthehatter.com.*

Fodor's Choice ★ **Rubensteins.** Known as one of the city's premier men's stores, this locally owned clothier also has a large selection of contemporary fashions for women. Labels include Brioni, Zegna, Burberry, Prada, Bruno Magli, Valentino, and Missoni. ✉ *102 St. Charles Ave., CBD* ☎ *504/581–6666* ⊕ *www.rubensteinsneworleans.com.*

Walking Co. New Orleans is a wonderful place to walk around, and it's imperative that you have comfortable shoes. Here's the place to find them, in stylish designs by makers like Birkenstock, Timberland, and Mephisto. There also are accessories such as canvas hats, folding canes, and hiking staffs. ✉ *Riverwalk Marketplace, 1 Poydras St., Warehouse District* ☎ *504/522–9255* ⊕ *www.walkingcompany.com.*

FOOD

Creole Delicacies & Cookin' Cajun. Accomplished and aspiring cooks will find a cornucopia of New Orleans's and Louisiana's spices, mixes, cookbooks, and cookware here, as well as cooking classes. Call for details, as class schedules and menus vary. ⊠*Riverwalk Marketplace, 1 Poydras St., Warehouse District* ☎*504/523–6425 or 800/786–0941* ⊕*www.cookincajun.com.*

JEWELRY

Adler's. Locally owned and operated, Adler's carries respected name brands in watches, engagement rings, jewelry with gemstones, wedding gifts, top-of-the-line silver, and more. ⊠*722 Canal St., CBD* ☎*504/523–5292* ⊕*www.adlersjewelry.com.*

Clock and Watch Shop. Master clock maker Josef Herzinger repairs and restores all types of new-, vintage-, and antique watches and clocks at his two-story shop, which is filled with time machines. The store also sells more than 15 brands of new clocks and watches, as well as an assortment timepieces ranging from miniature and mantle styles to large grandfather clocks. ⊠*824 Gravier St., CBD* ☎*504/523–0061.*

> ### A TASTE FOR PRACTICALITY
>
> Red beans and rice is a quintessential New Orleans comfort food. It's traditionally served on Monday throughout the city at fancy restaurants, casual establishments, and private homes. The tradition started in the days when Monday was wash day. The chore required lots of time and elbow grease, and red beans were a convenient meal because they could simmer on the stove unattended for hours. You can pick up red beans in the store (they're kidney beans)—but don't leave New Orleans without a box of Zatarain's red-bean seasoning mix.

7

MAGAZINE STREET

Magazine Street is a blossoming retail area of New Orleans, attracting new shops and eateries to meet the needs of local residents, university students, and visitors who flock to this historic area. Many of the stores are housed in shotgun houses and cottages that once served as residences. In addition to the original shops and galleries that have long graced the 6-mi street that curves from Canal Street to Carrollton Avenue, the area has become a prime spot for relocated businesses and branches for enterprises located in other areas of the city. One of the oldest and most-diverse shopping districts in the city—second only to the French Quarter—the area has antiques shops, art galleries, fashion boutiques, jewelers, home-furnishings shops, emporiums of vintage and local crafts, plus restaurants and coffee shops.

City buses provide transportation to and along Magazine Street, and streetcars travel along St. Charles Avenue, which runs parallel to Magazine Street. The easiest way to navigate this shopping district, however, is by car, which allows you to stop when you see something interesting and peruse clusters of shops within a block or two of each other at a time.

Most of the shops here can arrange to have your purchases sent directly to your home. Make sure you inquire about return policies before you make a purchase, as many of the smaller boutiques allow only in-store credit.

The **Magazine Street Merchants Association** (☎ *800/387–8924* ⊕ *www.mag azinestreet.com*) publishes a free brochure with maps and store descriptions; it's available in hotels and stores, or you can request one from the association's Web site. **Macon Riddle** (☎ *504/899–3027* ⊕ *www.new orleansantiquing.com*) shares her expertise in antiques and collectibles in half- or full-day shopping expeditions tailored to her clients' needs.

ANTIQUES

Antiques Magazine. Lighting is the specialty here, with nearly 200 lighting fixtures hanging from the ceiling, some dating back to the 1850s. The store also carries Victorian furniture, rare oyster plates, and accessories. The shop is closed Thursday and Sunday. ✉ *2028 Magazine St., Uptown* ☎ *504/522–2043.*

★ **As You Like It Silver Shop.** Everything you'd want in silver is available here, with a bounty of discontinued, hard-to-find, and obsolete American sterling-silver tea services, trays, and flatware. Victorian pieces, art-nouveau and art-deco pieces, and engraved pillboxes round out the selection. ✉ *3033 Magazine St. Uptown* ☎ *504/897–6915 or 800/828–2311* ⊕ *www.asyoulikeitsilvershop.com.*

Fodor's Choice ★ **Bush Antiques.** Antique beds are the specialty, but you'll also find religious artifacts, Continental furniture, architectural elements, ironwork, and lighting. The shop displays its beds, furniture, and accessories in vignettes on two floors. A courtyard in the back holds a bounty of antique garden accoutrements. ✉ *2109 Magazine St., Uptown* ☎ *504/581–3518* ⊕ *www.bushantiques.com.*

Home Hook & Ladder. The almost cavernous layout of this fire station–turned–antiques shop provides plenty of room for browsing through the shop's collection of 18th- and 19th-century French, English, and Continental antique furniture, accessories, garden art, and curios. The store is open by appointment only on Monday, but there are regular hours Tuesday through Saturday. ✉ *4100 Magazine St., Uptown* ☎ *504/895–4480 or 887/792–6169* ⊕ *www.homehookladder.com.*

Kevin Stone Antiques & Interiors. Unusual antique pieces, most from the 18th and early 19th centuries, fill this shotgun house; the collection includes many large, very ornate furniture pieces from the Louis XIV and -XV eras. The inventory ranges from small decorative bowls and ornate sconces to a large grand piano and armoires. ✉ *3420 Magazine St., Magazine Street* ☎ *504/891–8282* ⊕ *www.ksantiquer.com.*

La Belle Nouvelle Orleans. Elaborate stained-glass windows are mounted to the ceiling because the rest of the ample space is devoted to European antique furniture, artwork, porcelain, sculpture, and oddities from the 18th to 20th century. An open-air patio outfitted with garden benches, fountains, and other outdoor decor is linked to the main showroom by a warehouse-type gallery stacked almost floor to ceiling with furniture, salvaged doors, and other architectural items. ✉ *2112 Magazine St., Uptown* ☎ *504/581–3733* ⊕ *www.labellenouvelleorleans.com.*

Magazine Antique Mall. If you are easily intimidated, you should take a deep breath before you walk into this expansive shop, where every possible inch of counter and shelf space is filled with antiques and vintage goods. You find an array of costume- and fine jewelry, vintage photographs, antique clocks, home decor, glassware, clothing, silver, furniture, collectible china and ceramics, and a variety of other collectibles from a number of vendors. ✉ *3017 Magazine St., Magazine Street* ☎ *504/896–9994.*

ART & CRAFTS GALLERIES

Fodor's Choice
★ **Carol Robinson Gallery.** A Victorian house is home to contemporary paintings and sculpture by contemporary U.S. artists, with a special nod to those from the South. ✉ *840 Napoleon Ave., at Magazine St., Uptown* ☎ *504/895–6130* ⊕ *www.carolrobinsongallery.com.*

Cole Pratt Gallery. The contemporary paintings and sculptures of mid-career Southern artists are displayed at this modern gallery, which is open Tuesday through Saturday. ✉ *3800 Magazine St., Uptown* ☎ *504/891–6789* ⊕ *www.coleprattgallery.com.*

Thomas Mann Gallery I/O. The handmade jewelry of Thomas Mann, known for his unique style of "techno-romantic" pins, earrings, bracelets, and necklaces (which often feature hearts), is showcased alongside work by a changing slate of other artists, creating an eclectic mix of jewelry, housewares, sculpture, and unique gifts. ✉ *1812 Magazine St., Uptown* ☎ *504/581–2113* ⊕ *www.thomasmann.com.*

BOOKS

Garden District Book Shop. This small, one-room bookstore at the Rink shopping center is packed with works of history, fiction, and cookbooks by local, regional, and national authors; it was the first stop in novelist Anne Rice's book tours when she lived in New Orleans. Autographed copies and limited editions of her titles are usually in stock. ✉ *2727 Prytania St., Uptown* ☎ *504/895–2266* ⊕ *www.gardendistrictbookshop.com*

Octavia Books. The building itself gets attention because of its contemporary architecture, and an attractive layout inside invites leisurely browsing. The collection includes a strong selection of architecture, art, and fiction. ✉ *513 Octavia St., Uptown* ☎ *504/899–7323* ⊕ *www.octaviabooks.com.*

CLOTHING

Funky Monkey. Popular among local college students, the clothing exchange mixes new, used, and vintage clothing for men and women with hipster couture, custom-made T-shirts, handmade costumes, and lots of quirky accessories, all at affordable prices. ✉ *3127 Magazine St., Uptown* ☎ *504/899–5587.*

Fodor's Choice
★ **House of Lounge.** Opened by two women with backgrounds in film and costuming, the boutique is theatrical in its plush furnishings and fun, decadent special events. Merchandise includes high-quality bustiers, bras, slips, panties, hosiery, gowns, and sexy accessories. ✉ *2044 Magazine St., Uptown* ☎ *504/671–8300* ⊕ *www.houseoflounge.com.*

Jean Therapy. Popular among locals because of its diverse range of jeans—the shop carries more than 100 styles for men and women to fit

Magazine Street Shopping

Gen. Taylor St. to Louisiana Ave.

Mississippi River

Aidan Gill for Men **34**

Antiques Magazine **35**

As You Like It
Silver Shop **23**

Aux Belles Choses **14**

Blue Frog Chocolates **2**

Bush Antiques **29**

Cameron Jones for
Your Home **28**

Carol Robinson
Gallery **10**

Cole Pratt Gallery **16**

Dominique Giordano
Jewelry **6**

Fleur D'Orleans **18**

Funky Monkey **21**

Garden District
Book Shop **26**

Hazelnut **3**

Home Hook & Ladder **11**

House of Lounge **31**

Jean Therapy **4**

Jezebel's Art
and Antiques **9**

Jim Russell
Rare Records **37**

Katy Beh **17**

Kevin Stone
Antiques & Interiors **20**

La Belle
Nouvelle Orleans **30**

1st St. to St. Marys St.

see 1st St. to
St. Marys St.
inset for detail

see Gen. Taylor St.
to Louisiana Ave.
inset for detail

Kunflama	38	Perlis	1	Style Lab For Men	19
Magazine Antique Mall	24	Ray Langley Interiors	27	Thomas Mann Gallery	39
Metro Three	33	Savvy Gourmet	8	Winky's	32
Mon Coeur	12	Scriptura	5		
Neophobia	25	Shadyside Pottery	15		
Octavia Books	7	Southern Fossil &			
Orient Expressed		Mineral Exchange	36		
Imports	13	Sputnik Ranch	22		

0   1/4 mi

0   1/2 km

all body types—Jean Therapy also offers T-shirts, tops, lingerie, hats, jackets, handbags, and body products. ✉*5505 Magazine St., Magazine Street* ☎*504/897–5535* ⊕*www.jeantherapy.com.*

Kunflama. A clothing boutique for both sexes as well as an art gallery, Kunflama sells custom-fitted apparel and uncommon accessories, as well as furniture and decorative items. It also has a beverage bar that serves refreshments ranging from espresso to smoothies. ✉*1920 Magazine St., Uptown* ☎*504/586–1606* ⊕*www.kunflama.com.*

Metro Three. This is the place New Orleanians come when they want to wear their civic pride. The shop is dedicated to T-shirts that reflect the various personalities of the city, its neighborhoods, and its cultures, as well as Hurricane Katrina themes. Other fashions available include shorts, skirts, and casual shirts and blouses. ✉*2032 Magazine St., Magazine Street* ☎*504/558–0212* ⊕*www.metrothree.com.*

Perlis. The bottom floor of this New Orleans institution is devoted to outfitting men with classic suits, sportswear, shoes, ties, and accessories, as well as the store's signature crawfish-logo polo shirts. Upstairs, there's a children's section and dressy, casual, and formal apparel for women. ✉*6070 Magazine St., Uptown* ☎*504/895–8661* ⊕*www.perlis.com.*

Sputnik Ranch. Inspired by the fashions of yesteryear, this shop puts a contemporary spin on Western attire in clothing and boots for men and women. It also sells designer toys, lowbrow art, books, collectibles, and gifts. ✉*3029 Magazine St., Uptown* ☎*504/897–5446* ⊕*www.sputnikranch.com.*

Fodor'sChoice
★ **Style Lab for Men.** With a pool table in the back, this shop aims to dress the city's men well and make their shopping experience enjoyable and stress-free. The store stocks racks of fashions more commonly found in New York or Los Angeles, with an eye toward not-too-dressy business apparel and casual wear, as well as shoes, skin-care products, belts, and wallets. ✉*3641 Magazine St., Uptown* ☎*504/304–5072* ⊕*www.stylelabformen.com.*

↻ **Winky's.** This shop's fashions for men, women, and children have a decidedly retro influence, with a heavy dose of spunky New Orleans attitude. There's also a variety of toys and novelty gifts. Upstairs is Unique Products, an art gallery that specializes in lamps, clocks, jewelry, and decorative accessories made from recycled items such as cookie tins, melted Mardi Gras beads, and even laundry detergent bottles and vinyl records. ✉*2038 Magazine St., Uptown* ☎*504/568–1020.*

HOME FURNISHINGS

Fodor'sChoice
★ **Cameron Jones for Your Home.** Furniture, local art, home accessories, custom rugs, art glass, lighting, and a cadre of gift items here have a distinctly West Coast attitude melded with New Orleans flair. ✉*2127 Magazine St., Uptown* ☎*504/524–3119.*

Neophobia. Retro furniture and accessories for the home are the specialties at this shop, which carries furniture, clocks, lamps, tableware, glasses, jewelry, and vintage clothes from the 1920s to the 1970s. ✉*2855 Magazine St., Uptown* ☎*504/899–2444* ⊕ *www.neophobia-nola.com*

Ray Langley Interiors. Contemporary, eclectic, and elegant home furnishings include oversize sofas, colorful finishes, and uncommon accessories with modern European sensibilities. ✉*2302 Magazine St., Uptown* ☎*504/522–2284* ⊕*www.raylangley.com.*

Savvy Gourmet. Innovative kitchenware, equipment, and utensils from more than 50 vendors are available at this shop, which also houses a demonstration kitchen for cooking classes and serves lunch Tuesday through Saturday, brunch on Sunday. ✉*4519 Magazine St., Uptown* ☎*504/895–2665* ⊕*www.savvygourmet.com.*

JEWELRY

Dominique Giordano Jewelry. Local designer Dominique Giordano creates handmade contemporary jewelry designs in sterling silver and 18-karat gold with semiprecious and precious stones, pearls, and resin inlay. Styles range from casual to elegant. ✉*5420 Magazine St., Magazine Street* ☎*504/895–3909* ⊕*www.dgiordano.com.*

Fleur D'Orleans. Jewelry adorned with the fleur-de-lis is the main attraction here, but you'll also find items that carry other New Orleans icons such as crowns, masks, hearts, and more. In addition to jewelry, the store sells handbags, art, glassware, wood and ceramic boxes, batik scarves, ironwork, and more. ✉*3701-A Magazine St., Magazine Street* ☎*504/899–5585* ⊕*www.fleurdorleans.com.*

Jezebel's Art and Antiques. Past the shop's almost cartoonish mural and the cottage garden leading up to the entrance is an impressive collection of antique and estate jewelry by famous designers as well as more-affordable reproductions and new pieces by local artists. The store also carries new and vintage fashion furs, coats, and hats. ✉*4610 Magazine St., Uptown* ☎*504/895–7784* ⊕*www.jezebelscloset.com.*

Fodor's Choice ★ **Katy Beh Contemporary Jewelry.** The owner's penchant for unusual, finely crafted contemporary jewelry is evident in the display cases that hold national and emerging artists' delicate and sometimes bold pins, bracelets, earrings, rings, and pendants. ✉*3708 Magazine St., Uptown* ☎*504/896–9600* ⊕*www.katybeh.com.*

Mon Coeur by Janet Bruno-Small. Handmade jewelry crafted by Janet Bruno-Small from antique and vintage pieces is a specialty, but the showroom also has an assortment of distinctive jewelry by contemporary designers as well as antique and estate jewelry. ✉*3952 Magazine St., Uptown* ☎*504/899–0064* ⊕*www.moncoeurfinejewelry.com.*

MUSIC

Jim Russell Rare Records. Collectors love to browse through the endless bins of LPs, 78s, and 45s collected for more than 35 years, but the shop also stocks new recordings ranging from hip-hop to ragtime. ✉*1837 Magazine St., Uptown* ☎*504/522–2602* ⊕*www.jimrussell records.com.*

NOVELTIES & GIFTS

Fodor's Choice ★ **Aidan Gill for Men.** Relax in an old-fashioned barber chair while getting a contemporary cut by Aidan Gill, who also brings old and new together in his shaves, which feature the application of a number of hot towels. The front of the store is devoted to manly diversions, with new and reproduction shaving sets, contemporary and New Orleans–theme cuff links, cutting-edge pocket knives, wallets, bow ties (a specialty), grooming products for face and hair, and gifts. ✉*2026 Magazine St., Uptown*

☎504/587–9090 ⊠550 Fulton St., *CBD* ☎504/566–4903 ⊕*www. aidangillformen.com.*

Aux Belles Choses. This dreamy cottage of French and English delights has richly scented soaps, vintage and new linens, antique enamelware, collectible plates, and decorative accessories. It's open Wednesday through Saturday. ⊠*3912 Magazine St., Uptown* ☎*504/891–1009* ⊕*www.abcneworleans.com.*

Blue Frog Chocolates. Chocolates and other confections from all over the world are sold individually from an old-fashioned display case in the front of the store. Pack the goodies in gift boxes, arrangements, or on trays. Many of the candies are molded into novel shapes; candy-covered almonds form the petals of flowers gathered into sweet bouquets. ⊠*5707 Magazine St., Uptown* ☎*504/269–5707* ⊕*www.blue frogchocolates.com.*

Hazelnut. Founded by local actor Bryan Batt and his partner Tom Cianfichi, this shop sells eclectic accessories and gifts, including New Orleans toile pillows, decorative accessories and bags, stemware, tableware, accent furniture, frames, and more. ⊠*5515 Magazine St, Uptown* ☎*504/891–2424* ⊕*www.hazelnutneworleans.com.*

Orient Expressed Imports. Imported porcelain, vases, ceramics, jewelry, and the store's own line of smocked children's clothing are popular gift items. The store also has a showroom of home furnishings, including accent furniture, lamps, and antique accessories. ⊠*3905 Magazine St., Uptown* ☎*504/899–3060* ⊕*www.orientexpressed.com.*

Scriptura. Fitting tributes to the arts of writing and communication are evident in the Italian leather address books and journals, hand-decorated photo albums, specialty papers and stationery, handmade invitations, and a varied selection of glass and high-quality fountain pens sold here. ⊠*5423 Magazine St., Uptown* ☎*504/897–1555* ⊕*www. scriptura.com.*

Shadyside Pottery. Master potter Charles Bohn's studio and shop is filled with the functional and decorative stoneware, raku, and pottery he creates on-site as well as his custom wood tables. ⊠*3823 Magazine St., Uptown* ☎*504/897–1710* ⊕*www.shadysidepottery.com.*

Southern Fossil & Mineral Exchange. A wonderland for geologists or anyone enamored with natural history, this shop carries everything from inexpensive tumbled rocks to a table-size slab covered with fish fossils. In between you'll find crystals, bowls, vases, and other home decor fashioned from beautiful rocks, many with fossils, as well as alligator-skin knife sheaths, jewelry, mounted butterflies, and more. ⊠*2049 Magazine St., Magazine Street* ☎*504/523–5525.*

MAPLE STREET/RIVERBEND

Most of the shops and restaurants here are housed in turn-of-the-20th-century cottages, which lend an old-fashioned, small-town feeling to your shopping excursion. Once you're inside the shops, though, most of the wares are contemporary and modern. On Maple Street, the shops run about six blocks, from Carrollton Avenue to Cherokee Street, and in the Riverbend they dot the streets behind a shopping center on Car-

Angelique
& Victoria's
Shoes **6**

C. Collection **2**

Encore Shop **4**

Gae-Tana's **5**

Maple Street
Book Shop **9**

Maple Street
Children's
Book Shop **8**

N.O. Surf Shop ...**7**

Nuance/
Louisiana
Artisans
Gallery **1**

Yvonne
LaFleur **3**

Maple Street/
Riverbend
Shopping

KEY

🚋 Streetcar

0   1/4 m

0   1/4 km

rollton Avenue. St. Charles Avenue streetcars provide an easy way to get to the area.

ART & CRAFTS GALLERIES

Nuance/Louisiana Artisans Gallery. Mostly local and regional hand-blown glass artists are represented in the studio, which also carries dried-Spanish-moss dolls by Louisiana's Houma Indians, jewelry, pewter, ceramics, lamps, T-shirts, and more. ⊠*728 Dublin St., Uptown* 🕾*504/865–8463* ⊕*www.nuanceglass.com.*

BOOKS

Maple Street Book Shop. Local authors and touring ones stop here to catch up on literary trade news, perform readings, and autograph their work for readers. The store's focus is New Orleans and Louisiana, but you'll find most new titles in its maze of well-stocked small rooms. ⊠*7523 Maple St., Uptown* 🕾*504/866–4916* ⊕*www.maplestreet bookshop.com.*

🌀 **Maple Street Children's Book Shop.** Children find a comfortable introduction to literature here with shelves of books divided into age groups, stuffed animals tucked onto bookshelves, and toys to divert young non-readers while their parents and siblings shop. The store frequently hosts storytellers. ⊠*7529 Maple St., Uptown* 🕾*504/861–2105* ⊕*www. maplestreetbookshop.com.*

CLOTHING

Angelique & Victoria's Shoes. It's two stores in one, and both are trendsetters. Angelique provides apparel by designers such as Diane von Furstenberg, Nanette Lepore, and BCBG, and Victoria's covers the soles with shoes from top designers like Jimmy Choo, Chaplier and Jack Gomme, as well as jewelry and accessories from local and national artists. ⊠ *7725 Maple St., Uptown* ☎ *504/866–1092.*

C. Collection. Geared toward young adults, this store resembles a sorority-house closet jammed with hip, flirty women's clothes, shoes, handbags, and accessories ranging from casual to dressy by makers such as XOXO and ToTheMax. ⊠ *8141 Maple St., Uptown* ☎ *504/861–5002.*

Encore Shop. This fund-raising resale shop for the local symphony orchestra is stuffed with previously owned designer clothes, from casual to formal, for men and women, as well as shoes, handbags, and jewelry, all at yard-sale prices. The shop, which takes consignment as well as donated items, is open Tuesday through Saturday. ⊠ *7814 Maple St., Uptown* ☎ *504/861–9028.*

Gae-Tana's. Natural fabrics and stylish-but-comfortable clothing and hip designs make this a favorite stop for fashion-conscious mature women as well as college students looking for skirts, jeans, shorts, dressy skirts, blouses, fun shoes, handbags, and jewelry. ⊠ *7732 Maple St., Uptown* ☎ *504/865–9625.*

N.O. Surf Shop. There are no rolling waves in New Orleans, but this shop caters to the Crescent City's street surfers and sun lovers with a range of skateboards, hip beachwear, swimsuits, sunglasses, fashion accessories, and its own line of T-shirts that combine city icons such as fleur-de-lis and king-cake babies with surfer themes. ⊠ *7722 Maple St., Maple Street/Riverbend* ☎ *504/891–1616* ⊕ *www.nosurfshop.com.*

Yvonne LaFleur. Romantic fashions for women include lingerie, casual blouses, flirty dresses, ball gowns, tiaras, jewelry, handbags, and a whole room filled with wedding dresses in a variety of styles. Owner Yvonne LaFleur also custom-designs hats for all occasions, and her store is always infused with the sweet scent of her signature perfume line. ⊠ *8131 Hampson St., Uptown* ☎ *504/866–9666* ⊕ *www.yvonnelafleur.com.*

Side Trips from New Orleans

WORD OF MOUTH

"A truly authentic experience would have to include Breaux Bridge and a meal at Café des Amis. If you come on a Saturday, get there mighty early (at least 8 AM but I suggest earlier from what I've heard) for opening at 8:30 for the Zydeco breakfast."

—neworleanslady

By Sue
Strachan

NEW ORLEANS HAS NEVER BEEN A TYPICAL OLD SOUTH city. But look away to the west of town, and you can find the antebellum world conjured by the term Dixieland, which was coined here in the early 19th century. Between New Orleans and Baton Rouge, the romantic ruins of plantation homes alternate with the occasional restored manor, often open to visitors. Anyone with an interest in the history of the Old South or a penchant for a picturesque drive along country roads should spend at least half a day along the antebellum grand route, the Great River Road.

Popular day trips include tours of the swamps and bayous that surround New Orleans. *Bayou* comes from a Native American word that means "creek." The brackish, slow-moving waters of south Louisiana were once the highways and byways of the Choctaw, Chickasaw, and Chitimacha. Two centuries ago Jean Lafitte and his freebooters easily hid in murky reaches of swamp, which were covered with thick canopies of subtropical vegetation; pirate gold is said still to be buried here. The state has an alligator population of about 500,000, and most of them laze around in the meandering tributaries and secluded sloughs of south Louisiana. Wild boars, snow-white egrets, bald eagles, and all manner of other exotic creatures inhabit the swamps and marshlands. A variety of tour companies, large and small, take groups to swampy sites a half hour to two hours away from the city center. Guides steer you by boat through still waters, past ancient gnarled cypresses with gray shawls of Spanish moss, explaining the state's flora and fauna and the swamp traditions of the trappers who settled here. *(For swamp tour operators,* ⇨ *Alligators Up Close: Swamp Tours.)*

South Louisiana, cradle of the Cajun population, is decidedly French in flavor. In small communities along the coast and in the upland prairie, Cajun French is still spoken, although just about everyone also speaks English. After a hard day's work fishing or working crawfish ponds, rural residents of Cajun Country often live up to the motto *Laissez les bons temps rouler!,* which means "Let the good times roll!"

ABOUT THE RESTAURANTS

Part of the considerable charm of the region west of New Orleans is the Cajun food, popularized by Cajun chef Paul Prudhomme, a native of Opelousas. This is jambalaya, crawfish pie, and filé gumbo country, and nowhere else on Earth is Cajun food done better than where it originated. Cajun food is often described as the robust, hot-peppery country kin of creole cuisine. It is a cuisine built upon economy—heavy on the rice and the sauces, lighter on the meats—and heavily reliant upon African cooking traditions. Indigenous sea creatures turn up in étouffées, bisques, and pies, and on almost every Acadian menu are jambalaya, gumbo, and blackened fish. Alligator meat is a great favorite, as are sausages like andouille and boudin (stuffed with pork and rice). Cajun food is very rich, and portions tend to be ample. Biscuits and grits are breakfast staples, and many an evening meal ends with bread pudding.

IF YOU LIKE

MUSIC

Music beats at the heart of Cajun life. Ensembles of fiddles, accordions, and guitars produce eminently danceable folk music, with songs sung in a mélange of English and Cajun French. Zydeco, closely related to Cajun music, adds washboard and drums to the mix and has more of a blues-rock feel to it. Saturday morning and afternoon are devoted to Cajun music, played in small gatherings and in bars beginning at 8 AM. Zydeco music rocks back-road barns and country clubs on Friday and Saturday nights. Many Cajun clubs and restaurants host Sunday-afternoon jams.

HISTORIC HOMES

The sweeping artistry of the grand plantation houses stands in the eerie shadow of massive chemical plants that operate on the Mississippi today, and plantation ruins sometimes appear in the middle of a cow field or alongside a bayou, directly testifying to this clash between old and new. Some are low-slung, West Indies–style structures that are relatively humble, whereas others are grandly columned mansions.

Cajun cuisine extends beyond Cajun Country itself, and into many of the restaurants along River Road. North of Baton Rouge, however, in St. Francisville, more-typical Southern fare prevails. Here you will still find po'boys and sometimes gumbo, but barbecue is more common than boudin. *(For explanations of many Cajun foods, see Chapter 3.)*

ABOUT THE HOTELS

Some of the handsome antebellum mansions along River Road are also B&Bs in which you may roam the high-ceiling rooms before bedding down in a big four-poster or canopied bed. The greatest concentration of accommodations in Cajun Country is in Lafayette, which has an abundance of chain properties as well as some B&Bs. In nearby towns are charming B&Bs, where friendly hosts can give you insider tips about touring the region. St. Francisville is valued as one of the best B&B towns in the South.

WHAT IT COSTS					
	$$$$	$$$	$$	$	¢
RESTAURANTS	over $30	$23–$30	$16–$22	$10–$15	under $10
HOTELS	over $150	$121–$150	$90–$120	$50–$89	under $50

Restaurant prices are for a main course at dinner. Hotel prices are for two people in a standard double room in high season, excluding 8% sales tax.

PLANTATION COUNTRY

The area designated Plantation Country envelops a cascade of plantations along the Great River Road leading west from New Orleans, plus a reservoir of fine old homes north of Baton Rouge, around the town of St. Francisville. Louisiana plantation homes range from the grandiose

Southern Louisiana

MISSISSIPPI

Gulfport

Pearl R.

Bogalusa

Plantation Country

Covington

Lake Pontchartrain

New Orleans

Chalmette

Kenner

Lake Maurepas

Lake Salvador

Grand Isle

Burnside

Napoleonville

Houma

Baton Rouge

St Francisville

New Roads

False River

White Castle

Plaquemine

Morgan City

Patterson

Franklin

New Iberia

Marsh Island

Cajun Country

Opelousas

Lafayette

Eunice

Abbeville

Erath

White Lake

Grand Lake

Rockefeller Wildlife Refuge

Gulf of Mexico

Alexandria

Red R.

TEXAS

De Ridder

Toledo Bend Reservoir

Sabine River

Lake Charles

Sulphur

Vinton

Port Arthur

Lake Sabine

Lake Calcasieu

Grand Chenier

0   50 miles

0   75 km

Nottoway on River Road to the humble, owner-occupied Butler Green-wood near St. Francisville. Some sit upon an acre or two; others, such as Rosedown, are surrounded by extensive, lush grounds.

The River Road plantations are closely tied to New Orleans's culture and society: it was here that many of the city's most prominent families made their fortunes generations ago, and the language and tastes here are historically French. The St. Francisville area, on the other hand, received a heartier injection of British-American colonial culture during the antebellum era, evidenced in the landscaped grounds of homes such as Rosedown and the restrained interior of Oakley House, where John James Audubon lived while in the area.

Baton Rouge, the state capital, provides a midpoint between the River Road plantations and St. Francisville and has some interesting sights of its own. Chain hotels in Baton Rouge provide a convenient base for explorations in both directions and B&Bs are scattered nearer the plantations.

THE GREAT RIVER ROAD

The Old South is suspended in an uneasy state of grace along the Great River Road, where the culture that thrived here during the 18th and 19th centuries, both elegant and disturbing, meets the blunt ugliness of the industrial age. Between New Orleans and Baton Rouge, beautifully restored antebellum plantations along the Mississippi are filled with period antiques, ghosts of former residents, and tales of Yankee gunboats. Yet industrial plants mar the scenery, and the man-made levee, constructed in the early 20th century in a desperate ploy to keep the mighty Mississippi on a set course, obstructs the river views that plantation residents once enjoyed. Still, you can always park your car and climb up on the levee for a look at Ol' Man River.

Between the Destrehan and San Francisco plantations you will drive through what amounts to a deep bow before the might of the Mississippi: the Bonnie Carre Spillway is a huge swath of land set aside specifically to receive the river's periodic overflow, thus protecting New Orleans, 30 mi downriver.

The Great River Road is also called, variously, Route or LA 44 and 75 on the east bank of the river and Route or LA 18 on the west bank. "LA" and "Route" are interchangeable; we use Route throughout this chapter. Alternatives to the Great River Road are Interstate 10 and U.S. 61; both have signs marking exits for various plantations. All the plantations described are listed on the National Register of Historic Places, and some of them are B&Bs. Plantation touring can take anywhere from an hour to two days, depending upon how many houses you want to see.

Numbers in the margin correspond to points of interest on the Planta-tion Country map.

DESTREHAN PLANTATION
23 mi west (upriver) of New Orleans.

The oldest plantation left intact in the lower Mississippi Valley, this simple West Indies–style house, built in 1787 by a free man of color, is typical of the homes built by the earliest planters in the region. The plantation is notable for the hand-hewn cypress timbers that were used in its construction and for the insulation in its walls, made of *bousillage,* a mixture of horsehair, Spanish moss, and mud. Some days bring period demonstrations of indigo dying, candle making, or open-hearth cooking; an annual fall festival with music, crafts, and food is held during the second weekend in November. A costumed guide leads you on a 45-minute tour through the house, which is furnished with period antiques and some reproductions. You are free to explore the grounds, including several smaller structures and massive oak trees borne down by their weighty old branches. ✉ *13034 River Rd., Destrehan* ☎ *985/764–9315* ⊕ *www.destrehanplantation.org* 🎫 *$10* ⏱ *Daily 9–4.*

SAN FRANCISCO PLANTATION
18 mi west of Destrehan Plantation, 35 mi west of New Orleans.

An elaborate Steamboat Gothic house completed in 1856, San Francisco presents an intriguing variation on the standard plantation styles, with galleries resembling the decks of a ship. The house was once called St. Frusquin, a name derived from a French slang term, *sans fruscins,* which means "without a penny in my pocket"—the condition its owner, Valsin Marmillion, found himself in after paying exorbitant construction costs. Valsin's father, Edmond Bozonier Marmillion, had begun the project. Upon his father's death, Valsin and his German bride, Louise von Seybold, found themselves with a plantation on their hands. Unable to return to Germany, Louise brought German influence to south Louisiana instead. The result was an opulence rarely encountered in these parts: ceilings painted in trompe l'oeil, hand-painted "toilets" with primitive flushing systems, and cypress painstakingly rendered as marble. Tour guides impart the full fascinating story and more on the 45-minute tour through the main house. An authentic one-room schoolhouse and a slave cabin have been installed on the grounds, which you can tour at your leisure. Louisiana novelist Frances Parkinson Keyes used the site as the model for her book *Steamboat Gothic.* ✉ *2646 River Rd., Garyville* ☎ *985/535–2341 or 888/322–1756* ⊕ *www.sanfranciscoplantation.org* 🎫 *$15* ⏱ *Nov.–Mar., daily 9–4; Apr.–Oct., daily 9:30–4:30.*

LAURA PLANTATION
10 mi west of San Francisco Plantation, 57 mi west of New Orleans.

Laura Plantation provides a more-intimate, well-documented presentation of creole plantation life than any other property on River Road. The narrative of the guides is built on first-person accounts, estate records, and original artifacts from the Locoul family, who built the simple, creole-style house in 1805. Laura Locoul, whose grandmother founded the estate, kept a detailed diary of plantation life, family fights, and the management of slaves. The information from Laura's diary and the original slave cabins and other outbuildings (workers on the plantation grounds lived in the cabins into the 1980s) provide rare insights into slavery under the French. The plantation gift shop stocks a large selection of literature by and about slaves and slavery in southern Louisiana and the United States. Senegalese slaves at Laura are believed to have first told folklorist Alcee Fortier the tales of Br'er Rabbit; his friend Joel Chandler Harris used the stories in his Uncle Remus tales. ✉2247 River Rd. (Rte. 18), Vacherie ☎225/265–7690 or 888/799–7690 ⊕www. lauraplantation.com ⊠$15 ☉Daily 10–4.

> ## PACE YOURSELF
>
> Don't try to visit every plantation listed here—your trip will turn into a blur of columns. If you can, spend the night at one of the plantations, such as Oak Alley or Madewood, and then tour the region. St. Francisville is a weekend trip in its own right. If you're visiting from New Orleans and are strapped for time, Destrehan, one of the state's oldest plantations, might fit the bill; it's just 23 mi from the city.

WHERE TO EAT
¢–$ ✕**B&C Seafood.** This small shop and deli serves the tastiest seafood gumbo ever ladled into a Styrofoam bowl. Try it with a dash of hot sauce and a sprinkle of filé, or sample the alligator and garfish po'boys. Finish with a scoop of soft and chewy bread pudding. The deli has fresh and frozen catfish, crawfish, alligator, and turtle meat harvested from the nearby swamps. You can buy seafood packed to travel. ✉2155 Rte. 18, beside Laura Plantation, Vacherie ☎225/265–8356 ⊕www. bandcseafood.com ▤AE, D, MC, V ☉Closed Sun.

OAK ALLEY
3 mi west of Laura Plantation, 60 mi west of New Orleans.

Built between 1837 and 1839 by Jacques T. Roman, a French-Creole sugar planter from New Orleans, Oak Alley is the most famous of all the antebellum homes in Louisiana and an outstanding example of Greek Revival architecture. The 28 gnarled oak trees that line the drive and give the columned plantation its name were planted in the early 1700s by an earlier settler, and the oaks proved more resilient than the dwelling he must have built here. A guided tour introduces you to the grand interior of the manor, furnished with period antiques. Be sure to take in the view from the upper gallery of the house and to spend time exploring the expansive grounds. A number of late-19th-century cottages behind the main house provide simple overnight accommodations and a restaurant is open daily for breakfast (8:30–10) and lunch (11–3). ✉3645 River Rd. (Rte. 18), Vacherie ☎225/265–2151 or 800/442–5539 ⊕www.oakalleyplantation.com ⊠$15 ☉ Weekdays 10–4, weekends 10–5.

HOUMAS HOUSE
29 mi northwest from San Francisco Plantation, 58 mi west of New Orleans.

Surrounded by majestic 200-year-old oaks, Houmas House is a classic Louisiana plantation home—grand white pillars and all. The house here is actually two buildings, of quite different styles, joined together. In 1790 Alexander Latil built the smaller rear house in the French–Spanish creole style that was becoming popular in New Orleans. The Greek Revival mansion was added to the grounds in 1840 by John and Caroline Preston, who eventually connected the two structures with an arched carriageway. ⊠*40136 Rte. 942, 0.5 mi off Rte. 44, Darrow* ☎*225/473–7841 or 225/473–9380* ⊕*www.houmashouse. com* ⊠*Guided home and garden tour $20, self-guided garden tour $10* ☉*Daily 9–5.*

WHERE TO EAT
$–$$$$

✕**Latil's Landing Restaurant.** Set in the rear wing of Houmas House Plantation, Latil's Landing Restaurant is furnished with period antiques and reproductions that put you in the mood for the "nouvelle Louisiana" food, a mélange of traditional ingredients with more-contemporary cooking techniques and flavors. Try the bisque of curried pumpkin, crawfish and corn, rack of lamb, and the chocolate napoleon. ⊠*40146 Hwy. 942, Darrow* ☎*225/473–7841 or 888/323–8314* ☐*AE, D, MC, V* ☉*No dinner Mon.*

$–$$$

✕**The Cabin.** Yellowed newspapers and antique farm implements hang from the walls of this 150-year-old slave cabin, which was part of the Monroe Plantation. Crawfish étouffée and other Cajun seafood dishes are the specialties here, but you can also choose po'boys, burgers, or steaks. ⊠*5404 Rte. 44, at the corner of Rte. 22, Burnside* ☎*225/473–3007* ⊕*www.thecabinrestaurant.com* ☐*AE, D, MC, V* ☉*No dinner Mon.*

MADEWOOD
20 mi south of Houmas House, 74 mi west of New Orleans.

This galleried, 21-room Greek Revival mansion with its massive white columns was designed by architect Henry Howard and completed in 1854. The house, across the road from Bayou Lafourche, has an enormous freestanding staircase and 25-foot-high ceilings, and is best experienced overnight: the B&B experience is magnificent. Guests can arrange a tour with the owners; visitors should call to set up a time to visit the property. ⊠*4250 Rte. 308, 2 mi south of town, Napoleonville* ☎*985/369–7151 or 800/375–7151* ⊕*www.madewood.com* ⊠*$10* ☉*Daily 10–4.*

River Road African American Museum. This museum explores the contributions of African-Americans in Louisiana's rural Mississippi River communities through exhibits that explore their cuisine, the Underground Railroad, free people of color, jazz, and other topics. ⊠*406 Charles St., Donaldsonville* ☎*225/474–5553* ⊕*www.africanamericanmuseum.org* ⊠*$4* ☉*Wed.–Sat. 10–5, Sun. 1 PM–5 PM.*

WHERE TO STAY
★ $$$$

⌂**Madewood.** Expect gracious hospitality, lovely antiques, and canopied beds in both the 21-room main house and Charlet House, a smaller structure on the plantation grounds. Guests come here for the social experience as well as the elegant accommodations: a Southern

8

dinner is shared in the formal dining room at 7 PM, preceded by a cocktail hour in the library. The cost of a room includes breakfast, dinner, and a tour of the house. **Pros:** Quiet, beautiful, staying here is like stepping back in time—though with modern amenities. **Cons:** Some may find it too quiet, not the place to go for total seclusion—dinner is a group affair. ✉4250 Rte. 308, Napoleonville ☎504/369–7151 or 800/375–7151 ⊕www.madewood.com ⇔5 rooms, 3 suites ⊟AE, D, MC, V ⓘⓄⓘMAP.

$$–$$$$ ▥**Oak Alley.** Stay in 100-year-old cottages on Oak Alley Plantation's grounds. The furnishings have country charm—with brass beds and antiques or reproductions. Some cabins have full kitchens. **Pros:** Spectacular sunrise views from the levee in front of the plantation, serene quiet, charming rooms with comfortable Tempur-Pedic beds. **Con:** Few nearby options for supplies and food. ✉3645 River Rd. (Rte. 18), Vacherie ☎225/265–2151 or 800/442–5539 ⊕www.oakalleyplantation. com ⇔6 rooms ⊟AE, D, MC, V ⓘⓄⓘMAP.

NOTTOWAY

Fodor'sChoice
★
33 mi northwest of Madewood, 70 mi west of New Orleans.

The South's largest plantation house, Nottoway, should not be missed. Built in 1857, the mansion is a gem of Italianate style. With 64 rooms, 22 columns, and 200 windows, this white castle (the town of White Castle was named for it) was the crowning achievement of architect Henry Howard. It was saved from destruction during the Civil War by a Northern officer (a former guest of the owners, Mr. and Mrs. John Randolph). An idiosyncratic layout reflects the individual tastes of the original owners and includes a grand ballroom, famed in these parts for its crystal chandeliers and hand-carved columns. You can stay here overnight, and a formal restaurant serves lunch and dinner daily. ✉30970 Rte. 405, 2 mi north of White Castle ☎225/545–2730 or 866/527–6884 ⊕www.nottoway.com ⓘ$15 ⓄDaily 9–5.

WHERE TO   ▥**Nottoway.** The largest antebellum plantation in the South, this stun-
STAY   ner is fun to wander around at night. You can sit on the upstairs bal-
$$$–$$$$ cony and watch the ships go by on the river. In this antiques-filled B&B, three suites come with a bottle of champagne; if you stay in the other rooms—in the main house, its wings, and surrounding cottages—you receive a complimentary glass of sherry. Mornings begin with hot coffee and muffins delivered to your room, followed by a full breakfast on the ground floor. ✉30970 Rte. 405, White Castle ☎225/545–2730 or 866/428–4748 ⊕www.nottoway.com ⇔11 rooms, 3 suites ☖In-hotel: restaurant, pool, no elevator ⊟AE, D, MC, V ⓘⓄⓘBP.

BATON ROUGE

80 mi northwest of New Orleans via I–10.

Hemmed in as it is by endless industrial plants, Baton Rouge does not look like much from the road. Yet government history enthusiasts will want to stop here on their way through the south Louisiana countryside. Baton Rouge, the state capital, has several interesting and readily accessible sights, including the attractive state capitol grounds and an educational planetarium. This is the city from which colorful, cunning Huey P. Long ruled the state; it is also the site of his assassination. Even today, more than half a century after Long's death, legends about the controversial governor and U.S. senator abound.

The parishes to the north of Baton Rouge are quiet and bucolic, with gently rolling hills, high bluffs, and historic districts. John James Audubon lived in West Feliciana Parish in 1821, tutoring local children and painting 80 of his famous bird studies. In both terrain and traits, this region is more akin to north Louisiana than to south Louisiana—which is to say, the area is very Southern.

Louisiana Arts & Science Museum and Irene W. Pennington Planetarium. Housed in a 1925 Illinois Central railroad station near the Old State Capitol, this idiosyncratic but high-quality museum brings together a contemporary art gallery, an Egyptian tomb exhibit, a children's museum and discovery zone, and a state-of-the-art planetarium, which is also kid-friendly. The planetarium presents regular shows, as does the ExxonMobil Space Theater. The museum also hosts traveling exhibits, and houses the nation's second-largest collection of sculptures by 20th-century Croatian artist Ivan Mestrovic, many of which adorn the entrance hall. ✉*100 S. River Rd.* ☎*225/344–5272* ⊕*www.lasm.org* ✑*$6, $8 including planetarium show* ⊗*Tues.–Fri. 10–4, Sat. 10–5 (planetarium 10–8), Sun. 1–5.*

Louisiana State Museum—Baton Rouge. This museum showcases the history of Louisiana through two exhibits: "Grounds for Greatness: Louisiana and the Nation," which relates Louisiana history to the nation and the world, from the Louisiana Purchase to World War II; and the "Louisiana Experience: Discovering the Soul of America," a road-trip-like exhibit that courses through the different regions of the state. There is also a gallery for changing exhibits. ✉*660 N. 4th St.* ☎*800/568–6968* ✑*$6* ⊗*Tues.–Sat. 9–5, Sun. noon–5.*

Old Arsenal Museum. Only one Revolutionary War battle was fought outside the 13 original colonies, and it was fought on the state capitol grounds. These days the grounds are pleasantly landscaped, but this restored heavy-duty powder magazine, set atop a knoll beneath the towering state capitol, recalls the spot's bellicose history. The museum inside has informational exhibits held in powder kegs that open and light up and displays on Louisiana's Native American history. ✉*State capitol grounds* ☎*225/342–0401* ✑*$1* ⊗*Tues.–Sat. 9–4.*

Old Governor's Mansion. This Georgian-style home was constructed for Governor Huey P. Long in 1939, and nine governors have since lived there. The story goes that Long instructed the architect to design it to resemble the White House, representing Long's unrealized ambition to live in the real one. Notable features on the guided tour include Long's bedroom and a secret staircase. ✉*502 North Blvd.* ☎*225/387–2464* ⊕*www.fhl.org* ✑*$6* ⊗*Tues.–Fri. 10–3, or by appointment.*

Old State Capitol. When this Gothic Victorian fantasia was completed in 1850, it was declared by some to be a masterpiece, by others a monstrosity. No one can deny that the restored building is colorful and dramatic. In the entrance hall a stunning purple, gold, and green spiral staircase winds toward a stained-glass atrium. The building now holds the **Louisiana Center for Political and Governmental History,** an education and research facility with audiovisual exhibits. The "assassination room," an exhibit covering Huey Long's final moments, is a major draw. ⊠*100 North Blvd., at River Rd.* ⊕*www.sec.state.la.us/ osc* ☜*$4* ☉*Tues.–Sat. 10–4, Sun. noon–4.*

Rural Life Museum & Windrush Gardens. This 5-acre complex, run by Louisiana State University (LSU), is an outdoor teaching and research facility. Three major areas—the Barn, the Working Plantation, and Folk Architecture—with 25 or so rustic 19th-century structures represent the rural life of early Louisianians. The Barn holds an eclectic collection of items including old farm tools, quilts, 19th-century horse-drawn carriages, slave items, and much more. The working plantation's several buildings include a gristmill, a blacksmith's shop, and several outbuildings. The gardens cover 25 acres and were created by landscape designer Steele Burden. It's a truly unique place. ⊠*4650 Essen La., off I-10* ☎*225/765–2437* ⊕ *www.rurallife.lsu.edu* ☜*$7* ☉*Daily 8:30–5.*

Shaw Center for the Arts. This multicultural center houses the LSU Museum of Art, the Brunner Gallery, the Manship Theatre, the LSU-MOA museum store, the LSU School of Art Gallery, two sculpture gardens, and a rooftop terrace with great views of the Mississippi River. River views can also be appreciated from the on-site restaurant, Tsunami, a nightlife hot spot with Asian-fusion cuisine. ⊠*100 Lafayette St.* ☎*225/346–5001* ⊕*www.shawcenter.org* ☜*$8* ☉*Tues.–Sat. 9 AM–11 AM, Sun. 11–5*

State Capitol Building. Still called the "New State Capitol," this building has housed the offices of the governor and Congress since 1932. It is a testament to the personal influence of legendary Governor Huey Long that the funding for this massive building was approved during the Great Depression, and that the building itself was completed in a mere 14 months. You can tour the first floor, richly decked with murals and mosaics, and peer into the halls of the Louisiana legislature. Huey Long's colorful personality eventually caught up with him: he was assassinated in 1935, and the spot where he was shot (near the rear elevators) is marked with a plaque. At 34 stories, this is America's tallest state capitol; an observation deck on the 27th floor affords an expansive view of the Mississippi River, the city, and the industrial outskirts. ⊠*900 N. 3rd St.* ☎*225/342–7317* ☜*Free* ☉*Daily 8–4:30 (tower until 4).*

USS Kidd & Veterans Memorial Museum. A Fletcher-class destroyer, the USS *Kidd* is a World War II survivor restored to its V-J Day configuration. A self-guided tour takes in more than 50 inner spaces of this ship and also the separate **Nautical Center** museum. Among the museum's exhibits are articles from the 175 Fletcher-class ships that sailed for the United States, a collection of ship models, and a restored P-40 fighter plane hanging from the ceiling. The Louisiana Memorial Plaza lists more than 7,000 Louisiana citizens killed during combat. ⊠ *305 S. River Rd. (Government St. at the levee)* ☎ *225/342–1942* ⊕ *www. usskidd.com* ☞ *$7* ⊗ *Daily 9–5.*

WHERE TO STAY & EAT

★ $$-$$$$ ✕ **Juban's.** An upscale bistro with a lush courtyard and walls adorned with art, Juban's is a family-owned and -operated restaurant not far from the LSU campus. Tempting main courses of seafood, beef, and veal dishes, as well as roasted duck, rabbit, and quail, highlight the sophisticated menu. The Hallelujah Crab (soft-shell stuffed with seafood and topped with "creolaise" sauce) is a specialty, and Juban's own mango tea is delicious. The warm bread pudding is something to write home about. ⊠ *3739 Perkins Rd. (Acadiana Shopping Center)* ☎ *225/346–8422* ⊕ *www.jubans.com* ⊟ *AE, D, DC, MC, V* ⊗ *Closed Sun. No lunch Mon. and Sat.*

$$-$$$$ ✕ **Mike Anderson's.** This lively seafood spot manages to be a lot of things to a lot of people: first-daters, families, groups of friends, and solo diners all find a warm welcome here. Locals of every stripe praise the seafood, and it is true that the food is good, fresh, served in large portions, and consistent. But what Mike's does best is the comfortable, subtly rustic atmosphere, made a bit more special with oversize fish tanks. ⊠ *1031 W. Lee Dr.* ☎ *225/766–7823* ⊕ *www.mikeandersons. com* ⊟ *AE, D, MC, V.*

¢-$$$ ✕ **Ruffino's.** A broad, clubby dining room invites lingering over the best Italian cuisine in town. Local ingredients find their way into hearty Italian preparations, such as eggplant Parmesan and shrimp scampi. A romantic bar area includes some smoking tables just off the main dining areas. The restaurant is a few minutes east from downtown along Interstate 10. ⊠ *18811 Highland Rd., Exit 166 off I–10* ☎ *225/753–3458* ⊕ *www.ruffinosrestaurant.com* ⊟ *AE, D, DC, MC, V* ⊗ *No lunch Mon.–Sat.*

$$-$$$$ ⊡ **Hilton Baton Rouge Capitol Center. Pros:** Spectacular view of the river, near all the downtown sites. **Con:** Downtown Baton Rouge can sometimes feel like a ghost town. ⊠ *201 Lafayette St.* ☎ *225/344–5866* ⊕ *www.hiltoncapitolcenter.com* ⇌ *291 rooms, 7 suites* ⚷ *In-hotel: restaurant, room service, bar, gym, spa, laundry service, concierge, airport shuttle, no-smoking rooms* ⊟ *AE, D, DC, MC, V.*

$$-$$$$ ⊡ **Embassy Suites.** This centrally located property has two-room suites, with mahogany furniture and a wet-bar area with microwave, coffee-

8

maker, and mini-refrigerator. A two-hour cocktail happy hour and a full breakfast, cooked to order, are included in the room rate, and the service is quite good across the board. **Pros:** Great location if you're going to an LSU football game, comfortable rooms, lots of services. **Cons:** Chain property, downtown sights are not within walking distance, occasionally packed with conventioneers—or high-spirited LSU fans. ⊠*4914 Constitution Ave.* ☎*225/924–6566 or 800/362–2779* 🖷*225/923–3712* ⊕*www.embassysuites.com* ⇆*223 suites* 🕭*In-hotel: restaurant, room service, bar, pool, laundry service, airport shuttle* ⊟*AE, D, DC, MC, V* ⦿*BP.*

$$–$$$$ ⌨ **Marriott Baton Rouge.** This high-rise hotel has somewhat formal rooms and public spaces with traditional furnishings. The top four floors offer VIP perks such as continental breakfast and afternoon hors d'oeuvres and cocktails. **Pros:** Very accommodating for large groups, full-service hotel, lots of comforts. **Con:** Not centrally located. ⊠*5500 Hilton Ave.* ☎*225/924–5000 or 800/228–9290* 🖷*225/926–8152* ⊕*www.marriott. com* ⇆*300 rooms* 🕭*In-hotel: restaurant, room service, bar, gym, laundry service, concierge, airport shuttle, no-smoking rooms* ⊟*AE, D, DC, MC, V.*

ST. FRANCISVILLE

25 mi north of Baton Rouge on U.S. 61.

A cluster of plantation homes all within a half-hour drive, a lovely, walkable historic district, renowned antiques shopping, and a wealth of comfortable B&Bs draw visitors and locals from New Orleans to overnight stays in St. Francisville. The town is a two-hour drive from New Orleans, so it is also possible to make this a day trip.

St. Francisville's historic district, particularly along Royal Street, is dotted with markers identifying basic histories of various structures, most of them dating to the late 18th or early 19th century. The region's Anglo-Protestant edge, in contrast to the staunchly French-Catholic tenor of the River Road plantations, is evident in the prominent **Grace Episcopal Church,** sitting proudly atop a hill in the center of town and surrounded by a peaceful, Spanish moss–shaded cemetery. The smaller (though older) Catholic cemetery is directly across a small fence from the Episcopal complex.

Butler Greenwood Plantation. This home has been occupied by the same family since its construction in the 1790s, and with much of the same furniture. This renders the house a bit musty and quirky compared to other, more-showpiece-oriented plantations in the area, providing an intimate picture of day-to-day living in such a home. Butler Greenwood is relatively modest in size, and the tour focuses on details such as dress (several items of clothing worn by the family's ancestors are on display) and china (a beautiful set has been in the family for generations). A complete set of coveted rosewood furniture, still with the original upholstery, is of particular interest. The property is also a B&B. ⊠*8345 U.S. 61* ☎*225/635–6312* ⊕*www.butlergreenwood. com* ⛁*$5* ⦿*Mon.–Sat. 9–5, Sun. 1–5.*

OFF THE
BEATEN
PATH **Louisiana State Penitentiary Museum at Angola.** The notorious Angola prison is a half-hour drive from St. Francisville, at the dead end of Route 66. With a prison population of about 5,000 inmates, this is one of the largest prisons in the United States. Wryly nicknamed "The Farm," Angola was once a working plantation, with prisoners for field hands. The prison has been immortalized in countless songs and several films and documentaries, including *Dead Man Walking* and *Angola Prison Rodeo—the Wildest Show in the South*. A small museum outside the prison's front gate houses a fascinating, eerie, and often moving collection of photographs documenting the people and events that have been a part of Angola. Items such as makeshift prisoner weapons and the electric chair used for executions until 1991 are also on display. ⊠ *Hwy. 66* ☎*225/655–2592* ⊕ *www.angolamuseum.org* ✉*Free* ⊙*Tues.–Fri. 8–4:30, Sat. 9–5.*

The Myrtles. A 110-foot gallery with Wedgwood-blue cast-iron grillwork makes a lovely setting for the weddings and receptions frequently held at the Myrtles. The house was built around 1796 and has elegant formal parlors with rich molding and faux-marble paneling. The upper floor is a B&B, thus limiting the scope of the daytime guided tour. The house is reputedly haunted, and the fun Friday- and Saturday-night mystery tours (offered at 6, 7, and 8) are perhaps more of a draw than the daytime tours. The Varnedoe's Carriage House Restaurant, beside the house, is a fine place for dinner. ⊠*7747 U.S. 61, about 1 mi north of downtown St. Francisville* ☎*225/635–6277 or 800/809–0565* ⊕*www.myrtlesplantation.com* ✉*$8, mystery tours $10* ⊙*Daily 9–5; mystery tours Fri. and Sat. nights at 6, 7, and 8.*

OFF THE
BEATEN
PATH **Oakley House and Audubon State Historic Site.** John James Audubon did a major portion of his *Birds of America* studies in this 100-acre park. The three-story Oakley Plantation House on the grounds is where Audubon tutored the young Eliza Pirrie, daughter of Mr. and Mrs. James Pirrie, owners of Oakley. The simple, even spartan, interior contrasts sharply with the extravagances of the River Road plantations and demonstrates the Puritan influence in this region. The grounds, too, are reminiscent of the English penchant for a blending of order and wilderness in their gardens. You must follow a short path to reach the house from the parking lot. A state-run museum at the start of the path provides an informative look at plantation life as it was lived in this region 200 years ago. ⊠*11788 Rte. 965, 2 mi south of St. Francisville off U.S. 61* ☎*225/635–3739 or 888/677–2838* ⊕*www.lastateparks.com* ✉*Park and plantation $2* ⊙*Daily 9–5.*

★ **Rosedown Plantation and Gardens.** The opulent house at Rosedown dates from 1835, is beautifully restored, and nestles in 28 acres of exquisite formal gardens. The original owners, Martha and Daniel Turnbull, spent their honeymoon in Europe and Mrs. Turnbull fell in love with the formal gardens she saw there. She had the gardens at Rosedown laid out even as the house was under construction, and she spent the rest of her life lovingly maintaining them. The state of Louisiana owns Rosedown, and the beauties of the restored manor, including 90% of the original furniture, can be appreciated during a thorough one-hour tour led by park rangers. Be sure to allow ample time for roaming the grounds after the tour. ✉ *12501 I–10, off U.S. 61* ☎ *225/635–3332 or 888/376–1867* ⊕ *www.lastateparks.com* ⚑ *$10, grounds only $5* ⊘ *Daily 9–5.*

WHERE TO STAY & EAT

$$$ ✗ **The Magnolia.** This low-key and unassuming dining establishment is a St. Francisville hot spot on weekend nights. During the day, locals and tourists flock here for Southern specialties and pizza. At night, go for cocktails or dinner; on Friday evening there's always a live band. ✉ *5689 Commerce St., St. Francisville* ☎ *225/635–6528* ▤ *MC, V* ⊘ *No dinner Sun.–Wed.*

$–$$$ ✗ **Varnedoe's Carriage House Restaurant.** A fine-dining establishment in the shadow of the Myrtles Plantation, Varnedoe's is a boon to over-nighters in the St. Francisville area. The dining room is elegant yet intimate. The contemporary cuisine draws from a wealth of culinary traditions, courtesy of chef Scott Varnedoe. His "Upscale Down South" cuisine encompasses dishes ranging from Cajun Asian duck to fried green tomatoes with collard greens. Reservations are accepted for large parties only; it's best to arrive early to claim a table—and your share of specials. ✉ *7747 U.S. 61, at the Myrtles Plantation* ☎ *225/635–2635* ⊕ *www.varnedoes.com* ▤ *AE, D, MC, V* ⊘ *Closed Mon.*

★ ¢–$$ ✗ **Roadside BBQ & Grill.** Looking for Southern barbecue? Here it is—ribs, pork, and chicken grilled to perfection. If you're not in the mood for 'cue, they also have hamburgers, salads, and fried seafood po'boys. Most astonishing, though, are the sophisticated specials that hit the chalkboard on weekends, such as crab cakes topped with sautéed shrimp, and rib eye topped with lump crabmeat. A child's menu is also available. With all due respect to the many fine Cajun and creole establishments nearby, this is as good a meal as you'll find in these parts. ✉ *Colonial Dr. and U.S. 61, 9 mi south of St. Francisville* ☎ *225/658–9669* ▤ *AE, D, DC, MC, V* ⊘ *Closed Mon. No dinner Tues., Wed., and Sun.*

$$–$$$$ ▦ **Barrow House & Printer's Cottage.** Along St. Francisville's historic Royal Street, these two old houses hold some of the most comfortable B&B accommodations in the area, with antique furnishings in most of the rooms. Breakfast is continental; full breakfast is available for a small surcharge. A cassette walking tour of town is included. **Pros:** Good location in downtown St. Francisville, B&B ambience, friendly staff. **Con:** If you don't like antiques, you may feel like you're in a museum or your grandmother's home. ✉ *9779 Royal St.* ☎ *225/635–4791* ⊕ *www.topteninn.com* ⇥ *3 rooms, 3 suites* ▤ *AE, D, MC, V* ⛶ *CP.*

$$–$$$$ ▦ **The Myrtles.** If you don't mind a deep legacy of hauntings, the Myrtles is a pleasant and convenient place to stay, just a few miles beyond the center of St. Francisville. The guest rooms fill the second floor of the plantation house and a couple of outlying buildings. A tour of the home is included in your stay, as is a continental breakfast served beside the gift shop. In nice weather, many guests opt for the outdoor tables behind the house. The fine Varnedoe's Carriage House Restaurant serves excellent lunches and dinners and is another good reason to stay here. **Pros:** Historical property oozes atmosphere, ghost hunters' paradise, next door to Varnedoe's Carriage House Restaurant. **Cons:**

Feels like it's in the middle of nowhere, easily frightened travelers might want to stay elsewhere. ⊠7747 U.S. 61 ☎225/635–6277 or 800/809–0565 🖷225/635–5837 ⊕www.myrtlesplantation.com ⇘10 rooms, 1 suite ⊟AE, D, MC, V ⏀CP.

PLANTATION COUNTRY ESSENTIALS

To research prices, get advice from other travelers, and book travel arrangements, visit ⊕www.fodors.com.

AIR TRAVEL

Baton Rouge provides easy access to the region. Baton Rouge is served by American, Continental, Delta, and Northwest.

AIRPORT

New Orleans International Airport is off Interstate 10, just 20 minutes from Destrehan Plantation. Baton Rouge Metropolitan Airport is 7 mi north of downtown.

AIRPORT INFORMATION **Baton Rouge Metropolitan Airport** *(BTR)* ⊠ *9430 Jackie Cochran Dr.* ☎ *225/355-0333* ⊕ *www.flybtr.com.*

BUS TRAVEL

Greyhound Southeast Lines has frequent daily service from New Orleans to Baton Rouge, and limited service to surrounding areas.

BUS INFORMATION **Greyhound Southeast Lines** ☎ *800/231-2222* ⊕ *www.greyhound.com.*

CAR TRAVEL

From New Orleans, the fastest route to the River Road plantations is Interstate 10 west to Interstate 310 to Exit 6, River Road. Alternatives to the Great River Road are to continue on either Interstate 10 or U.S. 61 west; both have signs marking exits for various plantations. Route 18 runs along the west bank of the river, Route 44 on the east.

Interstate 10 and U.S. 190 run east–west through Baton Rouge. Interstate 12 heads east, connecting with north–south Interstate 55 and Interstate 59. U.S. 61 leads from New Orleans to Baton Rouge and north. Ferries across the Mississippi cost $1 per car; most bridges are free. Route 1 travels along False River, which is a blue oxbow lake created ages ago when the mischievous, muddy Mississippi changed its course. The route wanders past gracious homes and small lakeside houses.

EMERGENCIES

Dial 911 for assistance. Hospital emergency rooms are open 24 hours a day at Baton Rouge General Medical Center and Our Lady of the Lake Medical Center. Walgreens has a 24-hour pharmacy.

HOSPITALS **Baton Rouge General** Medical Center ⊠ *3600 Florida Blvd.* ☎ *225/387–7000* ⊕ *www.generalhealth.org.* **Our Lady of the Lake Regional Medical Center** ⊠ *5000 Hennessy Blvd.* ☎ *225/765-6565* ⊕ *www.ololrmc.com.*

24-HOUR PHARMACY **Walgreens** ⊠ *4747 S. Sherwood Forest Blvd.* ☎ *225/292-8975.*

VISITOR INFORMATION

TOURIST **Baton Rouge Visitors & Conventions Bureau** ⊠ *730 North Blvd., Baton Rouge*
INFORMATION ☎ *225/383–1825 or 800/527–6843* ⊕ *www.visitbatonrouge.com.* **Louisiana Visitor Information Center** ⊠ *900 N. 3rd St., Baton Rouge* ☎ *225/342–7317* ⊕ *www. louisianatravel.com.* **West Feliciana Tourist & Convention Information Center** ⊠ *1157 Ferdinand St., St. Francisville 70775* ☎ *225/635–4224 or 800/789–4221* ⊕ *www.stfrancisville.us.*

CAJUN COUNTRY

French Louisiana, lying amid the bayous, rice paddies, and canebrakes to the west of New Orleans, has become famous in the rest of the country for its food (jambalaya and blackened fish) and music (both Cajun and zydeco). The Cajun culture has its roots far from these parts in the present-day Canadian provinces of Nova Scotia and New Brunswick, where French settlers colonized a region they called l'Acadie at the start of the 17th century. The British seized control of the region in the early 18th century and the French were expelled. Their exile was described by Henry Wadsworth Longfellow in his epic poem "Evangeline." Many Acadians eventually settled in 22 parishes of southwestern Louisiana. Their descendants are called "Cajun," a corruption of "Acadian"; some continue the traditions of the early French settlers, living by fishing and fur trapping.

Cajun culture is decidedly rural, rooted in a smattering of tiny towns and in the swamps and bayous that wind among them. Driving from one village to the next, antiques shoppers and nature lovers alike will find bliss. Live oaks with ragged gray buntings of Spanish moss form canopies over the bottle-green bayous. Country roads follow the contortions of the Teche (pronounced *tesh*), the state's longest bayou, and meander through villages where cypress cabins rise up out of the water on stilts and moored fishing boats and pirogues scarcely bob on the sluggish waters. At the centers of these same villages are wonderful bakeries, historic churches, fresh oyster bars, and regional antiques for sale in small, weathered shops.

Many visitors to this region are surprised to hear the dialect for the first time. Cajun French is an oral tradition in which French vocabulary and approximate grammar encounter the American accent, and it differs significantly from what is spoken in France. English is also spoken throughout Cajun Country, but you will hear Gallic accents and see many signs that read ICI ON PARLE FRANÇAIS (French spoken here).

Numbers in the margin correspond to points of interest on the Cajun Country map.

LAFAYETTE

Lafayette (pronounced lah-fay-*ette*), 136 mi west of New Orleans and the largest city in Cajun Country, is a major center of Cajun life and lore, the "big city" in the middle of the countryside. It's an interest-

Acadian
Cultural
Center **8**

Acadiana Park
Nature Station . **10**

Alexander
Mouton House
and Lafayette
Museum **3**

Children's
Museum of
Acadiana.........**6**

Jefferson
Street
Market **4**

Lafayette
Courthouse **2**

Lafayette
Natural History
Museum and
Planetarium **5**

Paul and Lulu
Hilliard
University
Art Museum **7**

St. John the
Evangelist
Cathedral **1**

Vermilionville ...**9**

ing and enjoyable town, with some worthwhile historical and artistic sights. The simulated Cajun villages at **Vermilionville** and **Acadian Village** provide evocative introductions to the traditional Cajun way of life. Excellent restaurants and B&Bs make Lafayette a good jumping-off point for exploring the region. The city has also had an infusion of new restaurants and nightclubs—particularly downtown, which is lively even on weekend nights.

Numbers in the margin correspond to numbers on the Lafayette map and numbers in "A Good Walk."

WHAT TO SEE

③ Alexander Mouton House and Lafayette Museum. Built in 1800 as the *maison dimanche,* or "Sunday house," of town founder Jean Mouton, this galleried town house with a mid-19th-century addition now preserves local history. The older section is an excellent example of early Acadian architecture and contains artifacts used by settlers. The main museum contains Civil War–era furnishings and memorabilia and a Mardi Gras exhibit. ✉ *1122 Lafayette St.* ☎ *337/234–2208* 💲 *$3* 🕐 *Tues.–Sat. 9–4:30, Sun. 1–4.*

🐾 ⑥ Children's Museum of Acadiana. Good on a rainy day or to soak up extra energy in the kids, this museum is basically a large indoor playground, with some educational games and interactive exhibits such as a grocery store, a recycling arts projects, a bubble exhibit, and more. ⊠*201 E. Congress St.* ☎*337/232–8500* ⊠*$5* ⊘*Tues.–Sat. 10–5.*

❹ **Jefferson Street Market.** A collective of artists, artisans, and dealers fills the deep hall of this market. Antiques and mod kitsch, refined gifts and quirky artwork—this market has it all. Changing contemporary art exhibits claim the central gallery space. ⊠*538 Jefferson St.* ☎*337/233–2589* ⊘*Mon.–Sat. 10–5:30.*

❷ **Lafayette Courthouse.** The courthouse contains an impressive collection of more than 2,000 historical photographs of life in the Lafayette area. There are images of famous politicians such as Dudley LeBlanc and Huey Long working the stump and scenes from the great flood of 1927. Many of the pictures are displayed on the second floor. ⊠*800 Buchanan St.* ☎*337/233–0150* ⊘*Weekdays 8:30–4:30.*

☝ ❺ **Lafayette Natural History Museum and Planetarium.** Opened in 2003, this sparkling natural-history museum includes changing exhibitions and lots of fun hands-on science for kids. ⊠*433 Jefferson St.* ☎*337/291–5544* ⊕*www.lnhmpmuseum.org* ⊠*$5* ⊘*Tues.–Fri. 9–5, Sat. 10–6, Sun. 1–6.*

Murals. There are several outdoor murals by Robert Dafford in the center of Lafayette. A Louisiana swamp scene is across from **Dwyer's Café** (⊠*323 Jefferson St.*) (⇨ *Where to Eat*), and splashy cars and TVs with vignettes of Cajun life are on the **Jefferson Tower Building** (⊠*556 Jefferson St.*). The microcosm of Lafayette inside the garage at Parc **Auto du Centre Ville,** at the corner of Polk and Vermilion streets, is the work of local artist Tanya Falgout.

❶ **St. John the Evangelist Cathedral.** This cathedral, completed in 1916 (construction began in 1913), is a Romanesque structure with Byzantine touches. Union troops encamped on the grounds during the Civil War. In the cemetery behind the church are aboveground tombs that date back to 1820; interred here are town founder Jean Mouton, Civil War hero General Alfred Mouton, and Cidalese Arceneaux. Arceneaux is believed to be the daughter of Gabriel, the lost love of Longfellow's Evangeline. Next to the cathedral is the 400-year-old St. John Oak, one of the charter members of the silent but leafy Louisiana Live Oak Society. ⊠*914 St. John St.* ☎*337/232–1322.*

OUTSIDE DOWNTOWN ❽ **Acadian Cultural Center.** A unit of the Jean Lafitte National Historical Park and Preserve, the center traces the history of the area through numerous audiovisual exhibits of food, music, and folklore. Be sure to watch the introductory film, which is a dramatization of the Acadian exile. Black-and-white clips from the 1929 movie *The Romance of Evangeline* are incorporated in the film; aficionados of early motion pictures will love it. Ranger-guided boat tours of Bayou Vermilion take place March through June in a traditional Louisiana boat. ⊠*501 Fisher Rd.* ☎*337/232–0789* ⊠*Free* ⊘*Daily 8–5.*

8

OFF THE BEATEN PATH

Acadian Village. A re-creation of an early-19th-century bayou settlement, this park is on 10 wooded acres with a meandering bayou crisscrossed by wooden footbridges. Most structures here were constructed during the early 19th century; they were moved here to create this representative "village," though they actually represent a broad range of Acadian architectural styles. Each house is decorated with antique furnishings. The rustic general store, blacksmith shop, and chapel are replicas of 19th-century buildings. ⊠200 Greenleaf Dr., south of downtown ☎337/981–2364 or 800/962–9133 ⊕www.acadianvillage. org ⊑$7 ⊙Daily 10–4.

Acadiana Center for the Arts. This multicultural arts center hosts art exhibits, musical performances, lectures, and children's programs. ⊠101 W. Vermilion St. ☎337/233–7060 ⊕www.acadianacenterfort hearts.org ⊙Tues.–Fri. 10–5, Sat. 10–6.

❿ Acadiana Park Nature Station. Naturalists are on hand in the interpretive center at this three-story cypress structure, which overlooks a 42-acre park of natural forest. Discovery boxes help children get to know the wildflowers, birds, and other outdoorsy things they'll see on the 3.5-mi nature trail. Free guided trail tours take place every Saturday and Sunday at 1 PM. There is a guided evening hike on the last Saturday of the month ($2 per person). ⊠1205 E. Alexander St. ☎337/291–8448 ⊕www.naturestation.org ⊑Free ⊙Weekdays 8–5, weekends 11–3.

❼ Paul and Lulu Hilliard University Art Museum. A gleaming contemporary architectural gem, this museum features world-class exhibits—including works by Deborah Butterfield and Robert Rauschenberg—and a sculpture garden and bookstore. ⊠710 E. St. Mary Blvd. ☎337/482–2278 ⊕ www.louisiana.edu/uam ⊑$5 ⊙Tues.–Sat. 10–5.

❾ Vermilionville. Directly behind the Acadian Cultural Center, a living-history village re-creates the early life of the region's Creoles and Cajuns, focusing on the late 1800s to early 1900s. On select days visitors can see a blacksmith demonstration or weavers. There are exhibits in 19 Acadian-style structures, including a music hall where live Cajun or zydeco music is played every Sunday afternoon. A large rustic restaurant serves Cajun classics, and cooking demonstrations are held on weekends. ⊠300 Fisher Rd., off Surrey St. ☎337/233–4077 or 866/992–2968 ⊕www.vermilionville.org ⊑$8 ⊙Tues.–Sun. 10–4.

WHERE TO EAT

$$–$$$$ ✕**Café Vermilionville.** This 19th-century inn with crisp white napery and old-brick fireplaces serves French and Cajun fare to a well-dressed crowd. Among the specialties are pecan-crusted tilapia and Cajun-marinated seared duckling. This is a favorite spot for special occasions among Lafayette residents. ⊠1304 W. Pinhook Rd. ☎337/237–0100 ⊕www. cafev.com ⊟AE, D, DC, MC, V ⊙Closed Sun. No lunch Sat.

★ $–$$$$ ✕**Prejean's.** Oyster shuckers work in a cozy bar at this local favorite along Interstate 49, north of central Lafayette. Three meals are served in this cypress house with a wide front porch and a 50-foot shrimp boat parked outside. People gather at tables with red-and-white-check cloths to partake of Prejean's seafood platter (gumbo, fried shrimp, oysters, catfish, and seafood-stuffed bell peppers) as well as Cajun rack of elk, American buffalo au poivre, and steak and chicken prepared in various ways. There's live Cajun music, and usually dancing, nightly. ⊠*3480 U.S. I–49 N* ☎*337/896–3247* ⊕*www.prejeans.com* ⊟*AE, D, DC, MC, V.*

$$–$$$ ✕**Charley G's.** This chic yet friendly seafood grill is a popular spot for locals seeking a creative and delicious bite. Charley G's is famous for the smoked duck and andouille gumbo, grilled fish, crab cakes, and soft-shell crabs. Desserts are divine. ⊠*3809 Ambassador Caffery Pkwy.* ☎*337/981–0108* ⊕*www.charleygs.com* ⊟*AE, MC, V* ⊗*Closed Sun. No lunch Sat.*

$$$ ✕**Pamplona Tapas Bar.** Tapas have arrived in Lafayette—and with great success. An authentic interior (one wall is covered with bullfighting posters) creates just the right mood for Chef William Annesley's sophisticated dishes and one of the best wine lists in the area. On Saturday night, there's a DJ. ⊠ *631 Jefferson St.* ☎*337/232–0070* ⊟*AE, MC, V* ⊗*Closed Sun. and Mon.*

★ ¢–$$ ✕**Tsunami.** A stylish contemporary restaurant as chic as the crowd it attracts, Tsunami delivers fresh and innovative sushi and Japanese cuisine. Entrées include beef Negimaki, Chilean sea bass, and various tempura dishes. For a nightcap, go next door to the lounge—managed by the same owners—which has an L.A vibe. ⊠*412 Jefferson St.* ☎*337/234–3474* ⊕*www.servingsushi.com* ⊟*AE, MC, V* ⊗*Closed Sun. and Mon.*

¢–$ ✕**Café Bonjour.** The old Mello Joy coffee shop has a new name and coffee brand (CCs), but it's still a great place to perk up in the AM. For light bites, there are fresh-baked pastries and muffins, sandwiches, soups, and salads. ⊠*625 Jefferson St.* ☎*337/232–0006* ⊟*AE, MC, V* ⊗*No dinner Sun.*

¢–$ ✕**Dwyer's Café.** People jam this diner as early as 6 AM for hot biscuits and grits. Dwyer's serves red beans and rice, jambalaya, pot roast, burgers, and omelets. Be sure to try the hearty plate lunches which include an entrée, two sides, and bread. ⊠*323 Jefferson St.* ☎*337/235–9364* ⊟*AE, MC, V* ⊗ *No dinner.*

¢–$ ✕**T-Coon's Café.** This lively diner serves hearty (half orders are recommended) Cajun lunches such as smothered rabbit or stuffed pork chops with two vegetables, rice, and gravy. Locals gather in the back room for conversation, jokes, and raucous songs in French. ⊠*740 Jefferson St.* ☎*337/232–3803* ⊟*AE, MC, V* ⊗*Closed weekends. No dinner.*

WHERE TO STAY

★ $$–$$$ ⊡**Bois des Chênes Inn.** This B&B is housed in the 19th-century Mouton Plantation, in a quiet residential area of Lafayette. An upstairs suite can accommodate five, and has early Acadian antiques; downstairs, the Louisiana Empire Suite has a queen-size bed, and the Victorian Suite a double bed. Breakfast is prepared by owner Marjorie Voorhies, and her husband, Coerte Voorhies, conducts unusually informative boat tours through the surrounding swamps. A complimentary glass of wine and a tour through the home is included in the room rate. **Pros:** Nice owners, pretty grounds. **Con:** Rooms feel like they could benefit from a good airing out. ⊠*338 N. Sterling St.* ☎☎*337/233–7816* ⇖*5 rooms* ⊟*AE, MC, V* ⦙⦿⦙*BP.*

$–$$$ ▦ **Lafayette Hilton & Towers.** Traditional furnishings outfit the standard rooms and the beds are very comfortable; some rooms on concierge floors come with hot tubs and wet bars. Riverside rooms of this high-rise overlook the Bayou Vermilion, though the hotel is on a heavily commercialized strip. **Pros:** Typical Hilton amenities, good location is convenient for sightseeing, comfy beds. **Cons:** Reservations are hard to come by if there's a wedding or event, halls can be loud when the hotel is full, chain property. ⊠ *1521 W. Pinhook Rd.* ☎ *337/235–6111 or 800/332–2586* ⊟ *337/237–6313* ⊕ *www.hilton.com* ✎ *327 rooms* ⚬ *In-hotel: restaurant, bar, pool, gym, concierge, airport shuttle* ☰ *AE, D, DC, MC, V.*

> ## CAJUN VS. CREOLE
>
> Cajun cuisine relies on locally available ingredients, such as rabbit, mirliton, and rice. Most dishes have the "holy trinity" of celery, bell pepper, and garlic as a base; traditional examples include boudin and maque choux (a corn stew, usually served with crawfish tails). Creole cuisine is more cosmopolitan, incorporating French, Spanish, Italian, African, and French Caribbean influences. While many dishes use the same "holy trinity," creole dishes, like their French counterparts, are defined by their sauces. Examples include shrimp creole, crawfish bisque, and oysters Rockefeller.

$$ ▦ **T'Frere's House.** Built in 1880 of native cypress and handmade bricks, "little brother's house" has been a B&B since 1985. About 2 mi south of the Oil Center, the Acadian-style house with Victorian trim is furnished with French and Louisiana antiques. Additional accommodations are in an Acadian-style cottage behind the main house. You are greeted with a complimentary "T'julep" and "Cajun canapés," hors d'oeuvres made with boudin. The Cajun breakfast combines regional ingredients with traditional Southern cuisine. **Pros:** Charming decor, owners like to feed their guests well, great if you are looking to get away from it all but still want to be near 21st-century amenities. **Cons:** It feels a bit far from everything, not a good option if you're on a diet. ⊠ *1905 Verot School Rd.* ☎ *337/984–9347 or 800/984–9347* ⊕ *www. tfreres.com* ✎ *6 rooms* ☰ *AE, D, MC, V* ❘O❘ *BP.*

$$$$ ▦ **Juliet Boutique Hotel.** This new hotel (opened in late 2007) is the only boutique property in downtown Lafayette. All 20 rooms have fine bed linens and full baths; there's also a pool, and Wi-Fi and room service are available. **Pros:** Great location, extremely comfortable beds, you'll feel like you're staying in your own private hotel. **Cons:** Some rooms have structural poles, bathrooms have shuttered windows (and don't feel very private), checkout can take a while (since there's only one person at the front desk). ⊠ *800 Jefferson St.* ☎ *337/261–2225* ⊕ *www. juliethotel.com* ✎ *20 rooms* ☰ *AE, D, MC, V.*

NIGHTLIFE & THE ARTS

NIGHTLIFE   Pick up a copy of the *Times of Acadiana* or the trendier *Independent* to find listings for *fais-do-dos*, zydeco dances, and other events. These free weeklies are available in hotels, restaurants, and shops.

Major concerts are held at the **Cajundome** (⊠ *444 Cajundome Blvd.* ☎ *337/265–2100* ⊕ *www.cajundome.com*). The **Heymann Performing**

Arts Center (⌧*1373 S. College Rd.* ☎*337/291–5540* ⊕*www.heymann-center.com*) hosts concerts and theatrical productions of all types.

Downtown galleries are open and the streets are hopping during the popular **ArtWalks**, which are held on the second Saturday of each month.

On Friday evening from mid-March through June and September through November, **Downtown Alive!** (⌧*Jefferson St. at Main St.* ☎*337/291–5566* ⊕*www.downtownalive.org*) draws dancing crowds to downtown Lafayette, where bands play on an open-air stage. **El Sido's** (⌧*1523 N. St. Antoine* ☎*337/235–0647*) is a family-run zydeco club with music on weekends. Sid Williams manages the club while his brother's band, Nathan and the Zydeco Cha-Chas, performs frequently. **Randol's** (⌧*2320 Kaliste Saloom Rd.* ☎*337/981–7080 or 800/962–2586* ⊕*www.randols.com*), a good Cajun restaurant, also has music and dancing nightly.

FESTIVALS The biggest bash in this neck of the woods is the **Courir de Mardi Gras** (February or March, depending on when Lent occurs), which showcases colorful parades and King Gabriel and Queen Evangeline. For information, contact the Lafayette Convention and Visitors Commission (☎*337/232–3737 or 800/346–1958*).

★ Lafayette's **Festival International de Louisiane** (✉*Box 4008 70502* ☎*337/232–8086*), which takes place on the last weekend of April, is a free music festival, rivaling the New Orleans Jazz and Heritage Festival, that fills the streets with entertainers, artisans, and chefs from French-speaking nations and communities. The annual **Festival Acadiens** is a huge music-and-food fest in Lafayette, held in late September or early October. For information, contact the **Lafayette Convention and Visitors Commission** (☎*337/232–3737 or 800/346–1958*).

SHOPPING

ANTIQUES A cooperative of vendors sells antiques, as well as works by local artists and craftspeople in **Jefferson Street Market** (⌧*538 Jefferson St.* ☎*337/233–2589* ⊙*Mon.–Sat. 10–5:30*). Look for beautiful cypress pieces and handwoven textiles.

FOOD The fresh French bread and pastries baked at **Poupart's Bakery** (⌧*1902 Pinhook Rd.* ☎*337/232–7921* ⊙*Closed Mon.*) rival Paris's best.

Looking to bring home some authentic Cajun goodies? Then a stop at**Don's Specialty Meats & Grocery** (⌧*730 I–10 S. Frontage Rd., Scott* ☎*337/234–2528* ⌧*104 Hwy. 726, Carencro* ☎*337/896–6370* ⊕*www.donsspecialtymeats.com*) is a must. You can fill your cooler with boudin, cracklin's, stuffed pork chops, quail, a variety of sausages, and much more at Don's two locations—both just outside Lafayette.

GRAND COTEAU

11 mi north of Lafayette.

The tiny village of Grand Coteau may be the most serene place in south Louisiana. Nestled against a sweeping ridge that was a natural levee of the Mississippi River centuries ago ("grand coteau" means big hill), the town is oriented around a core of grand and beautiful religious institutions. Covering the hill itself is a peaceful cemetery, behind the stately St. Charles College, a Jesuit seminary. When the Mississippi overflowed its banks during the cataclysmic flood of 1927, the water stopped shy at the base of Grand Coteau's ridge, and the town was preserved. Today the entire town center is listed on the National Register of Historic Places, with dozens of historical structures including creole cottages, early Acadian-style homes, and the grand Academy and Convent of the Sacred Heart. Martin Luther King Drive (Route 93) is the main thoroughfare. Antiques stores line the main street.

A magnificent avenue of pines and moss-hung oaks leads to the entrance of the **Academy and Convent of the Sacred Heart,** founded in 1821 as the first of the international network of Sacred Heart schools, and the site of the only Vatican-certified miracle to occur in the United States. The miracle occurred when nuns at the convent said novenas to St. John Berchmans, a 15th-century Jesuit priest, on behalf of Mary Wilson, a very ill novice. St. John Berchmans subsequently appeared to Mary twice, and she was suddenly and unexpectedly cured. St. John Berchmans was canonized in 1888. You may enter a shrine on the exact site of the miracle and (by appointment only) tour a museum with artifacts dating from the school's occupation by Union troops during the Civil War. ⊠ *1821 Academy Rd., end of Church St.* ☎*337/662–5275* ⊕*www.ashcoteau.org* ⊠*$5* ⊙ *Weekdays 9–2.*

In one of Grand Coteau's historic cottages, the **Kitchen Shop** specializes in regional cookbooks and cooking supplies, in addition to a wide range of gifts and other merchandise. It also has prints and greeting cards by famed local photographer John Slaughter. In a tearoom, pastry chef Nancy Brewer prepares scones, cookies, and a rich torte she calls *gateau-na-na.* ⊠ *296 Martin Luther King Dr., at Cherry St.* ☎*337/662–3500* ⊙*Tues.–Sat. 10–5, Sun. 1–5.*

St. Charles College was the first Jesuit seminary in the South. You can drive or walk through the grounds and cemetery, though you can only visit the beautiful interior of the **Church of St. Charles Borromeo** by appointment. ⊠ *313 E. Martin Luther King Hwy., at Church St.* ☎*337/662–5251, 337/662–5279 to visit church.*

WHERE TO EAT

$$$–$$$$ ✕**Catahoula's.** This stylish yet simple restaurant in a renovated former dry-goods store serves ambitious contemporary cuisine prepared with Mediterranean flair, yet with Cajun roots ever in evidence. The menu changes seasonally, ensuring the freshest ingredients and preparations. Depending on the time of year, the menu includes such inventions as firm gulf shrimp wrapped in a flour tortilla with grilled onions, poblano peppers, and feta cheese, or smoked seafood–stuffed soft-shell crab with strawberry-fig butter. The decor is spare, and highlights artistic representations of the Catahoula Hound, Louisiana's state dog. ⊠ *234 Martin Luther King Dr.* ☎*337/662–2275 or 888/547–2275* ⊕*www.*

catahoulasrest.com ▭*AE, D, MC, V* ⊘*Closed Mon. No lunch Tues.–Thurs. and Sat. No dinner Sun.*

OPELOUSAS

15 mi north of Grand Coteau.

In the heart of St. Landry Parish, Opelousas is the third-oldest town in the state—Poste de Opelousas was founded in 1720 by the French as a trading post. It is a sleepy spot with a historic central square, a provincial museum, and several excellent zydeco clubs within spitting distance. Look for two murals located in a pocket park/parking lot adjacent to the St. Landry Bank & Trust Co. building. One depicts the history of the area and historical monuments in St. Landry Parish and the other depicts the legend of the Seven Brothers Oak, which is located south of Washington, a charming nearby town. Contact the **St. Landry Parish Tourist Commission** (🕾*337/948–8004* ⊕*www.cajuntravel. com*) for information about the entire area.

The **Opelousas Museum and Interpretive Center** (✉*315 N. Main St.* 🕾*337/948–2589* 🖃*Free* ⊘*Mon.–Sat. 9–5*) traces the history of Opelousas from prehistoric times to the present and includes an exhibit on the town's brief stint as state capitol, during the Civil War, and a doll collection of more than 400 dolls. The museum is also home to the Louisiana Video Library and the Southwest Louisiana Zydeco Festival archives.

Traveling exhibits from major museums and private art collections make up the **Opelousas Museum of Art** (✉*106 N. Union St.* 🕾*337/942–4991* 🖃*Suggested donation $3* ⊘*Feb.–Dec., Tues.–Fri. 1–5, Sat. 9–5*) inset in the Wier House, a rare Southern example of classic Federal architecture.

★ On the town square, you can step back in time at the **Palace Cafe** (✉*135 W. Landry St.* 🕾*337/942–2142* ⊘*Closed Sun.*), an old-style diner serving breakfast, lunch, and dinner. Try one or all of the six different types of gumbo on the menu.

At the intersection of Interstate 49 and U.S. 190, look for the **Opelousas Tourist Information Center** (🕾*337/948–6263* ⊘*Daily 8–4*), where you can get plenty of information, arrange for tours of historic homes, and see memorabilia pertaining to Jim Bowie, the Alamo hero who spent his early years in Opelousas.

8

WEEKEND ANTIQUES HUNTING

Antiques lovers will want to stop in Washington, located north of Opelousas. It is a short, 2-mi diversion from the main route if you are traveling from Opelousas to Ville Platte. Founded in 1770, Washington has many buildings on its main street that are on the National Register of Historic Places. More than 10 antiques stores cluster within walking distance of one another. Most of these stores are open only Friday to Sunday. For more information, contact the town's **museum and tourist information center** (🕾*337/826–3627*).

NIGHTLIFE & THE ARTS

The roads surrounding Opelousas are *the* place to catch authentic, sweaty zydeco music.

Beloved **Richard's** (⊠*U.S. 190, Lawtell* ☎*337/543–6596*) is a rural, wood-frame zydeco club west of Opelousas with music most weekends. Plaisance, on the outskirts of Opelousas, holds a **Southwest Louisiana Zydeco Music Festival** (☎*337/942–2392* ⊕*www.zydeco.org*) the Saturday before Labor Day.

SHOPPING

For Cajun, zydeco, and Swamp pop-music recordings and related products, **Floyd's Record Shop** (⊠*434 E. Main St., Ville Platte* ☎*337/363–2185* ⊕*www.floydsrecordshop.com*) is well worth the drive.

EUNICE

20 mi southwest of Opelousas.

As home to some of Cajun music's most prominent proponents and establishments, tiny Eunice lays claim to some heft within the Cajun music world. Saturday is the best time to visit: spend the morning at a jam at the **Savoy Music Center;** at midday move on to see Tante Sue de Mamou at Fred's Lounge; end the day at the variety show *Rendez-Vous des Cajuns*, in Eunice's Liberty Theatre.

The area surrounding Eunice is the major stomping ground for an annual event, **Courir de Mardi Gras,** which takes place on Mardi Gras Day. Costumed horseback riders dash through the countryside, stopping at farmhouses along the way to shout, "*Voulez-vous recevoir cette bande de Mardi Gras* (Do you wish to receive the Mardi Gras krewe)?" The answer is always Yes, and the group enlarges and continues, gathering food for the street festivals that wind things up.

The **Eunice Depot Museum** is in a former railroad depot and contains modest displays on Cajun culture, including Cajun music and Cajun Mardi Gras. ⊠*220 S. C. C. Duson Dr.* ☎*337/457–6540 or 337/457–2565* ⊡*Free* ⊗*Tues.–Sat. 8:30–4:30.*

The impressive **Prairie Acadian Cultural Center,** part of the Jean Lafitte National Historical Park, has well-executed exhibits tracing the history and culture of the Prairie Acadians, whose lore and customs differ from those of the Bayou Acadians south of Lafayette. Food, crafts, and music demonstrations are held on Saturday. ⊠*250 W. Park Ave.* ☎*337/457–8490* ⊡*Free* ⊗*Tues.–Fri. 8–5, Sat. 8–6.*

Fodor'sChoice
★ **Savoy Music Center and Accordion Factory** includes a music store and, in back, a Cajun accordion workshop. Proprietor Marc Savoy's factory turns out about five specialty accordions a month for people around the world. On Saturday morning, accordion players and other instrumentalists tune up during jam sessions in the shop. Musicians from all over the area drop in. ⊠*U.S. 190, 3 mi east of town* ☎*337/457–9563* ⊡*Free* ⊗*Tues.–Fri. 9–noon and 1:30–5, Sat. 9–noon.*

Cajun and Zydeco Music

It's 9 am on a typical Saturday morning in the Cajun prairie town of Mamou, and Fred's Lounge (⇨ Nightlife & the Arts in Eunice) is already so full that people are spilling out the door. Inside, Cajun singer Donald Thibodeaux gets a nod from the radio announcer, squeezes his accordion, and launches into a bluesy rendition of "Pine Grove Blues." Oblivious to the posted warning, THIS IS NOT A DANCEHALL, the packed bar begins to roll. Fred's Lounge may not be a "formal" dance hall, but plenty of dancing is done here; it gets especially lively during Mamou's Mardi Gras and Fourth of July celebrations. And every Saturday morning for more than 40 years, live Cajun radio shows have been broadcast from the late Fred Tate's lounge. Things get revved up at 8 AM and keep going till 1 PM, and the show is aired on Ville Platte's KVPI radio (1050AM).

Music has been an integral expression of Cajun culture since early Acadian immigrants unpacked stringed instruments and gathered in homes for singing and socializing. With the growth of towns, these house parties—called fais-do-dos (pronounced fay-doh-doh, from "go to sleep" in French. The term fais-do-do comes from words mothers murmured to put their babies to sleep while the fiddlers tuned up before a dance.)—were supplanted by dance halls. Accordions, steel guitars, and drums were added and amplified to be heard over the noise of crowded barrooms.

Cajun music went through some lean years in the 1940s and '50s when the state attempted to eradicate the use of the Cajun-French language, but today Cajun music is enjoyed at street festivals and restaurants such as Randol's, Prejean's, and Mulate's, which serve equal portions of seafood and song. These places not only keep the music and dance tradition alive but also serve as magnets for Cajun dance enthusiasts from around the world.

Zydeco, the dance music of rural African-Americans of south Louisiana, is closely related to Cajun music, but with a slightly harder, rock-influenced edge. The best place to find the music is in one of the roadside dance halls on weekends. Modern zydeco and Cajun music are both accordion-based, but zydeco tends to be faster and uses heavy percussion and electric instruments; electric guitars and washboards (called a frottoir), largely absent from Cajun music, are staples of zydeco. Zydeco bands often play soul- and rhythm and blues–inflected tunes sung in Creole French.

Dance is the universal language of Cajun Country, but don't worry if you're not fluent—there's always someone happy to lead you around the floor and leave you feeling like a local.

8

NIGHTLIFE & THE ARTS

★ **Fred's Lounge** (✉420 6th St., Mamou ☎337/468–5411 ✉Free) hops on Saturday from about 8 AM until about 2 PM, or for as long as the Cajun band jams and dancers crowd the tiny dance floor. A regular radio broadcast (on KVPI 1050AM) captures the event. Drive north from Eunice on Route 13 to Mamou, a town so small you can drive around it in five minutes.

In addition to showcasing the best Cajun and zydeco bands, **Rendez-Vous des Cajuns** (⊠ *Liberty Center for the Performing Arts, 200 Park Ave., at 2nd St.* ☎ *337/457–7389* ✑ *$5*), a two-hour variety program, presents local comedians and storytellers and even a "Living Recipe Corner." The show, mostly in French, has been dubbed the Cajun Grand Ole Opry; it's held every Saturday at 6 PM in a 1924 movie house and is broadcast on local radio and TV.

BREAUX BRIDGE

★ *10 mi northeast of Lafayette, 20 mi southeast of Grand Coteau.*

A dyed-in-the-wool Cajun town, Breaux Bridge is known as the Crawfish Capital of the World. During the first full weekend in May, the Crawfish Festival draws more than 100,000 visitors to this little village on Bayou Teche. Once a wild place, old Breaux Bridge has attracted a small arts community that includes renowned Louisiana photographer Debbie Fleming Caffery and has traded its honky-tonks for B&Bs, antiques shops, and restaurants.

This town of 8,000 has a Main Street (Route 31) occupied largely by antiques shops.

You can pick up a city map and information at the **Chamber of Commerce** (⊠ *314 E. Bridge St.* ☎ *337/332–5406* ⊕ *www.breauxbridgelive.com*), at the foot of the bridge that gives Breaux Bridge its name, about 0.5 mi south of Interstate 10.

WHERE TO STAY & EAT

★ $$–$$$$ ✕ **Café des Amis.** The culinary heart and soul of downtown Breaux Bridge rests in this large, renovated storefront just a block from Bayou Teche where locals and visitors gather to enjoy hospitality that is second only to the food. Sample the ambience over cocktails or coffee at the bar, or take a table and try the extraordinary turtle soup or the crawfish corn bread. Breakfast here should be savored, from the fresh-squeezed orange juice to the *oreille de cochon* (pastry-wrapped boudin), *couche-couche* (corn-bread-based cereal), and black java. Saturday mornings bring the popular Zydeco Breakfast, featuring a band and dancing. ⊠ *140 E. Bridge St.* ☎ *337/332–5273* ⊕ *www.cafedesamis.com* ⊟ *AE, D, MC, V* ⊗ *Closed Mon. and Tues. No dinner Sun.*

$–$$$ ✕ **Mulate's.** A roadhouse with flashing yellow lights outside and red-and-white-check plastic tablecloths inside, Mulate's is a tourist favorite. With a Cajun eatery and a dance hall (live Cajun music every night), it is a family gathering place that has been featured on many national TV programs. A dressed-down crowd digs into stuffed crabs and the Super Seafood Platter. ⊠ *325 Mills Ave. (Rte. 94)* ☎ *337/332–4648 or 800/422–2586* ⊟ *AE, MC, V.*

¢–$ ✕ **Poche's.** At this no-frills operation, order your authentic Cajun cooking at the counter, then eat in or take away. Daily specials are stick-to-your ribs Cajun food. Boudin, sausage, cracklings, and stuffed chicken are just a few of the items to take out. ⊠ *33015-A Main Hwy., 2 mi from center of Breaux Bridge* ☎ *337/332–2108.*

CLOSE UP

Alligators Up Close: Swamp Tours

The bayous, swamps, and rivers of south Louisiana's wetlands present a tantalizingly unfamiliar landscape to many visitors, and the best way to get better acquainted is by boat. Tour operators offer convenient departure times and hotel pickups in New Orleans. Most tour operators use pontoon boats, but—depending on the size of the group—a bass boat might be used. Anticipate from one to two hours on the water and 45 minutes to two hours' commute time to and from New Orleans. Prices generally range from $10 to $20 per person. Expect to see nutria, a member of the rodent family that resembles a beaver in appearance and size; egrets (a white, long-necked heron with flowing feathers); turtles; and the occasional snake. During the warmer months, alligator sightings are commonplace. Many of the guides use either chicken or marshmallows to attract them. Plant life includes Spanish moss, cypress, water oaks, and water hyacinths (a member of the lily family). In the summer months, be prepared for the heat and humidity—and don't forget the insect repellent.

Pontoon boats at **McGee's Landing** take passengers daily for 1½-hour tours of the Atchafalaya Basin. McGee's is a 25-minute drive east of Lafayette. Tour times are contingent upon the presence of at least four passengers. ⊠ *1337 Henderson Levee Rd., Henderson (from I–10, Exit*

115 at Henderson; 1 block south of the highway turn left on Rte. 352 and follow it more than 2 mi east over Bayou Amy; turn right atop the levee onto Levee Rd.), ☎ *337/228–2384* ⊕ *www.mcgeeslanding.com* 🍴 *Tour $18* ⊙ *Tours daily 10, 1, and 3. Additional tour at 5 during daylight saving time.*

Angelle's Whiskey River Landing (⊠ *1.75 mi south of Rte. 352, on the Levee Rd. on the left*) is the departure point for **Angelle's Swamp Tours** (☎ *337/228–8567* 🍴 *Tour $15* ⊙ *Tours daily 10, 1, and 3*).

Cajun Country Swamp Tours ⊠ *108 Mills Ave., Breaux Bridge* ☎ *337/319–0010* ⊕ *www.cajuncountryswamptours.com* ⊙ *Tours daily* uide Walter "Butch" Guchereau, who was born, raised, and still lives on the banks of Bayou Teche in Breaux Bridge. An experienced outdoorsman with a degree in zoology and biology, his ecotours use Cajun crawfish skiffs to be environmentally unobtrusive. **Doucet's Airboat Tours** ☎ 337/342–0382 or 337/342–2235)you'll see alligators, birds, and much more with guide Taco Doucet. Airboats can go through very shallow swamps where many motorboats cannot. Tours leave from Pat's Fishermans Wharf Restaurant in Henderson (⊠ *1008 Henderson Levee Rd.*). Six-passenger capacity per boat and reservations recommended. Call ahead for tour times and price.

8

$$–$$$$
Fodor's Choice
★

🍴 **Maison des Amis.** The owners of Café des Amis renovated this 19th-century house on the bank of Bayou Teche with comfort and relaxation in mind. Each room has a private entrance and a queen-size bed covered with luxurious linens and pillows. A pier and gazebo are perfect for watching moonlight over the bayou. The complimentary Cajun breakfast at Café des Amis is not to be missed. ⊠ *111 Washington*

St. ☎337/507–3399 ⊕*www.maisondesamis.com* ↩*3 rooms, 1 suite* ▭*AE, D, MC, V* ⫯*BP.*

NIGHTLIFE

La Poussière (✉*1215 Grand Point Rd.* ☎*337/332–1721*) is an ancient Cajun honky-tonk where local favorite Walter Mouton plays every Saturday. They also have live music on Sunday.

ATCHAFALAYA BASIN

5 mi northeast of Breaux Bridge, 12 mi east of Lafayette.

The Atchafalaya Basin is an eerily beautiful 800,000-plus-acre swamp wilderness, the storybook version of mystical south Louisiana wetlands. Boating enthusiasts, bird-watchers, photographers, and nature lovers are drawn by vast expanses of still water, cypresses standing knee-deep in marsh and dripping with Spanish moss, and blue herons taking flight. The basin is best viewed from one of the tour boats that ply its waters, but it is possible to explore around its edges on the 7 mi of Henderson's Levee Road (also known as Route 5; off Interstate 10, Exit 115), which provides several opportunities to cross the levee and access swamp tours, bars, and restaurants on the other side.

McGee's Cafe and Bar offers Cajun cuisine and is known for its boiled crawfish. For a rustic touch, rent one of the floating "Cajun Cabins" for a night on the swamp. ✉*1337 Henderson Levee Rd., Henderson (from I-10, Exit 115 at Henderson; 1 block south of the highway turn left on Rte. 352 and follow it just over 2 mi east over Bayou Amy; turn right atop the levee onto Levee Rd.),* ☎*337/228–2384* ⊕*www.mcgeeslanding.com.*

Angelle's Whiskey River Landing (✉*1.75 mi south of Rte. 352, on the Levee Rd. on the left*) is the site of the lively **Angelle's Atchafalaya Basin Bar** (☎*337/228–8567*). On Sunday afternoon, when the last tour boat comes in, Cajun bands play in a dance hall right over the water for the traditional Sunday fais-do-do. The music usually starts around 4 PM and attracts a crowd of fishermen, locals, and visitors. Beer and burgers are served. No credit cards are accepted.

WHERE TO EAT

$$ ✕**Pat's Fishermans Wharf Restaurant.** Adjacent to Bayou Amy, Pat's is
Fodor'sChoice the real deal, with platters heaping with seafood. On a cool night, get
★ a table on the porch overlooking the bayou. The Atchafalaya Club, which is the area hot spot for Cajun dancing on Saturday nights, is nearby. ✉*1008 Henderson Levee Rd.* ☎*337/228–7512.*

ST. MARTINVILLE

15 mi south of Breaux Bridge.

St. Martinville, along winding Bayou Teche, is the heart of Evangeline country. It was founded in 1761 and became a refuge for both Acadians kicked out of Nova Scotia and royalists who escaped the guillotine

Gone Fishin'

Legend has it that somewhere in the Atchafalaya swamp lives a catfish more than 6 feet long. Although that "whopper" may or may not be true, what can't be disputed is Louisiana's claim to be a sportsmen's paradise. Ever since chef Paul Prudhomme blackened his first redfish caught in local waters, the secret has been out—there are plenty of fish to be had almost everywhere in Louisiana.

The **Gulf of Mexico** and its brackish-water coastal marsh region have made Louisiana famous for shrimp, blue crab, oysters, and fish. And folks are looking for much more than just oil out at the rigs in the gulf. Whether you choose to troll around the rigs or to anchor for some casting, you'll find brag-size lemonfish, cobia, snapper, yellowfin tuna, speckled trout, Spanish and king mackerel, sailfish, wahoo, and even pompano. Many of the marinas in Grand Isle, Cocodrie, and Venice (due south of New Orleans) offer charter-fishing trips that include all fishing tackle, fuel, soft drinks, ice, and someone to bait your hook during the trip and clean your fish when it's

over. Prices range from $200 to $500 a day depending on where you fish, the length of the trip, and the number of passengers. Trips range from four to eight hours or overnight. If you're not inclined to pay for a charter, there are plenty of piers, wharves, bridges, and jetties like those at Grand Isle State Park to give you easy access to the open water.

If saltwater fishing isn't your thing, don't worry: there's plenty of fresh-water to go around. Top spots include the **Atchafalaya Basin,** Louisiana's magnificent 800,000-plus-acre natural swampland with facilities at Lake Fausse Point State Park; and **Toledo Bend Reservoir,** a 186,000-acre bass-fishing paradise lined with camp-grounds, marinas, and North Toledo Bend State Park. There are numerous oxbow lakes such as **False River,** north of Baton Rouge, and **Lake Bruin,** where you can find scads of bream, goggle-eye, and perch.

The New Orleans Convention and Visi-tors Bureau (⇨ *Visitor Information in New Orleans Essentials*) can provide a list of charter fishing companies.

8

during the French Revolution. Known as Petit Paris, this little town was once the scene of lavish balls and operas, and you can still roam through the original old opera house on the central square. St. Martin-ville is tucked away from the state's major highways and misses much of the tourist traffic. It is a tranquil and historically interesting stop, although neighboring towns are better for dining and nightlife. The St. Martinville Tourist Information Center is located across the street from the Acadian Memorial and African American Museum.

In all of Acadiana, St. Martinville is the spot where you can sense most vividly the tragic aspect of the Cajun story, whether in the tiny cemetery behind the main church, or at the bayou-side Evangeline Oak. Henry Wadsworth Longfellow's classic poem "Evangeline," about the star-crossed lovers Evangeline and Gabriel, is based on a true story. Accord-ing to the oft-told tale, the real-life lovers, Emmeline Labiche and Louis Arceneaux, met for the last time under the **Evangeline Oak.** Louis arrived in St. Martinville, a major debarkation port for the refugees, but it was

EVANGELINE

Henry Wadsworth Longfellow's epic poem "Evangeline" (1847) is based on historic documents that chronicle a couple's tragic separation, a result of the British expelling Acadians from Nova Scotia in 1755. Evangeline Bellefontaine and Gabriel Lajeneusse were taken from each other on their wedding day. Once Evangeline arrives in Louisiana, she finds out Gabriel has been there, but has left to live in the Ozarks. After years of searching for him, Evangeline finds Gabriel on his deathbed in Philadelphia. Many believe the two represent real-life counterparts Emmeline Labiche and Louis Arceneaux, though those names themselves are based on another fictional version of the legend. The story shows how the Cajuns faced oppression, separation, and adversity and made a new life for themselves in south Louisiana.

A video introduction, a wall of names of Acadian Louisiana refugees, and a huge mural relate the odyssey of the Acadians at the **Acadian Memorial.** Behind the small heritage center containing these memorials, an eternal flame and the coats of arms of Acadian families pay symbolic tribute to their cultural and physical stamina. ✉ *121 S. New Market St.* ☎ *337/394-2258* ⊕ *www.acadian-memorial.org* ⊑ *$2* ⊘ *Daily 10–4.*

The **African American Museum** traces the African and African-American experience in southern Louisiana in riveting detail. Videos, artifacts, and text panels combine to create a vivid, disturbing, and inspiring portrait of a people. It is an ambitious and refreshing balance to the often sidelined or romanticized references to slavery customary in this region. ✉ *121 New Market St.* ☎ *337/394–2250* ⊑ *$2* ⊘ *Daily 10–4.*

many years before Emmeline came. Legend has it that the two saw each other by chance just as she stepped ashore. He turned deathly pale with shock and told her that, having despaired of ever seeing her again, he was betrothed to another. *The Romance of Evangeline* was filmed in St. Martinville in 1929. The privately owned movie was never distributed, but clips from it are incorporated in the film presentation at the Jean Lafitte National Historical Park Acadian Cultural Center (⇨ *Acadian Cultural Center in Lafayette*). Its star, Dolores Del Rio, posed for the bronze statue of Evangeline that the cast and crew donated to St. Martinville; it is in the cemetery behind the church of St. Martin de Tours, near the final resting place of Emmeline Labiche. ✉ *Evangeline Blvd. at Bayou Teche.*

Shaded by giant live oaks draped with Spanish moss, the 157-acre **Longfellow-Evangeline State Historic Site** has picnic tables and pavilions and early Acadian structures. A small museum traces the history of the Acadians. The Evangeline legend claims that Louis Arceneaux, on whom Gabriel was based, lived in the **Maison Olivier,** a plantation house on the park's grounds, but there is no evidence that he did. The modest house was built in the early 18th century of handmade bricks, and it contains Louisiana antiques. A lively one-hour tour includes many interesting details about life on the indigo plantation. ✉ *1200 N. Main St. (Rte.*

31), 0.5 mi north of St. Martinville ☎*337/394–3754 or 888/677–2900*
⊕*www.crt.state.la.us/parks* ☜*$2* ⊘*Daily 9–5.*

The **Petit Paris Museum** on the church (St. Martin de Tours) square contains historical records, Carnival costumes, a video history of Mardi
Gras, and a chariot exhibit. The chariots are from an annual one-of-a-
kind event, the Chariot Parade—a colorful procession of wagons, made
by children, which depict anything from a streetcar to a castle. The
children and their fanciful chariots circle the church square beginning
at dusk on the third Sunday of August. ✉*103 S. Main St.* ☎*337/394–
7334* ☜*$1* ⊘*Call ahead for hrs.*

St. Martin de Tours is the mother church of the Acadians and one of the
country's oldest Catholic churches; the 1836 building was erected on
the site of an earlier church. Inside is a replica of the Lourdes grotto
and a baptismal font said to have been a gift from Louis XVI. Emmeline Labiche is buried in the small cemetery behind the church. ✉*123
S. Main St.* ☎*337/394–4203.*

WHERE TO STAY & EAT

¢–$ ✕**Le Petit Paris Café.** Creole and Cajun dishes are served at this charm-
ing café with high ceilings, a courtyard, and a mural. Open for breakfast and lunch, daily specials include red beans and rice and crawfish
étouffée, or try the house specialties of petit puffs, filled with crawfish
and seasonings; or Brandy's crawfish corn bread. ✉*116 S. Main St.*
☎*337/394–7159* ▭*AE, MC, V* ⊘*No dinner.*

$–$$$ ▦**Old Castillo Bed & Breakfast.** In the late 19th century the Castillo Hotel,
a two-story redbrick building next to the Evangeline Oak and Bayou
Teche, was an inn for steamboat passengers and a gathering place for
French royalists. Rooms are comfortable, with hardwood floors and the
odd early Louisiana antique. Some look over the bayou, and all have
access to a downstairs parlor and breakfast room. **Pros:** There's no better
place to stay in St. Martinville, as its right by a number of attractions;
friendly staff; delicious breakfast. **Cons:** If you have a downstairs room,
you hear everything that happens downstairs;decor is a little dated. ✉*220
Evangeline Blvd.* ☎*337/394–4010 or 800/621–3017* ▭*337/394–7983*
⊕*www.oldcastillo.com* ⇖*7 rooms* ▭*AE, MC, V* ⊙|*BP.*

8

NEW IBERIA

★ *14 mi south of St. Martinville.*

The town of New Iberia is the hub of lower Cajun Country, second
only to Lafayette as an arts-and-culture draw. The grand homes of
sugarcane planters dominate the residential section of Main Street, just
off Bayou Teche, pointing to a glorious past at the center of a booming
sugar industry and anchoring the current cultural revival taking place
here. Park downtown or stay in one of the numerous B&Bs here and
you can easily walk to the bayou, restaurants, art galleries, and shops
in the historic business district. Downtown stretches eight blocks east
and west on Main Street (Route 182) from the intersection of Center

Street (Route 14). The Shadows-on-the-Teche plantation home is at this intersection and is a good place to park.

Check with the **Acadiana Arts Council** (☎ *337/233–7060* ⊕ *www.acadiana artscouncil.org*) for the latest information on performances at the intimate **Sliman Theater for the Performing Arts** (☎ *337/369–2337*), on Main Street. It is the site for the "Louisiana Crossroads" concert series, which features mainly Louisiana musicians, but also showcases musicians from out of state who are influenced by the region.

The **Conrad Rice Mill** is the country's oldest rice mill still in operation, dating from 1912, and it produces a distinctive wild pecan rice. Tours are conducted on the hour between 10 AM and 3 PM. The adjacent **Konriko Company Store** sells Cajun crafts and foods. ⊠ *307–309 Ann St.* ☎ *337/364–7242 or 800/551–3245* ⊕ *www.conradricemill.com* ⊠ *Mill $4* ⊗ *Mon.–Sat. 9–5.*

★ **Shadows-on-the-Teche,** one of the South's best-known plantation homes, was built on the bank of the bayou for wealthy sugar planter David Weeks in 1834. In 1917 his descendant William Weeks Hall conducted one of the first history-conscious restorations of a plantation home. Truckloads of original documents were deliberately preserved. The result is one of the most fascinating tours in Louisiana. Weeks Hall willed the property to the National Trust for Historic Preservation in 1958, and each year the trust selects a different historical topic to emphasize. Surrounded by 2 acres of lush gardens and moss-draped oaks, the two-story rose-hue house has white columns, exterior staircases sheltered in cabinet-like enclosures, and a pitched roof pierced by dormer windows. The furnishings are 85% original to the house. ⊠ *317 E. Main St.* ☎ *337/369–6446* ⊕ *www.shadowsontheteche.org* ⊠ *$7* ⊗ *Mon.–Sat. 9–4:30, Sun. noon–4:30.*

WHERE TO STAY & EAT

$–$$$ ✕**Clementine.** Named for folk artist Clementine Hunter, with an insignia based on her signature, Clementine favors cuisine that might be called nouveau-Cajun: inspired by local ingredients and traditions, but subtly seasoned and artfully presented. Changing art exhibits by locals are introduced at bimonthly openings featuring wine and hors d'oeuvres. Clementine hosts live music on Friday and Saturday nights. ⊠ *113 E. Main St.* ☎ *337/560–1007* ⊕ *www.clementinedowntown.com* ☐ *AE, D, MC, V* ⊗ *Closed Sun. No lunch Sat. No dinner Mon.*

$$–$$$ 🏠**leRosier.** A gracious reception awaits at this 19th-century house across from Shadows-on-the-Teche plantation. Guest rooms, in the renovated service wing behind the main house, are small and simple, but the king-size beds are supremely comfortable. A delicious breakfast is served in the main house. ⊠ *314 E. Main St.* ☎ *337/367–5306 or 888/804–7673* ⊕ *www.lerosier.com* 🛏 *6 rooms* ☐ *AE, MC, V* �🍴*BP.*

$ 🏠**Bayou Teche Guest Cottage.** There could scarcely be a better way to appreciate the Queen City of the Teche than to spend a night in this simple, two-room 18th-century cottage on the bank of the bayou, down the road from downtown attractions. Guests are left on their own, with self-service breakfast items provided in the refrigerator. You can explore the 3 acres of quiet grounds or sit in the front-porch rocking chairs and watch towboats ply the waters. The house canoe is also at your disposal. **Pros:** Pretty views; good location to explore New Iberia; if you want to be alone, this is the place. **Con:** Depending on what you expect from a B&B, you'll either find it charming—or a bit worn around the edges. ⊠*100 Teche St.* ☎*337/364–1933* 🛏 *1 cottage* ▭*No credit cards.*

AVERY ISLAND

9 mi southwest of New Iberia.

The Louisiana coastline is dotted with "hills" or "domes" that sit atop salt mines, and Avery Island is one of these. They are covered with lush vegetation, and because they rise above the surface of the flatlands, they are referred to as islands.

Avery Island is the birthplace of Tabasco sauce, which pleases the Cajun palate and flavors many a Bloody Mary.

☾ The 250-acre **Jungle Gardens,** on Avery Island, have trails through stands of wisteria, palms, lilies, irises, and ferns and offer a lovely perspective on southern Louisiana wilderness. Birdlife includes ducks and geese, and there's also a 1,000-year-old statue of the Buddha. These gardens belonged to Edward Avery McIlhenny, who brought back flora from his travels: lotus and papyrus from Egypt, bamboo from China. **Bird City,** a bird sanctuary on the southeast edge of Jungle Gardens, is sometimes so thick with egrets that it appears to be blanketed with snow. The largest egret colony in the world (20,000) begins nesting here in February or March, and offspring remain until the following winter. Herons and other birds find refuge here as well. You can park your car at the beginning of the trails and strike out on foot, or drive through the gardens and stop at will. ⊠*Rte. 329* ☎*337/369–6243* ⊕*http://junglegardens.org* �*Jungle Gardens and Bird City $6.25, toll onto Avery Island $1* ☉*Daily 9–5.*

Tabasco was invented by Edmund McIlhenny in the mid-1800s, and the **Tabasco Factory** is presided over by the fourth generation of the McIlhenny family. Tabasco is sold all over the world, but it is produced and bottled only here, on Avery Island. You can take a factory tour, which lasts about 20 minutes and highlights the bottling process. The Jungle Gardens and Bird City are adjacent. ⊠*Rte. 329* ☎*337/365–8173* ⊕*www.tabasco. com* ▭*Tour is free; $1 toll to enter Avery Island* ☉*Daily 9–4.*

JEFFERSON ISLAND

4 mi from Avery Island, 9 mi from New Iberia.

Like Avery "Island," Jefferson Island is actually a salt dome. The highlight of a visit here is the magnificent 20-acre **Rip Van Winkle Gardens,** filled with semitropical vegetation and the sort of vistas that only a salt dome can offer in southern Louisiana. A café looks over Lake Peigneur and provides a restful and picturesque spot for refreshments following

PARLEZ-VOUS CAJUN FRANÇAIS?

It's not uncommon while traveling through Cajun country to still hear French—the Cajun version. Here's a few words that might help you enjoy and understand the lingo.

Allons: Let's go!

Bayou: A sluggish body of water, larger than a creek, but smaller than a river.

C'est la vie: Such is life.

Cher: Dear

Cochon de lait: A pig roast.

Étouffée: A stew mainly made with seafood, in which the "holy trinity" (celery, garlic, and bell pepper) is used.

Fais-do-do: A dance. French for "Go to sleep," which was what parents would whisper to their children so they could go dancing.

Lagniappe: A little something extra.

Laissez les bons temps rouler: Let the good times roll.

Roux: Flour browned in fat and used as a thickener in many Cajun dishes such as gumbo.

exploration of the gardens. Be on the lookout for the peacocks—if you're lucky, one of the males will open his feathers for you. Also on the grounds is the **Joseph Jefferson Home,** a highly personalized mansion that combines Steamboat Gothic, Moorish, and French-plantation styles. It was built as a country home for stage actor Joseph Jefferson in the mid-19th century and is open for 40-minute tours. There is also a bed-and-breakfast on the grounds should you like it so much you want to stay. ⊠ *5505 Rip Van Winkle Rd.* ☎ *337/359–8525* ⊕ *www. ripvanwinklegardens.com* 🖃 *Garden access and house tour $10, garden only $5* ☉ *Daily 9–5.*

ERATH

9 mi west of Jefferson Island.

The little town of Erath is a quintessential tiny Cajun village.

The several rooms of the **Acadian Museum** are filled to the rafters with memorabilia donated by local folks—everything from antique radios and butter churns to patchwork quilts and yellowed newspaper clippings. ⊠ *203 S. Broadway* ☎ *337/233–5832* ⊕ *www.acadianmuseum.com* 🖃 *Free; donations suggested* ☉ *Weekdays 1–4, weekends by appointment.*

WHERE TO EAT

$ ✕ **Big John's.** The menu in this barn-style eatery is a mere formality—nobody orders anything but boiled crawfish. In fact, Big John's is open only during crawfish season (roughly, November through May). Orders are placed by the pound (3, 5, or 10); prepare your sauces while you wait for your crustacean delights. ⊠ *3630 Broadview Dr., at Rte. 339* ☎ *337/937–8355* ☉ *Closed June–Oct. No lunch.*

★ $ ✕ **T-Bob's Seafood.** If you want a truly authentic Cajun experience, eat at T-Bob's. It's like dining in someone's home—one that's filled with Cajun memorabilia. Boiled seafood is served year-round. Crawfish is made per order, and homemade sauce is provided for dipping, if you wish. T-Bob's is open for lunch and dinner. ⊠*109 E. Lastie St.* ☎*337/937–4573* ⊟ *AE, MC, V.*

NIGHTLIFE

Wilbert "Smiley" Menard operates a popular 1950s-style dance hall—**Smiley's Bon Ami.** On a warm Saturday night, cars park on the moist meadow outside and an older crowd fills the dance floor, gliding in the way that only the elder generation of Cajun dancers seems to have mastered. There are jam sessions on Friday and an early show especially popular with senior citizens on Sunday after mass. ⊠*2206 Rte. 14, between Erath and Delcambre* ☎*337/937–4591.*

ABBEVILLE

5 mi west of Erath, 15 mi south of Lafayette.

Abbeville has a number of historic buildings and two pretty village squares anchoring the center of downtown. It is a good stop for pleasant town walks and for oysters on the half shell, a local fetish. The town sponsors the annual Giant Omelet Festival each November, when some 5,000 eggs go into the concoction. At other times, oysters are the culinary draw. It is also the base for Steen's Cane Syrup.

You can pick up a self-guided walking-tour brochure at the **Abbeville Tourist Office** (⊠*1905 Veterans Memorial Hwy.* ☎*337/898–4264*). Many buildings in the 20-block Main Street district are on the National Register of Historic Places.

St. Mary Magdalen Catholic Church (⊠*N. Main and Père Megret Sts.* ☎*337/893–0244* ⊙*Mon.–Sat. 8–5; Sun. mass 6:30* AM) is a fine Romanesque Revival building with stunning stained-glass windows.

WHERE TO EAT

$$$ ✕**Black's Seafood Restaurant.** In 2007 Black's returned after being closed for over a year—but the look, feel, and great food are the same. Boiled, fried, and steamed seafood are the specialties, and you'll find oysters, crab, shrimp, and crawfish prepared in a number of ways. ⊠*319 S. Main St.* ☎*337/740–4266.*

$–$$ ✕**Dupuy's Oyster Shop.** This small restaurant has been serving family-harvested oysters in the same location since 1869. Seafood platters feature seasonal specials. ⊠*108 S. Main St.* ☎*337/893–2336* ⊟*MC, V* ⊙*Closed Sun. and Mon.*

MAURICE

10 mi north of Abbeville, almost 11 mi south of Lafayette.

Maurice is considered the gateway to Vermilion Parish, and lies between Lafayette and Abbeville. Many overlook this small town but it's well worth the stop for Hebert's Specialty Meats' world-famous "turducken" and the Maurice Flea Market.

8

WHERE TO EAT

$-$$ ✕**Hebert's Specialty Meats.** A visit to Cajun country is not complete without stopping at Hebert's, rumored to be the spot where "turducken" was invented. A "turducken" is a turkey stuffed with a duck, stuffed with a chicken. Other to-go specialties include boudin, deboned chicken, and other regional delicacies. ⊠*8212 Maurice Ave. (Rte. 167)* ☎*337/893–5062*

SHOPPING

ANTIQUES   From fine antiques to slightly rusted kitchen utensils, the **Maurice Flea Market** (⊠*8701 Maurice Ave. (Rte. 167)* ☎*337/898–2282* ☉*Thurs.–Sat. 10–5*) is a treasure hunter's paradise.

CAJUN COUNTRY ESSENTIALS

To research prices, get advice from other travelers, and book travel arrangements, visit ⊕*www.fodors.com.*

BUS TRAVEL

Greyhound has numerous daily departures from New Orleans to Lafayette. The trip takes 3–3½ hours because of frequent stops along the way.

BUS   Greyhound ☎*800/231–2222* ⊕*www.greyhound.com.*
INFORMATION

CAR TRAVEL

Interstate 10 runs east–west across the state and through New Orleans. Take Interstate 10 west to the Lafayette exit, 128 mi from New Orleans. The interstate route takes about two hours. If you wish, return to New Orleans via U.S. 90, down through Houma, to take advantage of many scenic stopovers. This route takes around two hours.

EMERGENCIES

Dial **911** for assistance. The Medical Center of Southwest Louisiana has an emergency room.

HOSPITAL   Medical Center of Southwest Louisiana ⊠*2810 Ambassador Caffery Pkwy., Lafayette* ☎*337/981–2949.*

24-HOUR   CVS ⊠*1920 Kaliste Saloom Rd., Lafayette* ☎*337/984–1092.*
PHARMACY

TRAIN TRAVEL

Amtrak connects New Orleans and Lafayette via the *Sunset Limited.* Trains make the three- to four-hour scenic trip each way three times a week.

TRAIN   Amtrak ☎*800/872–7245* ⊕*www.amtrak.com.*

VISITOR INFORMATION

CONTACTS   Lafayette Convention and Visitors Commission ⊠*1400 N. W. Evangeline Thruway (Box 52066), Lafayette* ☎*337/232–3737 or 800/346–1958* ⊕*www.lafayettetravel. com.* La Remise ⊠*215 Evangeline Blvd., St. Martinville* ☎*337/394–2233.*

New Orleans Essentials

PLANNING TOOLS, EXPERT INSIGHT,
GREAT CONTACTS

There are planners and there are those who, excuse the pun, fly by the seat of their pants. We happily place ourselves among the planners. Our writers and editors try to anticipate all the issues you may face before and during any journey, and then they do their research. This section is the product of their efforts. Use it to get excited about your trip to New Orleans, to inform your travel planning, or to guide you on the road should the seat of your pants start to feel threadbare.

GETTING STARTED

We're really proud of our Web site: Fodors.com is a great place to begin any journey. Scan Travel Wire for suggested itineraries, travel deals, restaurant and hotel openings, and other up-to-the-minute info. Check out Booking to research prices and book plane tickets, hotel rooms, rental cars, and vacation packages. Head to Talk for on-the-ground pointers from travelers who frequent our message boards. You can also link to loads of other travel-related resources.

▌ RESOURCES

ONLINE TRAVEL TOOLS

All About New Orleans ⊕ www.neworleanscvb.com: locals' most recommended site for restaurants, accommodations, events, and activities; includes maps, information on music, nightlife, tours, weather, New Orleans history, and more. ⊕ www.crt.state.la.us: general overview of tourism in Louisiana, especially recovery efforts after Hurricanes Katrina and Rita. ⊕ www.neworleansonline.com: basic trip planning and travel tools. ⊕ www.cityofno.com: the city's official site; has updates on local issues and government affairs. ⊕ www.nojazzfest.com: the official site of the New Orleans Jazz & Heritage Festival. ⊕ www.nola.com: everything New Orleans; includes links to the Times-Picayune, New Orleans's daily newspaper, with news stories, nightlife, and more. ⊕ www.offbeat.com: site of OffBeat magazine, with Louisiana music coverage. ⊕ www.neworleans.com: general information about events, hotels, and restaurants. ⊕ www.experienceneworleans.com: links to a blog, podcast, and a fun video, in addition to the standard tourist sites. ⊕ www.mardigrasneworleans.com: devoted entirely to Mardi Gras and includes histories, parade schedules, and other specific Mardi Gras information. ⊕ www.frenchquarter.com: great links to event, accommodation, and parking information, as well as an interactive French Quarter map. ⊕ www.bestofneworleans.com: site of Gambit Weekly magazine with varying perspectives on life in New Orleans.

Safety Transportation Security Administration (TSA) ⊕ www.tsa.gov.

Time Zones Timeanddate.com ⊕ www.timeanddate.com/worldclock can help you figure out the correct time anywhere.

Weather Accuweather.com ⊕ www.accuweather.com is an independent weather-forecasting service with good coverage of hurricanes. **Weather.com** ⊕ www.weather.com is the Web site for the Weather Channel.

Other Resources CIA World Factbook ⊕ www.odci.gov/cia/publications/factbook/index.html has profiles of every country in the world. It's a good source if you need some quick facts and figures. To prepare for your trip to New Orleans, rent A Streetcar Named Desire, starring Marlon Brando and Vivien Leigh. Seedy, steamy, and emotionally charged, this is the quintessential New Orleans film. In Abbott and Costello Go To Mars, the two comedians think they're in a rocket ship to outer space. They end up in New Orleans during Mardi Gras, but don't realize the mix-up (an honest mistake). Also check out Elvis in King Creole, a music-filled noir tale set in the French Quarter. More-contemporary New Orleans films include Double Jeopardy, with Ashley Judd, and Déjà Vu, with Denzel Washington. For more films set in New Orleans, go to ⊕ www.classicmovies.org/articles/neworleans1.htm. A necessary read for any New Orleans visitor is John Kennedy Toole's A Confederacy of Dunces. Ingatius J. Reilly, the book's bumbling protagonist, is as quirky as the city itself. Andrei Codrescu's New Orleans, Mon Amour, a collection of memoirs written over the last 20 years, is a humorous and touching read. For a look into life in old New

Orleans, pick up anything by George Washington Cable or Barbara Hambly.

VISITOR INFORMATION

For general information and brochures, contact the city and state tourism bureaus below. The New Orleans Multicultural Tourism Network produces a variety of multicultural heritage directories. The New Orleans Convention & Visitors Bureau's Web site is a comprehensive source for trip planning, hotel and tour booking, and shopping; you can also download brochures, coupons, walking tours, and event schedules, as well as find links to other helpful Web sites.

Contacts Louisiana Office of Tourism Box 94291, Baton Rouge, LA 70804-9291 800/633–6970 www.louisianatravel.com. **New Orleans Convention & Visitors Bureau** 2020 St. Charles Ave., 70130 800/672–6124 or 504/566–5011 www.neworleanscvb.com. **New Orleans Multicultural Tourism Network** 1520 Sugar Bowl Dr., 70112 800/725–5652 or 504/523–5652 www.soulofneworleans.com.

▌THINGS TO CONSIDER

GEAR

New Orleans is casual during the day and casual to slightly dressy at night. A few restaurants in the French Quarter require men to wear a jacket and tie. For sightseeing, pack walking shorts, sundresses, cotton slacks or jeans, T-shirts, and a light sweater. In winter you'll want a coat or warm jacket, especially for evenings, which can be downright cold. In summer pack for hot, sticky weather, but be prepared for air-conditioning bordering on glacial, and bring an umbrella in case of sudden thunderstorms. Leave the plastic raincoats behind (they're extremely uncomfortable in the high humidity). In addition, pack a sun hat and sunscreen lotion, even for strolls in the city, because the sun can be fierce. Insect repellent will also come in handy if you plan to be outdoors on a swamp cruise or in the city dining alfresco, because mosquitoes come out in full force after sunset in warm weather.

TRIP INSURANCE

What kind of coverage do you honestly need? Do you even need trip insurance at all? Take a deep breath and read on.

We believe that comprehensive trip insurance is especially valuable if you're booking a very expensive or complicated trip (particularly to an isolated region) or if you're booking far in advance. Who knows what could happen six months down the road? But whether or not you get insurance has more to do with how comfortable you are assuming all that risk yourself.

Comprehensive travel policies typically cover trip-cancellation and interruption, letting you cancel or cut your trip short because of a personal emergency, illness, or, in some cases, acts of terrorism in your destination. Such policies also cover evacuation and medical care. Some also cover you for trip delays because of bad weather or mechanical problems as well as for lost or delayed baggage. Another type of coverage to look for is financial default—that is, when your trip is disrupted because a tour operator, airline, or cruise line goes out of business. Generally you must buy this when you book your trip or shortly thereafter, and it's only available to you if your operator isn't on a list of excluded companies.

If you're going abroad, consider buying medical-only coverage at the very least. Neither Medicare nor some private insurers cover medical expenses anywhere outside the United States (including time aboard a cruise ship, even if it leaves from a U.S. port). Medical-only policies typically reimburse you for medical care (excluding that related to preexisting conditions) and hospitalization abroad, and provide for evacuation. You still have to pay the bills and await reimbursement from the insurer, though.

Expect comprehensive travel insurance policies to cost about 4% to 7% or 8% of the total price of your trip (it's more like 8%–12% if you're over age 70). A medical-only policy may or may not be cheaper than a comprehensive policy. Always read the fine print of your policy to make sure that you are covered for the risks that are of most concern to you. Compare several policies to make sure you're getting the best price and range of coverage available.

Insurance Comparison Sites **Insure My Trip. com** (☎800/487–4722 ⊕www.insuremytrip. com). **Square Mouth.com** (☎800/240–0369 or 727/490–5803 ⊕www.squaremouth.com).

Medical Assistance Companies **AirMed International Medical Group** (⊕www. airmed.com). **International SOS** (⊕www. internationalsos.com). **MedjetAssist** (⊕www. medjetassist.com).

Medical-Only Insurers **International Medical Group** (☎800/628–4664 ⊕www.

imglobal.com). **Wallach & Company** (☎800/237–6615 or 540/687–3166 ⊕www. wallach.com).

Comprehensive Travel Insurers **Access America** (☎866/729–6021 ⊕www. accessamerica.com). **AIG Travel Guard** (☎800/826–4919 ⊕www.travelguard.com). **CSA Travel Protection** (☎800/873–9855 ⊕www.csatravelprotection.com). **HTH Worldwide** (☎610/254–8700 ⊕www.hthworldwide. com). **Travelex Insurance** (☎888/228–9792 ⊕www.travelex-insurance.com). **Travel Insured International** (☎800/243–3174 ⊕www.travelinsured.com).

■TIP→OK. You know you can save a bundle on trips to warm-weather destinations by traveling in the rainy season, but there's also a chance that a severe storm will disrupt your plans. The solution? Look for hotels and resorts that offer storm/hurricane guarantees. Although they rarely allow refunds, most guarantees do let you rebook later if a storm strikes.

BOOKING YOUR TRIP

WITH A TRAVEL AGENT

If you use an agent—brick-and-mortar or virtual—you'll pay a fee for the service. Know that the service you get from some online agents isn't comprehensive. For example Expedia and Travelocity don't search for prices on budget airlines like jetBlue, Southwest, or small foreign carriers. That said, some agents (online or not) *do* have access to fares that are difficult to find otherwise, and the savings can more than make up for any surcharge.

A knowledgeable brick-and-mortar travel agent can be a godsend if you're booking a cruise, a package trip that's not available to you directly, an air pass, or a complicated itinerary including several overseas flights. What's more, travel agents who specialize in a destination may have exclusive access to certain deals and insider information on things such as charter flights. Agents who specialize in types of travelers (senior citizens, gays and lesbians, naturists) or types of trips (cruises, luxury travel, safaris) can also be invaluable.

Agent Resources American Society of Travel Agents ☎703/739–2782 ⊕www.travelsense.org.

▌RENTAL CARS

When you reserve a car, ask about cancellation penalties, taxes, drop-off charges (if you're planning to pick up the car in one city and leave it in another), and surcharges (for being under or over a certain age, for additional drivers, or for driving across state or country borders or beyond a specific distance from your point of rental). All these things can add substantially to your costs. Request car seats and extras such as a GPS when you book.

Rates are sometimes—but not always—better if you book in advance or reserve through a rental agency's Web site. There are other reasons to book ahead, though: for popular destinations, during busy times of the year, or to ensure that you get certain types of cars (vans, SUVs, exotic sports cars).

Automobile Associations American Automobile Association (AAA) ☎315/797–5000 ⊕www.aaa.com; most contact with the organization is through state and regional members. **National Automobile Club** ☎650/294–7000 ⊕www.thenac.com; membership is open to California residents only.

Major Agencies Alamo ☎800/462–5266 ⊕www.alamo.com. **Avis** ☎800/331–1212 ⊕www.avis.com. **Budget** ☎800/527–0700 ⊕www.budget.com. **Hertz** ☎800/654–3131 ⊕www.hertz.com. **National Car Rental** ☎800/227–7368 ⊕www.nationalcar.com.

CAR-RENTAL INSURANCE

Everyone who rents a car wonders whether the insurance that the rental companies offer is worth the expense. No one—including us—has a simple answer. It all depends on how much regular insurance you have, how comfortable you are with risk, and whether or not money is an issue.

If you own a car and carry comprehensive car insurance for both collision and liability, your personal auto insurance will probably cover a rental, but read your policy's fine print to be sure. If you don't have auto insurance, then you should probably buy the collision- or loss-damage waiver (CDW or LDW) from the rental company. This eliminates your liability for damage to the car. Some credit cards offer CDW coverage, but it's usually supplemental to your own insurance and rarely covers SUVs, minivans, luxury models, and the like. If your coverage is secondary, you may still be liable for loss-of-use costs from the car-rental company (again, read the fine print). But no credit-card insurance is valid unless you use that card for *all* transactions, from reserving to paying the final bill.

■TIP➔Diners Club offers primary CDW coverage on all rentals reserved and paid for with the card. This means that Diners Club's company—not your own car insurance—pays in case of an accident. It *doesn't* mean that your car-insurance company won't raise your rates once it discovers you had an accident.

You may also be offered supplemental liability coverage; the car-rental company is required to carry a minimal level of liability coverage insuring all renters, but it's rarely enough to cover claims in a really serious accident if you're at fault. Your own auto-insurance policy will protect you if you own a car; if you don't, you have to decide whether you are willing to take the risk.

U.S. rental companies sell CDWs and LDWs for about $15 to $25 a day; supplemental liability is usually more than $10 a day. The car-rental company may offer you all sorts of other policies, but they're rarely worth the cost. Personal accident insurance, which is basic hospitalization coverage, is an especially egregious rip-off if you already have health insurance.

■TIP➔You can decline the insurance from the rental company and purchase it through a third-party provider such as Travel Guard (www.travelguard.com)—$9 per day for $35,000 of coverage. That's sometimes just under half the price of the CDW offered by some car-rental companies.

▌CRUISES

The *Delta Queen* Steamboat Company offers 3- to 11-night excursions up the Big Muddy and environs aboard the *Delta Queen,* a National Historic Landmark built in the 1920s, the *Mississippi Queen,* built in 1976; or the *American Queen,* the largest paddle wheeler ever built. Cruises up the Mississippi focus on the river's effect on history and historic onshore sites such as antebellum plantation houses, Vicksburg, and Natchez. Founded in 1890, the company operates out of an enormous and efficient waterfront terminal complex adjacent to the Ernest N. Morial Convention Center. Carnival Cruise Line, Norwegian Cruise Line, and Royal Caribbean International also depart from New Orleans.

For more information, visit the Port of New Orleans Web site at ⊕*www.portno. com.*

Cruise Lines **Carnival Cruise Line** ☎800/227–6482 or 305/599–2600 ⊕www. carnival.com. Delta Queen **Steamboat Company** ⊠Robin St. Wharf, 1380 Port of New Orleans Pl. ☎800/768–8946 or 504/586–0631 ⊕www.deltaqueen.com. **Norwegian Cruise Line** ☎800/327–7030 or 305/436–4000 ⊕www.ncl.com. **Royal Caribbean International** ☎800/327–6700 or 305/539–6000 ⊕www.royalcaribbean.com.

TRANSPORTATION

▮ BY AIR

Flying time is 2½ hours from New York, 2¼ hours from Chicago, 1¼ hours from Dallas, 4½ hours from Los Angeles, 4¼ hours from San Francisco, and 9¼ hours from London. Flights to the city have not reached pre-Katrina levels, so book early to ensure that you have as many options as possible. (Nonstop flights book early.)

Airlines & Airports **Airline and Airport Links. com** ⊕www.airlineandairportlinks.com has links to many of the world's airlines and airports.

Airline Security Issues **Transportation Security Administration** ⊕www.tsa.gov has answers for almost every question that might come up.

Air Travel Resources in New Orleans **Louis Armstrong New Orleans International Airport** ☎504/464–0831 ⊕www.flymsy.com.

AIRPORTS

The major gateway to New Orleans is Louis Armstrong New Orleans International Airport (MSY), 15 mi west of the city in Kenner. There's an Airport exit off I-10. Again, plan for about 45 minutes of travel time from downtown New Orleans to the airport (more at rush hour). An alternative route is Airline Drive, which will take you directly to the airport from Tulane Avenue or the Earhart Expressway. Be prepared for many stoplights, and possibly congestion (you'll have a lot of company if you take this route).

Airport Information **Louis Armstrong New Orleans International Airport** ✉900 Airline Dr., Kenner ☎504/464–0831 ⊕www.flymsy.com.

FLIGHTS

Airline Contacts **AirTran** ☎800/247–8726 or 678/254–7999 ⊕www.airtran.com. **Alaska Airlines** ☎800/252–7522 or 206/433–3100 ⊕www.alaskaair.com. **American Airlines** ☎800/433–7300 ⊕www.aa.com. **ATA** ☎800/435–9282 or 317/282–8308 ⊕www. ata.com. **Continental Airlines** ☎800/523–

3273 for U.S. and Mexico reservations, 800/231–0856 for international reservations ⊕www.continental.com. **Delta Airlines** ☎800/221–1212 for U.S. reservations, 800/241–4141 for international reservations ⊕www.delta.com. **jetBlue** ☎800/538–2583 ⊕www.jetblue.com. **Northwest Airlines** ☎800/225–2525 ⊕www.nwa.com. **Southwest Airlines** ☎800/435–9792 ⊕www.southwest.com. **United Airlines** ☎800/864–8331 for U.S. reservations, 800/538–2929 for international reservations ⊕www.united.com. **USAirways** ☎800/428–4322 for U.S. and Canada reservations, 800/622–1015 for international reservations ⊕www.usairways.com.

GROUND TRANSPORTATION

Shuttle-bus service to and from the airport and downtown hotels, as well as local hospitals and the uptown college campuses, is available through New Orleans Tours Airport Shuttle. Buses leave regularly from the ground-floor level near the baggage claim. To return to the airport, call 24 hours in advance of flight time. The cost one-way is $13 per person, and the trip takes about 40 minutes.

Louisiana Transit also runs a bus between the airport, the CBD, and Mid-City. The trip costs $1.60 in exact change ($1.10 from Carrollton and Tulane avenues) and takes about 45 minutes. Departures for the airport are every 10 to 20 minutes from Elks Place and Tulane Avenue across from the main branch of the New Orleans Public Library, and from the corner of Tulane and Carrollton avenues. The last bus leaves at 7:40 PM from Tulane and Elks Place, 11:45 PM from Tulane and Carrollton.

A cab ride to or from the airport from uptown or downtown New Orleans costs $28 for the first two passengers, then $12 for each additional passenger. Pickup is on the lower level, outside the baggage-claim area. There may be an additional charge for extra baggage.

NAVIGATING NEW ORLEANS

Getting around New Orleans requires a little bit of patience, but once you get your bearings and become familiar with a few major roads, getting around here isn't too difficult. It's best to know your location relative to the following thoroughfares: Canal Street (runs from the river to the lake), St. Charles Avenue (runs uptown/upriver/northwest from Canal), Interstate 10 (runs west to the airport, east to Slidell), and Interstate 90 (takes you across the river to the West Bank).

■ Knowing where you are in relation to the river and to the lake will also help you with your bearings, but keeping a visual on the Superdome is the surest way to know where the Central Business District is. The French Quarter lies just to the east of it over Canal Street.

■ Getting on and off the interstate can prove challenging for some. Coming from I-10 into the French Quarter takes specific attention to exits and off-ramps. Your hotel concierge can generally provide good inside tips to navigating the path to and from your accommodations, but if you go exploring, be sure to ask for explicit details if the interstate is involved.

■ Streets that start in the French Quarter and cross over Canal Street change names as they go upriver. For example, Decatur Street becomes Magazine Street and Royal Street becomes St. Charles Avenue. Also, making a U-turn on Canal Street can prove difficult. Not all crossovers allow left turns. Be patient, though, there are opportunities.

■ There is generally more than one way to get everywhere in New Orleans. Don't be afraid to take the long way up Canal Street or St. Charles Avenue if you feel more comfortable doing so. Be careful, however, that your wanderings are not too creative and keep to the main streets.

By car, take I-10 (from the CBD, go west to the Airport exit). Allow an hour for the drive during afternoon rush hour; without traffic, the drive takes a half hour.

Contacts Louisiana Transit ☎504/818–1077. **New Orleans Tours Airport Shuttle** ☎504/522–3500.

▌ BY BOAT

The ferry ride across the river to a part of New Orleans called Algiers is an experience in itself, offering great views of the river and the New Orleans skyline as well as the heady feeling of being on one of the largest and most powerful rivers in the world. Pedestrians climb the stairs (there is a ramp for wheelchair access) near the Spanish Plaza and the Riverwalk shopping area and board the Canal Street Ferry from above, whereas bicycles and cars board from below on the left of the terminal. The trip takes about 10 minutes; ferries leave on the hour and half hour from the east bank and on the :15 and :45 of every hour from the west bank—they run from 6 AM to midnight. Hours at night may vary, so be sure to check with the attendants if you are crossing in the evening—it is no fun to be stranded on the other side. There are wheelchair-accessible restrooms on the ferry.

Information Canal Street Ferry ⊠Foot of Canal ☎504/376–8100, $1 cash round-trip per car, free for pedestrians.

▌ BY BUS

Greyhound has one terminal in the city, in the Union Passenger Terminal in the CBD. Ask about special travel passes. Check with your local Greyhound ticket office for prices and schedules.

Within New Orleans, the Regional Transit Authority (RTA) operates a public bus and streetcar transportation system with interconnecting lines throughout the city. The buses are generally clean and on time. Bus and streetcar service runs 24 hours a day, though wait times can be as long as an hour or more in the morning's earliest hours. Smoking, eating, and drinking are not permitted on RTA vehicles. Those who violate this rule can find themselves paying a hefty fine in Municipal Court or, worse, pulled off the bus and arrested. Buses are wheelchair accessible; streetcars are not.

Bus and streetcar fare is $1.25 exact change plus 25¢ for transfers. Visiting senior citizens 65 or over who have a valid Medicare ID card may ride public transit for only 40¢. Unlimited passes cost $5 for one day, $12 for three days of unlimited rides, and $55 for a month. The daily passes are available from streetcar and bus operators; three-day passes are available at many hotels; monthly passes must be purchased from official vendors, including all local Whitney Banks.

Bus & Streetcar Information Greyhound Union Passenger Terminal ✉1001 Loyola Ave. ☎800/231–2222 or 504/525–6075 ⊕www.greyhound.com. **RTA** ☎504/248–3900, 504/242–2600 automated information ⊕www.norta.com.

▌ BY CAR

 Having a car in New Orleans is no problem—except at Mardi Gras and during other special events, including the Sugar Bowl (around New Year's) and the Bayou Classic (Thanksgiving weekend). During these times some or most of the French Quarter is closed to traffic.

A car is not needed for sightseeing around the most-visited areas of the city, however. You can get around many popular areas on foot or by streetcar or taxi. For excursions to surrounding areas, cars are advisable.

GASOLINE

Gas stations are not plentiful within the city of New Orleans. The downtown area is particularly short on stations. Head for Lee Circle if you need gas while in the downtown area. Most stations in the city and suburbs are open 24 hours.

PARKING

Finding a parking space is fairly easy in most of the city, except for the French Quarter, where meter maids are plentiful and tow trucks eager. If in doubt about a space, pass it up and pay to use a parking lot. Avoid parking spaces at corners and curbs: less than 15 feet between your car and the corner will result in a ticket. Watch for temporary NO PARKING signs, which pop up along parade routes and film shoots. At all times of the year, carefully read street signs in the French Quarter and CBD—tickets are quickly written and towings are frequent. Long-term and overnight parking are extremely expensive at hotels and garages, but some limited options are available for parking your car overnight safely and cheaply. There are some long-term lots around the edge of the Quarter, near Decatur Street.

Garages Central Parking ✉111 Iberville St., French Quarter ☎504/529–3327 ⊕www.parking.com. **Central Parking** ✉202 N. Peters St., French Quarter ☎504/299–9786 ⊕www.parking.com. **Standard Parking** ✉911 Iberville St.,French Quarter ☎504/524–5996 ⊕www.standardparking.com. **Towne Park** ✉530 Natchez St., CBD ☎504/525–8359 ⊕www.townepark.com.

FROM NEW ORLEANS TO	ROUTE	DISTANCE
Atchafalaya Basin	I–10	124 mi
Avery Island	I–10, U.S. 90	168 mi
Baton Rouge	I–10	80 mi
Breaux Bridge	I–10, U.S. 31	130 mi
Lafayette	I–10	136 mi
St. Francisville	I–10, U.S. 61	105 mi
Oak Alley	U.S. 44	60 mi
Opelousas	I–10, U.S. 49	162 mi
San Francisco Plantation	U.S. 44	35 mi

▮ BY STREETCAR

The riverfront streetcar covers a 2-mi route along the Mississippi River, connecting major sights from the end of the French Quarter (Esplanade Avenue) to the New Orleans Convention Center (Julia Street). Nine stops en route include the French Market, Jackson Brewery, Canal Place, the World Trade Center, the Riverwalk, and the Hilton Hotel. This streetcar operates daily 7 AM until 10:30 PM, passing each stop every 30 minutes.

The historic streetcars of St. Charles Avenue returned to operation at the end of 2007. Cars run from St. Charles Avenue at Common Street to the Riverbend at Carrollton Avenue every 10 minutes on weekdays and every 15 minutes on weekends.

A third streetcar line runs along Canal Street several blocks from the river to City Park and passes every 12 minutes.

TICKET/ PASS	PRICE
Single Fare	$1.25
One-day Visitor Pass	$5
Three-day Visitor Pass	$12

One-way fare is $1.25 (exact change); one-day and three-day visitor passes are available at $5 and $12, respectively, for unlimited rides on both the Canal Street and riverfront streetcar lines. Visitor passes apply to buses as well as streetcars. The one-day pass is available from streetcar operators.

Streetcar Information **RTA** ☎504/248–3900, 504/242–2600 automated information ⊕www.norta.com.

TAXI TRAVEL

■ If you need a cab from a major event, call and have one pick you up a few blocks away.

■ During Mardi Gras, it can be extremely difficult to get a cab.

■ If you're trying to hail a cab in New Orleans, try Decatur Street or Canal Street. Otherwise, call for a cab.

▮ BY TAXI

Cabs are metered at $2.50 minimum for two passengers, plus $1 for each additional passenger, $1 for fuel allowance, and $2 per mile.

Taxi Companies **United Cabs** ☎504/522–9771 **White Fleet-Rollins Cab Co.** ☎504/822–3800.

▮ BY TRAIN

Three major Amtrak lines run at New Orleans's Union Passenger Terminal. The *Crescent* makes daily runs from New York to New Orleans by way of Washington, D.C. The *City of New Orleans* runs daily between New Orleans and Chicago. The *Sunset Limited* makes the two-day trip from Los Angeles to New Orleans en route to Orlando. It departs from New Orleans traveling westward on Monday, Wednesday, and Saturday and leaves Los Angeles on Sunday, Wednesday, and Friday.

Information **Amtrak** ☎800/872–7245 ⊕www.amtrak.com. **Union Passenger Terminal** ✉1001 Loyola Ave. ☎800/872–7245 .

TRAIN ROUTE	SERVES	COSTS (APPROX.)
City of New Orleans	Chicago	$180
Crescent	New York	$230
Sunset Limited	Los Angeles	$130

ON THE GROUND

▌DAY TOURS & GUIDES

BUS TOURS

Gray Line conducts city, plantation, walking, and combination bus–paddle wheeler tours. Le'Ob's Tours runs prearranged group tours (20–30 people) of the swamp and plantations. Their tours are multicultural and focus particularly on the contributions of African-Americans. New Orleans Tours leads city, swamp, and plantation tours and combination city–paddle wheeler outings, and runs a Magazine Street Shopping Shuttle. Tours by Isabelle runs city, swamp, plantation, and combination swamp-and-plantation tours. Gray Line and Tours by Isabelle both offer tours of Hurricane Katrina devastation as well.

Fees and Schedules **Gray Line**
☎800/535–7786 or 504/569–1401 ⊕www. graylineneworleans.com. **Le'Ob's Tours**
☎281/751–7524 ⊕www.leobstours.com. **New Orleans Tours** ☎888/486–8687 ⊕www. notours.com. **Tours by Isabelle** ☎877/665–8687 or 504/391–3544 ⊕www.toursby isabelle.com.

ORIENTATION TOURS

Several local tour companies give two- to four-hour city tours by bus that include the French Quarter, the Garden District, Uptown New Orleans, and the lakefront. Prices range from $25 to $50 per person. Both Gray Line and New Orleans Tours offer a longer tour that combines a two-hour city tour by bus with a two-hour steamboat ride on the Mississippi River.

Tour Operators **Gray Line** ☎800/535–7786 or 504/569–1401 ⊕www.graylineneworleans. com. **New Orleans Tours** ☎888/486–8687 ⊕www.notours.com. **Tours by Isabelle** ☎877/665–8687 or 504/391–3544 ⊕www. toursbyisabelle.com.

RIVERBOAT CRUISES

The New Orleans Steamboat Company offers narrated riverboat cruises and evening jazz cruises up and down the Mississippi on the steamboat *Natchez,* an authentic paddle wheeler. The same company operates the *John James Audubon* riverboat, which makes several trips daily between the Aquarium of the Americas and the Audubon Zoo. Ticket sales and departures for the *Natchez* are at the Toulouse Street Wharf behind Jackson Brewery. The *John James Audubon* operates from in front of the aquarium and a dock at the levee behind the zoo. New Orleans Paddle Wheel has a Mississippi River cruise highlighting the port and French Quarter twice daily departing from the Riverwalk. There is also an evening jazz dinner cruise from 8 to 10 (boarding at 7 PM); tickets are available for the dinner and cruise, or just the cruise and live music. The ticket office is at the Poydras Street Wharf near the Riverwalk.

Cruise Operators **New Orleans Paddle Wheel** ☎800/445–4109 or 504/529–4567. **New Orleans Steamboat Company** ☎800/233–2628 or 504/586–8777 ⊕www. steamboatnatchez.com.

SPECIAL-INTEREST TOURS

Full-day plantation tours by bus from New Orleans, which include guided tours through two antebellum plantation homes along the Mississippi River and a stop for lunch in a Cajun-creole restaurant outside the city, are offered by Gray Line and New Orleans Tours. Tours by Isabelle includes lunch in its full-day plantation package that traces the history of the Cajun people. Also available is the Grand Tour: a full-day minibus tour that includes a visit to one plantation, lunch in a Cajun restaurant, and a 1½-hour boat tour in the swamps with a Cajun trapper.

Other special-interests tours focus on popular activities. Le'Ob's Tours leads large group jazz-history tours, complete with club recommendations for the week of your visit, and a Louis Armstrong tour. You can also take cooking classes or arrange a shopping tour.

Exploring an exotic Louisiana swamp and traveling into Cajun country is an adventure not to be missed. Dozens of swamp-tour companies are available. You can check at your hotel or the visitor center for a complete listing. Many do not provide transportation from downtown hotels; those listed below do. Full-day tours often include visiting a plantation home.

For highlights of African-American history and culture, contact Le'Ob's Tours.

African-American Tours Le'Ob's Tours
☎281/751–7524 ⊕www.leobstours.com.

Antiques Shopping Macon Riddle
☎504/899–3027 ⊕www.neworleansantiquing. com.

Cooking Classes Cookin' Cajun ✉1 Poydras St., Store 116, 3rd fl., Riverwalk ☎800/523–6425 ⊕www.cookincajun.com. **New Orleans School of Cooking** ✉524 St. Louis St. ☎800/237–4841 or 504/525–2665 ⊕www. thelouisianageneralstore.com. **Savvy Gourmet School of Cooking** ✉4519 Magazine St., Uptown ☎504/895–2665 ⊕www.savvy-gourmet.com.

Nightlife Le'Ob's Tours ☎281/751–7524 ⊕www.leobstours.com.

Plantations & Swamps Gray Line
☎800/535–7786 or 504/569–1401 ⊕www. graylineneworleans.com. **New Orleans Tours** ☎888/486–8687 or 504/529–4567 ⊕www. notours.com. **Tours by Isabelle** ☎877/665–8687 or 504/391–3544 ⊕www.toursbyisabelle. com.

Swamp Tours Gray Line ☎800/535–7786 or 504/569–1401 ⊕www.graylineneworleans.com. **Honey Island Swamp Tours** ☎985/641–1769 ⊕www.honeyislandswamp.com. **Tours by Isabelle** ☎877/665–8687 or 504/391–

3544 ⊕www.toursbyisabelle.com.**Westwego Swamp Adventures** ☎800/633–0503 or 504/581–4501 ⊕ www.westwegoswamp adventures.com.

WALKING TOURS

Free 1½-hour, general history tours of the French Quarter are given daily at 9:30 AM by rangers of the Jean Lafitte National Historical Park and Preserve. Each visitor may procure a ticket for the tour at the Park Service office at the National Park Visitor Center after 9 AM on the morning of the tour. Check the National Park Visitor Center for details. Tickets are free, but tours are limited to 25 people. Two-hour, general history tours, beginning at the 1850 House on Jackson Square, are given daily at 10 and 1:30 by Friends of the Cabildo (on Monday only the afternoon tour is offered).

Several specialized walking tours conducted by knowledgeable guides on specific aspects of the French Quarter are also available. Because some of these tours accommodate as few as two people, be sure to make advance reservations. Heritage Tours leads a general literary tour and others focusing on either William Faulkner or Tennessee Williams.

The cemeteries of New Orleans fascinate many people because of their unique aboveground tombs. The most famous, St. Louis Cemetery No. 1, is just outside the French Quarter; Save Our Cemeteries conduct guided walking tours. Reservations are generally required.

French Quarter Friends of the Cabildo
☎504/523–3939 ⊕www.friendsofthecabildo. com.

French Quarter & Garden District Gray Line ☎800/535–7786 or 504/569–1401 ⊕www.graylineneworleans.com. **Haunted History Tours** ☎888/644–6787 or 504/861–2727 ⊕www.hauntedhistorytours. com **Jean Lafitte National Historical Park and Preserve** ✉419 Decatur St., French Quarter ☎504/589–2636

Literary Heritage Tours ☎504/949–9805.

Voodoo, Ghosts, Vampires & Cemeteries **Haunted History Tours** ☎888/644–6787 or 504/861–2727 ⊕www.hauntedhistorytours. com. **Historic New Orleans Walking Tours** ☎504/947–2120 ⊕www.tourneworleans.com. **New Orleans Spirit Tours** ☎504/566–9877 ⊕ www.neworleanstours.net. **Save Our Cemeteries** ☎888/721–7493 or 504/525–3377 ⊕www.saveourcemeteries.org.

▌ EMERGENCIES

Doctors & Dentists. **Touro Infirmary** ☎504/897–7011 or 504/897–8250 has a physician-referral service available weekdays 8–5.

Hospitals & Clinics **Touro Infirmary** ✉1401 Foucher St., Garden District ☎504/897–7011 or 504/897–8250. **Tulane University Medical Center** ✉1415 Tulane Ave. ☎800/588–5800 or 504/988–5800 ⊕ www.tuhc.com.

Pharmacies **Rite-Aid** ✉2669 Canal St., Mid-City ☎504/827–1400 ✉3401 St. Charles Ave. Garden District ☎504/896–4575.**Walgreens** ✉900 Canal St., French Quarter ☎504/568–1271   ✉134 Royal St.French Quarter ✉3311 Canal St.Mid-City ☎504/568–1271 ✉1801 St. Charles Ave. (24-hr pharmacy), Garden District ☎504/561–8458.

▌ MAIL

Main Branches **Main post office** ✉701 Loyola Ave.☎800/275–8777. **Post office in French Quarter** ✉207 N.Peters St., Suite 200 ☎504/525–4896. **French Quarter Postal Emporium** ✉1000 Bourbon St.☎504/525–6651.

▌ MONEY

CREDIT CARDS

Throughout this guide, the following abbreviations are used: **AE**, American Express; **D**, Discover; **DC**, Diners Club; **MC**, MasterCard; and **V**, Visa.

Reporting Lost Cards **American Express** ☎800/528–4800 in the U.S., 336/393–1111 collect from abroad ⊕www.americanexpress.com. **Diners Club** ☎800/234–6377 in the U.S., 303/799–1504 collect from abroad ⊕www.dinersclub.com. **Discover** ☎800/347–2683 in the U.S., 801/902–3100 collect from abroad ⊕www.discovercard.com. **MasterCard** ☎800/627–8372 in the U.S., 636/722–7111 collect from abroad ⊕www.mastercard.com. **Visa** ☎800/847–2911 in the U.S., 410/581–9994 collect from abroad ⊕www.visa.com.

▌ SAFETY

New Orleans has long drawn unwelcome attention for its high crime rate. Tourists are seldom the target of major crimes but can, like other citizens, be the target of pickpockets and purse-snatchers. The New Orleans Police Department regularly patrols the French Quarter. Still, common sense is invaluable. Know where you're going or ask the concierge at your hotel about the best route. In the French Quarter, particularly if you are on foot, stay on streets that are heavily populated. After dark, walk with a sense of purpose; night is not the time for obvious sightseeing. In other, less-populated areas of the city it is always advisable to drive. High-end neighborhoods and derelict properties back up to one another throughout New Orleans, making aimless strolling a bad idea outside the Quarter. Try to stick to the recommended walks and areas in this book, and be aware of your surroundings. Take a taxi late at night or when the distance is too great to walk; this is even more important if you've been drinking.

FOR INTERNATIONAL TRAVELERS

CURRENCY

The dollar is the basic unit of U.S. currency. It has 100 cents. Coins are the penny (1¢); the nickel (5¢), dime (10¢), quarter (25¢), half-dollar (50¢), and the very rare golden $1 coin and even rarer silver $1. Bills are denominated $1, $5, $10, $20, $50, and $100, all mostly green and identical in size; designs and background tints vary. You may come across a $2 bill, but the chances are slim.

CUSTOMS

Information **U.S. Customs and Border Protection** (⊕ www.cbp.gov).

DRIVING

Driving in the United States is on the right. Speed limits are posted in miles per hour (usually between 55 mph and 70 mph). Watch for lower limits in small towns and on back roads (usually 30 mph to 40 mph). Most states require front-seat passengers to wear seat belts; many states require children to sit in the backseat and to wear seat belts. In major cities rush hour is between 7 and 10 AM; afternoon rush hour is between 4 and 7 PM. To encourage carpooling, some freeways have special lanes, ordinarily marked with a diamond, for high-occupancy vehicles (HOV)—cars carrying two people or more.

Highways are well paved. Interstates—limited-access, multilane highways designated with an "I–" before the number—are fastest. Interstates with three-digit numbers circle urban areas, which may also have other limited-access expressways, freeways, and parkways. Tolls may be levied on limited-access highways. U.S. and state highways aren't necessarily limited-access, but may have several lanes.

Gas stations are plentiful. Most stay open late (24 hours along major highways and in big cities) except in rural areas, where Sunday hours are limited and where you may drive for long stretches without a refueling opportunity. Along larger highways, roadside stops with restrooms, fast-food restaurants, and sundries stores are well spaced. State police and tow trucks patrol major highways. If your car breaks down on an interstate, pull onto the shoulder and wait for help, or have your passengers wait while you walk to an emergency phone (available in most states). If you carry a cell phone, dial *55, noting your location on the small green roadside mileage marker.

ELECTRICITY

The U.S. standard is AC, 110 volts/60 cycles. Plugs have two flat pins set parallel to each other.

EMBASSIES

Contacts **Australia** ☎ 202/797–3000 ⊕ www.austemb.org. **Canada** ☎ 202/682–1740 ⊕ www.canadianembassy. org. **United Kingdom** ☎ 202/588–7800 ⊕ www.britainusa.com.

EMERGENCIES

For police, fire, or ambulance, dial 911 (0 in rural areas).

HOLIDAYS

New Year's Day (Jan. 1); Martin Luther King Day (3rd Mon. in Jan.); Presidents' Day (3rd Mon. in Feb.); Memorial Day (last Mon. in May); Independence Day (July 4); Labor Day (1st Mon. in Sept.); Columbus Day (2nd Mon. in Oct.); Thanksgiving Day (4th Thurs. in Nov.); Christmas Eve and Christmas Day (Dec. 24 and 25); and New Year's Eve (Dec. 31).

MAIL

You can buy stamps and aerograms and send letters and parcels in post offices. Stamp-dispensing machines can occasionally be found in airports, bus and train stations, office buildings, drugstores, and convenience stores. U.S. mailboxes are stout, dark-blue steel bins; pickup schedules are posted inside the bin (pull down the handle to see them). Parcels weighing more than a pound must be mailed at a post office or at a private mailing center.

Within the United States a first-class letter weighing 1 ounce or less costs 42¢; each additional ounce costs 17¢. Postcards cost 27¢. Postcards or 1-ounce airmail letters to most countries cost 94¢; postcards or 1-ounce letters to Canada or Mexico cost 72¢.

To receive mail on the road, have it sent c/o General Delivery at your destination's main post office (use the correct five-digit ZIP code). You must pick up mail in person within 30 days, with a driver's license or passport for identification.

Contacts **DHL** ☎ *800/225–5345* ⊕ *www. dhl.com.* **Federal Express** ☎ *800/463– 3339* ⊕ *www.fedex.com.* **Mail Boxes, Etc./ The UPS Store** ☎ *800/789–4623* ⊕ *www. mbe.com.* **United States Postal Service** ⊕ *www.usps.com.*

PASSPORTS & VISAS

Visitor visas aren't necessary for citizens of Australia, Canada, the United Kingdom, or most citizens of European Union countries coming for tourism and staying for fewer than 90 days. If you require a visa, the cost is $100, and waiting time can be substantial, depending on where you live. Apply for a visa at the U.S. consulate in your place of residence; check the U.S. State Department's special Visa Web site for further information.

Visa Information **Destination USA** ⊕ *www.unitedstatesvisas.gov.*

PHONES

Numbers consist of a three-digit area code and a seven-digit local number. In the greater New Orleans area, the area code is 504; surrounding areas use 225 or 985. Within many local calling areas you dial only the seven digits; in others you dial "1" first and all 10 digits—just as you would for calls between area-code regions. The same is true for calls to numbers prefixed by "800," "888," "866," and "877"—all toll free. For calls to numbers prefixed by "900" you must pay—usually dearly.

For international calls, dial "011" followed by the country code and the local number. For help, dial "0" and ask for an overseas operator. Most phone books list country codes and U.S. area codes. The country code for Australia is 61, for New Zealand 64, for the United Kingdom 44. Calling Canada is the same as calling within the United States, whose country code, by the way, is 1.

For operator assistance, dial "0." For directory assistance, call 555–1212 or occasionally 411 (free at many public phones). You can reverse long-distance charges by calling "collect"; dial "0" instead of "1" before the 10-digit number.

Instructions are generally posted on pay phones. Usually you insert coins in a slot (usually 25¢–50¢ for local calls) and wait for a steady tone before dialing. On long-distance calls the operator tells you how much to insert; prepaid phone cards, widely available in various denominations, can be used from any phone. Follow the directions to activate the card (there's usually an access number, then an activation code), then dial your number.

CELL PHONES

The United States has several GSM (Global System for Mobile Communications) networks, so multiband mobiles from most countries (except for Japan) work here. Unfortunately, it's almost impossible to buy a pay-as-you-go mobile SIM card in the United States—which allows you to avoid roaming charges—without also buying a phone. That said, cell phones with pay-as-you-go plans are available for well under $100. The cheapest ones with decent national coverage are the GoPhone from AT&T and Virgin Mobile, which only offers pay-as-you-go service.

Contacts **AT&T** ☎ *888/333–6651* ⊕ *www. att.com.* **Virgin Mobile** ☎ *No phone* ⊕ *www. virginmobileusa.com.*

INDEX

A

Abbeville, *261*
Abita Springs, *26*
Academy and Convent of the Sacred Heart, *248*
Acadiana Arts Council, *258*
Acadiana Center for the Arts, *244*
Acadiana Park Nature Station, *244*
Acadian Cultural Center, *243*
Acadian Village, *244*
Acme Oyster and Seafood Restaurant ✕, *126*
Adams House, *68*
African American Museum, *256*
Aidan Gill for Men, *219*
Airports, *239, 269*
Air travel, *239, 269*
Alcee Fortier Park, *83*
Alexander Mouton House and Lafayette Museum, *242*
Algiers Point, *12, 91–92*
Algiers Point Library, *92*
Alligators, *253*
Ambassador Hotel 🏨, *158*
American Aquatic Gardens, *53*
American-Italian Museum, *65*
American-Italian Renaissance Foundation Museum and Library, *61*
Anatole's ✕, *129*
Angeli on Decatur ✕, *140*
Angelle's Atchafalaya Basin Bar, *254*
Angelle's Whiskey River Landing, *254*
Angelo Brocato's ✕, *141*
Anthemion, *77*
Antoine's ✕, *118*
Aquarium of the Americas, *22, 35*
Arcadian Memorial, *256*
Arnaud's ✕, *118*
Art for Art's Sake, *24*
Arthur Roger Gallery, *61, 210*
Ashton's Bed & Breakfast 🏨, *171*✕
Astor Crown Plaza 🏨, *147, 150*
As You Like Silver Shop, *214*
Atchafalaya Basin, *254*
Audubon Park, *77–78*
Audubon State Historic Site, *237*

Audubon Zoo, *22, 35, 79–80*
August ✕, *133*
Avenue Plaza Resort 🏨, *166–167*
Avery Island, *259*

B

Bacchanal Fine Wine & Spirits, *179*
Backstreet Cultural Museum, *55–57*
Balcony Bar & Café ✕, *140*
Banks Street Bar and Grill ✕, *192*
Barrow House & Printer's Cottage 🏨, *238*
Bars & lounges, *176–184*
  gay and lesbian, *186–187*
Basil Leaf ✕, *138*
Baton Rouge, *232–236*
Bayona ✕, *126*
Bayou St. John and Mid-City *restaurants, 85, 89, 139, 141–142*
Bayou St. John & Mid-City, *12, 83–89*
Bayou Teche Guest Cottage 🏨, *258–259*
B&C Seafood ✕, *230*
Beauregard-Keyes House, *44*
Bed and Breakfasts
  CBD & Warehouse District, 166
  French Quarter and Faubourg/ Marigny, 155–158
  Garden District/Uptown, 169–171
  Lafayette, 245–246
  Mid-City, 171–172
  New Iberia, 258–259
  St. Martinville, 257
  websites, 159
Benachi-Torre House, *85*
Benjamin House, *80*
Bennachin ✕, *114–115*
Best Western St. Charles Inn 🏨, *167*
Bienville House Hotel 🏨, *150*
Big Fisherman ✕, *81*
Big John's ✕, *260*
Bike travel
  Mardi Gras and Jazz and Heritage Festival, 109
Bistro at Maison de Ville ✕, *118*

Black's Seafood Restaurant ✕, *261*
Blaine Kern's Mardi Gras World, *22, 92*
Boat travel, *270*
Bois des Chênes Inn 🏨, *245*
Bombay Club (bar), *176*
Bon Maison Guest House 🏨, *155*
Bon Ton Café ✕, *128*
Boomtown Belle Casino, *185*
Borataria Preserve, *22*
Bourbon House ✕, *120*
Bourbon Orleans Hotel 🏨, *150*
Bourbon Pub (gay bar), *186*
Bourbon Street, *14, 45*
Bradish-Johnson House, *68*
Breaux Bridge, *252–254*
Breaux Bridge Crawfish Festival, *24*
Brennan's ✕, *120*
Brevard House, *68*
Bridge Lounge, *182*
Briggs-Staub House, *68*
Brigtsen's ✕, *136*
Broussard's ✕, *120*
Brown House, *80*
Buckner Mansion, *68–69*
Buddy Bolden's House, *57*
Bulldog, The (bar), *183*
Bultman Funeral Home, *80*
Bush Antiques, *214*
Bus travel
  Cajun country, 262
  Mardi Gras and Jazz and Heritage Festival, 109
  New Orleans, 270–271
  Plantation Country, 239
Butler Greenwood Plantation, *236*

C

Cabildo, *35, 38*
Cabin, The ✕, *231*
Cabrini High School and Mother Cabrini Shrine, *85*
Café Bonjour ✕, *245*
Café Degas ✕, *141*
Café des Amis ✕, *252*
Café du Monde ✕, *38, 115, 140, 184*
Café Lafitte in Exile (gay bar), *186*
Café Maspero ✕, *123*
Café Rose Nicaud ✕, *54, 184*

Café Vermilionville ✕, 244
Cajun Country, 12, 27, 240–262
Cajun culture, 66
Cajun French, 260
Cajun music, 251
Camelback Houses, 80
Cameron Jones for Your Home, 218
Canal Place, 38
Canal Street, 38
Carol Robinson Gallery, 215
Carousel Gardens, 85
Carousel Revolving Bar, 176
Carroll House, 69–70
Carrollton Station, 191
Car travel, 10, 271–272
Cajun country, 262
Mardi Gras and Jazz and Heritage Festival, 109–110
Plantation Country, 239
Casamento's ✕, 137
Castles House, 80
Catahoula's ✕, 248
Cat's Meow (bar), 176
CBD & Warehouse District, 12, 59–66
hotels, 158–166
nightlife & the arts, 177, 182–183, 191
restaurants, 63–64, 66, 128–133
shopping, 209–213
CC's Coffeehouse, 184
Celebration in the Oaks, 24
Cell phones, 277
Cemeteries, 26, 72–74
Central Grocery ✕, 123
Charley G's ✕, 245
Chart Room (bar), 176
Chateau Sonesta ☒, 150
Checkpoint Charlies (club), 190
Children, attractions for, 22
CBD & Warehouse District, 63, 65
Algiers Point, 92
Avery Island, 259
Baton Rouge, 233
Bayou St. John & Mid-City, 85, 89
hotels, 160
Jackson Square, 35, 38, 40–42
Jazz and Heritage Festival, 108
Lafayette, 242–244
Mardi Gras, 103
Metairie & the Lakefront, 90–91
restaurants, 123, 126–127, 137, 139, 142–143

shopping, 208–209, 212, 218, 221
Uptown, 79–80
Vieux Carré, 46
Children's Museum of Acadiana, 242–243
Chimes Bed & Breakfast ☒, 169
Chris Owens Club, 188
Christ Church Cathedral, 80
Christopher Porché-West Galerie, 53
Churches and cathedrals
Abbeville, 261
Algiers Point, 92
CBD & Warehouse District, 65
French Quarter, 42
Lafayette, 243
Tremé, 58
Uptown, 80
Circle Bar, 191
City Park, 22, 85–86
Claiborne Mansion ☒, 155–156
Clancy's ✕, 136
Clementine ✕, 258
Clementine's Belgian Bistrot ✕, 142
Clover Grill ✕, 140
Cochon ✕, 128
Coffeehouses, 184–185
Coissant d'Or Patisserie ✕, 122
Colonel Short's Villa, 70
Columns Hotel ☒, 80, 167, 183
Commander's Palace ✕, 136
Congo Square, 57
Conrad Rice Mill, 258
Contemporary Arts Center, 61
Cooking schools, 87, 171–172
Coop's Place (bar), 176
Corner Pocket (gay bar), 186
Cosimo's (bar), 176
Country Club New Orleans (gay bar), 186
Courir de Mardi Gras, 247, 250
Courtyard by Marriott ☒, 158
Cowpokes (gay bar), 186
Crabby Jack's ✕, 143
Credit cards, 275
Creole culture, 66
Crescent City Brewhouse, 178
Cruises, 268, 273
Currency, 276
Customs, 276
Customs House, 39
Cuvée ✕, 133

D

d. b. a (bar), 179
Dakota, 143
Dance, 193
Dance bars (gay and lesbian), 187
Danny Barker's Birthplace, 57
Dante's Kitchen ✕, 138
Dashka Roth Contemporary Jewelry, 205
Dauphine Orleans ☒, 151
Derby Pottery, 74
Destrehan Plantation, 229
Dickie Brennan's Steakhouse ✕, 126
Disabilities and accessibility
Mardi Gras and Jazz and Heritage Festival, 110–111
Dixon Hall, 192
Doll House, 81
Dominique's ✕, 118
Donna's Bar & Grill ✕, 188
Doubletree Hotel ☒, 158–159
Dr. Bob, 53
Drago's, 131–132
Driving, 276
Dry Dock Café and Bar ✕, 92
Dungeon, The (bar), 178
Dupuy's Oyster Shop ✕, 261
Dwyer's Café, 245

E

Edgar Degas House ☒, 86, 171
Eiffel Tower Building, 75
1850 House, 39
1896 O'Malley House ☒, 169
Electricity, 276
Eleven 79 ✕, 132
Elizabeth's ✕, 142
Elleone Gallery, 75
Elms Mansion, 81
Embassies, 276
Embassy Suites (Baton Rouge) ☒, 235
Embassy Suites (New Orleans) ☒, 159
Emergencies, 275
Cajun country, 262
Mardi Gras and Jazz and Heritage Festival, 111
Plantation Country, 239
Emeril's Delmonico ✕, 131
Emeril's ✕, 129
Entergy IMAX Theater, 35
Erath, 260–261
Ernie K-Does Mother-in-Lounge, 190

Ernst Cafe (bar), *182*
Essence Music Festival, *24*
Eunice, *250–252*
Evangeline legend, *255–256*
Evangeline Oak, *255*

F

Fair Grinds Coffeehouse ✕, *85*
Fair Grounds Race Course, *86*
Fat Harry's (bar), *183*
Faubourg Marigny & Bywater,
   12, 52–55
hotels, 147–158
nightlife & the arts, 177, 179,
   181, 190–191
restaurants, 54, 127–128
Faulkner House, *39*
Festival International de Loui-
   siane, *23, 247*
Festivals and seasonal events,
   23–24, 247
Film, *193*
Finn McCool's (bar), *184*
Fiorella's Café, *123*
Fishing, *255*
528 on Fulton, *191*
F&M Patio Bar, *183*
Franky & Johnny's ✕, *138*
Free events, *25*
French Antique Shop, The, *197*
French 75 (bar), *178*
French Market, *14, 40, 204*
French Quarter, *12, 28, 34–52*
hotels, 147–158
nightlife & the arts, 176–179,
   188–190
restaurants, 38, 42, 114–127
shopping, 197–209
tours, 274–275
French Quarter Festival, *23*
Freret's Folly, *70*
Fritzel's European Jazz Pub,
   188

G

Galatoire's ✕, *120*
Gallery for Fine Photography,
   A, *201*
Gallier Hall, *61*
Gallier House, *45*
Gambling, *61–62, 185*
Garden District, *12, 14, 28,*
   66–76
hotels, 166–171
nightlife & the arts, 177,
   183–184, 191–192
restaurants, 71, 75, 133–138
tours, 274–275
walking tour, 69

Gardens and courtyards
Avery Island, 259
Baton Rouge, 234
Bayou St. John & Mid-City, 83,
   85, 87, 89
Faubourg-Marigny, 53–54
French Quarter, 14, 35, 40, 42,
   44, 46–47
Jefferson Island, 259–260
Metairie & the Lakefront,
   90–91
St. Francisville, 237–238
Tremé, 56–57
Uptown, 77–78
Garlands Guest House & Cre-
   ole Cottages 🛏, *156*
Gauche House, *45*
Gay and lesbian nightlife,
   185–187
Gentilly, *19*
George Vitale "Papa Jack"
   Laine's House, *57*
Germaine Wells Mardi Gras,
   45
Golden Lantern (gay bar),
   186–187
Golf, *79*
Good Friends (gay bar), *187*
Goodrich-Stanley House, *75*
Grand Coteau, *247–249*
Grand Isle ✕, *128*
Grand Victorian Bed &
   Breakfast 🛏, *169*
Great River Road, *227–232*
Guesthouses
CBD & Warehouse District,
   166
French Quarter and Faubourg/
   Marigny, 155–158
Garden District/Uptown,
   169–171
Mid-City, 171–172
New Iberia, 258–259
Gumbo Shop ✕, *121*
GW Fins ✕, *126*

H

Hampton Inn and Suites-Con-
   vention Center 🛏, *159–160*
Hampton Inn 🛏, *159*
Handsome Willy's (bar), *182*
Harrah's New Orleans
   Hotel 🛏, *61–62, 160, 185*
Haunted House, *46*
Herbert's Specialty Meats ✕,
   262
Herbsaint ✕, *133*
Hermann-Grima House, *46*

Hilton Baton Rouge Capitol
   Center 🛏, *235*
Historic New Orleans Collec-
   tion, *46*
Holiday Inn - Chateau Le
   Moyne 🛏, *151*
Holiday Inn French
   Quarter 🛏, *151–152*
Holidays, *276*
Holy Name of Mary Church, *92*
Homewood Suites by
   Hilton 🛏, *160*
Horseracing, *86*
Hotel InterContinental 🛏, *160*
Hotel Le Cirque 🛏, *167*
Hotel Maison de Ville 🛏, *151*
Hotel New Orleans 🛏, *161*
Hotel Royal 🛏, *156*
Hotels, *6,* ⇨*See also* Bed and
   breakfasts, Guesthouses
Baton Rouge, 235–236
Breaux Bridge, 253–254
CBD & Warehouse District,
   158–166
children, 160
costs, 147
French Quarter/Faubourg Mari-
   gny, 147–158
Garden District/Uptown,
   166–171
Great River Road, 231–232
haunted hotels, 153, 238–239
Lafayette, 245–246
Mardi Gras and Jazz and Heri-
   tage Festival, 111, 154
Metairie, 172
Mid-City, 171–172
New Iberia, 258–259
price categories, 146, 225
reservations, 147
services, 147
side trips from New Orleans,
   225
St. Francisville, 238–239
St. Martinville, 257
Kenner/airport, 172
Hotel Villa Convento 🛏, *156*
Houmas House, *230–231*
House of Blues, *188*
House of Broel's Victorian
   Mansion and Dollhouse
   Museum, *70*
House of Lounge, *215*
House on Bayou Road 🛏, *87,*
   171–172
Hové Parfumeur, Ltd., *208*
Howlin' Wolf, *191*
Hubig's Pies, *52*
Hurricane Katrina, *8–9, 15–20,*
   88

I

Idea Factory, 207
International House ⊞, 161
Irene's Cuisine ✕, 122
Irene W. Pennington Planetarium, 233
Itineraries, 28–29

J

Jackson Brewery, 40
Jackson Square, 14
Jackson Square and the Riverfront, 35–44
Jacques-Imo's Cafe ✕, 135
Jean Lafitte National Park Visitor Center, 46–47
Jax Brewery, 197
Jazz and Heritage Festival, 103–109
bathrooms, 111–112
children at, 108
essential information, 109–112
food, 105–106
history, 104
music and heritage, 104–105
planning, 107–108
safety, 109
second line parade, 106
shopping, 106–107
tickets, 107
what to wear and bring, 108
Jazz National Historic Park, 57
Jefferson Island, 259–260
Jelly Roll Morton House, 53–54, 57
J&M Music Shop, 56
Joey Bonhage Gallery, 70
John Minor Wisdom United States Court of Appeals Building, 62
Johnny's Po'boys ✕, 123
Joint, The ✕, 140, 142
Josephine Guest House ⊞, 169
Joseph Jefferson Home, 260
Juan's Flying Burrito ✕, 140
Julia Street, 62
Juliet Boutique Hotel ⊞, 246
Jungle Gardens, 259

K

Katy Beh Contemporary Jewelry, 218
Kerry Irish Pub, 178
Kingpin, The (bar), 183
Kitchen Shop, 248

K-Paul's Louisiana Kitchen ✕, 115
Kyoto ✕, 137

L

LaBranche Houses, 47
La Crêpe Nanou ✕, 137
Lafayette, 242, 244–247
hotels, 245–246
nightlift and the arts, 246–247
restaurants, 244–245
shopping, 247
Lafayette Court House, 243
Lafayette Hilton & Towers ⊞, 246
Lafayette Hotel ⊞, 161–162
Lafitte Guest House ⊞, 156–157
Lafitte's Blacksmith Shop, 47, 178
Lake Pontchartrain, 90–91
La Madeleine ✕, 77, 135
La Peniche ✕, 140
La Petite Grocery ✕, 133, 135
La Provence ✕, 143
La Quinta Inn and Suites Downtown ⊞, 161
La Richelieu in the French Quarter ⊞, 152
Latil's Landing Restaurant ✕, 231
Latrobe House, 47
Latrobe Park, 40
Laura Plantation, 229–230
La Vita ✕, 141
Le Bon Temps Roulé, 191
Le Chat Noir (theater), 194
Lee Circle, 62–63
LeMieux Gallery, 212
Le Parvenu ✕, 143–144
Le Pavillon Hotel ⊞, 162
Le Petit Paris Café ✕, 257
Le Petit Salon, 47
Le Petit Théâtre, 47, 194
LeRosier ⊞, 258
Librairie Book Shop, 203
Lilette ✕, 135
Liuzza's by the Track ✕, 139
Loews New Orleans Hotel ⊞, 162
Loft 523 ⊞, 162
Longfellow-Evangeline State Historic Site, 256
Longue Vue House and Gardens, 90
Lonsdale House, 70–71
Louis Armstrong Park, 56
Louis Armstrong's birthplace, 57

Louisiana Arts & Science Museum, 233
Louisiana Children's Museum, 22, 63
Louisiana Music Factory, 206
Louisiana Office of Tourism, 41
Louisiana Philharmonic Orchestra, 193
Louisiana State Museum - Baton Rouge, 233
Louisiana State Penitentiary Museum at Angola, 237
Louisiana Strawberry Festival, 23
Louisiana Superdome, 63
Louisiana Supreme Court Building, 47
Lower Ninth Ward, 20, 55
Loyola University, 81
Lucullus, 200
Lucy's Retired Surfers Restaurant and Bar ✕, 63–64, 182
Luggage, 265
Luling Mansion, 87
Lüke ✕, 129

M

M. S. Rau, 200
Madame John's Legacy, 48, 51
Maddox House, 71
Madewood, 231
Madewood ⊞, 231–232
Magazine Street, 213–220
Magnolia, The ✕, 238
Mail service, 275–277
Maison des Amis ⊞, 253–254
Maison Dupuy ⊞, 152
Maison Olivier, 256
Maison Perrier Bed & Breakfast ⊞, 170
Mandina's ✕, 139
Maple Leaf, 192
Maple Street/Riverbend, 220–222
Mardi Gras, 23, 94–103
bathrooms, 111–112
Carnival royalty, 96
children at, 103
essential information, 109–112
history, 95–97
lingo, 95
parades, 97–100
safety, 102–103
shopping, 201
weekend activities, 99–100
where to watch, 101–102
Mardi Gras Day, 100–101
Mardi Gras Indians, 101
Margaritaville Café, 188

Markets, *4, 21, 40, 204, 243*
Marriott Baton Rouge 🏨, *236*
Martinique ✕, *135*
Maspero's Exchange, *48*
Maurice, *261–262*
McCarthy House, *81*
McGee's Cafe and Bar ✕, *254*
Melrose Mansion 🏨, *157*
Memorial Hall Confederate Museum, *64*
Mercury Injection Studio Arts, *54*
Metairie & the Lakefront, *12, 90–91*
   hotels, 172
Michalopoulos Galleries, *48*
Mid-City
   hotels, 171–172
   nightlife & the arts, 177, 184, 192
Mid-City Lanes Rock 'n' Bowl, *192*
Middle American Research Institute and Gallery, *81*
Mike Anderson's ✕, *235*
MiLa ✕, *129*
Miltenberger Houses, *48*
Milton H. Latter Memorial Library, *81–82*
Mimi's ✕, *140, 179*
Mississippi River, *41*
Mojo Coffee House ✕, *75*
Molly's at the Market (bar), *178*
Mona Lisa ✕, *123*
Mona's Café and Deli, *127*
Money, *275*
Monteleone Hotel 🏨, *152–153*
Morris House, *71*
Mosca's ✕, *144*
Mother's ✕, *132*
Mr. B's Bistro ✕, *121*
Mulate's (Breaux Bridge), *252*
Mulate's Cajun Restaurant ✕, *191*
Murals, *243*
Muriel's Jackson Square ✕, *121*
Musée Conti Wax Museum, *49*
Museums, *28–29*
   Algiers Point, 92
   Baton Rouge, 233–235
   Bayou St. John & Mid-City, 83–89
   CBD & Warehouse District, 61–66
   Erath, 260
   Eunice, 250

   Faubourg Marigny & Bywater, 52–55
   French Quarter, 39
   Garden District, 68–71, 74–76
   Great River Road, 231
   Lafayette, 242–244
   Metairie & the Lakefront, 90–91
   New Iberia, 258
   Opelousas, 249–250
   St. Francisville, 237
   St. Martinville, 255–257
   Tremé, 55–59
   Uptown, 77–83
   Vieux Carré, 44–51
   weird museums, 26
Music
   Cajun and Zydeco, 251
   classical music, 192–193
   history tour, 57
   shopping, 206
   venues, 187–192, 194
Musson House, *71*
Myrtles, The 🏨, *237–238*

N

Napoleon House Bar and Café, *49, 178–179*
Napoleon's Pub (gay bar), *187*
National World War II Museum, *64*
Navigating the city, *270*
New Iberia, *257–259*
New Orleans African-American Museum, *56*
New Orleans Airport Hilton 🏨, *172*
New Orleans Arena, *194*
New Orleans Ballet Association, *193*
New Orleans Botanical Garden, *87*
New Orleans Center for Creative Arts, *54, 193*
New Orleans Christmas, *24*
New Orleans Grill ✕, *128*
New Orleans Hilton Riverside 🏨, *162–163*
New Orleans Historic Voodoo Museum, *49*
New Orleans Jazz & Heritage Festival, *23*
New Orleans Marriott Hotel 🏨, *153*
New Orleans Marriott Metairie at Lakeway 🏨, *172*
New Orleans Metropolitan Convention and Visitors Bureau, *75*

New Orleans Museum of Art (NOMA), *87*
New Orleans Pharmacy Museum, *50*
New Orleans School of Glassworks and Printmaking Studio, *65*
New Orleans Wine & Food Experience, *24*
Nightlife & the arts, *174–194*
   bars & lounges, 176–184
   Breaux Bridge, 254
   Bywater, 177
   CBD & Warehouse District, 177, 182–183, 191
   classical music, 192–193
   closing hours, 182
   coffeehouses, 184–185
   dance, 193
   dance bars, 187
   Erath, 261
   Eunice, 251–252
   Faubourg Marigny & Bywater, 177, 179, 181, 190–191
   film, 193
   French Quarter, 176–179, 188–190
   gambling, 185
   Garden District/Uptown, 177, 183–184, 191–192
   gay & lesbian, 185–187
   Lafayette, 246–247
   Mid-City, 177, 184, 192
   music venues, 187–192, 194
   Opelousas, 250
   opera, 194
   practical matters, 175
   theater, 194
   tours, 274
Ninth Circle (gay bar), *187*
Ninth Ward, *20, 55*
Nola ✕, *121*
Nottoway, *232*
Nottoway 🏨, *232*

O

Oak Alley, *230*
Oak Alley 🏨, *232*
Oakley House, *237*
Ogden Museum of Southern Art, *65*
Old Absinthe House (bar), *179*
Old Arsenal Museum, *233*
Old Castillo Bed & Breakfast 🏨, *257*
Old Governor's Mansion, *233*
Old Mint, *50–51*
Old State Capitol, *234*
Old Ursuline Convent, *51*

Omni Royal Orleans Hotel 🏨, 153
One Eyed Jack's, 188–189
One ✕, 138
Opelousas, 249–250
Opelousas Museum and Interpretive Center, 249
Opelousas Museum of Art, 249
Opera, 194
Orientation tours, 273
Orleans Club, 82
Our Lady of Guadalupe, International Shrine of St. Jude, 58
Outdoor activities and sports, 21
Oz (dance bar), 187

P

Palace Café (New Orleans) ✕, 131
Palace Café (Opelouasas) ✕, 249
Palm Court Jazz Café, 189–190
Pal's (bar), 184
Pamplona Tapas Bar ✕, 245
Parade disco (dance bar), 187
Parades, 24, 64
  Mardi Gras, 97–100
Parasol's Restaurant & Bar ✕, 183–184
Parc St. Charles 🏨, 163
Parks, 14
Park View Guest House 🏨, 170
Parkway Bakery & Tavern ✕, 140–141
Pascal's Manale ✕, 137
Passports, 277
Pat O'Briens (bar), 179
Pat's Fishermans Wharf Restaurant ✕, 254
Paul and Lulu Hilliard University Art Museum, 244
Payne House, 71
Pelham Hotel 🏨, 163
Pelican Club ✕, 122
Peristyle ✕, 115
Petit Paris Museum, 257
Phones, 277
Piazza d'Italia, 65
Pirates Alley Caf[ac] ✕, 42
Pitot House, 87, 89
P.J.'s Coffee and Teas ✕, 66, 184–185
Plantation Country, 12, 14, 27–28, 225–240, 274
Poche's ✕, 252
Pontalba, Micaela, 45

Pontalba Buildings, 41–42
Port of Call ✕, 115
Praline Connection ✕, 127
Prejean's ✕, 244
Presbytère, The, 42
Preservation Hall, 189–190
Price categories
  hotels, 146, 225
  restaurants, 114, 225

Q

Quadroon Ballroom, 51
Queen & Crescent Hotel 🏨, 163

R

Ralph's on the Park ✕, 89, 139
Ramada Plaza Inn on Bourbon Street 🏨, 153–154
Rawhide (gay bar), 187
R Bar, 179
Rémoulade ✕, 122
Renaissance Art Hotel 🏨, 164
Renaissance Pere Marquette Hotel 🏨, 164
Rental cars, 267–268
Republic, 191
Restaurant des Familles ✕, 143
Restaurants, 6, 21
  Abbeville, 261
  African, 114–115
  Algiers Point, 92
  American, 115, 118, 128, 133, 135
  Atchafalaya Basin, 254
  Barbecue, 142, 238
  Baton Rouge, 235
  Bayou St. John and Midcity, 85, 89
  Belgian, 142
  Breaux Bridge, 252
  brunch, 116
  Bywater, 54, 127–128, 142
  cafés, 115, 135
  Cajun, 115, 128–129, 135, 139, 143, 246
  Caribbean, 118, 135
  CBD & Warehouse District, 63–64, 66, 128–133
  costs, 117
  Creole, 118–122, 127, 129, 131, 135–136, 139, 141, 143, 246
  dessert, 122–123, 141
  dress, 116
  eclectic, 122, 131
  Erath, 260

Faubourg Marigny & Bywater, 54, 127–128
food glossary, 124–125
for children, 123, 126–127, 137, 139, 142–143
French, 131, 137, 141, 143–144
French Quarter, 38, 42, 49, 114–127
Garden District, 71, 75, 133–138
Grand Coteau, 248–249
Great River Road, 230–231
Italian, 122–123, 131–132, 137, 144
Japanese, 127, 137
Lafayette, 244–245
Maurice, 262
mealtimes, 116
Mediterranean, 144
Mid-City, 139, 141–142
Middle Eastern, 127
New Iberia, 258
Opelousas, 249
outside city limits, 142–144
Po'boys and other sandwiches, 123, 126, 132, 141–142, 183–184
price categories, 114, 225
reservations, 116
seafood, 126, 132, 137–138, 230, 260–261
side trips from New Orleans, 224–225
Southern, 126, 133, 138, 142
St. Francisville, 238
St. Martinville, 257
steak, 126–127
Thai, 127, 138
tipping, 117
under $10, 140
Uptown, 77, 81, 133–138
Vietnamese, 144
RHINO Contemporary Crafts, 212
Rice, Anne, 71
Riche ✕, 131
Rink, The, 71
Rio Mar ✕, 132
Rip Van Winkle Gardens, 259–260
Ritz-Carlton New Orleans 🏨, 154
Riverbend, 220–222
Riverboat cruises, 268, 273
River Road African American Museum, 231
Rivertown, 22
Riverview Drive, 21

Riverwalk Marketplace, 65
Roadside BBQ & Grill, 238
Robinson House, 71
Rodrigue Studio, 51–52
Rosedown Plantation and Gardens, 237–238
Rosenberg House, 82
Royal Sonesta Hotel ☉, 154
Rubensteins, 212
Rue de la Course, 185
Ruffino's ✕, 235
Rural Life Museum & Windrush Gardens, 234

S

Sacred Heart Academy, 82
Safety, 11, 102–103, 109, 275
St. Alphonsus Art and Cultural Center, 75–76
St. Augustine Catholic Church, 58
St. Charles Avenue Streetcar, 14, 76–77
St. Charles College, 248
St. Charles Guest House ☉, 170
St. Francisville, 236–239
St. James Hotel ☉, 164
St. Joe's (bar), 184
St. John the Evangelist Cathedral, 243
St. Louis Cathedral, 42
St. Martin de Tours, 257
St. Martinville, 254–257
St. Mary Magdalene Catholic Church, 261
St. Patrick's Church, 65–66
St. Vincent's Guesthouse, 76
San Francisco Plantation, 229
Savoy Music Center and Accordion Factory, 250
Schlesinger House, 74
7 on Fulton ✕, 131
Seven Sisters House, 74
17th St. Canal, 18
Shadows-on-the-Teche, 258
Shakespeare Festival, 194
Shaw Center for the Arts, 234
Sheraton New Orleans ☉, 164–165
Shopping, 196–222
antiques, 197, 200, 214–215, 247, 249, 274
art & crafts galleries, 200–203, 209–212, 215, 221
books, 202–203, 215, 221
CBD & Warehouse District, 209–213

clothing and accessories, 203, 215, 218, 222
food, 204, 213, 247
for children, 208–209, 212, 218, 221
French Quarter, 197–209
home furnishings, 218–219
Jazz and Heritage Festival, 106–107
jewelry, 205, 213, 219
Lafayette, 247
Magazine Street, 213–220
Maple Street/Riverbend, 220–222
Mardi Gras, 201
masks, 205–206
music, 206
novelties and gifts, 207–208, 219–220
Opelousas, 249–250
perfumes, 208–209
to go shopping, 206
toys, 208–209
Side trips from New Orleans, 224–262
Smith House, 82
Sno-balls, 26
Snug Harbor (club), 190
Soniat House ☉, 157
Southern Decadence, 24
Southern Repertory Theater, 194
Spanish Plaza, 66
Special-interest tours, 273–274
Spoiled Cat (club), 191
State Capitol Building, 234
Staybridge Suites New Orleans ☉, 165
Stella!, 122
Sterling Silvia, 205
Still Perkin' ✕, 71
Storyland, 89
Storyville, 58–59
Streetcars, 22
Studio Inferno Glassworks, 54
Style Lab for Men, 218
Sukho Thai ✕, 127
Sully House, 82
Sully Mansion ☉, 170
Summer Stages Children's Theater, 22
Swamp tours, 253, 274
Sydney and Walda Besthoff Sculpture Garden, 89

T

Tan Dinh ✕, 144
Tara, 82
Taxis, 272

Mardi Gras and Jazz and Heritage Festival, 112
T-Bob's Seafood ✕, 260
T-Coon's Café, 245
Tennessee Williams/New Orleans Literary Festival, 23
T'Frere's House ☉, 246
Theater, 22, 38, 47, 194
Thomas Mann Gallery I/O, 76
Timing the visit, 11
Tipitina's, 192
Toby-Westfeldt House, 74
Tommy's Cuisine ✕, 132
Tours and guides, 273–275
Train travel, 10, 272
Cajun country, 262
Transportation, 10, 269–272
Garden District, 68
Trashy Diva Boutique, 203
Travel agencies, 267
Treasure Chest Casino, 185
Tremé, 12, 55–59
Trip insurance, 265–266
Trolley Stop Cafe ✕, 140
Tsunami ✕, 245
Tulane University, 82–83, 194
Two Sister's Kitchen ✕, 141

U

Ugly Dog Saloon, 183
Uptown, 12, 28, 76–82
hotels, 166–171
Mardi Gras watching in, 101–102
nightlife & the arts, 177, 183–184, 191–192
restaurants, 77, 81, 133–138
USS Kidd & Veterans Memorial Museum, 234–235

V

Varnedoe's Carriage House Restaurant ✕, 238
Vaughan's, 191
Vega Tapas Café ✕, 144
Vermilionville, 244
Vic's Kangaroo Café, 183
Vieux Carré, 44–52
Vieux Carré Palms ☉, 157
Visas, 277
Visitor information
Cajun country, 262
Mardi Gras and Jazz and Heritage Festival, 112
Plantation Country, 240
Vizard's on the Avenue ✕, 136
Voluntourism, 88

W

Walking tours, *274–275*
Wasabi ✕, *127*
Washington Artillery Park,
   42, 44
Washington Square Park, *54*
Web sites, *11, 264–265*
Bed and Breakfasts, 159
Mardi Gras and Jazz and Heri-
   tage Festival, 111
Wedding Cake House, *83*

Westin Canal Place ▦, *155*
Whisnant Galleries, *200*
Whitney, A Wyndham Historic
   Hotel, The ▦, *165*
W Hotel New Orleans French
   Quarter ▦, *154–155, 165*
Windsor Court Hotel ▦, *166*
Woldenberg Riverfront Park,
   35, 44
Women's Guild of the New
   Orleans Opera Association
   House, *74*

World Trade Center, *66*

Y

Ye Olde College Inn ✕, *139*

Z

Zoos, *22, 35, 79–80*
Zydeco music, *251*

NOTES

NOTES

ABOUT OUR WRITERS

Michelle Delio, who updated our French Quarter, Faubourg Marigny, Bywater, and Tremé coverage in Exploring New Orleans, splits her time living in Miami, New Orleans, and New York City. A freelance editor who covers art, pop culture, photography, travel, and technology, Michelle contributes to *Fodors.com*, *Fodor's New York City*, *Fodor's Essential USA*, and *Fodor's Guide to the Da Vinci Code*.

Jeanne Faucheux is the daughter of New Orleans natives. She has resided in Virginia, Georgia, Tennessee, Maryland, and New Jersey, but she recently came to her senses and moved back to Louisiana. Jeanne teaches Louisiana history and Social Studies to middle school students and travels as often as she can.

Paul A. Greenberg, who revised the Where to Stay and Where to Eat chapters, is a New Orleans-based writer and the Program Director for Journalism and Media Arts at Tulane University. Greenberg writes for local, regional, and national publications, and has been part of the Fodor's team for nine years. He has written extensively about the recovery efforts along the Gulf Coast since the 2005 hurricanes, and continues to promote New Orleans as a first-tier tourist and convention destination.

Molly Jahncke, who updated the CBD, Warehouse District, Garden District, Uptown, Bayou St. John, Mid-City, Metairie, lakefront, and Algiers Point portions of the Exploring chapter, has lived and worked as a writer in such exotic locales as France, Indonesia, Japan, Korea, Thailand, and even New Jersey. Though back now in hometown New Orleans, she still enjoys regular globetrotting as a freelance travel writer. Her journeys also inspire her mixed media artwork, which has sold pretty well—since she doesn't mind getting paid in gumbo, beignets, boudin, and etouffee.

Writer and reporter Russell McCulley—who wrote Experience New Orleans and the Arts and Jazz Fest coverage, as well as the Remembering Katrina feature—lived in New Orleans for the better part of two decades before moving back to his native Texas. His travel stories have appeared in *Islands* magazine and the *Miami Herald*, among other publications.

Sue Strachan is a freelance writer, as well as the public relations director for the Ogden Museum of Southern Art in New Orleans. She loves to travel, and she jouneyed to Louisiana's Cajun and Plantation regions to revise the Side Trips chapter, in addition to updating our Mardi Gras coverage. Laissez les bon temps roulez!